D1613855

SUCCESSFUL AGING

SUCCESSFUL AGING

Integrating Contemporary Ideas, Research Findings, and Intervention Strategies

By

DOUGLAS D. FRIEDRICH, PH.D.

Provost Emeritus and University Professor
University of West Florida

HQ
1061
.F734
2001
West

Charles C Thomas
PUBLISHER · LTD.
SPRINGFIELD · ILLINOIS · U.S.A.

Published and Distributed Throughout the World by

CHARLES C THOMAS • PUBLISHER, LTD.
2600 South First Street
Springfield, Illinois 62704

This book is protected by copyright. No part of
it may be reproduced in any manner without
written permission from the publisher.

© 2001 by CHARLES C THOMAS • PUBLISHER, LTD.

ISBN 0-398-07167-5 (cloth)
ISBN 0-398-07168-3 (paper)

Library of Congress Catalog Card Number: 00-054396

With THOMAS BOOKS *careful attention is given to all details of manufacturing
and design. It is the Publisher's desire to present books that are satisfactory as to their
physical qualities and artistic possibilities and appropriate for their particular use.*
THOMAS BOOKS *will be true to those laws of quality that assure a good name
and good will.*

Printed in the United States of America
MM-R-3

Library of Congress Cataloging-in-Publication Data

Friedrich, Douglas D.
     Successful aging : integrating contemporary ideas, research findings, and interven-
tion strategies / by Douglas D. Friedrich.
          p.cm.
     Includes bibliographical references and index.
     ISBN 0-398-07167-5 (cloth) -- ISBN 0-398-07168-3 (pbk.)
     1. Gerontology. 2. Aging. 3. Aged. I. Title.

HQ1061 .F734 2001
305.26--dc21   00-054396

PREFACE

Successful Aging: Integrating Contemporary Ideas, Research Findings, and Intervention Strategies is meant to provide useful information for practitioners dealing with older adults, as well as students interested in older adulthood. Since preventive intervention has become an accepted strategy for successful aging, the book can be helpful to seniors, as well as younger folks interested in preparing for successful aging. Regarding the latter objective, I do hope senior citizens and those approaching this status will find the book interesting enough to read it thoroughly and reflect upon the principles of aging and intervention strategies. One primary purpose in keeping the book at a readable level is to entice readers—discipline professionals, students, seniors, and younger cohorts—to learn more about the nature of growing older and give serious attention to personal skills for successful aging.

Fortunately, given the rather recent professional interest in **aging**, **gerontology**, and **geriatrics**, readers interested in the many aspects associated with growing older can choose among contemporary journal articles, professional texts, and websites. Unfortunately, given the fact that specialists in aging tend to publish research, theories, ideas, and intervention strategies in specialized publications or for other specialists in their field, much contemporary information about aging is not easy to understand. A practical example of the frustrations most of us have with technical jargon is in the field of medicine. Regardless of our chronological age, we find it very difficult to understand what an M.D. is telling us when the information is given in medical terminology. As we move from the general medical practitioner to medical specialist, our frustration with their technical jargon increases.

Specialists from many professional fields are involved in the study and practice of aging; e.g., medicine, psychology, sociology, social work, history, economics, demography, and genetics. Specialists in each of these professional fields usually use technical language rather specific to the field they are in. The study and practice of aging should be **multidisciplinary**, meaning that specialists from many professional fields are involved in better understanding. Since specialists from many professional fields are involved, using technical language specific to their respective professional field, is it any wonder that the average person is overwhelmed with new information about growing old? Yet, at the personal level, aging is **multifaceted**, including multiple functions and abilities in the physical, psychological, and social domains.

I have integrated important information about aging that reflects its multidisciplinary and multifaceted natures. The integrative language used, hopefully, will be understandable to nonspecialists, as well as specialists in areas other than their own. Noting these goals, I suggest that the reader use the standard of understanding information more so than detailed specificity when reading *Successful Aging*. Throughout the book, references are provided for those who desire more specificity; in fact, I have shared my personal preferences for journal articles and books dealing with more specificity (also more technical information).

Successful Aging is, for the most part, the result of two recent and very significant events in my life. Sharing the events with you will provide some insight into my biases as related to professional and personal aspects of growing older.

Current Event Number One

After 12 years as Provost and Vice President for Academic Affairs at the University of West Florida, I opted, at age 54, to transition back and up to full-time faculty status. The status is a bit different from the Professor role, as I transitioned to Provost Emeritus and University Professor. As part of my transition, I was provided a year's administrative leave. Such leaves are provided, and taken advantage of, for renewal of skills more typical of university teaching, scholarship, and professional service and less typical of academic administration. Prior to my academic administration tenure at the University of West Florida, I was in academic administration at another regional university–Central Michigan University. Before becoming an academic administrator, I was a professor of Psychology, specializing in lifespan development.

Throughout my professional career(s), I remained interested in a subspeciality of **lifespan development**, referred to as **developmental methodology**. This subspeciality deals with models and methods for organizing and/or interpreting lifespan research and models. For many of my years as an academic administrator, I longed for the more flexible work schedules and creative bursts associated with the professorial life. Perhaps reflecting my developmental biases, much of my academic administrative life dealt with the economic, social, and pedagogical impacts for higher education on people–students, their significant others, and higher education personnel. I was excited, in the last three years of my academic administration tenure, about the possibilities of returning to active research and practice in lifespan development.

Current Event Number Two

What to do with a year's worth of administrative leave? University policy is that such a leave deals with renewal of professional skills. Fortunately, I knew what I wanted to do with the rest of my professional life; i.e., become productive, again, in the scholarship, teaching, and service of lifespan development. What I wanted (and needed), however, was one thing; having good opportunities for renewal was another. I was so fortunate in being accepted as a visiting scientist at the Max Planck Institute, Berlin, Center for Lifespan Psychology. Director Paul B. Baltes, was most gracious in promoting my candidacy for the position at the Center. We became familiar with each other's work in developmental methodology over 30 years ago. Given the stature of the Max Planck Institute, Center for Lifespan Psychology, expertise and reputation of its permanent and visiting scientists, and my absence from lifespan development involvement for *some* time, Paul's decision was, I believe, not the easiest one to make.

My semester at the Center provided me many positive experiences related to professional and personal renewal. The Center community, its director, scientists, students—postdoctoral, doctoral, masters, and staff, is exceptional. What a collection of inquisitive, creative individuals. Director Baltes asked that I review the Center research projects, and I was eager to do so. The responsibility provided me with direct access to the principal investigators of projects, as well as motivating me to learn as much as I could, as quickly as possible, about the theories, methodologies, ideas, and practices related to the major research projects. One of the constructive suggestions I made with the review was that the Center should sponsor more activities related to practical aspects of the wonderful research conducted by Center scientists and, internationally, with research colleagues. I decided to act on this suggestion; hence the motivation for this book.

Successful Aging is meant to provide useful information about aging; useful information as we personally grow older, as well as about those with whom we engage. I have focused on integrating discipline-specific research and theory about aging, particularly aging in later adulthood, in language that is understandable to practitioners of diverse educational backgrounds. Those readers seeking more specificity of aging processes and intervention approaches are encouraged to read the primary references provided in this primer, especially books and book chapters.

Learning about the aging process is important for one's self, which includes the very important component of dealing with interpersonal relations, especially relations with significant others. Recently, I joined my mother, three sisters, and more distant relatives in caring for my father. Mom and Dad, in the category of old-old adults, have been very fortunate to have sister Joan, literally, at their sides. Joan lives in the same small Midwestern town and, it seems, has always been the child most caring for my parents. But, with Dad's serious life-threatening conditions, even Joan needed relief.

At 85 years of age, Dad had hip replacement surgery. Physical complications included postsurgery intestinal blockage—a terribly painful condition, followed rather quickly by hip dislocation. The next trauma for Dad and us was a violent episode of vomiting blood, the result of three stomach ulcers. Dad needed seven units of blood to stabilize. Diagnostics for the ulcers indicated abnormal stomach cells. After 49 hours of anxious waiting, the tests for cancerous cells came back negative. After seven days of physical therapy at a local rehabilitation hospital, dad returned to the family home. More than a few professionals and friends noted, during this terrible ordeal, that Dad was a "tough old bird." He was always both stoic and patient. These lifelong characteristics exemplify a lifespan principle that will be discussed in *Successful Aging*. The physical ordeal for my father was clearly traumatic. Psychological ordeals for him, and all of us, were, at times, seemingly unbearable. The hospital is 60 miles from my parents home. Mom, perhaps the strongest soul in the family, was beside herself. As the only member of my family fortunate enough to experience college education and professionalism, with training in gerontology, I was beside myself. Technical knowledge is one thing; dealing with traumas of the human condition is another. I have an understanding of aging, including normal, pathological, and successful aging. Involved with the life-threatening situation of my aging parents has provided another frame to appreciate the wonder of life. My hope is that this book will aid folks to deal with such human conditions as knowledgeably as possible.

Much of what is presented in *Successful Aging* is based upon the creative work of others. While I am becoming more aware of the aging process going on within me, at 56 years of age, I cannot share a lot of relevant personal experiences with later life. On the other hand, and as related to aging principles and intervention approaches to deal with the effects of aging principles, I certainly have personal biases to share.

A number of recent books provide very useful information about older adulthood targeted to the average reader. Tom Brokaw's (1999a,b) *The Greatest Generation* and *The Greatest Generation Speaks*, Mary Pipher's (1999) *Another Country: Navigating the Emotional Terrain of Our Elders*, and Studs Terkel's (1988) earlier published, *The Great Divide: Second Thoughts on the American Dream* are recommended reading for those interested in profiles of successful aging, historical and cultural impacts on one's life history, and, perhaps most importantly, personalized life stories which illustrate the principles of aging. Brokaw, Pipher and Terkel provide many illustrations of the principles of aging–the good, bad, and ugly. And then there is Mitch Albom's (1999), *Tuesdays with Morrie: An Old Man, a Young Man, and Life's Greatest Lesson.* Albom, a sports writer in Detroit, provides a beautiful summary of the life and death of his mentor, Professor Morrie Schwartz. The primary character in Albom's real life story provides much wisdom for living and dying from the perspective of a man dealing with death–and life. Each of these books–*The Greatest Generation, The Great Divide: Second Thoughts on the American Dream, Another Country: Navigating the Emotional Terrain of Our Elders,* and *Tuesdays with Morrie: An Old Man, a Young Man, and Life's Greatest Lesson*– provide us with personal accounts of real people and their gains and losses throughout life's course.

Successful Aging, though not providing personalized accounts of aging, illustrates an integration of contemporary ideas, research, and interventions that is, hopefully, both interesting to read and useful. While the integration of aging-related information spans the **physical**, **psychological**, **and social domains**, the lifespan development principles and interventions of Paul Baltes and associates are highlighted in the text. The ongoing creativity of Baltes and his associates, coordinated at the Max Planck Institute, Berlin, Center for Lifespan Psychology, provides, in the opinion of many lifespan and aging specialists, a contemporary focus on successful aging.

While at the Max Planck Institute, Center for Lifespan Development, Berlin, the need for a book like this was identified. Encouragement, as well as critical input, was provided throughout the project. My thanks to the many Max Planck Institute professionals. A second focused acknowledgment is for Neil Davis, a retired U.S. Navy Captain. While we were working together, Neil finished his MA in Psychology and moved into a doctoral program. Both Neil and I are middle-aged, though he is closer to older adulthood status than I. As colleagues, Neil and I are involved in a research project with over 400 older adults (dealing with life satisfaction and knowledge of aging), a University intervention program for systemic failing Freshman, preretirement seminars for University employees, and the completion of this book. Regarding the latter, Neil provided consistent critical review of successive drafts of the book. Practicing professionals in diverse fields of aging also provided such critical review. Neil also provided unique leadership in computer software expertise and practice. Given our relative strengths and weaknesses as related to the projects noted above, identifying us as colleagues is a fair representation. The last focused note of appreciation is for my partner, Kay, and our parents. Kay, with her own professional sense of self (ballet teacher) continues to share with me her gifts of emotional support and reality. Our parents continue to provide us divergent models of what may be ahead of us. The senior Thompsons (Kay's folks) and Friedrichs (my folks)—old-old adults—are relatively active. Bob Thompson continues his professional acting with the Wisconsin Peninsula Players and remains a successful stock market player; Margaret Thompson plays violin in the Downers Grove, Illinois area; Mel Friedrich, recovering from hip surgery and complications, is in his 25th year of retirement; and Christine Friedrich will remain focused on family relations and cleanliness. Each of our parents, for similar and different reasons, helped me finish the book. Their insight is somewhat different from those that follow them. Such is life.

D.D.F.

INTRODUCTION

Much of Chapter 1 requires your active participation in learning more about aging-related facts and issues. The chapter also deals with aspects of successful aging, with an emphasis on individual decisions impacting long-term lifestyles. Chapter 2 presents principles and ideas about aging, within the broader context of lifespan development. This chapter merges significant aspects of aging with lifespan development principles, promoting strategies for successful aging. Chapter 3 summarizes traditional and contemporary research methodologies for gerontology and lifespan development. Since *Successful Aging* is targeted to practitioner and students interested in older adulthood, applied research examples for each design are summarized. Chapter 4 highlights two models of lifespan development and aging; viz., *fluid/mechanical* abilities versus *crystallized/pragmatic* abilities (Horn & Cattell, 1967), and *selection-optimization-compensation* (Baltes, 1987). The Cattell-Horn model clearly illustrates age-related differences and changes among and within individuals in many capabilities. Baltes' model, perhaps the most accepted contemporary view integrating the phases of lifespan development, focuses on successful aging. Communal and personal intervention strategies for success throughout the lifespan are shared in Chapter 5. Intervention strategies are categorized into physical, psychological, and social domains. Chapter 6 deals with social policies impacting older adults, as well as projections of assistance in retirement from middle age citizens. Chapter 7 provides conclusions and ideas for normal and successful aging.

CONTENTS

SUCCESSFUL AGING

Chapter 1

FACTS ON AGING

Successful Aging: Integrating Contemporary Ideas, Research Findings, and Intervention Strategies, with seven chapters, integrates lifespan development and aging models and research, promoted by appropriate specialists, into a multidisciplinary perspective. This perspective, though including profiles of normal and pathological aging and associated determinants of age-related change, focuses on successful aging. Since the multidisciplinary approach deals with biological, psychological, and social aspects of age-related changes, successful aging profiles also include these three domains of development and aging.

While models of successful aging typically promote preventive interventions or positive lifestyles *before* one enters older adulthood, say 65 years of age, lifestyle decisions for successful aging can be effective within any period of the lifespan, including older adulthood. For an example within the physical domain, long-term cigarette smokers who stop smoking in older adulthood, compared to those who continue smoking, are at lower risks for lung cancer and other respiratory diseases such as emphysema during the remainder of their lifespan. For psychological aging, short-term memory loss becomes a significant problem for most older adults. Yet, those older adults who are flexible enough to use mnemonic devices such as written notes, tape recorders, and palm readers have significantly fewer short-term memory problems than their less cognitively flexible peers. *Successful Aging* illustrates we have many choices, almost daily, concerning the uses of compensatory strategies or maintenance of deteriorating abilities. An example of successful aging in the social domain deals with significant others or social convoys. For most of us, the older we get, the fewer significant others we have. Retirement often results in the loss of significant others, as do deaths of a spouse and friends. The more flexible, successful aging, older adult is able to reach out to potential new significant others.

Stanley Bing, a financial consultant, provided some wonderful advice for successful aging, albeit directed to the worlds of business and personal work. Since one's work throughout much of the lifespan (preparation, doing, retiring), is a primary source of a sense of self, Bing's advice to the young in business translates to the young in the lifespan. A young reader of *FORTUNE* asked Bing to share some wisdom about the things one must do to succeed in business. His advice, published in the May 1, 2000 (pp. 81, 82) issue of *FORTUNE* magazine, is augmented to suggest the multidisiciplinary approach for successful aging; i.e., generalizations for younger cohorts concerning better aging.

How To Succeed in Business: 15 Things Young Folks Need to Know about Comportment

1. Wear a gray or blue suit, with red or yellow silk tie with blue dots or a stripe. *In addition, regardless of gender, carry a soft briefcase, wear glasses, and do not wear a goatee or show underarm hair.* Bing's Point 1 illustrates the importance of "going with the contemporary flow," which, by the way, is usually defined and jealously maintained by those older—chronological age, work-related status, and/or overall importance—than you. It is more difficult to succeed at work and in life by being so unique that you alienate others, especially those who have some control over you. To expand Bing's first point, **seek a sense of balance between the need to be individualistic and the reality of the status quo.**

2. Never say what you really think. *Although very difficult for most of us, regardless of chronological age, history records many more successes for those who* **listen**, *than respond with what those in power* say, adding some of your own thoughts. For business workers, Bing's advice is worth quoting (p. 81): ". . . This listening is good practice for later, when you're in middle management and must be able to hear the secret thoughts of dangerous people before they kill you. Later still, you can stop listening altogether, but that day is a long way off." In work and in life, listening first (READY) provides us opportunities (AIM) for focused objectives (FIRE). Bing's Point 2 is expanded to suggest: **Express what you have reflected on, with a dose of perspective about others, like your boss, spouse, friend, or the obnoxious salesperson.**

3. Be nice to everyone you can be nice to. *Given the options of being nice or hurting someone, opt for being a nice person.* While Bing's advice fits well into corporate life, being nice to difficult people is less acceptable for us outside the work arena. And, even nice folks make decisions that negatively impact others. A generalization of Point 3 is the adage; **One is more successful in life using honey rather than vinegar.**

4. Never sacrifice friends and loved ones on the altar of Mammon. *". . . It's only business, you know. The people you love should be around long after you decide to hang it up and move to St. John. This means pushing back respectfully every* *time people with no life try to suck yours from you....*" (p. 81). To generalize Point 4, **reflect upon your priorities, more so for the long term as opposed to dealing with immediate, focused dilemmas.**

5. Be patient with your elders. *"... They have an incredibly hard job to do, most of them, and they're barely up to it.* Don't be too disappointed when they fail to get out of the way fast enough for your ambitions. In any event, never let them see you praying for their death. It makes them resent you. ..."* (p. 81). Bing's Point 4 needs no expansion in generalizing the work environment to life in general.

6. Have some insight about what you can and cannot do. *With some insight, fewer superiors, subordinates, and clients will have to deal with pointing out your faults.* The multidisciplinary inclusion of Point 6 is to **periodically use information to reflect upon strengths and weaknesses in the general domains of physical, psychological, and social well-being.**

7. Whatever you can do yourself, do. *In the world of work, don't pass off frustrating duties to someone else.* Experience and/or success result in greater responsibilities and, correspondingly, having subordinates deal with past issues of frustration. As will be illustrated throughout *Successful Aging*, Bing's Point 7 is generalized to all domains of aging—the physical, psychological, and social. For each of these domains, the successful aging person is one who maintains a positive lifestyle of relative independence. With advancing older age comes deterioration of capabilities. The successful ager is one who orchestrates a positive equilibrium among (a) deteriorating capabilities and corresponding adaptability, (b) compensatory actions to maintain adaptability, and (c) personal flexibility to deal with significant physical, psychological, and social changes impacting one's sense of self.

8. Don't be bitter at the success of others. The success of your business colleagues is theirs, not yours. *"... Their success has nothing to do with you, even though you may feel as if it does. There will always be people more successful than you, many of whom are less talented or worthy. ..."* (p. 81). Almost all of us use only one or two senses of self for assessment of self-worth during much of our life. Work, which includes the woman who cares for the children, is a primary evaluative category of self-worth. Commitment to a spouse is another. In both areas, much of our lifespan deals with mental exercises which include ascribing motives to the actions of others. These exercises often result in placing blame on others and produce long-term frustrations, if not lifestyle decisions. Most often, the person ascribing motives to the actions of others illustrates his or her motivations, not what motivates someone else. Point 8 is expanded to deal with ascribing motives: **When reacting to the actions of others, significant others like family members, friends, and work colleagues, don't ascribe motivation or harbor negative feelings for too long.**

9. Never go to a meeting when a phone call will do. *". . . Never place a phone call when an e-mail will do. Never launch an e-mail if 17 words in the e-levator will suffice. Don't travel just to show that you're an important person who must be places. Don't surround the activity of business with fruitless jabber and twaddle and rummaging around for no good purpose. Get things done expeditiously and move on, and if you must meet, bring your own pen. . . ."* (p. 82). Remember, Bing is giving advice to the novice businessperson! Perhaps Point 9 can be integrated in a multidisciplinary perspective with the following: **Avoid being pretentious and realize that the younger you are in life, the greater the possibility of dealing with folks who have been where you are trying to go**.

10. Be loyal, even when it is to your detriment. *Ahh, the naivete of youth. In work, a sense of loyalty includes superiors, colleagues, organization, and clients—more complex than a relationship of subordinate and superior. People notice reasonable loyalty, and the lack of it.* Generalizing Point 10 to all aspects of life suggests **a strong sense of positive reciprocity; i.e., do unto others, as you would have them do unto you**.

11. Don't blame others for your mistakes. *". . . In fact, don't blame others for **their** mistakes, even when you might avoid trouble by doing so. Just suck it up and never, ever make excuses, even when you have excellent ones. Big macho men and women who move gigantic furniture around for a living absolutely hate excuses, and they hate good excuses even more than bad ones. Everybody makes mistakes, but only losers make excuses. . . ."* (p. 82). A great arena illustrating the art of making excuses is politics (e.g., I never had sex with that woman . . .); unfortunately, the art permeates all of American society. Generalizing Point 11? **Better to deal honestly with significant issues, the sooner the better—for others and for yourself**.

12. Stay put until you absolutely cannot do so a moment longer. *". . . . Dig in. Hang tough. Cultures are deep. It takes time to negotiate them. People are the same everywhere. And careers can develop a rhythm only if you give them a chance to do so. Remember this: People who jump from job to job every two or three years from the beginning end up doing that for their entire careers, tinkers, skittering along on the surface of organizations that use but do not love them. Eventually, they become consultants. . . ."* (p. 82). While Bing's advice is good, young employees can expect to change jobs more than a few times during their work life. Point 12 for life in general may be reframed to suggest **working for a balance between (a) accepting the rewards of sustained relationships, habits, interests, and responsibilities, and (b) flexibility for adventure, trying new things, and dealing with unsuccessful attempts**.

13. Do not become a consultant. Well, becoming a consultant *after* many years of successes and failures *and* having reasonable financial and physical/mental health is probably okay. Related to a lifespan multidisciplinary frame of reference, Point 13 could suggest the following preventive strategy for successful aging: **Don't jump too soon from established reward systems, be they physical, psychological, or social; if you are impatient about dealing with one or more lifestyle frustrations, first test the alternatives.**

14. Don't be greedy. Bill Gates and at least a thousand others aside, youngsters in business do not become billionaires (or millionaires) overnight. *". . . . More probably you are destined to work hard, be given nothing for free, and earn every dime you require for the rest of your life. . . ."* (p. 82). For the young reader of *Successful Aging*, there is a contemporary lifespan analogy of Bing's advice about being greedy. Older adults with IRA's, pension plans, and personal stocks and bonds facilitate senses of well-being with daily fluctuations of Wall Street. Point 14 needs to be expanded, as being greedy has more to do with life than finances. **Don't be greedy with material wealth or personal strengths in ongoing relations with significant others and things significant to you.**

15. Have fun. *". . . And if you can't have fun, don't. Who said it was supposed to be fun? This is business, not windsurfing. . . ."* (p. 82). Interestingly, while many complain about work, most need work to maintain a sense of self-worth. Preretirees and recently retired older adults often express sustained anxiety with leaving their employment, citing concerns about an uncertain mental health future for themselves and spouse. Yet, most employees, regardless of job category or status, complain of job frustrations throughout their work life. In work, as well as the greater world of life, we tend to focus on the specifics of the tasks rather than adapting to diverse life obligations with a positive sense of well-being. Being positive, having fun with work, is associated with positive well-being; either the positivism from work transfers to life in general, or vice versa.

You may not agree with one or more of Bing's pieces of advice for the young businessperson. His tidbits are included, with some expansion, for several reasons. First, our work (probably starting with schoolwork) is a primary source of time and energy commitments, as well as a major portion of our sense of self. As will be presented in later sections of *Successful Aging*, too many of us, for too long, optimize our working existence. Such sustained focus with one's working self results in many lost opportunities in the many other aspects of life. Second, be it work or any other important life optimization, humans require many learning experiences to (a) really learn from mistakes, and (b) significantly change lifestyles for more successful development and aging. For each of the major domains of aging–physical, psychological, and social–much important information is available as we move through the lifespan. Yet, everyone admits (at least to himself/herself) to timidity in accepting advice for personal change.

How much do you know about older adulthood and aging? The following quiz (Palmore, 1998) may be useful in determining your Aging IQ. Answers to the FACTS ON AGING QUIZ are provided at the end of Chapter 1. Alternative FACTS ON AGING quizzes are provided in Appendix A.

FACTS ON AGING QUIZ

Mark the statements "T" for true, "F" for false, or "?" for don't know.

____ 1. The majority of old people (aged 65+) are senile (have defective memory, are disoriented, or demented).

____ 2. The five senses (sight, hearing, taste, touch, and smell) all tend to weaken in old age.

____ 3. The majority of old people have no interest in, or capacity for, sexual relations.

____ 4. Lung vital capacity tends to decline in old age.

____ 5. The majority of old people feel miserable most of the time.

____ 6. Physical strength tends to decline in old age.

____ 7. At least one tenth of the aged are living in long-stay Institutions.

____ 8. Aged drivers have fewer accidents per driver than those under age 65.

____ 9. Older workers usually cannot work as effectively as younger workers.

____10. Over three-fourths of the aged are healthy enough to do their normal activities without help.

____11. The majority of old people are unable to adapt to change.

____12. Old people usually take longer to learn something new.

____13. Depression is more frequent among the elderly than among younger people.

____14. Older people tend to react slower than younger people.

____15. In general, old people tend to be pretty much alike.

____16. The majority of old people say they are seldom bored.

____17. The majority of old people are socially isolated.

____18. Older workers have fewer accidents than younger workers.

____19. Over 20 percent of the population is now age 65 or over.

____20. The majority of medical practitioners tend to give low priority to the aged.

____21. The majority of old people have incomes below the poverty line (as defined by the federal government).

____22. The majority of old people are working or would like to have some kind of work to do (including housework and volunteer work).

____23. Old people tend to become more religious as they age.

____24. The majority of old people say that they are seldom irritated or angry.

____25. The health and economic status of old people will be about the same or worse in the year 2010 (compared with younger people).

(Answers are found on page 26)

Successful Aging presents information about age-related changes in adulthood, with an emphasis on successful aging. A lifespan perspective is also emphasized since significant parts of one's lifestyle are developed, then maintained, long before senior citizen status. Too few of us take a developmental (long-term) perspective earlier in our lifespan. Too many of us, in every phase of the lifespan, deal with our daily tasks and related short-term goals at the expense of long-term goals. Relatedly, most of us focus on our own agendas, more so than the agendas of others. These phenomena of the human species–focusing on the present and ourselves–are associated with a narrow lifespan perspective, limited by interpretations of personal experience.

Most of us would agree that the earlier in life one deals constructively with information about successful aging, the longer we will live and the better quality of life we will have. Earlier, rather than later, intervention correlates higher with successful aging. Unfortunately, too many of us, regardless of chronological age, do not make the effort to learn about ways to move through the lifespan more successfully or put the knowledge into practice. Fortunately, however, later life changes in personal habits can contribute to both longevity and quality of life.

An age-related myth is that you cannot teach elders–dogs or humans–new tricks. The reality is that older adults do learn new tricks, albeit with greater effort and additional assistance. Another reality is that most younger folks do not associate their current lifestyles or priorities to those in later life. These realities provide a foundation for the use of a lifespan development approach in interpreting age-related changes in adulthood. *Successful Aging* emphasizes, in addition to the lifespan development approach, a basic integration of discipline-specific information about aging in later adulthood and intervention strategies for successful aging.

What is a lifespan? It is every person's living existence, from conception to death. *How is the lifespan described?* Most often, the lifespan is described in terms of average characteristics of people at successive chronological ages, stages, or periods in the lifespan. These average characteristics are usually categorized into physical, psychological, and social domains. *What causes changes in characteristics over the lifespan?* Primary determinants of changes over the lifespan are as follows (Cavanaugh, 1999, p.2):

> ". . . *Biological forces* include all genetic, physiological, and health-related factors affecting development. Examples of biological forces include menopause, facial wrinkling, and changes in the major organ systems.
>
> *Psychological (behavioral) forces* include all internal, cognitive, emotional, and personality factors affecting development. Collectively, psychological forces provide the characteristics we notice most obviously about people that make them individuals.
>
> *Sociocultural factors* include interpersonal, societal, cultural, and ethnic factors that affect development. Sociocultural forces provide diversity and the network of people with whom we interact, and influence how the greater society is structured and operates.

Life-cycle forces reflect differences in how the same event or combination of biological, psychological, and sociocultural forces affects people at different points in their lives. Life-cycle forces provide the context for the developmental differences of interest in adult development and aging. Life-cycle forces are most often incorporated into biological, behavioral, and sociocultural theories of aging. . . ."

The following quizzes about aging augment the *Facts on Aging Quiz* presented at the beginning of the chapter. These quizzes, and the results at the end of the chapter, continue our introduction into the physical, psychological, and social aspects of aging. The *Facts on Aging and Mental Health Quiz* is from Palmore (1998), the *Berlin Aging Quiz* is from Baltes and Mayer (1999), and the *Life Satisfaction Index* is from Neugarten, Havighurst, and Tobin (1961). Alternatives for the *Facts on Aging Quiz and Mental Health and Life Satisfaction Index* are presented in Appendix A.

FACTS ON AGING AND MENTAL HEALTH QUIZ

Mark the following with a "T", "F", or "?" for don't know.

____ 1. The majority of persons over 65 have some mental illness severe enough to impair their abilities.

____ 2. Cognitive impairment (memory loss, disorientation, or confusion) is an inevitable part of the aging process.

____ 3. If an older mental patient makes up false stories, it is best to point out that he or she is lying.

____ 4. The prevalence of neurosis and schizophrenia increases in old age.

____ 5. Suicide rates increase with age for women past 45.

____ 6. Suicide rates increase with age for men past 45.

____ 7. Fewer of the aged have mental impairments, when all types are added together, than other age groups.

____ 8. The primary mental illness of the elderly is cognitive impairment.

____ 9. Alzheimer's disease (progressive senile dementia) is the most common type of chronic cognitive impairment among the aged.

____10. There is no cure for Alzheimer's disease.

____11. Most patients with Alzheimer's disease act the same way.

____12. Organic brain impairment is easy to distinguish from functional mental illness.

____13. It is best not to look directly at older mental patients when you are talking to them.

____14. It is best to avoid talking to demented patients because it may increase their confusion.

____15. Demented patients should not be allowed to talk about their past because it may depress them.

____16. The prevalence of cognitive impairment increases with old age.

____17. Isolation and hearing loss are the most frequent causes of paranoid disorders in old age.

____18. Poor nutrition may produce mental illness among the elderly.

____19. Mental illness is more prevalent among the elderly with less income and education.

____20. The majority of nursing home patients suffer from mental illness.

____21. The elderly have fewer sleep problems than younger persons.

____22. Major depression is more prevalent among the elderly than among younger persons.

____23. Widowhood is more stressful for older than younger women.

____24. More of the aged use mental health services than do younger persons.

____25. Psychotherapy is usually ineffective with older patients.

(Answers are found on page 31)

BERLIN AGING STUDY QUIZ

Answer each question as T (TRUE) or F (FALSE).

___ 1. The majority of old people are prescribed too many medications.

___ 2. Most old people have at least one illness.

___ 3. Most old people report that their health is poor.

___ 4. Old women live longer and therefore have fewer illnesses than men.

___ 5. The majority of very old women need assistance in bathing and showering.

___ 6. Most biochemical reference values do not change in old age.

___ 7. Depressive disorders become more frequent in old age.

___ 8. Most persons aged 70 and above have serious impairments in intellectual functioning.

___ 9. About half of those aged 90 years and over exhibit severe mental decline (dementia).

___10. Most old people receive too many psychotropic drugs.

___11. Everyday life for older adults consists mainly of passive activity and rest.

___12. Old people are preoccupied with death and dying.

___13. Memory gets worse with age.

___14. Most old people are no longer able to learn new things.

___15. A good education and a challenging job are protective against age-related intellectual decline.

___16. Most old people believe that they can no longer control what happens in their life.

___17. Only very few older persons still have life goals.

___18. Older adults live mainly in the past.

___19. Most old people have a confidant with whom they can talk about difficult problems.

___20. In West Berlin, many older adults are poor.

___21. The number of social relationships decreases with old age.

___22. Most persons aged 95 and above are institutionalized.

___23. People who were more socially active in their youth also participate more in social life when they are old.

___24. In old age, the rich are healthier than the poor.

___25. Women who were housewives for most of their lives are worse off in old age than women who were in paid employment.

(Answers are found on page 34)

LIFE SATISFACTION INDEX

Here are some statements about life in general that people feel differently about. Would you read each statement on the list and if you agree with it, put a check mark in the space under "AGREE." If you do not agree with a statement, put a check mark in the space under "DISAGREE." If you are not sure one way or the other, put a check mark in the space under "?" PLEASE BE SURE TO ANSWER EVERY QUESTION ON THE LIST.

	AGREE	DISAGREE	?
1. As I grow older, things seem better than I thought they would be.	_____	_____	__
2. I have gotten more of the breaks in life than most of the people I know.	_____	_____	__

3. This is the dreariest time
   of my life.   _____   _____   __

4. I am just as happy as when
   I was younger.   _____   _____   __

5. My life could be happier
   than it is now.   _____   _____   __

6. These are the best years
   of my life.   _____   _____   __

7. Most of the things I do are
   boring or monotonous.   _____   _____   __

8. I expect interesting and
   pleasant things to happen
   to me in the future.   _____   _____   __

9. The things I do are as interesting
   to me as they ever were.   _____   _____   __

10. I feel old and somewhat tired.   _____   _____   __

11. I feel my age, but it does not
    bother me.   _____   _____   __

12. As I look back on my life, I
    am fairly well satisfied.   _____   _____   __

13. I would not change my past
    even if I could.   _____   _____   __

14. Compared to other people
    my age, I've made a lot of
    foolish decisions in my life.   _____   _____   __

15. Compared to other people
    my age, I make a good
    appearance.   _____   _____   __

16. I have made plans for things
    I'll be doing a month or a
    year from now.   _____   _____   —

17. When I think back over my
    life, I didn't get most of the
    important things I wanted.   _____   _____   —

18. Compared to other people, I
    get down in the dumps too often.   _____   _____   —

19. I've gotten pretty much what
    I expected out of life.   _____   _____   —

20. In spite of what people say,
    the lot of the average man is
    getting worse, not better.   _____   _____   —

(Answers are found on page 38)

DEMOGRAPHIC FACTS ABOUT AGING IN AMERICA

Much of what is provided in this section is taken from recent summaries of the U.S. Administration on Aging and a special report from it by Hobbs and Damon (1996), **http://www.census.gov/prod/1/pop/p23-190/p,23-190 html**. Figure 1–1 illustrates growth of the 65 years and older American population by age groups, from 1900 to 2050. Figure 1–2 depicts alternative projections of the elderly. Projections vary because of mortality and international migrant assumptions. To reinforce the primary demographic information, I have summarized the Hobbs and Damon (1999) work by brief sentences. For those of you interested in detailed information about aging demographics, I suggest contacting the Executive Secretariat, Administration on Aging, U.S. Department of Health and Human Services, Washington, D.C. 20201 (phone number 202-619-0724; e-mail-aoa esec@ban-gate.aoa. dhhs.gov, and Internet Website **http://www.aoa.dhhs.gov**).

In 1860, half the population of the U.S. was under age 20; most of the population was not expected to reach age 65. In 1950, half the population was under age 30. As fertility declined and survival changes improved, the population became progressively older. Post-World War II baby booming (1946–1964) increased fertility, resulted in the population remaining a young one; since that time, however, the population has been aging. In 1994, 23

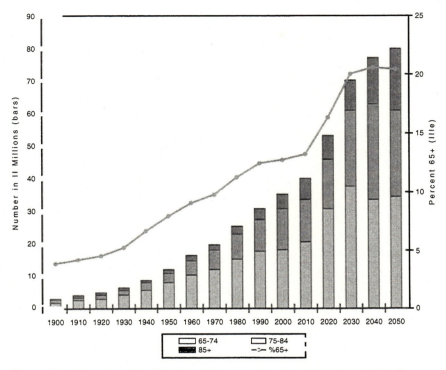

Figure 1-1. Growth of the 65+ Population, by Age Group: 1900 to 2050. Source: U.S. Bureau of the Census, Current Population Reports, Special Studies P–23–190, 65+ in the U.S. U.S. Government Printing Office, 1996.

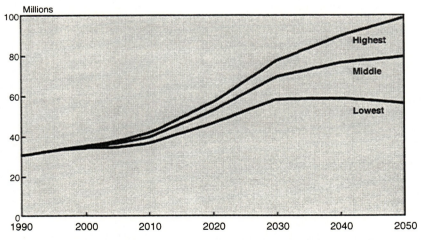

Figure 1-2. Projected Elderly Population–Alternative Series: 1990 to 2050. Source: U.S. Bureau of the Census. Data for 1990–92 shown in Population Paper Listing–8 (PPL-8), "U.S. Population Estimates, by Age, Sex, Race and Hispanic Origin: 1990–1993." Data for 1993 to 2050 shown in *Population Projections of the United States by Age, Sex, Race, and Hispanic Origin: 1993 to 2050*, Current Population Reports, P25-1104, U.S. Government Printing Office, Washington, DC, 1993.

percent of the population was under age 16 and 50 percent of the population was 34 years of age or older. In 2010, projections are that 50 percent of the population will be 37 years of age or older; in 2030, 39 years of age or older.

The elderly population growth rate has far exceeded the general population growth rate. In this century, the total population tripled; the population for those 65 years of age and older increased by a factor of 11 (3.1 million in 1900 and 33.2 million in 1994); by 2050, the number of persons 65 years of age and older will double. In 1994, one in eight Americans was 65 years or age or older; in 2030, one in five will be in that age group. A significant increase in the number of those 65 years of age and older will occur during 2010–2030, as the baby boomers will be entering the elderly category. In 1988, those 65 years of age or older totaled 30 million; by 2010, the total will be 40 million; by 2017, the total will be 50 million. Those 65 years of age or older grew by 82 percent from 1965 to 1995. From 1980 to 1985, the senior citizens population grew by 28 percent.

The oldest-old, defined as those 85 years of age or older, is the fastest growing segment of the senior citizen population. Since 1965, the oldest-old group, representing one percent of the total population, has doubled, and has grown 40 percent since 1980.

The number of centenarians (those 100 years of age or older) doubled during the 1980s. Figures 1–3, 1–4, 1–5, 1–6, and 1–7 show the U.S. population in the years 1905, 1975, 2010, 2030, and 2050, categorized by age and sex. The 1905 distribution (Figure 1–3) illustrates a population of youth

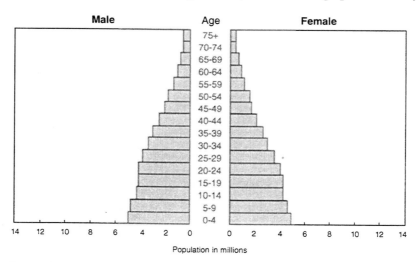

Figure 1–3. Population by Age and Sex: 1905. Source: U.S. Bureau of the Census, *Estimates of the Population of the United States, by Single Years of Age, Color, and Sex: 1900 to 1959*, Current Population Reports, Series P–25, No. 311. U.S. Government Printing Office, Washington, DC, 1965.

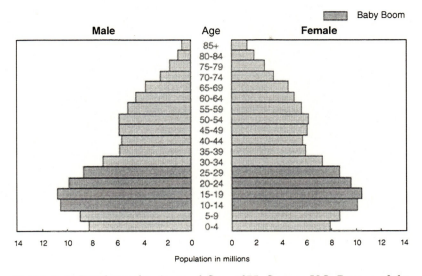

Figure 1–4. Population by Age and Sex: 1975. Source: U.S. Bureau of the Census, *Preliminary Estimates of the Population of the United States, by Single Years of Age, Color, and Sex: 1970 to 1981*, Current Population Reports, Series P–25, No. 917. U.S. Government Printing Office, Washington, DC, 1982.

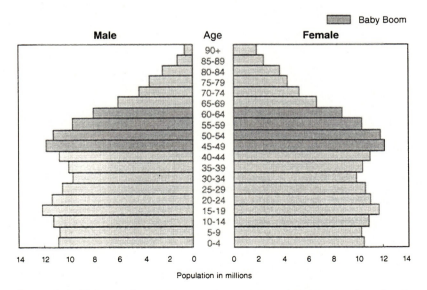

Figure 1–5. Projected Population by Age and Sex: 2010. Source: Jennifer C. Day, U.S. Bureau of the Census, *Population Projections of the United States, by Age, Sex, Race, and Hispanic Origin: 1993 to 2050*, Current Population Reports, P25–1104. U.S. Government Printing Office, Washington, DC, 1993 (middle series projections).

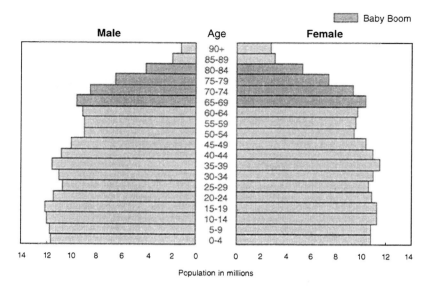

Figure 1–6. Projected Population by Age and Sex: 2030. Source: Jennifer C. Day, U.S. Bureau of the Census, *Population Projections of the United States, by Age, Sex, Race, and Hispanic Origin: 1993 to 2050,* Current Population Reports, P25–1104. U.S. Government Printing Office, Washington, DC, 1993 (middle series projections).

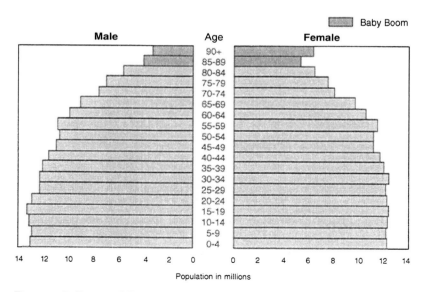

Figure 1–7. Projected Population by Age and Sex: 2050. Source: Jennifer C. Day, U.S. Bureau of the Census, *Population Projections of the United States, by Age, Sex, Race, and Hispanic Origin: 1993 to 2050,* Current Population Reports, P25–1104. U.S. Government Printing Office, Washington, DC, 1993 (middle series projections).

and rather high fertility; the pyramid shape of the 1905 population remained stable until the years 1921–1945, when there was a significant drop in birth rates. The 1975 population pyramid (Figure 1–4) illustrates a reduction in the age trends for ages 35–44. This is the result of significantly lower birth rates in the Depression years. The baby-boom effect is shown in the five year age groupings for ages 10 to 29 in the 1975 figure.

The 2010 population pyramid (Figure 1–5) illustrates what the baby boom effect will be in the years 46 to 64. As depicted in Figure 1–6, the baby boom effect is in the ages 65–74 (young-old) and 75–84 (older-old). Whereas elderly women now outnumber men by 3 to 2, in 2030, the ration will be 6 to 5. The rectangular shape of the 2050 (Figure 1–7) pyramid illustrates a population with sustained low fertility and mortality rates.

Figure 1–8 provides population estimates of older adults over 85 years of age. In 1990, those 85 years or older totaled 3 million, while the totals for 1900 and 2050 are 100,000 and 18.9 million, respectively. By 2050, the older-old adults will represent 5 percent of the total population. For those aged 100 or older (centenarians), 80 percent are female. The 1990 population census reported 36,000 centenarians. Figure 1–9 shows the relative percentages of

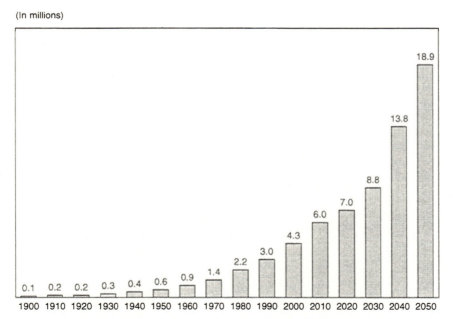

(In millions)

Figure 1–8. Population 85 Years and Over: 1900 to 2050. Source: U.S. Bureau of the Census, Decennial Censuses for specified years and *Population Projections of the United States by Age, Sex, Race, and Hispanic Origin: 1993 to 2050*, Current Population Reports, P25–1104, U.S. Government Printing Office, Washington, DC, 1993. Data for 1990 from *1990 Census of Population and Housing*, CPH-L-74, *Modified and Actual Age, Sex, Race, and Hispanic Origin Data*.

men and women in 1994 for successive elderly age groupings. As depicted in Figure 1–9, as age increases with the elderly, the percentage of men to women steadily declines.

On the other hand, as shown in Table 1–1, the percentage of males to females in the age category 85 or older, changes dramatically from 1930 to 2050.

Figure 1–10a graphically summarizes ethnic distributions of ages 65 or older, 65–69, and 80 or older in 1990 and 2050. As illustrated in Figure 1–10b, the elderly population of 2050 will be more diverse than that of 1990. In 1990, about ten percent of the elderly was non-white; in 2050, twenty percent of the elderly population will be people of color. Family support ratios for ethnicity are provided for year groups 1950 through 2050 (Table 1–2).

Relative to previous generations, more older adults are likely to have surviving parents, aunts and uncles. And, the increases in length of life will result in more adult children engaging with parents and older relatives. The parent support and sandwich generation ratios of Table 1–2 are used to estimate elderly generations. The parent support ratio, defined as the number of elderly 85 years or older per 100 50–64 year-olds, increases consistently and dramatically from 1950 to 2050. The need for physical, psychological, and social help by the former age group is most likely to be met by the latter age group. Yet, the latter age group, those 50 to 64 years of age, will also have to deal with the issues of personal aging. The sandwich generation ratio of

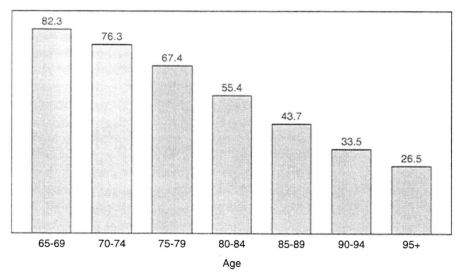

Figure 1–9. Number of Men per 100 Women by Age: 1994. Source: U.S. Bureau of the Census, data consistent with "U.S. Population Estimates by Age, Sex, Race, and Hispanic Origin: 1990 to 1993," Population Paper Listing-8 (PPL-8), 1994.

Table 1–1
Balance of Males and Females 85 Years and Over: 1930 to 2050
(Sex ratio is males per 100 females 85 years and over)

Year	Sex Ratio	Excess of females (thousands)
1930 ...	75.4	38
1940 ...	75.0	52
1950 ...	69.7	103
1960 ...	63.9	205
1970 ...	53.3	430
1980 ...	43.7	877
1990 ...	38.6	1,339
2030 ...	54.6 ·	2,599
2050 ...	60.1	4,705

Note: Data shown for 1930-1990 are for April 1, and data for 2030 and 2050 are for July 1.
Source: U.S. Bureau of Census, data for 1930 and 1940 shown in 1940 Census of Population, Volume IV, Part 1, Characteristics by Age, Table 2; data for 1950 shown in *Estimates of the Population of the United States and Components of Change, by Age, Color, and Sex: 1950 to 1960*, Current Population Reports, Series P-25, No. 310, U.S. Government Printing Office, Washington, DC, 1965; data for 1960 and 1980 shown in 1980 Census of Population, PC80-B1, *General Population Characteristics*, Table 45; data for 1970 shown in unpublished tables consistent with *United States Population Estimates by Age, Race, Sex, and Hispanic Origin: 1988*, P-25, No. 1045, U.S. Government Printing Office, Washington, DC, 1990; data for 1990 from 1990 Census of Population and Housing, Series CPH-L-74, *Modified and Actual Age, Sex, Race, and Hispanic Origin Data*; data for 2030 and 2050 shown in *Population Projections of the United States by Age, Sex, Race, and Hispanic Origin: 1993 to 2050*, Current Population Reports, P25-1104, U.S. Government Printing Office, Washington, DC, 1993.

Table 1–2, tracking the baby boomers, illustrates increases of dependents–their children and their parents–over the years 1950 through 2050. Middle-aged adults, compared to earlier years, will have a much higher percentage of children and parents to assist in the upcoming years. Support ratios reflect the percentages of youth (those under 20 years of age) and elderly (65 years or older) per those who are aged 20–64. Figure 1–11 depicts such ratios from 1990 to 1050.

The ratio of the elderly to those 20–64 years of age will almost double in the years from 1990 to 2050. The total support ratio (Figure 1–11, Total; youth plus elderly) will decrease a bit over the next several decades (because the youth ratio declines and the elderly ratio increases slightly). After 2010, the total support ratio will begin to increase as the baby boomers reach their elderly years. The elderly support ratio increase includes the fact that those 75 years or older are much more so than the elderly population in general. With increasing age in the elderly population comes more health and disability problems.

Aging population projections by age and sex is shown in Table 1–3, and are projected populations for countries are given in Table 1–4.
In 1994, 357 million persons were 65 years of age or older, representing six

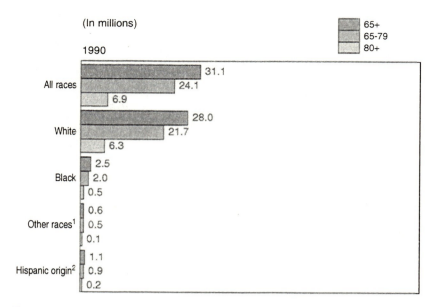

Figure 1–10a. Persons 65 Years and Over by Age, Race, and Hispanic Origin: 1990 and 2050.

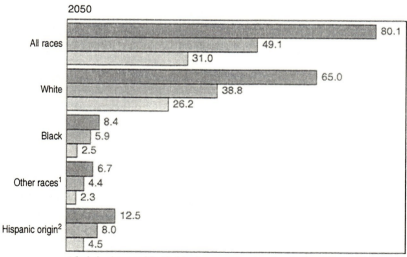

1 Includes Asian and Pacific Islanders, as well as American Indian, Eskimo, and Aleut.
2 Hispanic origin may be of any race.

Figure 1–10b. Source: U.S. Bureau of the Census, 1990 from 1990 Census of Population and Housing, CPH–L–74, *Modified and Actual Age, Sex, Race, and Hispanic Origin Data*, and 2050 from *Population Projections of the United States, by Age, Sex, Race, and Hispanic Origin: 1993 to 2050*, Current Population Reports, P25–1104, U.S. Government Printing Office, Washington, DC, 1993.

Table 1–2
Parent and Sandwich Generation Support Ratios: 1950 to 2050
(For meaning of abbreviations and symbols, see introductory text.)

Ratio and Race/Hispanic origin	1950	1993	2010	2030	2050
Parent Support Ratio[1]					
Total	3	10	11	16	29
White	3	11	11	17	33
Black	3	7	7	9	15
Other races	2	4	7	13	21
Hispanic origin[2]	(NA)	6	7	11	21
Sandwich Generation Ratio[3]					
Total	144	200	166	299	267
White	148	205	172	319	286
Black	[4]97	171	131	242	216
Hispanic origin[2]	(NA)	139	118	217	204

[1]Ratio of persons 85 years old and over to persons 50 to 64 years old.

[2]Hispanic origin may be of any race.

[3]Ratio of persons aged 18 to 22 enrolled in college plus persons aged 65 to 79 to persons aged 45 to 49 years. College enrollment for 2010-2050 is based on 1993 rates for 18-to-22-year olds (Total, 40.3 percent; White, 41.8 percent; Black, 27.8 percent; Hispanics, 26.2 percent).

[4]1950 data are for "Black and other races" combined. Over 90 percent of "Black and other races" were Black in 1950.

Source: U.S. Bureau of the Census, 1950 from 1950 Census of Population, Volume 2, Part 1, Chapter C, Tables 97 and 112; 1993 from Population Paper Listing (PPL-8), *U.S. Population Estimates, by Age, Sex, Race and Hispanic Origin: 1990 to 1993. 2010 to 2050 from Projections of the Population of the United States, by Age, Sex, Race and Hispanic Origin: 1993 to 2050*, Current Population Reports, P25-1104, U.S. Government Printing Office, Washington, DC, 1993 (middle series projections), table 2.

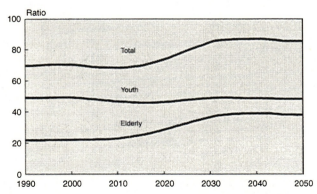

Figure 1–11. Total, Youth, and Elderly Support Ratios: 1990 to 2050. Note: Youth Ratio is the number of persons under age 20 divided by the number of persons aged 20 to 64 times 100. Elderly Ratio is the number of persons 65 years and over divided by the number of persons aged 20 to 64 times 100. Total Support Ratio is the sum of the Youth Support Ratio and the Elderly Support Ratio. Source: U.S. Bureau of the Census, 1990 from 1990 Census of Population and Housing, CPH–L–74, *Modified and Actual Age, Sex, Race, and Hispanic Origin Data*; 2050 from *Population Projections of the United States, by Age, Sex, Race, and Hispanic Origin: 1993 to 2050*, Current Population Reports, P25–1104, U.S. Govern,ment Printing Office, Washington, DC, 1993. (Middle series projections.)

Table 1–3
World Population by Age and Sex: 1994 and 2000

Year and age	Population (millions)			Percent			Males per 100 females
	Both sexes	Male	Female	Both sexes	Male	Female	
1994							
All ages	5,640	2,841	2,798	100.0	100.0	100.0	101.5
Under 15 years	1,790	917	873	31.7	32.3	31.2	105.1
15 to 64 years	3,492	1,771	1,722	61.9	62.3	61.5	102.9
65 years and over ..	357	153	204	6.3	7.3	7.3	75.2
2000							
All ages	6,161	3,103	3,057	100.0	100.0	100.0	101.5
Under 15 years	1,877	962	915	30.5	31.0	29.9	105.2
15 to 64 years	3,866	1,959	1,907	62.7	63.1	62.4	102.8
65 years and over ..	418	182	236	6.8	5.9	7.7	77.1

Source: U.S. Bureau of the Census, International Data Base.

percent of the international population (Table 1–4). In 2000, there will be approximately 418 million elderly, representing about seven percent of the international population. As shown in Table 1–5, the growth of those 65 years of age or older is in both developed and developing countries. In 1994, 55 percent of the elderly lived in developing countries; in 2020, 65 percent of the elderly will be living in developing countries. While the developed countries represented 22 percent of the total international population, the majority of the elderly aged 80 years or older lived in developed countries. In 2020, the projection is that the majority of the elderly aged 80 years or older will live in developing countries.

AGING QUIZZES DOCUMENTATION

The following documentation of the aging quizzes comes from Palmore (*Facts on Aging Quiz*, 1998, pp. 9–13), Woolf (*Woolf Aging Quiz*, 1999), Palmore (*Facts on Aging and Mental Health Quiz*, 1998, pp. 30–34), Mayer et. Al (*Berlin Aging Quiz*, 1999, pp. 476–485), Neugarten, Havighurst, and Tobin (*Life Satisfaction Quiz*, 1961), and Schulz (*Longevity Test*, 1978).

Facts on Aging Quiz (answers)

1. The majority of old people (age 65+) are senile (have defective memory, are disoriented, or demented. **FALSE**. The majority of older people (a) are not senile, (b) do not have defective memories, (c) are not disoriented, and (d) are not demented. About 10 percent of older people have some form of dementia or severe mental illness; another 10 percent have mild to moderate mental impairment.

Table 1–4
Projected Population for Countries With More Than Two Million Elderly: 1994 and 2020

Country/area	Rank		Population aged 65 years and over	
	1994	2020	1994	2020
China, Mainland	1	1	71,073	168,318
India	2	2	36,282	87,797
United States	3	3	33,169	53,348
Russia	4	5	17,384	26,050
Japan	5	4	17,140	32,231
Germany	6	7	12,476	18,551
Italy	7	9	9,259	13,012
United Kingdom	8	11	9,175	12,018
France	9	10	8,924	12,969
Ukraine	10	13	7,155	9,917
Brazil	11	8	7,098	18,084
Indonesia	12	6	6,875	19,476
Spain	13	16	5,768	8,086
Pakistan	14	14	5,078	9,448
Poland	15	19	4,216	7,536
Mexico	16	12	3,882	10,625
Bangladesh	17	15	3,727	8,949
Vietnam	18	22	3,570	6,610
Canada	19	24	3,401	6,287
Argentina	20	27	3,246	5,022
Turkey	21	17	3,141	7,835
Nigeria	22	18	2,818	7,666
Thailand	23	20	2,809	7,234
Romania	24	29	2,700	4,398
Philippines	25	21	2,603	6,631
Iran	26	25	2,368	5,199
South Korea	27	23	2,367	6,607
Australia	28	32	2,116	3,857
Egypt	29	26	2,094	5,047
Netherlands	30	34	2,040	3,467
Colombia	*	28	*	4,446
South Africa	*	30	*	4,253
Burma	*	31	*	4,028
China, Taiwan	*	33	*	3,490
Ethopia	*	35	*	3,224
Morocco	*	36	*	2,924
North Korea	*	37	*	2,734
Sri Lanka	*	38	*	2,584
Peru	*	39	*	2,535
Venezuela	*	40	*	2,486
Saudi Arabia	*	41	*	2,475
Algeria	*	42	*	2,413
Greece	*	43	*	2,348
Zaire	*	44	*	2,332
Chile	*	45	*	2,274
Czech Republic	*	46	*	2,205
Belgium	*	47	*	2,199
Hungary	*	48	*	2,181
Malaysia	*	49	*	2,133
Uzbekistan	*	50	*	2,132
Kazakhstan	*	51	*	2,084
Serbia	*	52	*	2,078
Portugal	*	53	*	2,061
Belarus	*	54	*	2,021
Sweden	*	55	*	2,016

Source: U.S. Bureau of the Census, International Data Base
Note: * Indicates population in 1994 was less than two million.

2. The five senses (sight, hearing, taste, touch, and smell) all tend to weaken in old age. **TRUE**. Disease, medications, and smoking may be involved in age-related declines of taste and smell. Many studies have illustrated age-related decline in the senses of sight, hearing, and touch.

3. The majority of old people have no interest in, nor capacity for, sexual relations. **FALSE**. The majority of older persons have interest in, and capacity for, sexual activity.

4. Lung vital capacity tends to decline in old age. **TRUE**. Pulmonary disease, lack of exercise, and smoking enhance decline of lung vital capacity, but volume of air that is forcibly expelled in one breath declines three to four deciliters per decade.

5. The majority of old people feel miserable most of the time. **FALSE**. Psychological well-being (happiness, morale, life satisfaction) research shows either no age-related differences or that one-fifth to one-third of the elderly score low on happiness or morale instruments.

6. Physical strength tends to decline in old age. **TRUE**. From about the third decade of life, muscle strength measurements indicate decreases.

7. At least one-tenth of the aged are living in long-stay institutions (such as nursing homes, mental hospitals, homes for the aged, etc.). **FALSE**. For ages 65–74, five percent are residents of long-stay institutions, and for those over 75, nine percent are residents. Forty percent of the elderly, however, are residents in such facilities at some point in life.

8. Aged drivers have fewer accidents per driver than those under 65. **TRUE**. While older drivers have about the same accident rate as middle-aged drivers, older drivers have a significantly lower accident rate than drivers 30 years old or younger. Older drivers, compared to the younger groups, drive significantly fewer miles per year.

9. Older workers usually cannot work as effectively as younger workers. **FALSE**. On most measures of work productivity, older workers perform as well, if not better than younger workers. Work demanding speed and accuracy of movement results in younger workers performing better than older workers. On the other hand, older workers perform better than younger workers when productivity is defined with such criteria as job turnover, accidents, and absenteeism—fewer for older workers.

10. Over three-fourths of the aged are healthy enough to do their normal activities without help. **TRUE**. Over 85 percent of the elderly are able to care for themselves in terms of such daily activities as eating, bathing, and dressing. This percentage drops with advancing age and with older individuals who have serious chronic illnesses.

11. The majority of older people are unable to adapt to change. **FALSE**. Older adults do change in dealing with serious matters such as retirement, loss of spouse and significant others, the "empty nest," serious illness, and relocation. They do, like younger adults, change positions on political and social issues. Older dogs, cats, and humans do learn new tricks!

12. Old people usually take longer to learn something new. **TRUE**. While such factors as chronic illness, motivation, learning style, lack of relevant practice, and energy level contribute to the relative slowness in learning for older persons, the reduction in biological functioning and reserve is a very important influence, particularly for advanced old age.

13. Depression is more frequent among the elderly than among younger people. **FALSE**. Clinically diagnosed depression is less among the elderly than among their younger cohorts.

14. Older people tend to react slower than younger people. **TRUE**. This finding is one of the most consistent and significant, especially in technologically-advanced societies. While there are different ideas concerning the reasons for increased reaction time (receiving, processing, and/or emitting information), older persons, in the laboratory and real life, just don't respond as quickly as younger persons.

15. In general, old people tend to be pretty much alike. **FALSE**. In fact, recent studies strongly suggest that as people age they tend to become less alike and more heterogeneous on many dimensions.

16. The majority of old people say they are seldom bored. **TRUE**. Studies have shown that from 79 to 87 percent of older persons expressed not being bored. Even in advanced older age, elders are occupied with matters to avoid boredom.

17. The majority of old people are socially isolated. FALSE. While it is true that there are age-related reductions in the number of significant others, it is not true that the majority of older adults, even advanced older adults, are socially isolated. Most older adults live with their spouse. Widows (a

much higher percentage than widowers) and widowers live with family members and/or have significant others to socialize with.

18. Older workers have fewer accidents than younger workers. **TRUE**. This holds true probably because older workers are more cautious, tend to avoid dangerous situations and hazardous work, and, because of seniority in such work environments, are supervisory.

19. Over 20 percent of the population is now age 65 or over. **FALSE**. In 1997, 12.8 percent of the population was 65 and older. In 2040, the projection is that the percentage will be 21.

20. The majority of medical practitioners tend to give low priority to the aged. **TRUE**. Medical folks are no different than fellow citizens when it comes to negative stereotypes about older individuals. M.D.'s, in general, prefer patients who are younger adults or children. M.D.'s, trained to cure illnesses, often find it difficult to deal with older adults who have chronic, incurable illnesses.

21. The majority of old people have incomes below the poverty line (as defined by the federal government). **FALSE**. The majority of older adults have income significantly above the poverty line. About 11 percent of adults over 65 are under the poverty line, which is similar to the percentage of adults under 65.

22. The majority of old people are working or would like to have some kind of work to do (including housework and volunteer work). **TRUE**. Over 75 percent of older adults are working, including volunteer work, or would like to work. Seven percent are employed, 17 percent work as homemakers, and 19 percent are volunteers.

23. Old people tend to become more religious as they age. **FALSE**. A cohort or generation effect indicates that present senior citizens are more religious than younger adults. Such a difference was not found for senior citizens in previous generations. Perhaps the present cohort of older adults was more religious throughout their lives; perhaps this cohort finding is the result of living through the Great Depression and World War II.

24. The majority of old people say they are seldom irritated or angry. **TRUE**. Self-reports of most older people, relative to younger adults, indicate less anger.

25. The health and economic status of old people will be about the same or worse in the year 2010 (compared with younger people). **FALSE**. Health, income, occupation, and education measures of older adults, relative to younger adults, indicate a positive increase. Successive differences between older and younger adults in these areas will be significantly less.

Facts on Aging and Mental Health Quiz (answers)

1. The majority of persons over 65 have some mental illness severe enough to impair their abilities. **FALSE**. From 15 to 25 percent of the elderly suffer from mental illness.

2. Cognitive impairment (memory loss, disorientation, or confusion) is an inevitable part of the aging process. **FALSE**. Only five to 15 percent of the elderly have any kind of dementia. The percentage rises to almost 50 percent for those aged 85 or older.

3. If an older mental patient makes up false stories, it is best to point out that he or she is lying. **FALSE**. The elderly with clinically diagnosed mental illness do not consciously lie. Thus, confrontation over a false story can lead to further inappropriate engagement on the part of all those involved in the conversation.

4. The prevalence of neurosis and schizophrenia increases with age. **FALSE**. These clinical illnesses decrease, rather than increase, with older age.

5. Suicide rates increase with age for women past 45. **FALSE**. Although suicide is a problem with older persons, relative to younger ones, suicide rates do not indicate significant increases for women.

6. Suicide rates increase with age for men past 45. **TRUE**. Suicide rates show dramatic age-related increases for older males, especially the very old males. Men, using more violent means than females, are more successful than women with attempted suicide.

7. Fewer of the aged have mental impairments, when all types of impairments are added together, than other age groups. **TRUE**. Adding over the most common mental impairments (affective disorders, panic and obsessive/compulsive disorders, substance abuse or dependency, somatization disorders, antisocial personality disorders, schizophrenia, phobia, and severe cognitive impairments), older persons have the lowest prevalence rates.

8. The primary mental illness of the elderly is cognitive impairment. **TRUE**. Fourteen percent of older persons have mild cognitive impairment, and four percent have severe cognitive impairment.

9. Alzheimer's disease (progressive senile dementia) is the most common type of chronic cognitive impairment among the aged. **TRUE**. Over half of the aged with dementia have Alzheimer's disease. Vascular dementia, directly linked to cardiovascular disease, is the second most prevalent type of dementia with older persons.

10. There is no cure for Alzheimer's disease. **TRUE**. Alzheimer's disease is defined as a progressive dysfunction. A dementia that is cured cannot be Alzheimer's disease.

11. Most patients with Alzheimer's disease act the same way. **FALSE**. Impaired memory and confusion are characteristic of patients with Alzheimer's disease. With that, much diversity exists among those with Alzheimer's disease' viz., age of onset, severity at disease stages, and number and severity of symptoms. Alzheimer's disease can be diagnosed with certainty only after death and physical analysis of the brain.

12. Organic brain impairment is easy to distinguish from functional mental illness. **FALSE**. It is very difficult to make distinctions, given that some criteria for organic brain impairment are the same or similar for functional mental illness. Also, diagnostic measures are neither valid nor reliable enough to easily distinguish organic brain impairment from functional mental illness. Multiple diagnostic measures, as well as complete patient history, increase the ability to distinguish between the two broad diagnostic categories, as well as within each.

13. It is best not to look directly at older mental patients when you are talking to them. **FALSE**. It is best to establish eye contact and attempt to maintain it; doing so allows for assessing if the patient is attending to you.

14. It is best to avoid talking to demented patients because it may increase their confusion. **FALSE**. Talking and listening can be pleasurable to the patient and significant other.

15. Demented patients should not be allowed to talk about their past because it may depress them. **FALSE**. Triggering memories and having the elderly talk about their past is often enjoyable to them and the significant other.

16. The prevalence of cognitive impairment increases in old age. **TRUE.** Severe mental impairment increases from one percent in people younger than the mid-40's to four percent for those aged 65 and older; mild cognitive impairment for these groups is two percent and 14 percent, respectively.

17. Isolation and hearing loss are the most frequent causes of paranoid disorders in old age. **TRUE.** In addition to these primary causes are those associated with adverse conditions like institutionalization, physical impairments, and substance abuse.

18. Poor nutrition may produce mental illness among the elderly. **TRUE.** A cycle may occur, where poor nutrition contributes to forms of mental illness which, in turn, contribute to even poorer nutrient intake.

19. Mental illness is more prevalent among the elderly with less income and education. **TRUE.** Mental illness is significantly greater for older persons from lower socioeconomic conditions, defined by income, education, or former occupation.

20. The majority of nursing home patients suffer from mental illness. **TRUE.** Three-fourths of nursing home patients have dementia or dementia with other types of mental illness.

21. The elderly have fewer sleep problems than younger persons. **FALSE.** While such problems are more severe for elderly with depression or anxiety, older people (a) take longer to get to sleep, (b) awaken from sleep more often, and (c) have significantly less deep sleep.

22. Major depression is more prevalent among the elderly than among younger persons. **FALSE.** Prevalence for major depression for the elderly is less than half that for the general population.

23. Widowhood is more stressful for older than for younger women. **FALSE.** Widowhood is more expected in older age, and older widows face fewer problems than younger widows (e.g., childbearing, child rearing, finding another spouse, employment, and age-similar widows).

24. More of the aged use mental health services than do younger persons. **FALSE.** Older persons have a lower prevalence of mental illness and are less willing to admit to, and seek assistance for, mental illness.

25. Psychotherapy is usually ineffective with older patients. **FALSE**. Psychotherapy is often effective with the elderly.

Berlin Aging Quiz (answers)

The following documentation is summarized from Mayer, P. Baltes, M. Baltes, Borchelt, Delius, Helmchen, Linden, Smith, Staudinger, Steinhagen-Theissen, & Wager (1999, pp. 476–485). Keep in mind, while reviewing the documentation, that these authors answer the questions based upon longitudinal research of elderly West Berliners. The study included 516 elderly, aged 70 to over 100 years of age. The sample was stratified by age and gender.

1. The majority of old people are prescribed too many medications. **FALSE**. While most older adults received regular prescription drugs (92 percent took at least one drug and 24 percent took five or more drugs simultaneously), only 14 percent were judged (by a medical team approach) as taking drugs not indicated by the case diagnosis or drugs that were contraindicated.

2. Most old people have at least one illness. **TRUE**. From medical diagnosis, almost all of the Berlin Aging Study participants aged 70 and older had at least one moderate to severe internal, neurological, or orthopedic illness as defined by the International Classification of Diseases, World Health Organization. Only 33 percent of the participants, however, had a life-threatening illness (e.g., coronary heart disease, congestive heart failure).

3. Most old people report that their health is poor. **FALSE**. Self reports of participants in the longitudinal study were: 29 percent rated their physical health as good or very good; 38 percent as satisfactory; 19 percent as fair; and 14 percent as poor. Also of interest is that when asked to compare their physical health to age peers, 62 percent replied that their health was better or much better.

4. Old women live longer and therefore have fewer illnesses than old men. **FALSE**. While women live longer than men, the former's physical health profile is not significantly different from men.

5. The majority of very old women need assistance in bathing and showering. **TRUE**. While 60 percent of women aged 85 and older needed such assistance, 32 percent of very old men did. Only 16 percent of the

participants, aged 70 and older, needed assistance in bathing and showering.

6. Most biochemical reference values do not change in old age. **TRUE**. With exceptions of kidney functioning, blood formation, and calcium metabolism, no significant age-related deviations from younger adults was found. Medications could have influenced this general finding.

7. Depressive disorders become more frequent in old age. **FALSE**. From ages 70 to over 100, the diagnosed prevalence of clinical depression did not differ significantly.

8. Most persons aged 70 and above have serious impairments in intellectual functioning. **FALSE**. While 17 percent of the participants illustrated some significant cognitive impairment, the majority of them, showing general decline in intellectual functioning, did not show significant impairment.

9. About half of those aged 90 years and over exhibit severe mental decline (dementia). **TRUE**. While no case of dementia was diagnosed for participants aged 70 to 74, 43 percent of those aged 90 and over were diagnosed as exhibiting severe mental decline. For both diagnostic and personal reasons, as suggested by the authors, it is very important to distinguish the old from the very old in matters of dementia. And, as suggested by the Berlin Aging Study researchers, again and again, it is very important to distinguish between averages and individuality, regardless of chronological age.

10. Most old people receive too many psychotropic drugs. **FALSE**. Seventy percent of the prescribed psychotropic drugs was judged medically necessary; only 13 percent of the prescriptions was judged to be possible of definite contraindications. No evidence in the longitudinal study was found of overdosage.

11. Everyday life for older adults consists mainly of passive activity and rest. **FALSE**. Only 19 percent of participants' daily waking hours was for resting, though the younger-older adults (88 percent) spent more time than older-older adults (74 percent) in nonresting activities.

12. Old people are preoccupied with death and dying. **FALSE**. Seventy percent of the participants occupied their thoughts and actions with family and relatives, and 60 percent with intellectual pursuits. About 30

percent thought about death and dying, with little difference between the young-old and older-old.

13. Memory gets worse with age. **TRUE**. Within the Berlin Aging Study group, there was a dramatic negative correlation between memory performance and aging. One study example of this conclusion: With testing on a list of eight pairs of words, 35 percent of participants 90 years and older, versus nine percent of those 70–79 years of age, could not remember any of the eight pairs.

14. Most old people are no longer able to learn new things. **FALSE**. Despite significant memory decline, most older participants without dementia were able to learn new things. The test for this was Enhanced Cued Recall–a list of 16 words memorized in three trials. About two-thirds of the participants were able to improve performance over three trials.

15. A good education and a challenging job are protective against age-related intellectual decline. **FALSE**. Although participants with above average education, prestigious and cognitively demanding professions, and relatively higher incomes did, on average, demonstrate a higher level of intellectual functioning, the rate or amount of intellectual decline for these participants was about the same as participants with below-average demographic levels. The key to the correct answer to this question is rate or amount of intellectual decline, as older adults with above average education, prestigious and cognitively demanding occupations, and relatively higher incomes did perform better than their below-average demographic resource peers.

16. Most old people believe that they can no longer control what happens in their life. **FALSE**. Seventy percent of the participants indicated that they felt in control of their lives, and 27 percent noted that to some extent they controlled their lives, but to a larger degree were dependent upon others.

17. Only very few older persons still have life goals. **FALSE**. Ninety-four percent of the participants talked about their future that dealt with a wide range of life domains and goals.

18. Older adults live mainly in the past. **FALSE**. Forty percent of the Berlin Aging Study participants reported thinking mostly about the present, 30 percent about the past, and 25 percent about the future.

19. Most old people have a confidant with whom they can talk about

difficult problems. **FALSE**. Forty-five percent of the participants reported that there was no one to talk to about personal problems. Even though, with this population, many significant others have died, it is tragic that many of the older adults had no confidant or significant other judged to be close enough for the discussion of personal problems.

20. In West Berlin, many older adults are poor. **FALSE**. Only three percent of the study population met poverty standards.

21. The number of social relationships decreases with old age. **TRUE**. The average number of persons in the social network was 10. While 70–74 year-olds identified 13 people in their network, those aged 95 and older named seven. Interestingly, though even the very old identified people in their social network, many Berlin Aging Study participants (45 percent) said that they had no one to talk to concerning difficult problems.

22. Most persons aged 95 and above are institutionalized. **FALSE**. Only nine percent of the participants were institutionalized, though those aged 95 and older had a percentage of 37. With advancing age, institutionalization becomes more of a possibility.

23. Children are the main caregivers of old persons in private households. **FALSE**. Children are not the primary caregivers for elderly parents. The prime sources of regular assistance and care at home are spouses (mostly female) and professional community or nursing services. However, parents who need care reported that their children provided other forms of support: 65 percent indicated that their children helped with practical matters and 40 percent said their children gave much emotional support.

24. People who were more socially active in their youth also participate more in social life when they are old. **TRUE**. Based upon retrospective accounts, those who were more socially active earlier in life continued to be so.

25. In old age, the rich are healthier than the poor. **FALSE**. There were few differences between the rich and poor in the areas of physical and mental health. Two explanations were provided for this finding. First, selective mortality may have benefitted both the rich and poor. Second, the German health insurance system promotes access to medical services, regardless of personal financial security.

26. Women who were housewives for most of their lives are worse off in old age than women who were in paid employment. **FALSE**. Years of employment of married and widowed participants did not correlate with family financial status in older adulthood. This lack of relationship, as noted by the authors, may be due to the German social welfare system.

Life Satisfaction Quiz (answers)

1. As I grow older, things seem better than I thought they would be. AGREE

2. I have gotten more of the breaks in life than most of the people I know: AGREE

3. This is the dreariest time of my life. DISAGREE

4. I am just as happy as when I was younger. AGREE

5. My life could be happier than it is now. DISAGREE

6. These are the best years of my life. AGREE

7. Most of the things I do are boring or monotonous. DISAGREE

8. I expect some interesting and pleasant things to happen to me in the future. AGREE

9. The things I do are as interesting to me as they ever were. AGREE

10. I feel old and somewhat tired. DISAGREE

11. I feel my age, but it does not bother me. AGREE

12. As I look back on my life, I am fairly well satisfied. AGREE

13. I would not change my past life even if I could. AGREE

14. Compared to other people my age, I've made a lot of foolish decisions in my life. DISAGREE

15. Compared to other people my age, I make a good appearance. AGREE

16. I have made plans for things I'll be doing a month or a year from now. AGREE

17. When I think back over my life, I didn't get most of the important things I wanted. DISAGREE

18. Compared to other people, I get down in the dumps too often. DISAGREE

19. I've gotten pretty much what I expected out of life. AGREE

20. In spite of what people say, the lot of the average man is getting worse, not better. DISAGREE

Much of Chapter 1 dealt with your active participation in learning more about practical aging-related issues. The aging quizzes and corresponding findings provide us a better understanding of aging processes, as well as contemplating personal approaches to age more successful. In the *Preface*, Mary Pipher's (1999) book, *Another Country: Navigating the Emotional Terrain of Our Elders*, was suggested as appropriate reading. The book, sharing interviews mostly of Midwestern white and African Americans, presents stories of older persons and Pipher's notions of ageism in American society. Her opinions about ageism, as related to the quizzes in this chapter, are pointed:

1. Older persons are segregated for multiple reasons, including ignorance, prejudice, and a culture without prescriptions for dealing with older adults.
2. Older people are expected to be at the end of their lifespan. Many of us avoid significant relations with older adults, fearing the emotions associated with losing a loved one. A death of someone is easier to deal with in the abstract.
3. Our culture and its members reinforce ageism by negatively reinforcing the value of older individuals and positively reinforcing the values of youth and personal successes associated with academics, athletics, employment, and appearance.
4. The human condition seems to be one of focus on short-term goals and an emphasis on personal gains and loses, rather than long-term goals and a balance between personal and communal gains and losses.

Atchley (2000) provided research summaries on ageism. His summaries, noted below, are informative:

1. Stereotypes allow us to easily categorize people. Diversity and individual differences are not acknowledged.
2. Stereotypes of older people are positive and negative, with an emphasis on the negative.
3. For the physical domain, older adults are stereotyped as being frail or more vulnerable, with diminished capabilities in all aspects of physical functioning. Older adults with one or more obvious physical disabilities are viewed as very vulnerable in all aspects of their lives, including the psychological and social. Negative stereotypes of older people in the psychological domain include perceptions of significant intellectual decline, personality changes, inflexibility, loss in life satisfaction, and reduced motivation. Positive stereotypes for the psychological domain include perceptions of wisdom and persistence.
5. For the social domain, negative stereotypes of elders are those of loneliness, financial insecurity, fear of crime, institutionalization, dependency, and elitism. Positive stereotypes are those of caring grandparent, conservative, and volunteerism.
6. Since older adults and those at the beginning of the lifespan are more variable among themselves than adolescents and young and middle   aged adults, perceptions of diversity among older adults are much more accurate than stereotypes assuming commonalities.

It is very difficult for us to combat the youth-oriented reinforcers of society and ourselves, especially without reliable and valid information of changes in adaptive capabilities throughout the lifespan, and, as importantly, factors that contribute to the changes. There is an interesting dialectic about aging. On the one hand, aging is most often characterized by loss of capabilities, especially those directly associated with biological (physical) well-being. After adolescence and young adulthood, the physical lifespan profiles are those of stability (maintenance) and less of previously developed capabilities. Lifespan and gerontological research continues to illustrate, as does daily life, that loss of optimal functioning is inevitable in adulthood. There are differences among individuals as they age, related to losses in specific capabilities; viz., type of loss, timing of loss, rate of loss, and inter-relationships among types, timing, and rate of loss. Yet, all of us will die, and most of us will die due to one or more chronic illnesses associated with aging.

The other hand of the aging dialectic is that with inevitable loss in the functioning of capabilities, most older adults are able to function, albeit with additional assistance, in complex contexts. Throughout the lifespan, each of us adapt to successive changes in our physical, psychological, and social capabilities. During the earlier stages of the lifespan, many of these changes are associated with maturation and development (gains), whereas in later stages of the lifespan, many changes are associated with deterioration (losses).

Putting stereotypes aside, the dialectic about human aging–dilemma, really, throughout the lifespan–is associated with decisions made about personal life-style. For every period of the lifespan, decisions made (by others or personally) result in personal gains and losses. Chapter 4 includes illustrations of gains and losses, as well as conceptual points of view. For example, parental and/or child emphasis on the youngster's talent for ballet can result in gains for the child such as successively enhanced status through childhood, adolescence, and young adulthood as a talented ballerina. Losses for such a progeny could include significantly reduced opportunities and, correspondingly, skills in other physical performance capabilities, constricted peer relationships, and a restricted sense of self. A second example of the developmental dialectic and gains and losses comes from young adulthood. With marriage and children, young married partners gain a nuclear family, extended intimacy with each other and children, and more independence from their parents. Potential losses for the young married partners include separation from friends who are single, reduction of personal time to engage in previously enjoyed activities, and increased stress related to finances. Middle age provides a third example. Gains associated with middle age include financial security, renewal of intimacy or more engagement with a spouse when children leave the family nest, and recognition of accomplishment in work and/or communal organizations. Possible losses include financial insecurity associated with loss of employment, empty nest depression when children leave home, and significantly reduced physical fitness. The dialectic of gains/losses in older adulthood? Gains include the sense of freedom from years of work, enhanced extended family relations, and financial security. Losses may be insecurity without the financial and/or social support of employment, chronic illness, and deaths of significant others.

Successful Aging is about the later stages of the lifespan. But, how each of us arrives at the later stages contribute significantly to the rest of the adventure. The examples of gains and losses shared earlier illustrate both the dialectic of aging and one's ongoing contribution to normal, pathological, and/or successful aging.

Chapter 2

LIFESPAN DEVELOPMENT

INTRODUCTION

One can gain an appreciation of aging processes in adulthood from a number of perspectives. Two points of view have received much acceptance from professionals interested in adulthood and older age. The study of **gerontology**, the first perspective, has had a longer *sustained* history than the study of **lifespan development**, the second perspective. Both perspectives are well represented in Bengtson and Schaie's (1999) *Handbook of Theories of Aging*.

The gerontology and lifespan development points of view are helpful in that both provide a sense of organization for aging education, research, and practice. Both points of view offer theories or models that deal with age-related phenomena. The theories or models of aging provide various senses of age-related changes and corresponding intervention ideas. *Successful Aging: Integrating Contemporary Ideas, Research Findings, and Intervention Strategies* will emphasize the lifespan development approach as it includes aging as one facet of developmental changes throughout the lifespan. Given that successive periods of development and developmental phenomena are, to greater and lesser degrees, dependent on preceding periods and phenomena, it seems reasonable to opt for an aging point of view that is inclusive rather than exclusive.

It is timely to address **types of aging**. Two types of aging are presented; the first deals with definitions of aging, while the latter focuses on conditions of aging.

Definitions of Age

1. Chronological age. Chronological age refers to time, in number of years, for a person since birth. Sometimes we make this definition even more general by the use of terms like levels, periods, phases, or stages. Chronological age is a rather crude unit of measure of development; it doesn't directly cause any condition or behavior. One can argue that such a phenomenon as mandatory or self-imposed retirement, based upon chronological age, has an impact on a person's life. Yet, such an impact would be only an indirect one. Interestingly, the overwhelming majority of research studies in lifespan development and gerontology use chronological age as a variable to segregate individuals, with one research focus being on age-related differences in other study variables. This practice has resulted in chronological age being a dependent or generic variable, with a multitude of research task performances and related constructs classified according to chronological ages or more general categories such as levels, periods, phases, and stages.

Fry (1999, pp. 279–281), discussing anthropological theories of age and aging, provided interesting ideas about the concept of age, as summarized:

> . . . Chronological age as a marker of behavior had to be invented and needed a good reason to be created. We often look to the record keeping of churches and the emergence of vital statistics and demography in Europe as the origin of chronological age as a measuring point. The Romans were among the first to use age as a defining term, for conscription into their military forces.
>
> Chronological age is clearly associated with state-level societies. Age defined chronologically becomes the basis for universalistic (in contrast to particularistic) norms in regulating a large population. Age defines the responsibilities of citizenship. With capitalism and industry, age has further been used to define adulthood and labor force participation. Legal norms prevent children from working and force them into educational institutions. Legal norms define when one can enter into adult activities—voting, military service, marriage, driving, drinking, and so on. Legal norms also define if and when one is pensionable and expected to retire from the labor force. Legal norms gauge the life course and calibrate a social clock of role entrances and exits. At minimum there is a stage of preparation, a stage of participation, and a stage of retirement.
>
> Preparatory stages are ones of enculturation and skill acquisition for an adult life of work and a career in the labor market. What begins at home, with nurturance by parents, is completed in formal educational institutions, with finely age-graded classes defined by chronological age. Children are launched into adulthood once they have completed their schooling and have attained the chronological age-defined legal norms of adult privilege. Especially relevant are the norms concerning age of work and age of marriage as thresholds into the stage of adult participation. Retirement from

participation in the labor force is similarly guided by chronological legal norms, most notably the age of eligibility for state social security programs or pensions. . . .

Age and aging are clearly temporal phenomena at the core of gerontology and theories about becoming old. But on second thought, is age really a variable? The answer is yes and no. On the negative side, age is time, and time is not a variable. Time is a property of the universe. Time never caused anything. It is what happens in time that is of importance to theories of aging. Indeed, most research on aging in biology, psychology, and the social sciences has focused on what happens in time. Bodies are transformed and societies respond to individuals who are very young and those who have been here a long time. Age becomes a variable only insofar as it is culturally conceptualized and incorporated into social life. Age also becomes a variable when a society becomes aware of its own demographics and begins to worry. . . .

2. Physical or biological age. Physical age refers to the biological, physiological, and/or cellular integrities of the person's structures, systems, and processes. Most often, physical age refers to vital organ structure and function capacities such as those associated with the cardiovascular, nervous, and pulmonary systems. Generally, the "younger" one's physical age, the better the biological quality of life, as well as length of life. One's physical or biological age is not necessarily highly correlated with his or her chronological age. It is common to witness individuals of the same chronological age, especially in older adulthood, who differ greatly in terms of physical age. Particularly in adulthood and old age, the idea of "use it or lose it" rings true.

As will be discussed in later sections, the negative effects of physical age are noticeable by middle adulthood. These effects are enhanced if the individual becomes less active. The enhanced deterioration is not so subtle! Recently, I had outpatient surgery to strip a varicose vein in my left leg. At 56 years of age, I have been an avid bicyclist for 15 years–some friends assess my devotion to the exercise as neurotic. Following the surgeon's orders, I refrained from any formal exercise for two weeks, with my left leg supported with compression bandages. During the two weeks of relative physical inactivity, I gained 10 pounds, had difficulty sleeping at night, and was, in general, rather grouchy. After the compression bandages were removed, I started my biking routine–which, by the way, begins daily at 5:15 a.m. The first week of biking was, I believe, more frustrating than the frustration of being relatively inactive for two weeks after surgery. My legs, shoulders, and lower back were sore from the daily exercise. I could not, at the start of my retraining, meet the usual standard of two hours of exercise.

Ever so slowly, it seemed, I regained my endurance and the soreness went away. At 30 years of age, I had major knee surgery, resulting in a full length leg cast for six weeks. After the third day of surgery, I was less inactive, with less pain, than two weeks after the varicose vein surgery. With the post-operative knee surgery, I did not gain weight, slept as usual, and was never grouchy. While my left leg had atrophied during its six weeks in a cast, I was able to resume running (albeit more slowly) two days after the cast was removed. What a difference 26 years make. The relevant points are that physical aging means deterioration of biological structures and functions, as well as the requirement of using what physical abilities one does have to retard the erosion of such abilities.

3. **Psychological age**. This definition of age refers to one's intellectual, emotional/personality, and motivational adaptive capabilities. A person's intellectual, emotional/personality, and motivational capabilities, unlike physical or biological capabilities, are more difficult to assess. Psychological abilities or phenotypes are inferred from behaviors in varying situations, including real-life, laboratory, and test settings. These psychological abilities are referred to as latent variables or higher order constructs in that they are not directly observable and usually include more than one specific measure of assessment. For example, intelligence is a very complex latent or higher order variable. Intelligence is defined by many adaptive abilities and is, most often, assessed with a standardized intelligence test. Like physical or biological age, psychological age is not necessarily highly correlated with chronological age. And, physical and psychological ages are not necessarily highly correlated. For example, we find older adults—defined by chronological age—who differ significantly on measures of biological, intellectual, emotional, and motivational "fitness." Intellectual abilities are usually measured by standardized intelligence tests. The most often used intelligence tests are the Wechsler Scales (Wechsler Preschool Primary Scale of Intelligence, Wechsler Intelligence Scale for Children, and Wechsler Adult Intelligence Scale) and the Stanford-Binet Intelligence Tests. As suggested by the Wechsler scale titles, different scales are used for different periods of the lifespan. Both the Wechsler and Stanford Binet intelligence tests, like most standardized tests, are statistically controlled for chronological age and gender variables. Both tests, like most tests of psychological abilities, however, have been criticized for not statistically controlling for cultural or ethnic factors.

Emotional/personality abilities refer to behavioral dispositions. Baltes, Lindenberger, and Straudinger (1998) have recently integrated emotional/personality, self-concept/identity, and self-regulatory processes into Baltes' views of self and personality in his lifespan model. While motivational and intellectual factors are linked to self and personality, Baltes and his associates focus on self and personality as abilities which the person uses in monitoring himself, others, and experience in general. Baltes' views of self and personality, as well as Costa and McCrae's (1995) Big Five personality factors (neuroticism, extroversion, openness, agreeableness, and conscientiousness) will be discussed within a lifespan framework of successful aging in Chapter 4.

Motivational abilities are usually categorized as intrinsic (internal motivation) or extrinsic (external motivation). In terms of lifespan development, Schulz and Heckhausen (1996; Heckhausen & Schulz, 1995) have provided a motivational model of the lifespan which differentiates primary control from secondary control. An individual's primary control focuses on changing the environment for personal gain or avoidance of loss, while secondary control focuses on maintaining or enhancing one's sense of self. This model will be presented in Chapter 4 within a lifespan framework of successful aging, as will facts and ideas about self-efficacy.

4. Sociological age. This age is defined by social roles. It deals with social expectations and roles associated with such significant phenomena as schooling, peer relations, marriage, parenting, work, retirement, loss of spouse, and dying. What are the roles of parents (mother, father), grandparents, and retirees? Social age, clearly, is not the same as chronological, physical, or psychological age, though social roles do, indirectly relate to the other ages. Social roles and, correspondingly, social ages, differ among cultures and subcultures. Primary aspects of sociological aging, discussed more fully in Chapters 5 and 7, are social convoys (quantity and quality of significant others), intergenerational familial relationships, and financial status (real, perceived, and projected).

5. Historical or contextual age. Rather recently, this definition has been recognized as important in the understanding of lifespan development. Historical or contextual age refers to one's developmental age markers in the context of history. For example, in the nineteenth century, regardless of culture, the human lifespan was much shorter than the twentieth century. Specific reasons for the difference will be provided in later parts of *Successful Aging*, but advances in medicine, personal and communal health practices, and education should come to mind. Aging, regardless of definition, should be appreciated in the context of history. Preventive intervention for successful aging, for example, makes sense in the twentieth century, given the research and public dissemination of findings related to tobacco use, drug abuse, poor nutrition, overeating, sustained high levels of stress, and lack of physical exercise.

Within any period of history, it is also important to appreciate cultural differences among and within countries. Lifespan developmentalists have attempted to delineate such differences with attention to such factors as sex, race, ethnicity, sexual preference, socioeconomic status, geographic regions, and education. Given the significant advances related to more successful lifestyles made over historical time, it is no wonder that all types of age—definitions and conditions—have changed.

6. Functional age. This definition incorporates the definitions of physical, psychological, social, and historical ages. Functional age refers to all significant capabilities allowing a person to adapt in the environment. The better your functional age, the more able you are to function.

Perhaps it was Satchel Page, a glorious African American baseball player often questioned about his age while playing the competitive sport, who stated that ". . . if you didn't know when you were born, you wouldn't know how old you were. . . ." With the above definitions of age, it is important to grasp what definition of age is being used in describing someone. To make matters even more interesting, Carstensen, Isaacowitz, Charles (1999), provided a theory of socioemotional selectivity as related to time or age markers. In their article, *Taking Time Seriously*, (pp. 165, 166), the authors provide useful ideas about definitions of age throughout the lifespan:

> . . . As people move through life they become increasingly aware that time is in some sense, "running out." More social contacts seem superficial—trivial—in contrast to the ever-deepening ties of existing close relationships. It becomes increasingly important to make the "right" choice, not to waste time on gradually diminishing future payoffs. Increasingly, emotionally meaningful goals are pursued. . . . we argue that the perception of time as constrained or limited as opposed to expansive or open-ended has important implications for emotion, cognition, and motivation. In particular, we argue that the approach of endings is associated with heightened emphasis on feelings and emotion states. Activities that are unpleasant or simply devoid of meaning are not compelling under conditions in which time is perceived as limited. Interest in novel information, because it is so closely intertwined with future needs, is reduced. Instead, when endings are primed people focus on the present rather than on the future or the past, and this temporal shift leads to an emphasis on the intuitive and subjective rather than the planful and analytical. The argument . . . is that a temporal emphasis on the present increases the value people place on life and emotion, importantly influencing the decisions they make. Subsequently . . . the perception of time is inevitably linked to the selection and pursuit

of social goals. . . . Because chronological age is inextricably and negatively associated with the amount of time left in life, age-related patterns do emerge, but even these patterns can be altered when individuals adopt a time perspective different from what is predicted by their place in the life cycle. . . .

Carstensen, Isaacowitz, and Charles' ideas of time, as related to one's perception of the lifespan remaining, suggest that regardless of the definitions of age we apply to ourselves and others, our major decisions about what is important in life are dependent upon that perception of personal longevity. At the early stages of the lifespan, the perception of personal longevity is, if anything, a vague concept unworthy of much attention or factoring into important decisions. While many of us may encounter a mid-life crisis dealing with the remaining years of life, Carstensen, Isaacowits, and Charles' notions focus on the probable limiting effects of restricted personal time remaining in older adulthood. Perceived limited life in older adulthood can certainly motivate the older individual to be more reflective (e.g., Erikson's final stage of psychosocial development), being intimate with long-term significant others, and, in general, getting one's house in order. Perceived limited life can also, however, motivate the older person to disengage from lifelong pursuits. The disengagement option could shorten one's real, instead of perceived, lifespan.

Three Age Conditions

1. Normal aging refers to the average course of development and is simply, the average of individual assessment on any measure and with any definition of age. Much of what is presented in the professional and popular presses about lifespan development and aging focuses on normal or average aging. Given statistical probability, most of us are closer to the mean or average, on any given measure, than significantly away from normal. Yet, two facts of development are important to remember. First, lifespan development deals with a multitude of variables, with complex interactions. Second, there is much variability in development, at any period of the lifespan. Thus, one needs to avoid the assumption of normal or average aging being a standard for self or other comparisons.

2. Pathological aging is an expression of either acute or chronic disease in which normal aging patterns are not followed. Usually with pathological aging, there is more rapid deterioration of certain structures and capabilities and more rapid deterioration of the person in general. Alzheimer's disease is the most illustrative pathological condition of the present Zeitgeist. Pathological aging can occur at any stage of the lifespan, with Down's

Syndrome (mutagenic or genetic dysfunction) and AIDS (contractible at any age).

3. Successful aging, like normal and pathological aging, is a concept or generalization. Successful aging refers to characteristics of aging individuals, who live long, productive, and satisfactory lives. While pathological aging can certainly reduce life expectancy, such abnormal physical aging need not retard a person from having a productive, satisfying life. Some professionals have used optimal or exceptional aging instead of successful aging in articulating the realities of maximizing one's potentials, especially during older adulthood. It is fair to share that few individuals fit into any of the three aging conditions—normal, pathological, and successful—for all capabilities. That is, as we age, it is likely that we will exhibit all three aging conditions in one or more capabilities. Perhaps the objective is to minimize pathological aging and maximize successful aging in those capabilities we have most direct control over. Another objective is to assume control for those capabilities as early in our lifespan as we can; i.e., use preventive rather than alleviation self-control strategies early on in coping with substantiated age-related declines in capabilities.

The study of gerontology was first organized and integrated for professional dissemination in the works of Cowdry (*Problems of Ageing,* 1942) and Birren (*Handbook of Aging and the Individual,* 1959). Much of the study of aging deals with characteristics of the changing older person, though some gerontologists do include earlier lifespan factors as determinants of behavior in later periods of the life. Birren and Renner (1977, p. 4), offered the following definition of gerontology or the study of aging: "Aging refers to the regular changes that occur in mature genetically representative organisms living under representative environmental conditions as they advance in chronological age."

As an example of successful professional aging, Birren (1999) recently provided a personal perspective on theories of aging. Bengtson and Schaie's (1999) *Handbook of Theories of Aging* ". . . was conceptualized as a *Festschrift* in honor of James E. Birren's 80th birthday, commemorating his remarkable career as a scientist, scholar, teacher, and institution builder in the field of gerontology. . . ." (p. 475). Birren, in his *Handbook of Theories of Aging* chapter, articulated the difference between the study of aging and the study of lifespan development. The study of aging—gerontology—deals with forces that result in decline of physical, psychological, and social structure and function. The study of lifespan development deals with the development, stability, and erosion of physical, psychological, and social structure and function. As noted by Birren (1999, p. 466), ". . . In the developing organism the systems move toward more differentiation and from less to more capacity for self-repair. In aging, or senescence, the organism moves toward less repair capacity and greater likelihood of developing a fatal illness from which it cannot protect itself. A question for contemporary thought about theory is whether it is desirable to attempt to blend both processes into a single conceptual system. . . ." One answer to the question is to support the blend, which is what lifespan development is about.

Lifespan development is a professional field of inquiry that has its origins with the German psychologist Johann Nikolaus Tetens (see Baltes, 1979). Tetens wrote a two-volume work on human nature and development, titled, *Menschliche Natur und ihre Entwicklung* (1777). What is remarkable about this work, in terms of the present professional field of lifespan development, is that Tetens advocated lifespan principles that were, for the most part, abandoned until the 19th century. As summarized by Baltes, Lindenberger, and Staudinger (1998, p. 1032), Tetens' second volume included the following chapters:

> On the perfectibility of human psyche (Seelennatur) and its development in general
> On the development of the human body
> On the analogy between the development of the psyche (mind) and the development of the body
> On the differences between men (humans) in their development
> On the limits of development and the decline of psychological abilities
> On the progressive development of the human species
> On the relationship between optimization (Vervollkommnung) of man and his life contentment (Glueckseligkeit)

As noted by Baltes, Lindenberger, and Staudinger (1998), lifespan development was not reinvented with a receptive professional audience until the late 1960s. Paul Baltes, Director of the Lifespan Psychology Center, Max Planck Institute for Human Development, Berlin, has the distinction of being the most durable, to date, of the lifespan development advocates. He, with his many colleagues, past and present, earned the reputation of being the modern era advocate of lifespan development. More importantly for the purposes of *Successful Aging*, Paul Baltes represents a model of successful aging. Later in the book, characteristics of successful aging will be identified, but I note here that having a sense of wisdom is one of the characteristics. Until the late 1960s, particularly in American professional literature and practice, the lifespan was dealt with as segmented rather than continuous. With this segmentation, professional and practical interests were focused on infancy and childhood. Much later, professional and practical interests focused on later adulthood (geriatrics, gerontology). For those interested in reviewing contemporary summaries of lifespan segments, I recommend Lerner's (1998) opus, *Handbook of Child Psychology*, volumes 1–4. Although the Handbook's title identifies child psychology, Lerner's edited volumes provide, albeit with technical verbiage, up-to-date literature reviews of primary age-related characteristics in all lifespan development periods. The chapters in the Handbook are produced by leading scholars, written for scholars and advanced students of various segments of the lifespan. Another way to review a segmented lifespan development approach to aging is to read one of the excellent undergraduate lifespan psychology texts, such as Santrock's (1999), *Life-Span Development*, 7th edition. Santrock's lifespan text includes older age, middle-age, young-adulthood, adolescence, and child-hood as an important parts of the lifespan. *Successful Aging*, on the other hand, focuses on older adulthood within the context of lifespan development, rather than one of many periods or stages of the lifespan. If you are interested in detailed information about aging theories, I recommend Birren's (1996) *Encyclopaedia of Gerontology* and Bengtson and Schaie's (1999) *Handbook of Theories of Aging*.

From our personal points of view, most of us, especially during the formative years, do not appreciate a lifespan development perspective. Given that many of us are most focused on the present, regardless of chrono-logical age, an argument can be made that one's lifespan perspective is not appreciated throughout the lifespan. This segmentation of one's lifespan seems to be a part of the human condition. As we develop, most of us focus on that segment or part of the lifespan that we find ourselves in, with two obvious exceptions. As parents, we also focus on the period of the lifespan that our offspring are in. As our parents age, we then focus, to some degree, on older adulthood. For most of us, however, much of our reflection, at any given point of personal development, centers upon ourselves and our present contexts of place and time. The effects of this human condition are relative. For example, regardless of age, if we do not concentrate on the goals and correlated gains and losses associated with a present state of affairs, then we place ourselves and significant others in jeopardy. But, if we concentrate too much on specific goals and correlated gains and losses that are self-serving, then we jeopardize ourselves, significant others, and relationships with them.

BRIEF OVERVIEW OF AGE-RELATED THEORIES OF AGING

Most integrative texts of gerontology summarize, to a greater or lesser extent, (a) normative or descriptive information about aging and (b) categorical determinants of aging in older adulthood. The following summaries of determinants and norms are provided as introductions to contemporary information. More detailed presentations are made by Belsky (1999) at the introductory level and Bengtson and Schaie (1999) at the advanced level. *Successful Aging* deals primarily with successful aging, and the model of choice is Baltes' views of lifespan development. Given these biases, a brief overview of aging theories will illustrate the diversity of views in the disciplines of lifespan development and gerontology. These theories, including hypotheses of age-related changes can be categorized several ways. First, some theories emphasize more distant cause-effect relationships for determinants of aging in adulthood and corresponding changes in abilities. Second, and as important, theories of age-related changes usually reflect the theorists' primary interest in aging, e.g., genetic and biological theories deal with physical aging, psychological theories deal with cognitive aspects of aging, and sociological theories deal with social roles and aging. Baltes' model of successful aging is an integrative or eclectic one; it includes important viewpoints of biological, psychological, and sociological aging

Physical Aging Theories

As all normal adults realize, physical aging, starting in young adulthood with many abilities covers almost all physical characteristics and all physical systems (such as the cardiovascular, pulmonary, skeletal, and nervous systems). The aging process of physical systems and abilities is one of erosion, deterioration, and loss. While there are significant differences among individuals regarding the initiation, rate, and successive levels of physical aging of individual abilities and more complex physical systems, the undeniable facts are that physical aging and corresponding disease and disability are inevitable. Even with the best hereditary contributions of our parents and the best environments for ourselves available, the super human will illustrate physical aging patterns and die. Why is physical aging inevitable?

Physical aging and diseases and physical disabilities correlated with physical aging are the focus of biological theories of aging. Biological theories of aging usually focus on cells or connective tissues among cells (Belsky, 1999). Cristofalo, Tresini, Francis, and Volker (1999) distinguish between stochastic and programmed theories of aging. Stochastic theories of physical aging stress random damage as determinants, while programmed theories stress the importance of genetic and developmental regulators as determinants. An interesting notion linked to genetic regulator determinants is that the phenomenon of natural selection (survival of the fittest) may include not only genetic selectivity (positively correlated with long-term environmental selectivity) to enhance reproduction, but genetic selectivity that is deleterious to both longevity and quality of physical aging. Or, genetic selectivity for reproductive purposes early in adulthood may not be so highly, positively correlated with physical aging in middle and late adulthood. Biological theories are so appealing because of the finite lifespan of species, regulatory physical aging in all members of a given species, primary diseases of species, and regulatory progression of these diseases.

As summarized by Belsky (1999), the two most advocated random damage biological theories of aging are *DNA Damage* and *Free Radical Damage.* DNA Damage is a random damage theory that postulates that the accumulation of cellular errors or mutations interferes with the production of normal proteins and protein synthesis. These mutations are presumed to be the result of both environmental insults and successive cellular activity. With more mutations, more defective proteins, and more cells malfunctioning, aging, disease, and death occurs. Free Radical Damage theory postulates that cellular waste products accumulate inside and outside cells, attach to other cells, and impair cellular functioning. Free radicals are included in cellular waste products.

Programmed biological theories of aging postulate that aging, like maturation, is the result of a set plan, which includes timing of effects from determining causes. The three most discussed programmed biological theories are: *Rate of Living, Aging -Hypothalamus and Aging - Immune System.* For Rate of Living proponents, rate of metabolism is genetically determined. Increases and decreases in rate of metabolic functioning, according to this theory, correspond to differential rates of aging and longevity. Though metabolic rate in some species has been shown to be related to longevity, specific causal agents have not been identified (Cristofalo, Tresini, Francis, & Volker, 1999). A related notion for aging, Restriction of Calories suggests that diet is related to metabolic function. As noted by Belsky (1999), dietary restrictions relate to:

- Retardation of chronic diseases
- Resistance to infection by retarding loss of immune function
- Improvement in capacity to deal with extreme heat
- Retardation of age-related biochemical changes in organs
- Enhancement of glucose metabolism, retarding onset of diabetes
- Improvement of muscle strength

Aging-Hypothalamus and hormonal theories of aging are primarily descriptive in nature, as support for such ideas are based upon correlation of hormonal changes, typically reductionary, and aging. As noted by Belsky (1999, p. 69), ". . . The hypothalamus is definitely responsible for the aging of one body system. By shutting off the production of the ovarian hormone estrogen at about the age 50, it ushers in menopause, and so ends a woman's capacity to conceive a child. . . ." The hypothalamus is one of several structures producing hormones. As reported by Cristofalo, Tresini, Francis, and Volker (1999), other neuroendocrine system structures may contribute to the aging process; viz., adrenal cortex and pituitary gland. From immunological theories come the notion that the decline in the immune system results in aging and death. Atchley (2000, p. 79) notes the following about changes in the immune system and subsequent changes in physical functioning:

> . . . If the immune system over time loses its capacity to recognize deviations in substances produced within the body, then mutated cells that formerly would have been destroyed by the immune system survive to the potential harm of the organism. This could explain why susceptibility to cancer increases with age.

> . . . Sometimes the immune system produces antibodies that destroy even normal cells, a process known as *autoimmune reaction.* The prevalence of autoimmune antibodies in the blood increases with age. Autoimmune reactions have also been linked with several age-related diseases, including rheumatoid arthritis and late-onset diabetes.

> . . . A failure of the immune system to defend against disease or to slow an immune response can increase the physical debilitation associated with both acute and chronic diseases. . . .

Atchley (2000, p. 80), summaries the range of biological theories as follows. ". . . Aging may result from:

1. A hereditary genetic program that sets limits on growth, aging, and longevity.
2. Age-related changes in the functioning of the genetic program.
3. An age-related buildup of cross-links or free radicals resulting in lowered molecular functioning.
4. An age-related lowered efficiency of the immune system in identifying and destroying harmful or mutated cells.
5. An age-related increase in autoimmune reactions in which antibodies that destroy normal cells are produced.
6. An age-related decline in the capacity of the nervous system to speedily and efficiently maintain bodily integration and prevent bodily deterioration. . . .

Psychological Age-Related Theories

There are a number of psychological theories of aging. These theories are different from both biological and sociological ones in that psychological concepts and behavioral adaptiveness are emphasized in the former. There are both age-related and non-age-related psychological theories of aging. Age-related psychological theories incorporate at least two principles. First, aging is part of the developmental continuum. Second, causal agents for changes in adaptability can be both distal (occurring earlier in the lifespan) or proximal (occurring in later adulthood). The following age-related theories are presented in order of historical entrance to the fields of lifespan development and gerontology:

1. **Freud's** *Psychoanalytic Perspective.* Freud's writings (e.g., *A General Introduction to Psychoanalysis,* 1917) about the unconscious in the early 1900s continue to have pervasive impact in psychology and related disciplines. As related to aging, the psychoanalytic perspective, if offering any light on what contributes to psychological adaptiveness in later life, suggests that our basic personality and self identify is forged in childhood. These crucial aspects of cognitive adaptability, having matured in childhood, should illustrate relative stability throughout adolescence and the stages of adulthood. While Freud's ideas about the importance of unconscious motivation remain of interest to lifespan developmentalists and gerontologists, the notion of a fixed personality throughout most of the lifespan does not generate much interest.

2. **Carl Jung's** *Midlife Shift Theory.* A contemporary of Freud, Jung (1933) suggested that after childhood and early adolescence, individuals moved through two phases of adulthood. The first phase, from puberty to the early periods of adulthood, is characterized by self-generated needs, ambitions, and focus; viz., attention to one's own agendas of success and failure. In the second phase, starting in middle adulthood, the individual reflects upon personal agendas and those of significant others. Such personal reflection includes introspection of one's self, relations with others, and personal insight into some meaningfulness in life—one's own and others. As summarized by Labouvie-Vief and Diehl (1999), research has not, in general, supported Jung's notions about major reorganizations around midlife, especially centering around a midlife crisis.

3. **Erikson's** *Psychosocial Theory.* Drawing upon Freud's notion of identification, Erickson (1963, 1982) proposed eight stages of psychosocial development. Of the psychological age-related theories of aging, Erikson's is by far the most widely accepted by lifespan developmentalists and gerontologists. Identification, for Erikson, deals with characteristics of self

which persist, yet are subject to changes, over the lifespan (Atchley, 2000). While Freud promoted identification of self as being a derivative of parental modeling in childhood, Erikson suggested cultural or contextual influences beyond childhood as molding one's sense of self. For his eight stages of psychosocial development, Erikson provided eight crises or primary tasks for the individual to deal with. As summarized by Belsky (1999) and Santrock (1999), the stages and corresponding crises of adulthood are as follows:

DEVELOPMENTAL STAGES	*CRISIS*
Early Adulthood	Intimacy versus Isolation
Middle Adulthood	Generativity versus Stagnation
Later Adulthood	Integrity versus Despair

Young adults have the task, according to Erikson's psychosocial development ideas, of forming intimate, deeply meaningful relationships with one or more individuals. The primary focus for intimacy is forming an intimate relationship with a long-term partner. Young adults who do not form intimate relationships become isolated individuals, shallow in establishing and maintaining meaningful interpersonal relationships. During middle adulthood, the primary task for positive self-identity is to be generative; viz., nurturing the positive development of successive generations, be it with children and grandchildren or broader aspects of one's sense of community. For those unable to meet this challenge of self-identity, one is left with a sense of stagnation or unmet obligations to others. In later adulthood, the primary task is to establish and maintain a sense of ego integrity; viz., positive reflections upon one's life and acceptance of both life's inevitabilities and one's own personal accomplishments and failures. If we do not develop and maintain ego integrity in later adulthood, the alternative is to be depressed and fearful of upcoming death.

Sociological Theories of Aging

Bengtson, Burgess, and Parrott (1997), reviewing relevant research articles from 1990 to 1994, identified seven theoretical perspectives most often referenced in journal articles dealing with issues of social gerontology. These seven perspectives, summarized by Hillier and Barrow (1999, p. 68), are categorized in Table 2.1. In addition to the Bengtson et al. (1997) recent survey of social gerontology orientations, Disengagement Theory and Activity Theory remain important contributions for a sociological perspective of aging. Disengagement Theory, promoted in Cumming and Henry's (1961), *Growing Old*, suggests that with advancing age in adulthood comes the normal decrease in physical, mental, and social activity. Disengagement provides reciprocity in the withdrawal of the individual from society and, correspondingly, the society from the individual. This sociological-based notion of older age, refined by Streib and Schneider (1971) to be one of differential disengagement, was, and is, at odds with contemporary research findings and attitudes about aging. While older adults, and younger ones too, for that matter, will disengage from certain long-lasting activities and/or relations, the disengagement is based upon specific contributing factors and need not generalize to other activities and/or relations. Activity Theory (Atchley, 2000; Hillier & Barrow, 1999), focuses on the findings of earlier positive physical, mental, and social lifestyles and adaptability in the later stage of life. Simply put, the more active—physically, psychologically, and socially—one is over the lifespan, the more successful one is at aging.

The brief review of biological, psychological, and sociological theories of aging albeit incomplete, sets the stage for a contemporary lifespan perspective that is both interdisciplinary and progressive. Baltes' lifespan perspective is interdisciplinary in that appropriate concepts and facts from many disciplines are incorporated into a more diverse model of development, including the gains often associated with maturation and the losses often associated with aging. Baltes' perspective is progressive in that the gains and losses within the lifespan are associated with an appreciation for successful aging.

BALTES' EIGHT PRINCIPLES OF LIFESPAN DEVELOPMENT

Baltes (1987, 1997), Baltes, Lindenberger and Staudinger (1998), and Baltes, Staudinger, and Lindenberger (1999) have summarized primary principles of lifespan development. The following summary is based upon the 1998 and 1999 works.

Principle 1: Lifespan Development

Individual or ontogenetic development is a lifelong process; no age, stage, period, or phase is any more important than any other. Berk (1998) has provided the following short summaries of lifespan stages:

> *Prenatal life (conception to birth).* This period illustrates the most rapid and pervasive of the lifespan, with life starting as a one-celled organism.
> *Infancy and toddlerhood (birth to two years of age).* During this period, there are dramatic changes, with special emphasis given to motor, perceptual, and intellectual abilities.

Successful Aging

Table 2–1
Theoretical models in social gerontology

Theory	Description	Key Concepts
Social constructionist	Focuses on individual agency and social behavior within larger structures of society; interest in understanding individual processes of aging as influenced by social definitions and structures	Labeling, social breakdown theory; situational features of aging
Social exchange theories	Examines exchange behavior between people of different ages as a result of the shift in roles, skills, resources that accompanies aging	Social costs and benefits; social resources; interaction; reciprocity; social power
Life course perspective	Explains the dynamic, context, and process nature of aging; age-related transitions; social meaning of aging as a process; focus on individuals, cohorts, and groups	Developmental tasks; social time clocks; social ecology; life trajectories and transitions, age roles and norms
Feminist theories	As a primary organizing principle for social life across the life course, gender is a primary consideration in understanding aging and the aged	Gender stratification; power structures; macrolevel analysis of social institutions; social networks and caregiving; family work
Age stratification	Focuses on role of social structures in the process of aging, looking at age cohort movement across time; asychrony between structural and individual change over time; interdependence of age cohorts and social structures	Age cohorts; social structures; structural lag; cohort flow
Political economy of aging	Explains how interaction of economic and political forces determines how social resources are allocated; how variations in treatment and status of elderly are reflected in policy, economic trends	Structural constraints, control of social resources, marginalization, social class
Critical theory	Focuses on humanistic dimensions of aging; structural components of aging; interested in understanding subjective and interpretive dimensions of aging, processes creating practical change, and knowledge that helps people change	Positive models of aging; power, social action, and social meaning in aging

Source: Bengtson, & Parrott, Tonya M. (1997). Reprinted with permission.

Early childhood (two to six years of age). In these four years children become more refined in their abilities, and are more self-controlled and self-sufficient; thought and language develop at an exceptional rate.

Middle childhood (six to 11 years of age). This period is the start of the school years; children learn more about the outside world and rules, participate in organizations and games, and develop more logical thought processes and senses of self and morality.

Adolescence (11 to 20 years of age). A bridge between childhood and adulthood, this period deals with puberty, adult physical abilities, and sexuality; thought becomes more abstract and idealistic; and, the later adolescent establishes autonomy from the family.

Early adulthood (20 to 40 years of age). This lengthy period is characterized by adults leaving home, finishing formal education, having an occupation, and obtaining financial independence; young adults seek a career path, mature intimate relationships, marriage, and raising children.

Middle adulthood (40 to 60 years of age). Another lengthy period, this is characterized by maximum responsibility for family, work, and community.

Late adulthood (60 years and older). Fortunately, another lengthy period for many, it deals with retirement, being a senior citizen, and reflecting upon one's meaning of life.

Burnside, Ebersole, and Monea (1979) expanded the period of late adulthood to include:

Young-old adulthood (60–69 years of age). Pre-retirement and retirement issues are the focus, with physical strength and endurance declines.

Middle-aged old adulthood (70 to 79 years of age). Loss of friends and family members occurs, social contacts and obligations are reduced, and chronic illness problems increase.

Old-old adulthood (80 to 89 years of age). Frailty characterizes this period, and more care is needed for personal and social demands.

Very old-old adulthood (90 years of age and older). Health problems are more severe in this final stage, yet, those who survive to this stage are usually more agile and fit than those who did not survive early stages of older adulthood.

To best understand development and/or any particular period within it, one needs to appreciate the processes and change throughout the lifespan. For those interested in earlier phases life, for example childhood or adolescence, having an appreciation for lifespan processes and changes provides for a better grasp of how earlier phases relate to later phases of life. For those interested in later phases of life, for example adulthood or old age, having a lifespan appreciation provides for both relationships among phases and possible distal determinants of later life.

For those interested in later adulthood and old age, as well as individuals in these stages of life, it may not be surprising to learn that most younger people are more interested in matters associated with their own periods of development and much less interested in issues associated with periods before and after their own. While some younger persons illustrate genuine interest in matters of older persons, a fair statement is that most of us focus on ourselves, regardless of stage of development.

Principle 2: Lifespan Changes in the Dynamic between Biology and Culture

Fundamental to a person's life and more observable during adulthood and old age, is the divergence between biological aging and aging that is more directly related to learning and environmental influences on developmental change. Baltes (1997), in his 1996 address for the Distinguished Contributions to the International Advancement of Psychology award, shared an interesting treatise on the incomplete architecture of human ontogeny. The following is from his introductory remarks, as presented in *American Psychologist*, 1997, p. 366):

> Drawing on both evolutionary and ontogenetic perspectives, the basic biological-genetic and social-cultural architecture of human development is outlined. Three principles are involved. First, evolutionary selection pressure predicts a negative age correlation, and, therefore, genome-based plasticity and biological potential decrease with age. Second, for growth aspects of human development to extend further into the life-span, culture-based resources are required at ever-increasing levels. Third, because of age-related losses in biological plasticity, the efficiency of culture is reduced as life-span development unfolds. Joint application of these principles suggests that the lifespan architecture becomes more and more incomplete with age. . . .

Relatedly, Baltes, Lindenberger, and Staudinger (1998, p. 1041) share four factors critical to the principle of lifespan changes in the dynamic between biology and culture:

1. An age-related general reduction in the amount and quality of biology-based resources as individuals moves toward old age.
2. The age-correlated increase in the amount and quality of culture

needed to generate higher and higher levels of growth.

3. The age-associated biology-based loss in efficiency with which cultural resources are used.
4. The relative lack of cultural, old age-friendly, support structures.

Baltes and Smith (1999) have elaborated on Baltes' earlier notions of the architecture of human development, an architecture Baltes and associates believe is incomplete. Figure 2–1 illustrates three general factors of the dynamics between biology and the environment throughout a person's lifespan.

> First, . . . Evolutionary selection benefits decrease with age. The first foundational lifespan principle [the first panel of Figure 2–1] refers to the role of evolutionary-based genetic functions and their expression across the life span. It states that the benefits resulting from evolutionary selection decrease with age. Support for this principle comes from population geneticists, who argue in a similar vein (i.e., that there was an evolutionary neglect of old age). A related fact is associated with ontogenetic biological theories of aging that emphasize an age-associated loss in biological potential (Finch & Tanzi, 1997; Martin, Austad, & Johnson, 1996; Rose, 1991) . . . In humans, evolutionary selection pressure has operated primarily during the first half of life to ensure reproductive fitness (Partridge & Barton, 1993). Moreover, in earlier historical time few people lived to be old. As a consequence, compared to younger ages, it is likely that the "modern" human genome in older age groups contain a larger number of deleterious genes and dysfunctional genetic expressions. One concrete illustration of this age-based weakening of the benefits of evolutionary selection is the existence of late-life illnesses such as Alzheimer dementia (for other examples see Martin, et al., 1996). . . .

A second factor is that ". . . there is an age-related increase in the need (demand) for culture. The second lifespan principle is depicted in the middle panel of Figure 2–1. For human development to extend itself farther and farther into the lifespan, there was an age-related increase in the need or demand for culture and its associated factors. Culture in this context refers to the entirety of psychological, social, material (environmental and technological), and symbolic (knowledge-based) resources that humans have generated and transmitted across generations (Cole, 1996; Durham, 1991; Shweder, 1991). . . ."

A first aspect of the age-related increase in the need for culture is that ". . . biological-genetic factors alone do not ensure the optimal expression of human development. Prerequisites for the fact that, over historical time, human ontogenesis has achieved higher and higher levels of functioning and longevity has been a conjoint evolutionary increase in the content and dissemination of culture. This idea of biological and cultural co-evolution (Durham, 1991) is illustrated in the changes in average life expectancy in industrialized countries during the twentieth century. Life expectancy increased from an average of about 45 years in 1900 to about 75 years in 1995. This increase is much more likely attributable to economic and technological innovations during this period than to changes in the genetic makeup of the population (Olshansky, 1995).

The second aspect underlying the age-related increase in demand for culture relates to the changing dynamic between biology and culture in the production of outcomes of adaptive fitness. As individuals approach old age, their biological potential declines (left part of Figure 2–1), so the demand for culture-based compensations (material, social, economic, psychological) to generate and maintain high levels of functioning increases. Examples of interactive tradeoffs between biological characteristics and culture can be found in research on cognitive aging. With increasing age, individuals need more environmental support to perform at the same level of achievement, for instance in the memory domain (Craik & Jennings, 1992); Dixon & Backman, 1995; Kliegl, Smith, & Baltes, 1989; Lindenberger & Baltes, 1994; Salthouse, 1991).

There is an age-related decrease in the efficiency of culture. The right-most panel of Figure 2–1 illustrates the third cornerstone of the overall lifespan architecture. With this foundational pillar, we argue that the relative

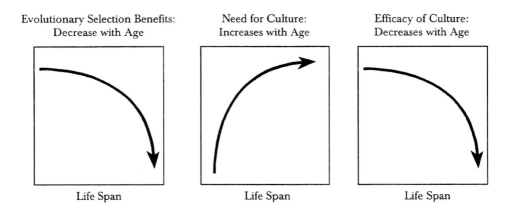

Figure 2–1. The incomplete architecture of human ontogeny. Schematic representation of three principles governing the dynamics between biology and culture across the ontogenic lifespan. Source: Baltes (1997). Reprinted with permission.

efficiency (effectiveness) of psychological, social, material, and cultural interventions or inputs wanes during the lifespan, beginning at least in the middle years if not earlier (P.B. Baltes et al., 1997). This is not to deny that there continues to be plasticity in the second half of life. Indeed, the extent of plasticity within different domains of functioning and on an individual may be larger than typically believed (P.B. Baltes et al., 1997; Schaie, 1996; Willis, 1990). Rather, this third pillar draws attention to the proposal that the score of plasticity of the human organism declines with age (see also Magnusson, 1996).

There are many examples from cognitive training studies to support this proposal of a negative lifespan script in cultural efficiency or efficacy (P.B. Baltes; Salthouse, 1991; Schaie, 1996). The older the adult, the more time, practice, and effort it takes to attain the performance levels and learning gains shown at younger ages. Moreover, when it comes to high, asymptotic levels of performance of memory functioning, for instance, older adults may never be able to reach the same levels of functioning that younger adults reach, even after extensive training (e.g., Kliegl et al., 1989; Lindenberger & Baltes, 1994). . . . The architectural plan of human ontogeny is essentially incomplete in two respects (P.B. Baltes, 1997). Incompleteness results from the fact that biological and cultural co-evolution (Durham, 1991) is not completed but continues. Second, incompleteness results from the fact that, relatively speaking, old age is young; therefore neither biological nor cultural evolution has had sufficient opportunity to evolve a full and optimizing scaffolding (architecture) for the later phases of life. (Baltes & Smith, 1999, pp. 157–158)."

Baltes, with assistance from his associates, has provided a compelling foundation or meta-theory for grasping, at a conceptual level, the evolution of lifespan development. His idea of the incomplete architecture of individual development raises an interesting question. Given the value of human life, at least for most individuals, will we ever attain a complete architecture? As the human species evolves—biologically and culturally— more of us should be able to attain a qualitatively higher level of longer life. A fair assumption is that in the industrialized countries, with increasing percentages of individuals living longer than those of preceding generations, more private and public funds will be made available for both research and intervention in older age disabilities. Cardiovascular, pulmonary, arthritic, dementia, and cancer illnesses come to mind, as do psychological and social impairments and interventions. With the co-evolution of contributing factors to individual development, it would seem that the architecture would never be complete—at least in terms of one's hopes. Perhaps Baltes' idea of the incomplete architecture of human development, based upon contemporary research and creative organization of existing information, is similar to the old notion of the Fountain of Youth. At the personal level, there is a relationship. Regardless of how much we know about the strengths and weaknesses of ourselves as we age, there remains the notion that one's life can continue, if only for a limited time. As will be discussed in Chapter 5, 6, and 7 older individuals, like younger ones, tend to compare their physical, psychological, and social situations more favorably than their peers. This wonderful ability relates to the ability of separating one's life end from both normative human data about the lifespan and realities of life-threatening illnesses.

Principle 3: Lifespan changes in allocation of resources to distinct functions of development: Growth vs. maintenance vs. regulation of loss

Use of personal and cultural/environmental resources change as the individual progresses through his or her lifespan. Growth, maintenance, and recovery, as well regulation of loss are evident in all stages of life, but the relative need and impact of each of these resources changes over the lifespan. Growth or maturation is most evident during the earliest phases of the lifespan—prenatal, postnatal, childhood and adolescence—and is illustrated by physical and physiological maturation. Growth or maturation is also illustrated by successive intellectual, emotional, and motivational changes. Use of resources for growth or maturation results in the person reaching higher levels of functioning and adaptive capacity.

Use of resources for maintenance and recovery (resilience) of one's systems and functions is most characteristic of adulthood, particularly middle and young-old adulthood. Adaptivity and use of resources for maintenance and recovery are for maintaining one's functioning and/or recovering from losses in functioning. Maintenance of functions includes such important aspects of life as physical fitness, physical and mental wellness, and positive social networks. Recovery adaptability is illustrated by successful remediation to such traumas as serious accidents, acute or chronic illnesses, and divorce or loss of significant others.

Use of resources for regulation of loss refers to adaptability in functioning at lower levels or at lower standards than previous functioning associated with growth of maintenance and recovery. Adaptability for regulation of loss is associated with older adulthood, and can be illustrated in one's physical, psychological, and social environments. As will be discussed in subsequent chapters, with older age come significant functional decreases in physical health, certain cognitive abilities, and significant others networks. A generic index of adaptability in older age is how successful one is in enhancing the meaning of life within a context of functional decreases in a number of important capabilities related to physical, cognitive, and social well-being.

Principle 4: Development as Selection (Specialization) and Selective Optimization in Adaptive Capacity

Development, rather than being general and universal, is a multidirectional, multifunctional, and predicted discontinuous set of processes that is based upon selection and selective adaptation. Selection of individual potentials is based upon biological (including genetic), psychological, cultural, and environmental factors. Selective adaptation or optimization of a potential by the person also results in the negation or erosion of other potentials. This principle, which will be discussed in more detail later, is the cornerstone of the general Selection-Optimization-Compensation (SOC) developmental model advocated by Baltes and his associates (Baltes, 1997; M. Baltes & P.B. Baltes, 1990). Paraphrasing Baltes, 1997, p. 371), Principle 4 incorporates the following agendas:

1. Development has specific targets or goals.
2. Development proceeds, but with limited capacity, based on time and resources.
3. Because development is linked to genetics, selection is limited by physical and psychological dispositions.
4. Development is limited or conditioned by age-related modifiability or plasticity and associated losses in potential.
5. Development illustrates a movement toward increased efficacy and higher levels of functioning or optimization.
6. Developmental optimization for enhanced adaptive capacity and functioning is directly related to biological, psychological, and social influences.
7. Developmental compensation occurs when optimization for enhanced adaptive capacity and functioning is no longer possible by a given means to achieving a goal.

Baltes (1997) has shared several examples of selection, optimization, and compensation. During the earlier periods of the lifespan, examples of the three are as follows. Parents and/or a child *select* the piano or ballet for artistic expression; parents and/or child *optimize* piano playing or ballet training at the expense of time, effort, and advancement in other artistic expressions, and, perhaps, socializing with a more diverse set of friends. If the piano playing or ballet training does not result in previously set goals of professional expertise, then the child-now-adult (and, most often, the parents) may *compensate* by establishing different goals for creative expression, such as becoming a teacher or using the artistic skills for pleasure.

During the middle periods of the lifespan, examples of selection, optimization, and compensation are as follows. A young adult, with an education in business management, selects small business accountancy as an occupation. During the early career phases, he/she optimizes accountancy expertise by attending graduate school, majoring in accountancy, and also enrolls in yearly accountancy workshops. In addition, optimizing his/her career, the accountant remains in the same small business. When the small business is consumed by a multinational corporation and the accountant's position is terminated because of downsizing, he/she compensates by negotiating a year's leave with pay, with the resulting training in international aspects of accountancy. With a different set of specializations, yet similar core accountancy skills, the accountant is hired by another multi-national firm. A very enjoyable book of fiction dealing with selection, optimization, and compensation within the context of multinational business intrigue is Stanley Bing's (1998), *Lloyd What Happened: A Model of Business.* In addition to learning more about the practical aspects of selection, optimization, and compensation, a review of Bing's book can help in one of many intervention strategies for successful aging; i.e., continued interest and practice of learning about new things.

For older adulthood, as with earlier stages of the lifespan, selection, optimization, and compensation deal with both cumulative effects of one's past as well as one's present context. Older adults, given a longer history of cumulative effects, are less likely to willingly accept lifestyle changes associated with selection, optimization, and compensation. Yet, lifestyle changes are inevitable, certainly for older adults interested in aging successfully. For example, retirement is a primary concern for the older worker and his/her spouse. For the worker, selection must involve options other than full-time employment; for the spouse, selection should include what options are available given that the partner is no longer spending much of his or her time at work. The pre-retiree could select among many options, including part-time employment, lifelong learning pursuits, hobbies/interests, and family relations. The spouse could select among similar options, though one of necessity is spending more time with the partner. Optimizing selections for retired couples, given the loss of work-related experiences of one or both of the partners, can be difficult. If employment of one or both partners maintained self-efficacy of one or both, then retirement poses a problem. The partners will have to learn to spend more time together or reframe avenues of maintaining distance. Compensation is required with both partners; if only to accept new patterns of maintaining earlier individual lifestyles.

Principle 4 makes a lot of common sense. Throughout the lifespan, each of us make decisions related to selection, optimization, and compensation. Most of the time, these decisions are made without much, if any, thought. Yet, other times, we are very deliberate about selecting, optimizing, and/or compensating in relation to present and future goals.

Principle 5: Development as Gain/Loss Dynamic

With the development of the individual, there is no gain without loss, and correspondingly, no loss without gain. Conceptually, it is easier to reflect upon the idea of no gain without loss. The idea is that when a person selects and acts upon a certain goal or objective, there is a loss in the selection and action for other goals and objectives. The idea that there is no loss without gain means that when a person's losses are enough to sustain a goal or objective, then he or she has the potential gain to select and act upon other goals or objectives. Baltes and his colleagues illustrate Principle 5 with examples of fluid and crystallized intellectual changes over the lifespan. Fluid and crystallized abilities will be discussed in detail later in this text.

One can think of many examples of the gains-losses relationship for any stage of the lifespan. In childhood, for example, the goals and actions related to formal education result in relative losses of time, action, and goal-attainment of previously appreciated goals and actions related to physical and psychological attachment to parents. These losses made for concentrated objectives and actions related to formal education and peer relations. In young adulthood, new gains deal with such goals/objectives and related actions as marriage, parenthood, and employment. Relative losses are single adulthood status, personal freedom, and the legal and social protectorate provided by parents. In middle adulthood, new gains could reflect financial, familial, social, and personal goals and related actions. Relative losses are declining physical abilities, increased stress (partially based upon declining physical abilities), and parents. In older age, new gains may include such goals/objectives and related actions of retirement and "empty nest" opportunities. Relative losses are declining physical abilities as well as frustrations related to retirement and the "empty nest." Baltes and Smith (1999) suggest that in older adulthood the balance between gains and losses in adaptability becomes less positive. They also suggest that even with more losses than gains, older adults are able to pursue gains from losses, either through compensating with other capabilities or enhancing intervention efforts for those abilities subject to declining performance.

Principle 6: Plasticity

For Baltes and his colleagues, the important points about plasticity or variability within the person are the range of plasticity and the relationship of the range of plasticity over successive periods of the lifespan. Although research indicates that within person variability (intraindividual variability) is greater in older age, compared to younger stages of adulthood (Baltes and Mayer, 1999), Baltes' plasticity principle includes the idea that variability for individual **potential** decreases in the last stages of adulthood. In later sections of *Successful Aging*, the idea of plasticity, with corresponding illustrations and research summaries, will be given specific attention. Plasticity, as defined by Baltes and his associates, is distinct from the other variabilities noted in that it includes not only boundaries or range of reaction, but emphasizes potential or the positive range of reaction. Relatedly, if a person, within any period of the lifespan, follows one course of development, then it is only one of many potential courses of development. Baltes, Lindenberger, and Staudinger (1998, p. 1047), provide the following reasons for why lifespan professionals included plasticity in models of lifespan development:

> First, as many life-span researchers did work in the field of aging, plasticity-related ideas such as modifiability were important to them, to counteract the prevailing negative stereotype of viewing aging as a period of universal decline with no opportunity for positive change.
> . . . Second, the use of the concept of plasticity accentuated the view that life-span development did not follow a highly constrained (fixed) course, especially where culture- and knowledge-based characteristics were concerned. . . .

Principle 7: Ontogenetic and Historical Contextualism

The idea for this principle is that both biological and environmental contributors to individual change, as well as individual change itself, are subject to the context of the individual and his/her environment. The context is defined as reflecting both historical and cultural effects. The life course and the contributing factors to it, are dependent upon the history and culture. Identical twins reared apart illustrate the notion of different cultures, as does siblings of different gender; siblings of different ages, reared in the same family, illustrate the notion of different histories, as does the life course of a parent and child.

Baltes, Lindenberger, and Staudinger (1998) distinguish among three contextual factors (biological and environmental influences) which cause both similarities and differences among individuals:

> 1. *Normative age-graded influences.* These biological and environmental influences are assumed to affect development in relatively

normative ways. Why? Because the effects of these influences are highly and positively correlated with chronological age. Examples of normative age-graded influences are developmental tasks such as bonding with parents and siblings, establishing and maintaining peer relations, marriage, parenthood, retirement, and older parents-older children dependencies. Maturational examples of normative age-graded influences include development of primary and secondary sex characteristics, height and weight increases within infancy, childhood, and adolescence, and physical deterioration and chronic illnesses during older adulthood. Since all individuals illustrate such developmental regularities, within rather prescribed life periods, these regularities are regarded as normal and subject to normative age-graded influences. A culture or subculture may incorporate normative age-graded influences that differ in timing of occurrence and effect from other cultures and subcultures.

2. *Normative history-graded influences.* These biological and environmental influences contribute to individual development differences among individuals because of historical factors. According to Baltes and colleagues, historical factors deal with cohort and historical periods. A cohort identifies the relative period one was born in, which can be defined as date of birth (specific year) or generation. Humans can, and do, make for significant changes in their environments; significant changes like world and regional wars, financial depressions, technological advances (educational, medical, financial, social), and significant illnesses (Polio, AIDS). One or more significant changes contribute to normative history-graded influences, as most people are affected. What period of the lifespan one is in during the impact of normative history-graded influences also makes a difference. For example, the age of the personal computer has had varying impacts on individuals, partially depending upon the period of lifespan they are in.

3. *Non-normative (idiosyncratic) influences.* These influences are, by definition, unique to the individual. With the uniqueness also comes the problem of not being able to predict the impact of the unique influence on the individual. Examples of unique influences that can have a dramatic effect through the remainder of one's lifespan are: major illness, winning the lottery, relocation, losing one's job, or loss of a significant other, and since non-normative influences are unique to the individual, the pool of such influences is both wide and deep. An influence that is significant for one person may not be for another.

These three influences help articulate the importance of the individual and the contextual influences on both individual development and historical (cultural, subcultural) changes. That is, individuals contribute to contextual changes, and vice versa.

Principle 8: Effective Coordination of Selection, Optimization, and Compensation

This principle is an expansion of Principle 4, and for Baltes and his associates, leads to a general and functional theory of development (Baltes, Lindenberger, and Staudinger, 1988, p. 1043):

> . . . successful development, defined as the (subjective and objective) maximization of gains and minimization of losses, can be conceived of as resulting from collaborative interplay among three components: Selection, optimization, and compensation. The ontogenetic pressure for this dynamic increases with age, as the relative incompleteness of the biology- and culture-based architecture of human development becomes more pronounced. . . .

As noted previously, the Selection-Optimization-Compensation model will be provided in more detail later in this text. Noteworthy is that Baltes and his associates, with their eight **Principles** present a more positive view of aging than most professionals of aging and laypersons. M. Baltes and Carstensen (1999, pp. 218–219) recently discussed the expansion of individual selection, optimization, and compensation to collective selection, optimization and compensation:

> Through selection, a given individual or group of individuals chooses from an array of possibilities or opportunities. Selection refers to a restriction of one's involvement to fewer domains of functioning as a consequence of new demands and tasks (elective selection) or as a consequence of or in anticipation of losses in personal and environmental resources (loss-based selection) . . . Selection can be proactive or reactive. It may be directed at environmental changes (i.e., relocation), active behavior changes (reducing the number of social partners), or passive adjustment (not climbing the stairs). Compensation, the second component factor facilitating adaptation to loss in resources, becomes operative when specific behavioral capacities or skills are lost or reduced below the level required for adequate functioning. Compensation involves a response to a loss in goal-relevant means. . . . Compensatory efforts can be automatic or planned and are not necessarily dependent on existing means. Compensation might require the acquisition of new

skills, of new means not yet in the repertoire. Compensation thus differs from selection in that the target, the domain, the task, or the goal is maintained but other means are sought to compensate for a behavioral deficiency in order to maintain or optimize prior functioning. Optimization, the third component factor, involves the probability, level, and scope of desirable outcomes or goal attainment (viz., the minimization of losses and maximization of gains). Therefore, the central themes of optimization are the generation and refinement of goal-relevant means (resources) associated with the generation and production of goal attainment (desired outcomes). Optimization and growth may relate to the perfection of existing goals and expectations (e.g., in the domain of generativity) but may also reflect new goals and expectations in line with developmental tasks of the third phase of life (such as acceptance of one's own mortality). . . .

Recently, Park, Nisbett, and Hedden (1999) have expanded the model of Baltes and his associates to highlight culture in the lifespan approach. These lifespan developmental thinkers give recognition to Baltes' ideas of fluid/mechanical and crystallized/pragmatic abilities, as well as corollary ones of primary and secondary cognitive processes identified by Geary and Lin (1996). Fluid/mechanical abilities or primary cognitive abilities refer to human characteristics that are more directly tied to biological (and, correspondingly, genetic) determinants that fit into the evolutionary concepts of species development. Given the biological and genetic links to these abilities, the assumption is that as one ages, cultural or experiential determinants would have relatively little influence. On the other hand, crystallized/pragmatic abilities or secondary cognitive processes, which are more susceptible to learning and experiential factors, should illustrate cultural effects and be less subject to unilateral aging than fluid/mechanical abilities or primary cognitive processes. Park, Nisbett, and Hedden (1999) make an important point in noting that most theorizing for lifespan development and aging is based upon research done on samples in Western cultures. While such research promotes the ideas of Baltes and Geary and Lin, it is important to note the constructive criticism of Park, Nisbett, and Hedden. As will be shared in more detail in later sections of *Successful Aging*, Park, Nisbett, and Hedden argue, and provide some research suggesting, that even fluid/mechanical abilities (Baltes idea) and primary cognitive processes (Geary and Lin's idea), are impacted by culture. Park, Nisbett, and Hedden also provide some research which supports their suggestion that cultural effects do not always increase with age, and that for some cognitive abilities, advancing age minimizes, rather than enhances cultural differences. The recent ideas of Park, Nisbett, and Hedden, in general, support the earlier theorizing of Baltes and his associates. Park, Nisbett, and Hedden add, I believe, a significant dimension to the creative work of Baltes and his associates. That dimension is to integrate the sparse cross-cultural (or limited multicultural sampling) research into one of the best articulated models of lifespan development that extends to both adulthood and old age. Baltes and his associates' agenda promote *successful development*, including aging. This promotion is, I suggest, not only unique. It is also realistic, with as much research support as the more pessimistic views (theories) of development and aging. Perhaps the more optimistic view is also based upon the optimism of its promoter, Paul Baltes. Remember, an individual can influence his own development as well as the development of others! It is fair to note that much of the literature (popular and scientific) and common thought about aging reflects more of the negative and less of the positive aspects of later adulthood. For many years, childhood, adolescence, young adulthood, and even middle adulthood were viewed as periods of progression, albeit with episodic negatives. Older adulthood, on the other hand, was viewed, if not with negativity, then reflecting mostly decline, with episodes of stability or enhancement. The beauty of the Baltes model, for both lifespan development and aging, is that of options, both personal and communal.

Reflect a bit on the Baltes model, including the eight **Principles**. Surely you have many examples to fit each of the principles. Regardless of one's state of affairs—period of the lifespan, culture/subculture, historical era, definition or type of age—there are options for the individual. Depending upon each of these parts of one's state of affairs and the permutations, the options for one's future are limited (range of reaction). Also, the options are dependent upon both one's personal resources (physical, psychological, sociological) and the contextual resources discussed above. Your state of affairs, regardless of what period of the lifespan you are in, depend, to a significant extent, on the personal resources you have and, as part of the personal resources, your willingness to select, optimize, and compensate. To paraphrase several well worn (preventative strategic) pieces of advice, (a) the glass is half full or half empty, (b) life is what you make of it, and (c) the only person you have to settle with at the end of life is yourself. Each of us makes decisions every day; sometimes, those decisions are to not make a decision. My appreciation for the Baltes view of lifespan development, which includes aging, is that I, like you, make for differences—for myself and others. Those differences are both good and bad for me and for others. The Baltes approach assumes personal responsibility for the development of one's self, as well as for the development of one's relations (real or virtual) with others (which is quite different from being responsible for the development of others).

CONCLUSION: THEORETICAL NOTIONS
ABOUT OLDER ADULTHOOD

As suggested earlier, theories of aging have been included within both lifespan development and gerontology. Bengtson, Rice, and Johnson (1999, pp. 9,10), in the following summary, share what professionals have to deal with in analyzing and understanding the aging process:

> . . . The first set of issues concerns *the aged*: populations of those who can be categorized as elderly in terms of their length of life or expected lifespan... The vast majority of gerontological studies in recent decades have concentrated on the functional problems of aged populations, seen in human terms of medical disability or barriers to independent living..." A second set of problems involve aging as a *developmental* process occurring over time. Here the focus is on how individuals of a species grow up and grow old–the processes of development, growth, and senescence over time–and the biological, psychological, and social aspects of that process, including it variable rates and consequences. . . .
>
> . . . A third problem involves the *study of age* as a dimension of structure and behavior within a species. This is of obvious interest to sociologists and other social scientists examining human populations, and the social organization they create and modify, in response to the age-related patterns of birth, socialization, accession to adult status, and retirement or death within the human group. The phenomena to be explained here concern how age is taken into account by social institutions; examples include the labor market, retirement, pension systems, and health care organizations. . . .

Lifespan development emphasizes the second set of problems identified by Bengtson, Rice, and Johnson (1999). Lifespan developmentalists, regardless of their primary interest within the lifespan (genetics, prenatal, childhood, adolescence, adulthood), advocate a lifespan perspective in dealing with their issues of interest. Thus, lifespan developmentalists with an interest in older adulthood advocate principles of change and potential determinants of change that can apply throughout the life course. In a sense, the first and third problems noted by Bengtson, Rice, and Johnson (1999), for lifespan developmentalists interested in aging are secondary. Gerontologists, on the other hand, have a primary interest in the first and third problems noted by Bengtson, Rice, and Johnson (1999). Gerontologists may use lifespan development principles in attempts to better understand the aging process, but they are most interested in describing and explaining what is going on in older age. To bring the continuum of lifespan development and gerontology into a circle, some gerontologists advocate a lifespan perspective and some lifespan developmentalists concentrate their efforts almost solely on aging in older adulthood.

Salthouse (1999) has provided a concise differentiation among theories of aging, focusing on cognitive aging. While his focus is on cognitive aging, the differences among theoretical positions hold for psychological, cognitive, physical, and social aspects of getting older and old. Some time is taken here to share Salthouse's differentiations, as theories of aging provide guideposts for research, practice, and intervention. Salthouse differentiates between distal and proximal explanations of aging. Distal explanations of aging, noted below, refer to contributing factors of present individual structures, processes, and behaviors that occurred at earlier, more distal periods in the lifespan. Since time itself does not cause change, it may be these distal factors which contribute to change over time. Proximal explanations of aging concentrate on current factors in one's lifespan that contribute to age-related changes.

Distal Explanation One: Changes occurring in the social and physical environments, more so than changes occurring within the person, result in aging effects. **Cohort effects** refer to factors in the social, cultural, and physical environments that contribute to changes within individuals born in different historical periods or eras. The cohort effects explanation for aging– really a description–suggests that the reason old people perform differently from younger folks is because both the former and later have grown up under different macro environments at different ages of the lifespan. Some credence is given to this idea, as significant global or national advances have certainly impacted individuals living through them. At the international level, wars, financial depressions, plagues, technological breakthroughs, and political persuasions come to mind. At the national level, rather recent examples of cohort impacts include computerization, medical advances, and educational technologies. One complicating aspect of cohort effects is that environmental changes associated with particular historical periods can impact, directly or indirectly, individuals of different lifespan periods as they move through the era(s). Significant environmental effects (cohort effects) do make a difference; that's the reason some historical period or cohort influences are identified. The reasoning isn't circular; it is descriptive and can help in understanding some chronological age-related differences. What macro or major environmental/cultural/national/international impacts made a difference for you? Make a list of them. With the list, go back and note what period of your lifespan you were in. Identify those impacts which stayed with you until now. Note those that you think were positive; those negative. Why do you think these influences are so sustainable?

Distal Explanation Two: Amount and type of relevant experience result in aging effects. This idea is a refinement of the first explanation of aging. How much is experienced, and what, also makes sense in trying to understand how we age. How much we experience and what we experience is related to what stage or period of the lifespan we are in. The stage of development of a person has a direct relation to both the amount and type of experience that can be dealt with. The assumption is that as the individual matures into adulthood, the integrities of human structures and functions allow for greater amounts of experience, as well as many types of experience, to have both positive and negative effects.

Proximal Explanation One: Some type of strategic mechanism change results in age-related differences or changes. With older age, a strategic mechanism deficiency results in less efficiency or effectiveness of performance. The production deficiency proximal explanation proposes that for some reason, as we move into older age we do not use optimal strategies as often as in the past and that even when we do, we are not as efficient with optimal strategies.

Proximal Explanation Two: Again, some type of strategic mechanism change results in age-related differences or changes. With older age, a strategic mechanism deficiency results in less efficiency or effectiveness of performance. The specific deficit explanation proposes that differences between younger and older adults on cognitive tasks are the result of one or more specific information processing components. Salthouse (1999) gives the example of short-term memory performance. Relative performance on a short-term memory task includes the components or abilities of encoding, storage, and retrieval of information. Inefficiencies (based upon structural or functional reasons) in each of the short-term components or abilities of encoding, storage and retrieval could result in age-related differences in short-term memory performance.

Proximal Explanation Three: One or more elementary (cognitive primitive) cognitive components or abilities result in pervasive inefficiencies, across a number of cognitive processes. Although the cognitive primitives explanation is similar to the specific deficit explanation above, the former explanation deals with inefficiencies (based upon structural and/or functional reasons) of (a) basic or elementary cognitive components which (b) are pervasive in that multiple cognitive processes are effected and, correspondingly, performances on a variety of cognitive tasks are reduced.

Salthouse (1999) identifies the cognitive primitives of attention, working memory, and processing speed as the most often suggested in the literature. As will be discussed in Chapter 3, these cognitive primitives do appear to account for much of the differences in certain cognitive abilities of younger and older adults.

Salthouse (1999, p. 204) cautions us in the use of theories or explanations dealing with age-related changes (within the individual over time) or differences (between younger and older adults) in cognition. Explanations of cognitive aging, even the mechanistic one of cognitive primitives, are often examples of circular reasoning: ". . . age-related cognitive differences are attributed to a reduction in processing resources, but the reduction in processing resources is inferred, on the basis of the same age-related differences in performance (Salthouse, 1991). . . ." In Chapter 3, contemporary theories or explanations of aging, based upon appropriate research methodologies, will be discussed. Perhaps the most important reason to review such theories is that they provide us guidelines for both understanding aging processes and, as important, selecting intervention strategies to deal effectively with aging phenomena. Such understanding and selection should also be based upon reliable research that can be generalized.

Chapter 3

METHODS OF RESEARCH, ISSUES, AND GENERALIZATIONS

INTRODUCTION

The primary audiences for *Successful Aging: Integrating Contemporary Ideas, Research Findings, and Intervention Strategies* are practitioners dealing with older adults and prospective practitioners enrolled in higher education. Thus, an overview is given for each primary developmental design. Emphasis is given to illustrate the strengths and weaknesses of each design. One example of the detail concerning lifespan development and aging research methods is provided in **Appendix B**; it is the detail of research design and statistics which tends to frustrate practitioners who are much more concerned about research applications. The best text on developmental research methodology is Baltes, Reese, and Nesselroade's (1988), *Life-span developmental psychology: An introduction to research methods.* Other relevant works on developmental research methodology include those of Friedrich and Van Horn (1976), Hertzog and Dixon (1996), and Schaie (1977, 1996). Since the primary purpose of *Successful Aging* is to share contemporary information about aging processes and corresponding interventions for successful aging, the presentation of developmental research methodology will focus on typical research designs which include chronological age as a variable. Since each of these research designs within developmental methodology has strengths and weaknesses as related to the internal validity of the research and external generalizability of study findings, it is worthwhile to share the typical research designs. For those interested in specific internal and external validities or data analytic techniques, the Baltes, Reese, and Nesselroade (1988) text, as noted, is the best there is.

In Chapter 2, some summary information was provided concerning theories and principles of lifespan development and aging. Theories, models, and principles, though different in terms of levels of abstraction, provide general guidelines or propositions about relationships among variables of interest. Such general guidelines, as noted by Baltes, Reese, and Nesselroade (1988, p. 17):

> . . . are (1) to organize or integrate knowledge and (2) guide research designed to increase knowledge. Theories fulfill the organizational function by showing that some facts or laws (theorems) are deducible from other, more general laws (axioms), or by showing that all of the known facts and laws are interrelated to form a coherent pattern. Theories fulfill the research function by suggesting fruitful lines of further experimentation. A scientific theory is evaluated on the basis of how well it fulfills these two functions."

Bengtson, Rice, and Johnson (1999, pp. 5–7), provide us another view of theories:

> . . . We define theory as *the construction of explicit explanations in accounting for empirical findings.* . . . There may be other ways to describe this, such as telling a story about empirical findings, or developing a narrative accounting about observations. . . . Nevertheless, the principal focus of theory is to provide a set of lenses through which we can view and make sense of what we observe in research. And the principal use of theory is to *build knowledge and understanding,* in a systematic and cumulative way, so that our empirical efforts will lead to integration with what is already known as well as a guide to what is yet to be learned (Bengtson, Parrott, & Burgess, 1996). . . . In addition to the depth of understanding that theoretically-based research provides, the breadth of pragmatic justifications for theory can be seen in four ways: *Integration of knowledge:* A good theory summarizes the many discrete findings from empirical studies and incorporates them into a brief statement that describes linkages among the crucial observations, variables, or theoretical constructs.
>
> *Explanation of knowledge:* A useful theory provides not only description of the ways empirically observed phenomena are related (that is what "models" reflect) but also *how* and especially *why* they are related, in a logically sound account of incorporating antecedents and consequences of empirical results.
>
> *Predictions about what is not yet known or observed.* Research based on theory can lead to subsequent discoveries based on principles proposed by earlier theory. Examples from the history of science include Darwin's theory of natural selection in biology; Mendeleev's theory leading to the periodic table of elements in chemistry; and Einstein's theory of relativity in physics.

Interventions to improve human conditions: Theory is valuable when we attempt to apply and advance existing knowledge in order to solve problems or alleviate undesirable conditions. The practical utility of scientific theory is evident in the advancement of instant communications from the telegraph to the world-wide Internet. . . .

. . . Another kind of intervention is social: governments intervene through public policy, attempting to ameliorate problems of poverty in old age, delaying institutionalization of older persons through home assistance provisions like Meals-on-Wheels, and providing enriched educational opportunities to disadvantaged children through "Head Start" programs. . . .

DEVELOPMENTAL DESIGNS

Lifespan development researchers are most often interested in age-related findings related to normal, pathological, and successful aging, as well as determinants of such aging. Regardless of abilities studied, lifespan development researchers are interested in differences in abilities among chronological age groups or changes in such abilities as the individual ages. While chronological age can be manipulated by researchers in terms of (a) including people of different ages in a study and testing them at the same time of measurement or (b) testing the same people over time (and thus age), it is important to note that chronological age does not cause anything. Chronological age is best defined as a **dependent**, rather than **independent, variable**. Chronological age is defined as a dependent variable because, like a developmental stage or level, it provides a marker for many levels of abilities reviewed at a particular chronological age, stage, or level. Correspondingly, researchers include chronological age in studies so as to measure ability levels that are age-related. A dependent variable is one whose changes are presumed to be caused by changes in one or more independent variables. Dependent variables, other than chronological age, often included in lifespan development and aging research are gender, socioeconomic status, education, and physical or mental health.

An independent variable is one which is manipulated or controlled in research and is presumed to have some effect on one or more dependent variables. For example, a geriatric study could include cigarette smoking as an independent variable and chronic pulmonary illness as a dependent variable. Study subjects could be categorized into smokers versus non-smokers (independent variable). Within the smokers category, decades of smoking could be manipulated; 10, 20, 30, 40 years of smoking. Usually, this type of research also controls for possible confounding factors which could jeopardize the validity of study findings. Thus, gender, socioeconomic status, education, and ethnicity would be balanced between the groups of smokers and non-smokers. Chapters 6 and 7 include research summaries dealing with negative life-styles (such as tobacco use) and corresponding limitations in quality of life. For the present hypothetical study of cigarette smoking and quality of life, a realistic summary is that prolonged smoking (independent variable) results in one or more chronic pulmonary diseases, and correspondingly, reduced quality and length of life.

Until fairly recently, the primary developmental designs used to assess age-related differences or changes were the **cross-sectional** and **longitudinal** designs. For both of these developmental designs, three variables are always involved; viz.,

1. Chronological age
2. Cohort
3. Time of measurement

Levels of chronological age refer to different chronological ages (usually in years). For example, a lifespan development researcher may be interested in testing intelligence at different periods in the lifespan. One way of looking at intelligence at different periods in the lifespan is to test people of different chronological ages on an IQ test; for example, looking at IQ scores of individuals aged 50, 70, and 90 years of age in 2000. Chronological age differences are assumed to correlate with changes due to processes associated with development and aging (Hertzog & Dixon, 1996).

Levels of cohort refer to different times of birth or generational membership. Particularly when cohort levels are distant (e.g., 10 or 20 years), cohort effects are assumed to correlate with environmental factors (as those in the same cohort have more common age-related environmental experiences) (Hertzog & Dixon, 1996). Using the intelligence test example above, a lifespan developmentalist may review research on intellectual abilities of 70-year-olds who were born in the successive cohorts of 1920 (tested in 1990), 1930 (tested in 2000), and 1940 (tested in 2010).

Levels of time of measurement refer to different times of assessment (usually years). Time of measurement effects are assumed to correlate with specific periods or historical sections of time (Hertzog & Dixon, 1966). Again, with the intelligence test example, a researcher may test 70-year-olds in 1990, 2000, and 2010.

As you may have detected, the three components of simple developmental designs—chronological age, cohort, time of measurement—cannot be manipulated independent of each other. This is a major problem with the cross-sectional and longitudinal designs, resulting in findings about developmental differences and change that often cannot be easily interpreted or generalized. Hertzog & Dixon (1996, p. 80), provide the following summary of the confounding problem with chronological age, cohort, and time of measurement or period:

> Despite the fact that age, cohort, and period effects are distinct and independent concepts, any developmental design relying on time-based sampling quickly confronts an unhappy problem in attempting to measure such effects empirically. At any particular point in time (T), age (A) and birth year, which defines the birth cohort (C), are perfectly confounded: in the year 2000, a person born in 1950 must, by definition, be 50 years old. Knowing any two of the numbers of the set (A,C,T) determines the remaining number; there are only two degrees of freedom among them.

Figure 3–1 depicts basic developmental designs:

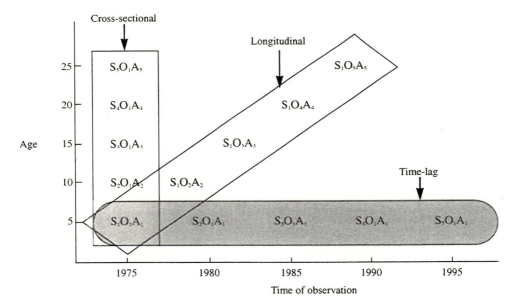

Figure 3-1. A cross-sectional method involves multiple samples (S_1-S_5) of different ages (A_1-A_5) at one point in time, each measured once (O_1). A longitudinal design involves following the same sample (S_1) through all ages (A_1-A_5), using repeated observations (O_1-O_5). The figure also illustrates the time-lag method (Schaie, 1965), which involves contrasting same-age (A_1) but different-cohort samples (S_1-S_5), using one-shot observations (O_1) at different points in time. The time-lag method illustrates the potential significance of historical-evolutionary change in studying development. Based on Baltes (1968) and Schaie (1965). Source: Baltes, Reese, & Nesselroade (1988). Reprinted with permission.

CROSS-SECTIONAL DEVELOPMENTAL DESIGN

The cross-sectional design is the most often used research design in lifespan development, including gerontology. The reason for its widespread use is that, in comparison to other developmental designs, the cross-sectional one is the most economical in terms of being time-efficient. The cross-sectional design is illustrated in Figure 3–1 as the perpendicular block; samples of individuals from different chronological ages (5, 10, 15, 20, 25) are tested on one or more measures at one point in time (1975 time of measurement). Referring to the Quizzes presented in Chapter 1, an example of the cross-sectional study is the Davis and Friedrich study (2000). About 400 older adults completed the nine Facts on Aging and Psychological Well-being quizzes. The chronological age categories of 50–54, 55–59, 60–64, 65–69, 70–74, 75–79, 80–84, 85–89, 90–94, and 95 or older were used. Other variables, such as gender, ethnicity, occupation, socioeconomic status, and physical health were included. The study was a cross-sectional one because diverse age groups were included and the project was conducted in a relatively brief time of measurement (1999–2000).

Demographic Variables cataloged in the Davis and Friedrich study:

• AGE

• GENDER

• LIVING ARRANGEMENT
 Living independently
 Assisted living
 Nursing home

• EDUCATION

• ETHNIC GROUP

• GENERAL HEALTH
 Excellent
 Above average
 Average
 Below average
 Poor

FINANCIAL WELL-BEING
More than enough, completely satisfied
Can always meet expenses, satisfied
Moderate debt, usually meet expenses
Heavily in debt, have needed assistance
Need assistance often, very dissatisfied

• RETIRED (YES or NO)

• VOLUNTEER (YES or NO)

• OCCUPATION
 (Respondents chose from 13
 major occupational groups)

Another example of the cross-sectional design is the report of the Berlin Aging Study by Mayer and Baltes (*The Berlin aging study: Aging from 70 to 100,*

1999). In this book, multiple authors present cross-sectional design results of the aging process. Although the Berlin Aging Study is a longitudinal study, the results presented in this first comprehensive summary of aging West Berliners were based on the cross-sectional design. The Mayer and Baltes book deals only with the first wave (cross-section of an ongoing project. As noted previously, the Berlin Aging Study is a multidisciplinary one, with age groupings of 70–74, 75–79, 80–84, 85–89, 90–94, and 95 years of age or older. In addition to age groupings, Berlin Aging Study researchers grouped participants on many other variables, including gender, education, family structure, residence, occupation, and income.

Political polls use a cross-sectional design, though chronological age is only one of many variables manipulated. These polls, almost always including chronological age as a variable, are conducted at a specific time of measurement.

For example, Belsky (1999, p. 49) described the following:

> . . . if we were interested in finding out whether people become more politically conservative as they age, we might use the following approach. We would randomly select equal numbers of young-adult, middle-adult, and elderly people (for instance 100 subjects aged 20, 100 aged 40, and 100 aged 60), taking care to match our groups for extraneous influences that might affect their scores, such as social class, educational level, or ethnic background. We would then give a scale of conservatism to each group and compare their scores. If we found a statistically significant trend toward conservatism in successively older groups, we would conclude that as people grow older, they become more skeptical of government efforts to help its needy citizens or effect social change.
>
> However, our conclusion would be wrong. Because we are not following people over time, we cannot assume that these differences *between* age groups reflect changes that actually occur as people advance in years. For instance, although a study carried out 30 years ago might have shown that young people were the most liberal, today the same hypothetical study might reveal the opposite trend . . . Because of the political climate in recent years, young adults might have the most conservative views. The most liberal attitudes might be held by the middle-aged and young-old subjects, who developed this political philosophy when they were young adults during the 1960s. . . .

A final example of cross-sectional design research comes from the Berlin Aging Study. As reported by Lindenberger and Reischies (1999), chronological age relations were summarized for five intellectual abilities. As depicted in Figure 3–2, the intellectual abilities of reasoning, knowledge, perceptual speed, memory, and fluency were studied.

Studying older old adults, the cross-sectional findings illustrated in Figure 3–2 show an age-related decrease in functioning; that is, from 70 to 100 years of age, there is a steady decline in performance. Interestingly, three of the intellectual abilities–perceptual speed, reasoning, and memory–indicated a more pronounced age-related effect than the other two–knowledge and fluency. As will be discussed in a later section, the perceptual speed, reasoning, and memory abilities are included in intellectual abilities that are categorized as fluid or mechanical. The intellectual abilities of knowledge and fluency are intellectual abilities categorized as crystallized or practical. Fluid abilities are directly linked to neurological and physiological integrities, while crystallized abilities are based more on learning. Thus, it makes sense that the fluid abilities, relative to crystallized ones, would show a more dramatic age-related decrease in older age.

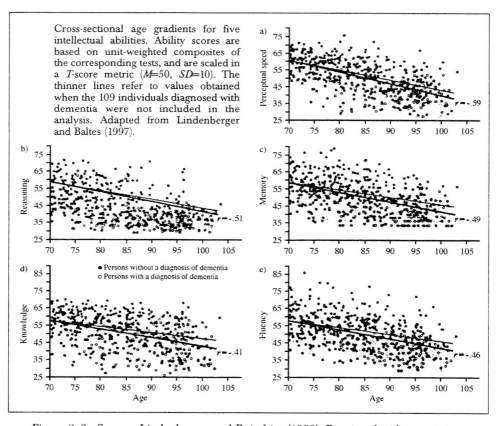

Cross-sectional age gradients for five intellectual abilities. Ability scores are based on unit-weighted composites of the corresponding tests, and are scaled in a *T*-score metric (*M*=50, *SD*=10). The thinner lines refer to values obtained when the 109 individuals diagnosed with dementia were not included in the analysis. Adapted from Lindenberger and Baltes (1997).

Figure 3–2. Source; Lindenberger and Reischies (1999). Reprinted with permission.

When lifespan developmentalists and gerontologists use cross-sectional designs, age differences found may be assumed to reflect chronological age changes associated with principles of maturation or deterioration. Since people of different ages are tested at about the same time of measurement, this assumption is a precarious one. Just because one finds chronological age differences in a cross-sectional study, it does not mean that the age-related differences are the result of factors contributing to maturation or deterioration. The cross-sectional design allows us to look at interindividual differences; that is, differences among individuals of different chronological ages. Interindividual age-related differences found in cross-sectional studies do not allow us to jump to the conclusion that such differences reflect intraindividual change. Why? Because cross-sectional designs, testing individuals of different ages at the same time of measurement, confound chronological ages with cohorts. As seen in the perpendicular block of Figure 3–1, the age groups are 5 to 25; these age groups come from cohorts 1970 (age 5), 1965 (age 10), 1960 (age 15), 1955 (age 20), and 1950 (age 25). Baltes, Reese, Nesselroade (1986, p. 123), explain the chronological age x cohort confound as follows:

> . . . if you can justify the largely untestable assumption that the different age groups in a cross-sectional study indeed come from the same parent population and differ only in age, then you can interpret cross-sectional age differences as average, intraindividual changes. That is, cross-sectional age differences are equivalent to age changes (Schaie, 1967) only if, for example, the 1975 5-year-olds would behave in 1980 (when they are 10) like the 1975 10-year-olds, if in 1985 the 1975 5-year-olds would behave like the 1975 15-year-olds, and so on.

Baltes, Reese, & Nesselroade (1986) continue, noting that age-related research findings from cross-sectional designs or studies only infer *group averages;* i.e., age differences or similarities from cross-sectional designs cannot provide information about intraindividual changes or stability. Cross-sectional studies, comparing chronological ages, do not compare the same individuals as they age. This is an important point, given that many cross-sectional studies do find differences between young adults, middle-aged adults, young-old adults, and old-old adults. Since cross-sectional designs confound chronological age and cohort, chronological age differences among groups may include differential generational differences and experiences.

Typical cross-sectional design findings—especially in the physical and psychological aging domains—are that average older adults do less well than average younger adults. The chronological age comparisons may be any of the following: *Young adults, middle-age adults, older adults, old-old adults.*

Since chronological age in itself is not a causal factor in findings about such age comparison, what are the contributing factors? Given that the cross-sectional design compares age groups at about the same time of measurement (day, month, year), the contemporary time of comparison is not a determining factor of any age differences. It may be that age differences found in a cross-sectional design are due to human functions directly associated with normal development (e.g., maturation) and aging (e.g., deterioration). The normal age differences could be the result of different environments in historical time for the various age groups. More likely, normal age differences found in cross-sectional studies reflect both maturation-deterioration and history-bound contextual principles. A hypothetical example of the confounding of maturation-deterioration and history-bound principles with cross-sectional design findings is use of personal computers. If groups of young, middle-aged, and older adult college graduates were evaluated on ability to use personal computers for personal communication (email), then the result would be one of progressively inferior speed performance over the three age groups. Even if the participants in the three age groups used personal computers, the result would not change. Why? First, the younger age group has better sensorimotor and processing speed skills than the the middle-aged adult group, which, in turn, has better sensorimotor and processing skills than the older age group. Such is the nature of maturation-deterioration. Second, the younger age groups have more experience with personal computers, and correspondingly more expertise. This result represents the successive historical opportunities of technology favoring the younger cohorts. Third, even the most experienced personal computing older adults will be less adept with personal computers than their younger cohorts, because of a combination of loss in relevant abilities and competing objectives based upon other skills, interests, and habits.

The cross-sectional study remains the study of choice by most lifespan developmental and aging researchers. Though this design confounds chronological age with cohort, it is relatively inexpensive to conduct and allows for inclusion of a number of independent and dependent variables. The most serious problem with cross-sectional studies is that lifespan changes within the individual cannot be measured. The traditional way of assessing change within the person over time, is the longitudinal design. Unlike the cross-sectional developmental design (focusing on interindividual differences), the longitudinal design allows for focus on the individual's functioning over successive times of assessment.

LONGITUDINAL DEVELOPMENTAL DESIGN

The longitudinal design is depicted in the triangular block of Figure 3–1. This design is a repeated measurement one, allowing for assessment of changes within the individual over time as well as differences among individuals over time. Changes within the individual over his or her lifespan is referred to as intraindividual change; differences among individuals over time is referred to as interindividual differences in change. In Figure 3–1, the longitudinal design includes individuals from one cohort (1970), tested in 1975 (5-years-olds), 1980 (10-year-olds), 1985 (15-year-olds), 1990 (20-year-olds), and 1995 (25-year-olds). The key idea about a longitudinal design is that individuals are tested repeatedly, over times of measurement, and usually on many variables. While any repeated measures design is longitudinal in nature, lifespan developmentalists and gerontologists are interested in repeated measurement designs that evaluate the same individuals over relatively long periods of time. Long-term longitudinal studies allow for assessment of proximal and distal determinants of development and aging. This interest in lengthy study of the same individuals, satisfied by the longitudinal design, unfortunately, has some serious practical problems. Belsky (1999, p. 51), identifies them:

> Longitudinal studies have practical problems, They require a huge investment of effort, time, and funds. The investigator or research team must remain committed to the study and available to continue it over years or, as in studying aging, decades. Imagine keeping your enthusiasm about a topic for 20 or 40 years. Even if you stayed interested, your question might become outmoded. Even the way you choose to measure conservatism is likely to become obsolete over the years! Imagine getting subjects to make the same demanding commitment. Then, think of the time it would take to search them out each time an evaluation is due. All of these impediments become more serious the longer a study goes on. For this reason, longitudinal studies covering decades are not common. Longitudinal studies spanning all of adult life are very rare. . . .

Fortunately, there are more than a few longitudinal studies that have included adulthood. One of the most famous is Terman's study of gifted children (Terman, 1925). Initiated in 1921, the study included 1,528 boys and girls who tested as gifted on standardized intelligence tests. One of the original objectives of this longitudinal study was to deal with myths about intellectually gifted children. As summarized in the study description from the Terman Life-Cycle Study of Children website (**artemis.calstatela.edu/Abstracts/ICP8092htm**):

. . . In 1922, the children were identified on the basis of an intelligence test as being in the top one percent of the population. Their development was followed over the next sixty years via questionnaires, personal interviews, and various test instruments. Questions were asked about their health, physical and emotional development, school histories, recreational activities, home life, family background, educational, vocational, and marital histories.

Questions were also asked about income, emotional stability, and socio-political attitudes. The follow-up questionnaires were concerned with the evolution of the respondents' careers, activity patterns, and personal adjustment. Since 1972 there has been special emphasis on the aging process. These longitudinal data will continue to be collected as long as living members of the original cohort contribute data. . . .

Friedman, Tucker, Schwartz, Tomlinson-Keasey, Martin, Wingard, and Criqui (1995) summarized psychosocial and behavioral predictors of longevity from the longitudinal *termites* study. As reported in 1995, half of the termites are dead. The objectives of Terman's longitudinal study of the gifted has changed from countering myths about intellectually gifted children to addressing . . . intriguing questions about the role of psychosocial variables in physical health and longevity through a life span prospective design. . . ." (Friedman, et al., 1995, p. 69). Summaries from the *termite* longitudinal study will be integrated in later sections dealing with successful aging.

Some conclusions of Friedman, et al. (1995), are presented now,

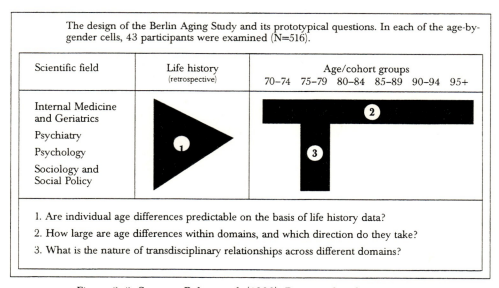

The design of the Berlin Aging Study and its prototypical questions. In each of the age-by-gender cells, 43 participants were examined (N=516).

Scientific field	Life history (retrospective)	Age/cohort groups 70–74 75–79 80–84 85–89 90–94 95+
Internal Medicine and Geriatrics Psychiatry Psychology Sociology and Social Policy	1	2 3

1. Are individual age differences predictable on the basis of life history data?

2. How large are age differences within domains, and which direction do they take?

3. What is the nature of transdisciplinary relationships across different domains?

Figure 3–3. Source: Baltes et al. (1999). Reprinted with permission.

however, to illustrate the advantages of longitudinal designs in lifespan development and gerontology fields. First, the authors highlighted the importance of longitudinal designs in articulating change within the individual as he/she ages. Second, evidence was found suggesting that both personality and social stress factors were independent predictors of longevity. For examples, divorce of parents during childhood or adolescence predicted premature mortality. So did the *termites* personality (defined by trait ratings from parents and teachers). Third, neither personality nor social factors predicted specific causes of death of *termites*, though both predicted mortality. Fourth, women outlived men, and childhood and adolescent psychosocial effects on men, relative to women, were more pronounced in later life. Fifth, ". . . the unhealthy patterns that have emerged thus far in our study predominantly involved being impulsive, imprudent, and arrogant rather than anxious, shy, pessimistic, and unsociable. . . ." (p. 76).

Another ongoing longitudinal study of adults is the Berlin Aging Study (Baltes & Mayer, 1999). Figure 3–3 illustrates the design of the study and primary research questions. This longitudinal study was and is funded by the German Federal Ministry for Research and Technology (1989–91) and the Federal Ministry for Family Affairs, Senior Citizens, Women, and Youth. Initiated in 1990 with periodic repeated measurement, the study of 516 older adults, 70 to over 100 years of age, the Berlin Aging Study is unique in terms of (a) focusing on older adults and (b) emphasizing an interdisciplinary research team. Regarding the latter, a summary of the various assessment instruments is provided. This summary, depicted in Tables 3–1 through 3–5, highlights the comprehensiveness of the interdisciplinary team.

The third example of a longitudinal study of adults is the Seattle Longitudinal Study (Schaie, 1996). This longitudinal study, initiated as a cross-sectional study in 1956, has been provided significant financial support from the National Institute of Child Health and Human Development and the National Institute on Aging. As noted by Director Schaie (1996), the objectives of the Seattle Longitudinal Study are:

1. Does intelligence change uniformly through adulthood, or are there different life course ability patterns?
2. At what age is there a reliably detectable decrement in ability, and what is its magnitude?
3. What are the patterns of generational differences, and what is their magnitude?
4. What accounts for individual differences in age-related change in adulthood?
5. Can intellectual decline with increasing age be reversed by educational intervention?

Table 3–1
The multidisciplinary BASE Intake Assessment (session 1)

Internal Medicine and Geriatrics	Psychiatry	Psychology	Sociology and Social Policy
Objective health Body Mass Index Drug consumption Last doctor's appointment	**Assessment of psychiatric age-related morbidity** SMMS[b] Self-reported depressivity Fears and worries	**Intelligence** Digit Letter test Backward digit span	**Socioeconomic status** Educational level Social prestige Income and savings Family members Housing conditions
Subjective health	**Dealing with psychiatric age-related morbidity**	**Social relationships** Number of close companions Loss of close companions	
Functional capacity ADL[a] Grip strength Wrist measurement Subjective walking distance Vision and hearing	Drug consumption Yesterday Interview (short form) Previous contact with psychiatrist	**Self and personality** PGCMS[c] (life satisfaction, satisfaction with aging, emotional balance) Control beliefs	**Social participation** Voting behavior

Concurrent observation of study participant by field staff
Health risk factors Disability/frailty Behavior and speech characteristics Housing conditions Residential environment

[a]ADL: Activities of Daily Living.
[b]SMMS: Short form of the Mini Mental State Examination.
[c]PGCMS: Philadelphia Geriatric Center Morale Scale.
Source: Baltes et al. (1999). Reprinted with permission.

Measures used in the Seattle Longitudinal Study include the following: *cognitive ability* battery inductive reasoning, spatial orientation, number skills, verbal ability, word fluency, perceptual speed, verbal memory; *composite indexes of intellectual ability* and *educational aptitude*; *self-reported cognitive change*; *everyday problem solving*; *cognitive style* (perseveration/rigidity, flexibility); *lifestyle* and *demographic characteristics*; *health styles*; *subjective environment*; and *personality traits* and *attributes*.

Schaie is very well known and appreciated for his creativity in developmental methodology, as well as tremendous productivity in lifespan development and gerontology. The design of his Seattle Longitudinal Study reflects that creativity and is summarized in **Appendix B**. The first six testing cycles or waves of the Seattle Longitudinal Study are clarified in Schaie's (1996), *Intellectual development in adulthood: The Seattle longitudinal study*, and

Table 3–2
Topics examined by the Sociology and Social Policy Unit and a
selection of the instruments used to measure them in the Intensive Protocol.

Main topics/constructs	Detailed example	Instruments
Life history and generational dynamics		
Social background	*Career mobility*	Magnitude Prestige Scale
Migration history	*Labor force participation*	Life history instrument
Educational history	*Career continuity*	
Employment history	*Unemployment*	
Partnership history	*Transitions (employment/*	
Family life history	*retirement)*	
Later phases of the family life cycle		
Current social structure	*Size of the family*	Family history inventory
of the family	*Living distance and contacts*	Social relations and support
Social structure of	*Household structure*	questionnaire
the generations	*Familial support*	
Changes of familial		
social structure		
Economics situation and social security		
Assets	*Savings*	German Socioeconomic
Sources of income	*Property*	Panel questionnaire
Transfers		(SOEP)
Income expenditure		
Consumer sovereignty		
Social resources and social participation		
Social status	*Formal and informal care*	Inventory of care needs
Housing standards/	*Household help*	
environment	*Institutionalization*	
Social care	*Institutionalization career*	
Social and cultural		
participation		

Note: To illustrate the depth of assessment, more details are given for selected topics or constructs (in italics). Cf. Mayer et al., Chapter 8, for references and further details. Baltes et al. (1999). Reprinted with permission.

the seventh testing cycle is summarized on the website for the study (**geron.psu.edu/research1.htm**).

Participants of the Seattle Longitudinal Study were/are members of a group health cooperative. The original population base for the study, in 1956, was about 18,000 potential participants aged 22 or older. Twenty-five men and 25 women were randomly selected for the first cycle or wave of the longitudinal study, and these participants were also stratified for chronological age. Cohorts or years of birth were from 1882 to 1934. In 1963, the second study cycle began. In addition to the longitudinal study participants

Table 3–3
Topics examined by the Psychology Unit and a selection
of the instruments used to measure them in the Intensive Protocol.

Main topics/constructs	Detailed example	Instruments
Intelligence and intellectual functioning		
Mechanics of intelligence	*Reasoning*	Letter Series
Pragmatics of intelligence	*Memory*	Figural Analogies
	Perceptual speed	Activity Recall
		Paired Associates
		Digit Letter test
Self and personality		
Self-concept	*Personal life investment*	"Who am I?"
Personality dimensions	*Changes in life investment*	Possible selves
Emotional state/affect	*Control beliefs*	NEO[a]
Self-regulatory processes	*Coping patterns*	PANAS[b]
Social relationships		
Network structure	*Closeness/distance*	Social network and support
Social support	*Size*	questionnaire
Changes of the network	*Age structure*	
Negative aspects	*Losses*	
Satisfaction with relationships	*Homogeneity*	
Relationships in retrospect		

Note: To illustrate the depth of assessment, more details are given for selected topics or constructs (in italics). Cf. Smith & Baltes, Chapter 7, for references and further details.
[a]NEO: Neuroticism, Extraversion, Openness.
[b]PANAS: Positive and Negative Affect Schedule.
Source: Baltes et al. (1999). Reprinted with permission.

selected in 1956, the 1963 cycle included 997 new male and female participants, ranging in age from 22 to 77. In 1970, the third cycle of the study included surviving participants from the 1956 and 1963 cycles, as well as a new, randomly selected sample, of 705 male and female participants. For the fourth cycle, started in 1977, potential participants came from what was then a 210,000 member health plan. In addition to testing those surviving participants of the 1956, 1963, and 1970 cycles, 609 new male and female participants were included in the study. In 1984, the fifth cycle included surviving participants of the earlier cycles, as well as 629 new male and female participants. The 1991 sixth cycle included surviving participants of earlier cycles and 693 new male and female participants. The successive cycles, with corresponding new participants, extended the cohorts from the late 1890s to 1959. The seventh, 1998 cycle, includes surviving participants of earlier cycles and 700 new male and female participants.

As presented in *Intellectual Development in Adulthood: The Seattle Longitudinal Study* (1996), Schaie provides some answers to the objectives of

Table 3–4
Topics examined by the Psychiatry Unit and a selection
of the instruments used to measure them in the Intensive Protocol.

Main topics/constructs	Detailed example	Instruments
Spectrum of age-related psychiatric morbidity		
Mental illness	*Clinical diagnosis*	GMS-A/HAS[a]
Depression syndrome	*Degree of depression*	DSM-III-R[b]
Dementia syndrome	*Differential diagnosis with*	ICD-10[c]
Psychopathology	*respect to somatic health or*	HAMD[d]
(subdiagnostic)	*dementia*	CES-D[e]
Predictors of psychiatric morbidity		
Previous illnesses	*Psychopathological morbidity*	Psychiatric history/diagnosis
Multi-/comorbidity	*Somatic morbidity*	Medical history/diagnosis
	Subdiagnostic morbidity	Consensus conference
Consequences of psychiatric morbidity		
Health/illness behavior	*Utilization of medical care*	Health behavior question-
Everyday competence	*Drug consumption*	naire
Self-efficacy	*Health perception*	Interview with family
	Illness concepts	physician

Note: To illustrate the depth of assessment, more details are given for selected topics or constructs (in italics). Cf. Helmchen et al., Chapter 6, for references and further details.
[a]GMS-A/HAS: Geriatric Mental State, Version A/History and Aetiology Schedule.
[b]DSM-III-R: *Diagnostic and Statistical Manual of Mental Disorders*, third revision.
[c]ICD-10: *International Classification of Mental and Behavioural Disorders*, 10th version.
[d]HAMD: Hamilton Depression Scale.
[e]CES-D: Center for Epidemiologic Studies–Depression Scale.
Source: Baltes et al. (1999). Reprinted with permission.

the longitudinal study noted above.

Does intelligence change uniformly through adulthood, or are there different life course ability patterns?

Uniform patterns of change in intelligence, at the levels of specific cognitive tests and higher order factors or concepts, were not found. Providing data which argues against use of cross-sectional research findings on intellectual changes over adult aging, Schaie's successive longitudinal research findings indicate that different cognitive abilities illustrate different age-related profiles and, importantly, even these unique profiles can change when different cohorts are studied in a longitudinal design.

At what age is there a reliably detectable decrement in ability, and what is its magnitude?

Schaie's data indicates that for some cognitive abilities, significant but modest declines are observable in 50-year-olds. He argues, however, that

Table 3–5
Topics examined by the Internal Medicine Geriatrics Unit and a
selection of the instruments used to measure them in the Intensive Protocol.

Main topics/constructs	Detailed example	Instruments

Objective health
Cardiovascular system
Musculoskeletal system
Immune system
Dental status
Multimorbidity
	Symptoms
	Objective status
	Cardiovascular risk factors
	Comorbidity
		Standardized medical history
		Medical and neurological
		  examination
		Resting ECG, blood
		  pressure
		Color-coded ultrasound

Subjective health
Subjective physical
  health
Subjective vision and
  hearing
	Retrospective interindividual
	  comparison
	Comparison with age peers
		Standardized subjective health
		  interview

Functional capacity
Activities of Daily Living
Physical performance
	Objective coordination and
	  balance
	Subjective ratings
	Compensation strategies
		Subjective walking distance
		Grip strength
		Use of aids
		Bending, turning
		Standing and walking with
		  closed eyes

Risk profile *Cardiovascular risks*	*Smoking* *Diet* *Lipid metabolism* *Hypertension*	Medical anamnesis and examination Diet questionnaire Blood chemistry

Treatment needs
Medication
Dental treatment
Integration of treatment
  needs
	Drug treatment needs
	Dental treatment needs
	Needs for medical and nursing
	  care
		Analysis of medication
		Dental examination
		Interview with family
		  physician
		Consensus conferences

Reference values Physical performance *Organ functioning* Metabolism	*Pulmonary function* *Renal function* *Hepatic function* *Immune function*	Spirometry Blood chemistry Immunological analysis

Note: To illustrate the depth of assessment, more details are given for selected topics or constructs (in italics). Cf. Steinhagen-Thiessen & Borchelt, Chapter 5, for references and further details. Source: Baltes et al. (1999). Reprinted with permission.

individual decline on the cognitive abilities studies prior to age 50 is probably due to pathological precursors or conditions. By the mid-70s, significant average decline is observable for all cognitive abilities studied; by the 80s almost all cognitive abilities studies indicate severe decline. Based upon his findings, Schaie concluded that in the late 60s and early 70s many individuals begin to illustrate noticeable declines in cognitive abilities.

What are the patterns of generational differences, and what is their magnitude?

Schaie's research has illustrated consistent cohort or generational effects. As he notes, not only does one observe individual aging in the lifespan, one detects significant changes in successive environments. Schaie's longitudinal program has clearly shown the dramatic effects of substantial generational trends in chronological age-related cognitive changes in adulthood. While many of the generational trends are positive, indicating better performance in successive cohorts, some trends are not. As will be presented in a later Chapter 3 section, Schaie is a leading proponent of sequential developmental designs. Such designs allow for unambiguous interpretations of chronological age, cohort/generation, and time of measurement effects. Schaie (1996, p. 354) has illustrated the importance of unambiguous interpretations as related to his research:

> . . . An understanding of these cohort differences is important in order to account for the discrepancy between longitudinal (within-subject) age changes and the cross-sectional (between-group) age differences reported. . . . In general, I conclude that cross-sectional findings will overestimate declines whenever there are positive cohort gradients and will underestimate decline in the presence of negative cohort gradients. Curvilinear cohort gradients will lead to temporary dislocations of age-difference patterns and will over- or underestimate age changes, depending on the direction of differences over a particular time period. . . .

What accounts for individual differences in age-related change in adulthood?

Schaie, an advocate of individual differences in intellectual change throughout the lifespan, summarized from his Seattle longitudinal study numerous factors accounting for such differences in cognitive change in adulthood:

1. genetic endowment
2. presence or absence of chronic diseases (cardiovascular disease, diabetes, neoplasms, arthritis) and overall health
3. survival of malignancies and late onset of cardiovascular disease and arthritis are associated with higher levels of cognitive functioning
4. seeking competent medical intervention and seeking it early

5. complying with preventive and remedial interventions, as well as advice
6. lack of engagement in high-risk life-styles
7. live in favorable environmental circumstances (socioeconomic status, education, occupational pursuits of complexity)
8. substantial involvement in stimulating environments (extensive reading, travel, cultural events, lifelong learning, membership in organizations)
9. live in intact families
10. spouse of high cognitive abilities
11. flexible rather than rigid personality style at midlife
12. high levels of perceptual and response speed
13. satisfaction with life's accomplishments

Can intellectual decline with increasing age be reversed by educational intervention?

With research colleague Sherry Willis, Schaie conducted cognitive interventions with some of the participants of the Seattle longitudinal study. Their conclusions from laboratory intervention studies are that (a) cognitive decline for many older individuals is the result of disuse, (b) cognitive training is beneficial to older adults, and (c) such training has long-term, yet ability specific effects. As will be discussed in Chapter 4, Schaie's cognitive intervention research with laboratory training procedures leads to the generalization of positive intervention effects in everyday living circumstances for older adults.

Schaie (**geron.psu.edu/research1.htm**, pp. 1,2) has identified the following contemporary sub-projects of the Seattle Longitudinal Study:

1. The seventh wave longitudinal and new participant data collection, with a focus on effects of repeated testing of individuals and attrition.
2. Neuropsychological assessment of older participants to study the relationship between psychometric abilities and measures used by clinicians to determine neuropsychological deficits, develop new methods for detection of very early signs of eventual dementia.
3. Update health records of the longitudinal participants and survey health behaviors to study health behaviors, disease experience and cognitive decline; relate objectively recorded disease occurrences, reported health behaviors, and the occurrence and timing of cognitive decline.
4. Longitudinal follow-up and new study of families to assess if family similarity persists in rate of cognitive aging.

5. Longitudinal follow-up and new study of participants involved in cognitive training to assess long-term persistence of training effects.
6. Permission to perform autopsies for all participants given neuro-psychological battery to assess behavioral change antecedents of changes in anatomical brain structure as well as other organ systems, like vascular changes.

Longitudinal studies do not have to take as long as those of Terman, Baltes and Mayer, and Schaie. Small, Dixon, Hultsch, and Hertzog (1999) summarized longitudinal changes in quantitative and qualitative indicators of word and story recall in young-old and old-old adults. As shared by these authors (1999, pp. 108, 109):

> . . . The participants consisted of 242 adults who participated in three waves of the VLS [Victoria Longitudinal Study]. Participants in the VLS were initially aged 55 to 85 years and were examined at 3-year intervals over a period of six years. At baseline, 487 adults (290 women and 197 men) participated in the testing sessions. Approximately three years later 335 individuals returned for retesting. At a third time of testing, 250 individuals returned approximately 3 years later. . . .
>
> Because of missing data, the final sample in the present study consisted of 242 adults (143 women and 99 men). The sample was divided, based on the age at entry into the study, into two groups: young-old ($n = 158$; 55–70 years. . .) and old-old ($n = 84$; 71–86 years. . .). In general, the young-old and old-old age/cohort groups were well educated . . . and rated their health to be good to very good. . . .

Small, et al. looked at multiple measures of word recall and narrative story recall with individuals of various chronological ages over a six-year period. The researchers found significant three-occasion longitudinal declines for both young-old and old-old groups on quantitative word recall; with qualitative word recall, varying profiles of longitudinal change were found, with decline being most predominant. For quantitative narrative story recall, age-related declines over testing times were not found. For qualitative narrative story recall, both young-old and old-old adults continued to be able to identify and use underlying organizations of stories over the three times of testing. What is unique about the Small et al. study, and the reason their work is presented in this section, is that it is one of very few longitudinal studies of memory for specific ongoing events, or any type of memory, for that matter. Almost all memory research, particularly short-term memory, is investigated using the cross-sectional design. In the cross-sectional design, groups of different chronological ages are tested on one or more measures at one particular time. In the Small et al. longitudinal study, different chronological age groups (young-old and old-old) were tested on memory tasks three times over a six-year period.

The longitudinal developmental design, invaluable for assessing intra-individual change (individual change over successive times of assessment), like the cross-sectional developmental design, has a methodological confound. With a longitudinal developmental design, the cohort(s) of the study remain constant, but with successive changes in chronological age there is, correspondingly, successive changes in time of measurement. Schaie (1996, p. 20), articulated this problem: ". . . Unless the behavior to be studied is impervious to environmental influences, it must be concluded that a single-cohort longitudinal study will confound age-related (maturational) change with time-or-measurement effects that are specific to the particular historical period over which the behavior is monitored (Schaie, 1972). The time-of-measurement effects could either mask or grossly inflate maturational changes. . . ."

Four sources of invalidity or confounding (see Campbell and Stanley, 1963 for threats to design internal and external validity) are pertinent to the longitudinal design; viz., *practice effects, selective attrition, time of measurement effects, and instrumentation.* Practice effects are defined as effects which are based upon the longitudinal study participants' repeated encounter with particular assessment measures or assessment measures that, though perhaps not exactly the same from one testing to the next, are very similar. Since the same individuals are tested repeatedly on the same or similar measures over repeated times of measurement, there is a possible confound of age and practice effects. Did the particular cohort group, tested over a 50-year period, show age-related profiles of change, practice effects, and/or a combination of age and practice effects?

Another bias with a longitudinal developmental design is selective attrition. Participants drop out of longitudinal studies. Participants who remain in longitudinal studies, especially over long periods of time, are more motivated and healthier than those who drop out. A particular type of attrition—selective mortality—results in the least healthy participants dropping from the study. Thus, as a longitudinal study continues over years, the selective attrition results in participants who do not represent the average person from their cohort. Such selective attrition results, particularly over study testings, minimize negative aging effects and maximize positive aging effects. Especially with long-term longitudinal studies, researchers must be very careful to assess changes within the individual over time as resulting from age-related changes, selective attrition effects, and a combination of both effects.

The third bias with a longitudinal developmental design with special impact on intraindividual change findings over time are time of measurement effects. As the longitudinal study progresses, certain significant environmental effects, in a particular year, for example, may influence how individuals respond to study assessments. The most often cited examples of time of measurement effects are economic depression and war. If one or both occur between times of testing participants in a longitudinal study, the changes found between testings may be the result of age-related effects, economic depression and/or war, and a combination of effects.

The fourth bias with a longitudinal developmental design is instrumentation. Long-term longitudinal studies often include many different types of assessments of the participants. Since the cost of longitudinal studies, compared to cross-sectional ones, is so high, longitudinal researchers often include many tests of different types of abilities, with the objective of detecting age-related changes in biological, psychological, and sociological development. For each of these developmental changes, specific tests are administered to study participants. Unfortunately, over time, these specific tests may become outdated, revised, or replaced by other tests. Studying the same individuals over time, changes in assessment tools could result in developmental changes that are due, in part, to changes in the assessment instruments used at different times of measurement.

By now, some readers may be concerned about the detail being given to the cross-sectional and longitudinal developmental designs, and corresponding problems. These designs are the most often used for age-related research, and cross-sectional design research far exceeds longitudinal design research. Lifespan developmentalists and gerontologists, like researchers in general, are held responsible by peers for doing their best to (a) control for confounding effects in their research designs, and (b) indicate limitations to generalizations of findings that are based on design limitations. The average citizen is not held to such a standard. Rather, individuals are interested in information that is relevant to personal responsibilities of daily life. Lifespan developments and gerontologists, unlike public opinion pollsters, are interested in identifying age-related phenomena that have rather long-lasting effects. Thus, it is important that lifespan developmental and gerontological research findings be as free from confounding effects as possible or that such effects are recognized and shared.

TIME-LAG DEVELOPMENTAL DESIGN

This design, identified in the horizontal block of Figure 3–1, compares subjects of the same chronological age, who come from different cohorts

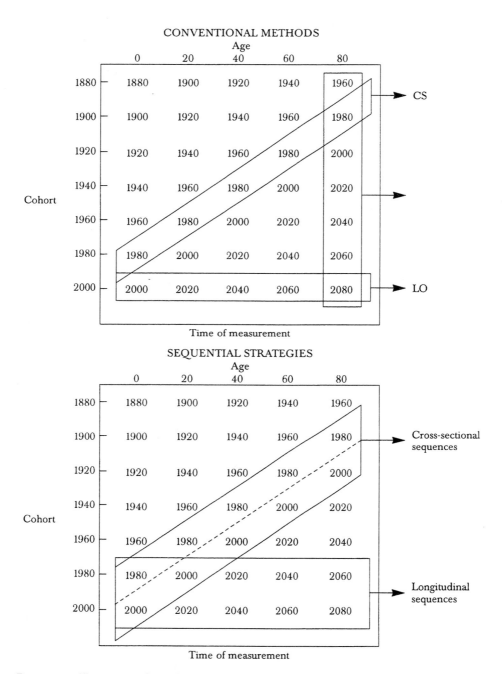

Figure 3–4. Illustration of simple cross-sectional, longitudinal, and time-lag designs (top) and cross-sectional and longitudinal sequences (bottom). Modified from Baltes (1968) and Schaie (1965). Source: Baltes, Reese and Nesselroade (1988). Reprinted with permission.

and, correspondingly, are tested at different times of measurement. In Figure 3–1, the age is 5, with one cohort born in 1970 and tested in 1975, a second cohort born in 1975 and tested in 1980, a third cohort born in 1980 and tested in 1985, a third cohort born in 1985 and tested in 1990, and the last cohort born in 1990 and tested in 1995. The time-lag design, seldom used, was thought to be an effective way to measure environmental change effects. As with the cross-sectional and longitudinal designs, however, the time-lag design has a confounding factor. Since time of measurement and cohort changes are not independent of one another, time of measurement effects cannot be unconfounded from cohort effects. Schaie (1996, pp. 21,22) clarified the advantages and disadvantages of the time-lag developmental design:

> . . . The hypothesis to be tested is whether there are differences in a given behavior for samples of equal age but drawn at different points in time. This strategy is of particular interest to social and educational psychologists. It is particularly appropriate when one wishes to study performance of individuals of similar age in successive cohorts (e.g., comparing baby boomers with the preceding generation). The simple time-lag design, however, also confounds the cohort effect with time-of-measurement effects and therefore may provide cohort estimates that are inflated or reduced, depending on whether the temporal interval between the cohorts represents a period of favorable or adverse environmental influences. . . .

SEQUENTIAL DEVELOPMENTAL DESIGNS

Schaie (1965) introduced sequential developmental designs, and these were provided more clarity by Baltes (1968) and Schaie and Baltes (1975). Figure 3–4 shows both the conventional and sequential developmental designs. Comparing the two sets of figures in Figure 3–4, each of the conventional developmental designs (top figure) is a special case of sequential developmental designs (bottom figure). *Cross-sectional sequences* and *longitudinal sequences* are identified in the bottom figure of Figure 3–4. For cross-sectional sequences, independent samples are obtained for all cohorts and all ages included in the design. In Figure 3–4, the cross-sectional sequences involve 1980 and 2000 cohorts sampled and tested at ages 0, 20, 40, 60, and 80 years of age. Notice with these two cross-sectional sequences that for the two cohorts, with successive ages come successive times of measurement. In Figure 3–4, the longitudinal sequences, requiring repeated measurement for each cohort, involve both the 1980 and 2000 cohorts, with repeated measurements of each cohort group from 1980 to 2060 for the 1980

birth cohort and from 2000 to 2080 for the 2000 birth cohort. As noted by
Baltes, Reese, and Nesselroade (1988) and Schaie (1996), longitudinal
sequences can include repeated testing of the sample individuals,
independent samples of individuals from the same cohorts at one or more
times of measurement, or both repeated and independent sampling of
participants. They also suggest that in the ideal lifespan development or
gerontology methodology, simultaneous application of cross-sectional and
longitudinal sequences results in maximizing the benefits of longitudinal
designs articulating changes within the individual and cross-sectional,
independent sampling of cohorts articulating possible age-related group
changes independent of biases, such as practice effects, associated with
longitudinal studies. Schaie (1996, pp. 29–30), provides the following
strategy for combining cross-sectional and longitudinal sequences in a systematic way:

> . . . the researchers begin with a cross-sectional study including
> multiple age groups. Then, after a period of years, all those subjects
> that can be retrieved are retested, providing longitudinal data on
> several cohorts (a longitudinal sequence). At the same time a new
> group of subjects over the same age range as the original sample is
> tested. The new sample together with the first cross-sectional study
> forms a cross-sectional sequence. This whole process can be
> repeated over and over (ideally with the groups and time intervals
> identical), retesting the previously tested subjects (adding to the
> longitudinal data) and initially testing new subjects (adding to the
> cross-sectional data). . . .

While the advantages of sequential designs for the investigation of
developmental phenomena are both significant and of interest to developmental methodologists, the fact is that very few research projects include
these designs. Like the simple longitudinal developmental design, the cross-
sequential and longitudinal sequential designs require monetary and time
resources that few researchers have. The Baltes, Reese, and Nesselroade
(1988) text on research methods for developmental psychology is the most
articulate and comprehensive one for professionals interested in age-related
research designs. I encourage those inclined to read this excellent text, if
only to educate us about the many factors that do contribute to questionable
research findings in lifespan development and gerontology. Likewise,
Appendix B presents examples of the cross-sectional and longitudinal
developmental sequential designs. These examples provide research results
that are about as "clean" as can be for age-related research. Because of the
monetary and time prohibitions, however, such examples are few and far
between in lifespan development and gerontology investigations.

META-ANALYSES IN THE SOCIAL SCIENCES

The final lifespan developmental and gerontological research tool discussed is known as *meta-analysis*. Technically, meta-analysis is neither a design nor research methodology (Hedges and Olkin, 1985). Rather meta-analysis represents statistical procedures in which findings from independent research studies are integrated. Such statistical procedures allow for summaries of age-related findings on specific abilities or constructs from many past studies. This is a useful technique, as individual research studies dealing with lifespan development and gerontology usually use a cross-sectional design, include few cognitive abilities for assessment, and have restricted chronological age ranges and sample sizes. Three meta-analyses are briefly summarized to illustrate the importance of integrating independent studies with appropriate statistical procedures. Both meta-analyses deal were completed by Paul Verhaeghen as the principal author.

The first brief summary is from Verhaeghen, Marcoen, and Goossens' (1993) article, *Facts and Fiction about Memory Aging: A Quantitative Integration of Research Findings.*

> . . . A meta-analytic literature review of adult age differences in speed of search in short-term memory (12 studies), memory span (40 studies), list recall (68 studies), paired-associate recall (21 studies), and prose recall (39 studies) is presented . . . (p. P157)
>
> . . . The present analysis is focused on the published literature from 1975 on. The core developmental and gerontological journals (*Developmental Psychology, The Gerontologist, International Journal of Aging and Human Development, The Journals of Gerontology,* and *Psychology and Aging*) were searched systematically. . . . In the meta-analysis, studies were included that (a) compared a young group (central tendency of age between 16 and 30) with a group of older subjects (central tendency of age 60 or over), both groups being free from cognitive problems caused by organic pathology; (b) assessed performance speed of search on STM (short-term memory) span tasks, recall of word lists, paired-associate recall (of verbal stimuli) or prose recall, or any combination of these; and (c) presented sufficient statistical data for the computation of effect sizes . . . Selection of studies was concluded in November, 1990. A total of 122 relevant research papers were retrieved. . . . (p. P157)

For their statistical analyses, Verhaeghen, Marcoen, and Goossens (1993) used two steps. First, they calculated the effects sizes of the individual studies, comparing relevant statistics of the young and old groups. From such calculations, an effect size resulted for each study. A positive effect size for a study indicated that the older group performed better than the younger, while a negative effect size indicated the reverse group relationships. The second step for Verhaeghen, Marcoen, and Goosens involved specific statistical comparisons of relevant subsamples for the five memory tasks reviewed. The five memory tasks included by these researchers were:

1. Speed of search in short-term memory
      latency
      intercept
      slope
      error
2. Memory Span
      digit span forward
      digit span backward
      digit span combined
      working memory
      other span measures
3. List Recall
4. Paired-associate Recall
5. Prose Recall

The conclusions of Verhaeghen, Marcoen, and Goossens quantitative literature review are striking. Rather large age differences in short-term memory and episodic memory performances were found. The use of moderating variables, interpreted to reflect strategy use, did not yield significant differences in the overall effect sizes for age. Specifically, speed of search in short-term memory was significantly different between young and older adults. The rate of search and the speed of other cognitive processes involved in the memory search task slow down significantly with older age. For speed of search in short-term memory and prose recall, differences were greater between young adults versus old-old adults than for young adults and young-old adults. Response latency increases sharply with aging. For memory span, the elderly performed significantly worse with working (short-term) memory, which includes both structural capacity and processing abilities. With episodic memory also, older adults performed significantly poorer than younger adults. The effect of moderator variables on age differences was also analyzed by the researchers. Moderator variables such as characteristics of to-be-remembered material, characteristics of presentation, learning instruction, recall conditions, and level of propositions had little effect on the significant age differences noted above.

Given the results of their comprehensive study, Verhaeghen, Marcoen, and Goossens (1993, pp. P167–P168) suggested that a general factor could well be responsible for the consistent memory differences between young and older adults.

> . . . The explanation most often advanced for this age main effect is the processing resource deficiency hypothesis (Salthouse, 1988, 1991). This hypothesis states that the decline in memory functioning over the adult life span is caused by limitations in information processing resources. A processing resource can be defined as any internal input essential for processing (e.g., locations in storage, communication channels) that is available in quantities that are limited at any point in time, (Navon, 1984, p. 217). Usually, processing resources are conceptualized in terms of space (e.g., working memory capacity), energy (e.g., mental effort), or time (e.g., processing speed) (Cohen, 1988; Salthouse, 1985, 1988, 1991).
>
> Limitations in resources can result in a decline in performance either because memory processes are carried out less efficiently (e.g., because information gets lost from short-term memory or because it has to be transferred to long-term memory, or because they lead to a shift toward less efficient mnemonic processes or strategies that require less space, energy, or less time for their execution. . . .

Verhaeghen, Marcoen, and Goossens noted that not all their findings support the processing resource deficiency hypothesis. The vast majority of their findings, however, do support it. Verhaeghen and Salthouse (1997) reviewed 91 studies in a meta-analysis including chronological age, speed of processing, primary/working/episodic memories, reasoning, and spatial ability. With age as a continuous variable (from young adulthood to old age; ages of 18 to 80), Verhaeghen and Salthouse (1997, pp. 232–233) categorized the dependent variables as follows:

> . . . Speed variables consisted largely of measures of reaction time or paper-and-pencil tests of perceptual speed, and variables reflecting working memory and primary memory consisted of measures representing the number of items that could be remembered immediately either with (working memory) or without (primary memory) additional processing requirements. Measures of episodic memory were derived from a variety of free recall, list learning, and paired associates tests. Measures of reasoning and spatial abilities were obtained from a mixture of psychometric tests (e.g., Raven [1960] Progressive Matrices and Shipley [1940] Abstraction for reasoning: Surface Development and Paper Folding [Salthouse & Mitchell, 1990] for spatial ability) and experimental tasks requiring abstraction and induction (reasoning) or integration and transformation (spatial) operations. . . .

Verhaeghen and Salthouse's (1997) statistical analyses and structural equation modeling were based upon correlation coefficients between age and each of the five dependent variables. In discussing their results, the authors provided a number of interesting findings related to (a) meta-analysis estimates between age and the five cognitive variables and (b) structural models of the nature of the age and measures of cognitive functioning relations. The largest age-related effects were on measures of speed, with older adults performing much slower than younger adults. Within the older adult group, performance trends declined significantly as chronological age increased for perceptual speed and reasoning. For the other cognitive variables, the trends in the older age group were similar, but not significant. While age-related declines in performance were stronger in the older adult group (aged 50 and over) than the younger group (aged 49 and younger), age-related declines with the five cognitive measures were found in both age groups. This suggests that, for the cognitive variables studied, cognitive performance starts to decline in adulthood before the age of 50.

Verhaeghen and Salthouse (1997) also subjected two explanatory models to the enhanced data analysis of the 91 studies; viz., single/common and mediational models for age-related changes in the cognitive abilities studied. These authors were interested in articulating primary determinants of such changes. Both models were supported, as (a) all cognitive abilities studied shared substantial age-related variance (supporting the common cognitive factor model) and (b) the mediational and interrelated factors of speed of processing and working memory were more prominent than other cognitive variables. In Chapter 4, more will be discussed concerning such model analyses in summarizing general determinants of aging.

The final example of meta-analysis is from Salthouse, Hambrick, and McGuthry (1998). These researchers shared analyses of new and previously published data dealing with shared chronological age-related influences on cognitive and noncognitive abilities. These researchers have provided a significant focus for lifespan and aging researchers seeking common determinants of aging. Until recently, much of the research on common determinants of aging dealt with cognitive variables. Salthouse, Hambrick, and McGuthry (1998) have expanded this agenda to assess relations among cognitive and noncognitive factors. The original data reported, with adults ranging from 18 to 87 years of age, included the following measures:

Cognitive Variables	**Noncognitive Variables**
Pattern comparison	Systolic blood pressure
Letter comparison	Diastolic blood pressure
Number matching	Grip strength

Pattern matching   Visual acuity
Matrix reasoning
Cube assembly
Free recall

Salthouse, Hambrick, and McGuthry also analyzed data on similar and different cognitive and noncognitive variables from research of Salthouse, Hancock, and Hambrick (1996), Clark (1960), Dirken (1972), and Heron and Chown (1967). These data were analyzed in an attempt to replicate the findings of the Salthouse, Hambrick, and McGuthry (1998) study. The general findings from all of the data analyses supported, with reservations, a factor common to all the study variables as a function of age. A finding consistent with past research by Salthouse and colleagues was that most of the age-related variance of the *cognitive variables* studied is shared. Since no significant quantitative or qualitative differences were found for age groupings under or over age 50 and before and after partialing age from the variables, what is shared by the cognitive variables studied changes very little, if at all, with advancing age. Also consistent with past research findings was the results of noncognitive variables sharing age-related variance with cognitive variables , and thus supporting a common determining factor. Two analyses in the Salthouse, Hambrick, and McGuthry (1998) study, however, led the researchers to suggest that the relationship of noncognitive and cognitive variables was spurious and the result of a relation all the study variables have with chronological age. First, when analyses were restricted to ages below and above age 50, the noncognitive variables had insignificant or reduced relations with the common factor. Second, when the common factor relations with the study variables were compared before and after partialing age-related variance in the variables, the relations were significantly reduced for the noncognitive variables, but minimally reduced for the cognitive variables.

The meta-analyses noted above have created contemporary interest in articulating specific organismic determinants of aging: determinants that have direct or mediating effects on age-related changes in specific human abilities. As will be discussed in Chapter 4, articulating reliable and valid influences on aging abilities impacts both theory and intervention in lifespan development and gerontology.

Chapter 4

MODELS AND GENERALIZATIONS

INTRODUCTION

It should not be surprising to read that there are many theories and points of view in the fields of lifespan development and gerontology. To complicate the matter, in terms of grasping age-related changes, there are many different human structures, abilities, and processes involved in lifespan development and aging. To illustrate, the following is a partial listing of chapter headings from Bengtson and Schaie's 1999 *Handbook of Theories of Aging*:

Biological and Biomedical Concepts and Theories of Aging
• Stress Theories of Aging
• Biological Theories of Senescence
• Theories of Neuropsychology and Aging
• The Role of Aging Processes in Aging-Dependent Diseases
• Psychological Concepts and Theories of Aging
• Multilevel and Systemic Analyses of Old Age: Theoretical and
  Empirical Evidence for a Fourth Age
• Theories of Everyday Competence and Aging
• Theories of Cognition
• Social-Psychological Theories and Their Applications to Aging:

From Individual to Collective
• The Self-Concept in Life Span and Aging Research
• Emotions in Adulthood

Social Science Concepts and Theories of Aging
• Anthropological Theories of Age and Aging
• Constructionist Perspectives on Aging
• Paths of the Life Course: A Typology
• The Aging and Society Paradigm
• The Political Economy Perspective in Aging

Belsky's (1999) *The Psychology of Aging: Theory, research and interventions,* provides the following breakdown of age-related summaries:

Normal Aging and Disease Prevention
• Biological Theories of Aging
• Normal Aging
• Lifestyle, Aging, and Disease
• Interventions

Sensory and Motor Functioning
• Vision
• Hearing
• Taste and Smell
• Motor Performance
• A General Strategy of Enhancing Sensory-Motor Functioning
  In Old Age

Disease Disability, and Health Care
• Chronic Disease Versus Disability
• Dealing With Disability

The Cognitive Dimension
• Intelligence
• Memory and Dementia

The Emotional Dimension
• Personality
• Psychopathology
• Interventions

The Social Dimension
• The Older Family
• Life Transitions: Retirement and Widowhood

I've provided partial listings of contemporary aging texts to illustrate the diverse ways to organize information about significant age-related changes in the physical, psychological, and social domains. The authors of these and other acknowledged lifespan development and gerontology books are to be complimented for integrating information about aging. Readers of such texts could be critical of the amount of information presented and the frames of reference in which the information is presented. But, one should pause, then give credit to those who are able to integrate massive amounts of information for professional and educational dissemination. My task is much simpler, as the goal is to share information about successful aging and keeping one's wits and wit. That goal, however, needs to be reached within the context of relevant information and professionally accepted summaries of normal, pathological, and successful aging. A related goal for this chapter is to provide, albeit with a focus on psychological aspects of aging, a summary of models and generalizations about aging that integrate, within limits, the multitude of aging-related research findings. The models and generalizations included in Chapter 4 not only make intuitive sense, the creators of such integration have used research to support their notions. While life is certainly much more complex than portrayed in any model, making sense out of the complex endeavor of life is aided by principles that integrate relevant information. Such is the case for professionals interested in lifespan development and gerontology, as well as individuals interested in better understanding their own, and others, paths over the life course.

For the last four decades, one of the most professionally accepted summaries of normal, pathological, and successful aging, accepted in terms of professionals from diverse lifespan development and gerontology disciplines, is the simple dichotomy of **fluid abilities** versus **crystallized abilities**. This dichotomy has been expanded to be **fluid mechanical abilities** and **crystallized pragmatic abilities**. Particularly from a focus on successful aging, the fluid mechanical versus crystallized pragmatic abilities model offers a good integration of information about aging. Pieces of information about this model of aging has been presented in earlier sections of this book. The following sections provide more detailed information for this model of lifespan development and aging.

FLUID AND CRYSTALLIZED ABILITIES

Raymond Cattell is the genius who initiated the model of fluid and crystallized abilities. Starting with a hint of the model in 1941, Cattell (1941, 1943) was interested in expanding upon the unitary or general intelligence factor by (a) articulating primary intellectual abilities (e.g., more than a single, unitary concept of intelligence), (b) using new statistical techniques allowing for more refined analyses of higher-order ability constructs or concepts, and (c) studying age-related changes in multiple indicators of intellectual functioning. Cattell, along with John Horn (e.g., Cattell, 1950, 1963; Horn & Cattell, 1966, 1967), developed a model of primary intellectual abilities–fluid and crystallized–which has gained wide acceptance in psychology in general, and in lifespan development and gerontology, specifically for integrating information about human abilities. Horn and Cattell, 1967, pp. 108,109) shared that their model of fluid and crystallized abilities:

... is an attempt to integrate evidence converging from some five kinds of studies of intellectual performance, viz., studies dealing with: (1) the effects of brain damage on abilities, particularly the differential effects associated with early (in development) as compared with late brain damage; (2) the relationships between test scores and opportunities to acquire knowledge; (3) the construction of intelligence tests which will be more nearly fair for all persons regardless of their social class of origin; (4) the factor structure among sets of tests said to measure various aspects of intelligence; and (5) the changes in intellectual performances associated with aging, both in childhood and in adulthood. The principal conclusion deriving from analysis of the evidence in these various areas is that intellectual abilities are organized at a general level into two general intelligences, viz., fluid intelligence and crystallized intelligence. These represent the operation of somewhat different—i.e., independent—influences in development. On the one hand there are those influences which directly affect the physiological structure upon which intellectual processes must be constructed—influences operating through the agencies of heredity and injury: these are most accurately reflected in measures of fluid intelligence. And on the other hand there are those influences which affect physiological structure only indirectly through agencies of learning, acculturation, etc.: crystallized intelligence is the most direct resultant of individual differences in these influences. . . .

Horn and Cattell (1967) provided specific abilities, based on empirical study and factor analytic techniques, for both fluid and crystallized abilities:

Fluid Abilities
letter groupings and series—Inductive Reasoning
figure classifications, topology, and matrices—Figural Relations
common word analogies—Semantic Relations
nonsense equations and paired associates memory—Associate Memory
span of attention and processing speed—Intellectual Speed

Crystallized Abilities
vocabulary and general information—Verbal Comprehension
syllogistic reasoning and inferences—Formal Reasoning
social situations—Experiential evaluation
arithmetic reasoning and distinctions—General Reasoning
ideas and things—Ideational Fluency

Horn (1982, p. 850), defined the two primary cognitive abilities as follows:

Crystallized Intelligence. This form of intelligence is indicated by a very large number of performances indicating breadth of knowledge and experience, sophistication, comprehension of communications, judgment, understanding conventions, and reasonable thinking. The factor that provides evidence for Gc (crystallized abilities) is defined by primary abilities such as verbal comprehension, concept formation, logical reasoning, and general reasoning. Tests used to measure the ability include vocabulary (what is a word near in meaning to temerity?), esoteric analogies (Socrates is to Aristotle as Sophocles is to _____?), remote associations (what word is associated with bathtub, prizefighting, and wedding?), and judgment (determine why a foreman is not getting the best results from workers). As measured, the factor is a fallible representation of the extent to which an individual has incorporated, through the systematic influences of acculturation, the knowledge and sophistication that constitutes the intelligence of a culture. . . .

Fluid Intelligence. The broad set of abilities of this intelligence includes those of seeing relationships among stimulus patterns, drawing inferences from relationships, and comprehending implications. The primary abilities that best represent the factor, as identified in completed research, include induction, figural flexibility, integration, and cooperatively with Gc (crystallized abilities), logical reasoning and general reasoning. Tasks that measure the factor include letter series (what letter comes next in the following series d f i m rx e _), matrices (discern the relationships among elements of 3-by-3 matrices), and typology (from among a set of figures in which circles, squares, and triangles overlap in different ways, select a figure that will enable one to put a dot within a circle and square but outside a triangle). The factor is a fallible representation of such fundamental features of mature human intelligence as reasoning, abstracting, and problem solving. In Gf (fluid abilities) these features are not imparted through the systematic influences of acculturation but instead are obtained through learning that is unique to an individual or is in other ways not organized by culture. . . .

In addition to fluid and crystallized abilities, Horn and Cattell (1967) included four additional general or primary factors in their model of cognitive abilities. They suggested that the following four factors are more specific than the broader fluid and crystallized primary abilities:

Visualization Ability . . . is a general visualization function producing some variance on all intellectual tasks which involve imaging the way objects may change in appearance as they move in space, maintaining orientation with respect to objects in space, keeping spatial configurations in mind, finding the Gestalt among disparate parts in a visual field, maintaining flexibility concerning other possible structurings of elements of space, etc. . . . (p. 112). *Speeded Ability* . . . picks up variance from most speeded ability tests and in this sense represents a function determining the rate at which ability problems are solved. This function is largely independent of those indicating the level of complexity one reaches in problem solving, as represented in the Gf (fluid abilities) and Gc (crystallized abilities) factors. But beyond this, the nature of the Gs (speeded ability) is not clear. It would seem to stem either from a test-taking effortfulness or from a more physiologically-based capacity, but the research which would provide for a clear distinction between these, and possibly other, interpretations has yet to be done. Meanwhile it is recognized as merely a speediness function which produces some variance on intellectual tasks but which is not an essential aspect of the functioning of intelligence, as such . . . (pp.112, 113).

As will be illustrated later in *Successful Aging: Integrating Contemporary Ideas, Research Findings, and Intervention Strategies*, the speeded ability, as well as Intellectual Speed, has become a major descriptive factor in consistent age-related differences on cognitive ability measures.

> *Carefulness* . . . is a dimension of unwillingness to give an incorrect answer to ability-test problems. Here again, the essential nature of the function is obscure. Logically, it would appear to be the inverse of the speediness function described above, but in fact the two factors have been quite independent in the research upon which their definition is based . . . (p. 113). Finally, *Fluency* . . . would appear to involve, principally, a process of quickly bringing concept labels— i.e., mainly words—from a long-term storage unit into immediate awareness. This, in turn, could represent either the size of store of concept labels—something that could be expected to increase with aging—or the degree of short-circuiting of pathways from storage centers to immediate awareness. And, of course, it could represent an interrelation of these two kinds of function. . . . (p. 113)

Fluid abilities, though defined are more directly linked to physiological and neurological processes and functions, while crystallized abilities are less directly linked to these biological aspects of aging and much more related to accumulative effects of experience and learning. Horn (1970) provided a clear illustration of fluid and crystallized abilities and age-related changes (see Figure 4–1). Figure 4–1 illustrates a general summary of age-related changes for overall, crystallized, and fluid abilities. At the earlier stages of life(infancy and childhood), the curves for crystallized and fluid abilities are about identical, but as development continues, the curves for crystallized and fluid abilities become disparate. According to Horn(1970, p. 466):

> . . . The accumulation of CNS (central nervous system) injuries is masked by rapid development in childhood, but in adulthood the effects become more obvious. Fluid intelligence, based upon this, thus shows decline as soon as the rate of development of CNS structures is exceeded by the rate of CNS breakdown. Experience and learning accumulate throughout development. The influence of these is felt in the development of crystallized intelligence, which increases throughout much of adulthood. It, too, will decline after the rate of loss of structure supporting intelligent behavior exceeds the rate of acquisition of new aids to compensate for limited analog function. . . .

Horn and Cattell (1967, pp. 113–115) provided explanations for why fluid abilities increase through childhood and adolescence, then level off and decline, whereas crystallized abilities increase throughout most of the lifespan:

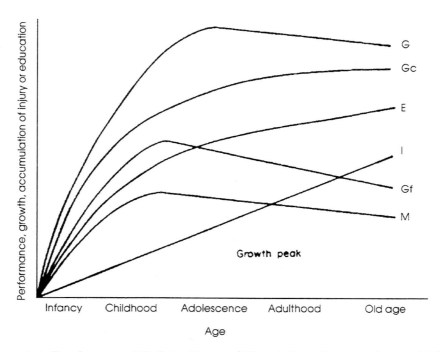

Figure 4–1. Development of fluid intelligence (Gf) and Crystallized intelligence (Gc) in relation to maturational growth and decline of neural structures (M), accumulation of injury to neural structures (I), accumulation of educational exposures (E), and overall ability (G). Source: Horn (1970). Reprinted with permission.

1. The neural and other physiological structures upon which intellectual functioning is based mature by growth and increase in complexity until the late teens or early twenties, at which time they reach their full growth and complexity. This maturation is reflected directly in an increase in Gf (fluid abilities), for although the development of Gf is a function of learning, the particular learning here involved is mainly dependent upon the adequacy of the physiological structure which supports learning. This maturation is reflected also, though indirectly, in an increase in Gc (crystallized abilities), because the development of Gc is based in part on the development of Gf and on the same physiological structures which support learning in general.

2. Injuries to the structures that support intellectual functioning occur throughout life and are irreversible. These injuries are usually so small and few in number during the course of a perceptible time span that they are not noticed, either subjectively by the person himself or by others. Moreover, in childhood the larger effects resulting from neural growth, learning and other development in this period mask the effects of such injuries on intellectual performances. But such injuries accumulate nevertheless and have a long-term limiting influence on the development of intelligence. Again, as in the case of maturational influences, this influence is felt most directly in the development of Gf and somewhat more indirectly in the development of Gc. In adulthood, when the masking influences referred to above cease to be potent, the effects of accumulation of neural damage become more evident in intellectual behavior. Hence, because fluid intelligence is most sensitively dependent upon the functioning of the physiological structures which support intellectual behavior, there will tend to be a decline in Gf with aging in adulthood, this reflecting a gradual degeneration of structure due to accumulation of irreversible injuries.

3. Large injuries to the structures that support intellectual functioning will have occurred more frequently in the population of older people than in the population of younger people. This is likely simply because injury results from exposure in living, and older persons would have had more such exposure. It means that, analogous to the accumulation with aging of small injuries within a particular person, there is an accumulation of large injuries within a sample of people. And because the effects of these larger injuries are also manifested most sensitively in Gf, the mean Gf level for older adults will in general be lower than the mean Gf for younger adults. . . .

4. In the human, particularly, but in all organisms to some extent, some learning occurs incidentally, without much effort being expended either on the part of the individual or on the part of those who would educate him. It is this learning which is manifested primarily in Gf, although, as noted, Gc is constructed on top of this learning. But some—perhaps much—learning occurs less incidentally, particularly in the formal agencies for acculturation such as the school. A kind of intensive acculturation can occur and this is likely to be particularly intensive during childhood, hence the principal work of the young person is seen to be that of acquiring enough of the knowledge of the culture to be able to maintain it. And since the acquisition resulting from this acculturation is shown mainly in Gc, crystallized intelligence increases at a rapid rate in childhood. But the work of preparing people to maintain a culture is never done; adults learn in their attempts to pass knowledge on to the young; and there are numerous inducements and incentives that encourage adults to acquire more and more of the collective intelligence of their culture. Hence, insofar as various acculturation influences continue to operate throughout adulthood, Gc can increase with aging. . . .

Cattell and Horn's research and views on fluid and crystallized abilities, emphasizing the psychological domain articulate many abilities involved in human development and aging. In fact, the fluid abilities of their model are directly associated with the physical domain of aging, particularly parts of the domain dealing with the central nervous system. Also articulated in the Cattell-Horn model is the fact that with so many abilities, there are different patterns of development, stabilization, and deterioration. The beauty of the Cattell and Horn model is that a two-factor approach (a) simplifies the general trends of fluid and crystallized abilities, and (b) categorizes possible determinants of the fluid versus crystallized abilities trends over the lifespan. We need to be careful, however, as to avoid oversimplifying patterns of abilities over the lifespan or factors contributing to general patterns. While fluid abilities patterns, as compared to crystallized abilities patterns show a different overall pattern of change over the lifespan, the multitude of abilities within either fluid or crystallized categories illustrate individuality of change patterns throughout the lifespan. Likewise, while genetic factors are more directly related to fluid abilities and environmental determinants to crystallized abilities, specific abilities can illustrate unique interactive effects of heredity and environment, differentially in one's lifespan. The Cattell/Horn model continues to be promoted by lifespan and gerontology professionals because of successive research which supports the delineation of fluid and crystallized abilities over the lifespan, differential patterns of change, differential determinants on these abilities, and differential importance of the determinants or causal factors in different periods of the lifespan.

The Cattell-Horn model, often cited by developmentalists and gerontologists, is primarily a model of differential cognitive abilities. Their creative model building and subsequent associated research by others, awaited creativity on the part of others for integration into a substantive approach to development and aging.

BALTES' MODEL OF SUCCESSFUL AGING

The Baltes model, represented in his **Eight Principles of Lifespan Development** (see Chapter 2), enhances the Cattell/Horn model to include such important concepts as the following:

> *Dynamic between Biological and Cultural Factors in Development* **(Principle Two)**
> Changes in Allocation of Resources over the Lifespan **(Principle Three)**
> *Adaptive Capabilities of Selection, Optimization, and Compensation* **(Principles Four and Eight)**
> *Plasticity* **(Principle Six)**
> *Fourth Stage of the Lifespan* **(Old-old Age)**

Baltes is consistent in his advocacy for successful aging in research and model-building for both lifespan development and aging (Baltes, Lindenberger, & Staudinger, 1998). While he continues to enhance his views on lifespan development, including reviews of physical, psychological, historical, and cultural aging-related research, Baltes offers generalizations about aging that articulate individual and cultural potentials for successful development. This positive approach, balanced by his promotion of the scientific method in investigating lifespan development, is remarkable. Recently, Paul and Margaret Baltes (1998, p. 13) provided an illustration of the Baltes' emphasis on successful aging:

> One of the great challenges of the next century will be to complete the architecture of the human life course, to transform old age into a period where the gains outnumber the losses, where labeling old age as the "golden years" is more than a dream. We have not yet reached that point. Most of us want to become old, but we worry about being old. We have succeeded in adding years to our lives, but

we are uncertain of our ability, as a society and as individuals, to add life to the years we have gained. Aging well from a psychological point of view lags behind the increase in sheer biological longevity. . . .

Earlier, Paul Baltes (1993, p. 592), shared the following as a guide to successful aging endeavors:

> . . . I conceptualize the two prototypes of intellectual functioning, the cognitive mechanics and the cognitive pragmatics, as exemplars of two fundamentally different streams of influence on the nature of aging: The genetic and the cultural. In the neurophysiological architecture of the mind (the cognitive mechanics), the evolution-based genome and the biology of aging are dominant. The central story in this hardware-like domain is one of aging as decline. In the software-like content component of the mind, the cognitive pragmatics, the enriching and compensatory power of knowledge and culture can unfold. With the principles of culture and cultural evolution, it is possible to have a larger vision that includes the possibility of 'outwitting' the biological limitations and deficits of old age. In this sense, a surprising conclusion about the nature of old age holds true: Because of the relative recency of culture for old age, old age is still "young". . . .

Dynamic Between Biological and Cultural Factors in Development

Perhaps the most important aspect of this lifespan principle is an attempt to integrate facts and ideas about (a) differential patterns of ability changes over the lifespan, (b) primary determinants of those differential patterns, and (c) intervention efforts to retard erosion of abilities subject to physiological decline, enhance abilities subject to environmental remediation or prevention, and/or enhance certain abilities to compensate for inevitable loss in other abilities. Chapter 2 included the following four factors of importance to the dynamic between biological and cultural factors in development:

1. A chronological age-related reduction in biological resources over the lifespan.
2. An increase in contextual support over the lifespan to compensate for reduced biological resources.
3. Continued reduction of biological resources in later stages of the life pan, even with enhanced cultural support.
4. Relative lack of communal (societal, communal, familial) support for older individuals.

The integration effort is a difficult one, given the complexity of life, at any stage of the lifespan. The following are issues of integration:

1. From an individual or societal perspective, what are the primary human attributes in the physical, psychological and social domains of importance? Those associated with length and quality of life quickly come to mind. Length of life becomes more in focus the older we become—older in terms of physical, psychological and social age. Quality of life is defined differently at successive stages of the lifespan. As with each of the three issues noted above for the Dynamic Between Biological and Cultural Factors in Development, *identification* of those primary human attributes for a long and positive life should be of interest to professionals in aging and aging persons.

2. What are the primary human attributes associated with length of life? The answers to this question usually emphasize physical aging, fluid abilities, and the integrity of biological and physiological systems and functions. In particular, *pathological aging* associated with chronic illnesses illustrates the importance of physical attributes for longevity. Another illustration of the importance of physical attributes for length of life is the genetic pre-disposition to cause of natural death; e.g., heart disease, cancer. Yet, one's psychological and social environments impinge upon those physical attributes most often identified with length of life. For example, cigarette smoking is positively correlated with lung cancer. Cigarette smoking in Japan and European countries is much higher than in the United States, reflecting different social contexts. Also, even with evidence linking cigarette smoking to lung cancer, many intelligent people continue to smoke. This phenomenon reflects the importance of psychological factors in longevity, as well as quality of life. With *normal aging*, many significant declines in physical attributes are detected; some well before age 50 (e.g., Salthouse, 1999). Visual and hearing declines are the most often described in middle adult-hood, but hair loss, skin deterioration, muscle mass/tone decline, physical strength deterioration, reduction in information processing speed, and declines in the integrity of sensory-motor, hormonal, cardiovascular, ner-vous, respiratory, and skeletal systems are also significant (Belsky,1999). In older age, deterioration in these physical attributes becomes much more pronounced. Clearly, physical attributes associated with such age-related changes contribute to both length of life and quality of life. While it is useful to review updates on average age-related changes in physical attributes, it is very important to appreciate the fact that averages do not reflect variability among individuals at any period of the lifespan or variability within the individual over the lifespan on any attribute. Findings of ongoing research (e.g., Baltes and Mayer, 1999; Schaie, 1996) and summaries of research studies (e.g., Baltes, Lindenberger, and Staudinger, 1998; Belsky, 1999; Santrock, 1999) illustrate that there is much variability in age-related abilities (interindividual variability) and, as important, increased variability (intraindividual variability) within the person in the later stages of the

lifespan. As with developmental progression of human abilities during childhood and adolescence, developmental deterioration of human abilities is illustrated by variability among individuals in onset of decline, rate of decline, and asymptote of functioning. In addition to these variabilities among and within individuals, we also have the phenomenon of variation among abilities in terms of ability onset, rate of development, and level of functioning. Thus, reported average age-related changes in human abilities, particularly those attributes associated with longevity and quality of life, should be guides, not grading scales, for individual assessments of normal, pathological, and successful aging. In industrialized nations, and certainly for the United States, significant professional attention has focused on pathological aging and chronic illnesses associated with cancer and the cardiovascular and skeletal systems (especially arthritis and osteoporosis). In addition, visual and hearing problems receive attention. Are the physical attributes associated with such problems the primary attributes of interest in aging? Are these attributes the most important in terms of longevity and/or quality of life? What are the primary human attributes associated with quality of life? Psychological attributes and cultural conditions are often identified in differentiating among quality of life levels, but physical attributes are also important factors. Many psychological attributes have been identified, to varying degrees, as correlating with quality of life; e.g., crystallized abilities, psychological well-being, life satisfaction, intelligence, motivation, personality, and lifestyle. Social correlates of quality of life are such factors as ethnicity, culture/subculture, living arrangements, occupation, social status, significant others, membership in social organizations, volunteerism, and income. Psychological and social factors are important in quality of life, as illustrated by the contemporary American issues of access to, and acceptance of, medical treatment, and death with dignity or controlling the timing of death.

3. For those primary attributes associated with longevity and quality of life, what determinants, singularly or in combination, contribute most? Throughout the history of lifespan development, an accepted proposition is that any human attribute—physical or psychological—is the result of an interaction between one's genetic makeup and environment. But, this proposition is only a starting point in identifying contributors important to physical and psychological changes over the lifespan. While research has shown that certain age-related changes are due more to biological factors (e.g., primary sex characteristics, eye color, and race) and other changes to environmental ones (e.g., peers, occupation, and income level), it has also been found that biological and environmental factors have differential influence over the lifespan. Also, more complex human attributes, like fluid and crystallized cognitive constructs or constructs such as memory, sensory-motor functioning,

motivation, and personality are determined by a complex interaction of biological (including genetic) and environmental determinants. Finally, with decline in some important abilities, humans are able to compensate for such loss by either remedial strategies or the use of other abilities. For example, optic surgery (structural remediation) or eyeglasses (prosthetic remediation) can compensate for loss of visual acuity. Hearing loss can be compensated for by hearing aids (prosthetic remediation). Short-term memory loss can be compensated for via use of a tape recorder (prosthetic remediation) or writing notes (cognitive remediation).

Given the complexities of human life, primary attributes associated with longevity and quality of life, and interaction of biological and environmental determinants on primary attributes, why focus on the dynamic between biological and cultural factors in lifespan development and aging? Realistically, professionals in lifespan development and aging will continue to pursue their interests in such factors, and some will continue to focus on the dynamics or interactions. In discussing the Berlin Aging study, Mayer, et al. (1999, p. 510) noted: ". . . As age simultaneously constitutes a biological, psychological, social, and institutional phenomenon, gerontological studies should be designed to include a wide range of disciplinary and interdisciplinary research". . . . Such efforts are mandatory for understanding the complex nature of development. More importantly, with the inclusion of primary human abilities for longevity and quality of life, the search for determinants of growth, stability, and decline leads to attempts at intervention for age-related declines.

4. Intervention related to age-related decline in important human abilities should be of interest to both professionals of lifespan development and aging, as well as those of us concerned with our own longevity and quality of life. Since life is finite, as are personal and societal funding sources, it is reasonable to focus on primary abilities, change in these abilities over the lifespan, factors contributing to changes, and ways to intervene.

Intervention strategies are either proactive (prevention, enhancement) or reactive (remedial). Intervention strategies related to aging will be detailed in Chapter 5 (Intervention Approaches). Preventive age-related interventions usually focus on lifestyle approaches such as moderation in the use of prescription drugs, alcohol, food consumption, and significant others, as well as physical/mental exercise, and annual medical evaluations. Enhancement age-related interventions focus on either government-regulated supplemental programs for the disadvantaged or self-initiated activities for educational (lifelong learning), occupational, or social improvement. Remedial age-related interventions have focused on physical impairments or deterioration, with the use of surgery, drug intervention, prosthetic devices, dietary controls, and moderate exercise.

Changes in Allocation of Resources Over the Lifespan

In our younger years, particularly during childhood, adolescence, and young adulthood, much effort was given to learning new things, while in later years, the emphasis shifts to retaining our abilities–physical, psychological, and social. The focus of personal attention to adaptiveness, termed resources by Baltes (1997, pp. 369–370), shifts as we age:

> . . . With the adaptive function of growth, I refer to behaviors involved in reaching higher levels of functioning or adaptive capacity. Under the heading of maintenance and recovery (resilience), I classify behaviors involved in maintaining levels of functioning in the face of a new contextual challenge or loss in potential. Finally, regarding regulation of loss or management, I mean behaviors that organize functioning at lower levels when maintenance or recovery (resilience) is no longer possible . . . Because of the architecture outlined above, my colleagues and I argue that there is a systematic life span shift in the relative allocation of resources to these three functions . . . In childhood, the primary allocation is directed toward growth; during adulthood, the predominant allocation is toward maintenance and recovery (resilience). In old age, more and more resources are directed toward regulation or management of loss. Such characterization of the life span, of course, is an oversimplification, as individual, functional (domain), contextual, and historical differences need to be taken into account. Note in this context that the reallocation of resources toward maintenance of functioning and regulation of loss is facilitated by the tendency of individuals to prefer avoidance of loss over enhancement of gains. . . .

Given Baltes' *Lifespan Principles* discussed earlier, it makes sense to note that his idea of age-related human allocations shifting is not independent of principles dealing with multiple human resources and differential age-related changes in primary human attributes. Abilities categorized as reflecting primarily physical, psychological, and social aging, though illustrating Baltes' principle of changes in resources over the lifespan, show uniqueness in progression, stability, and decline. We can differentiate among singular abilities reflecting physical, psychological, and social aging. Santrock (1999, pp. 388–389), for example, notes that we ". . . reach our peak physical performance under the age of 30, often between the ages of 19 and 26. . . . Not only do we reach our peak physical performance during early adulthood, but during this time we are also the healthiest. Few young adults have chronic health problems, and they have fewer colds and respiratory problems than when they were children". . . . In terms of athletic prowess, the choice of sport relates to peak performance. International Olympic competitions dramatically illustrate this differential. Medal gymnasts are young adolescents; the best basketball players are late-adolescents or young adults; and internationally recognized polo players are young- and middle-aged adults. The more sensorimotor abilities and processing speed play a role in competitive sporting activities, the younger are the champions; the more experience plays a role, the older, to the point of imbalance between fluid and crystallized abilities, are the winners. As was presented earlier, the lifespan profiles of fluid and crystallized abilities show different age-related changes. While fluid abilities start to decline relatively early in adulthood, crystallized ones either stabilize or continue to improve through most of adulthood. Social skills, heavily dependent upon crystallized, learned abilities, need not decline until very old age. The complex human ability of wisdom is determined within a social context. While the concept of wisdom has a number of definitions, almost all criteria for wisdom include experience within a cultural perspective. Wisdom, often associated with older and/or more experienced individuals, reflects accumulations of both expertise and personal-social histories. Thus, a developmental profile of wisdom should show a peak in the later stages of life.

Give some thought to your changes in allocation of resources over your lifespan. Think of some basic abilities important to you, such as relative speed of processing information. Remember, information important to you also changes in your lifespan! In childhood, even adolescence, you were able to process lots of information requiring immediate attention. You may have made mistakes in dealing with the information in a short period of time, but you did process lots of information. In middle adulthood, you are not able to process as much information in the same period of time as you did at a younger stage of development. In older adulthood, you will be able to process even less information in a limited period of time. Why is this so? Processing relevant information in a short period of time, and relatedly, not processing irrelevant information at the same time, is directly associated with the integrity of sensation, perception, and short-term memory structures and functions. These structures and functions begin to decline in young adulthood. In middle adulthood, even young adulthood, you cannot successfully compete with an adolescent in physical sports such as gymnastics, sprint running, and roller-blading or mental sports such as short-term remembrance of novel information lists, sensorimotor reactions to stimulation, and dealing with multiple stimuli in a short period of time. In later life, you will perform even less satisfactorily, compared to younger individuals on such fluid abilities activities. There are two important caveats to the general decline of physical abilities. First, the better one's physical abilities (some or many, based upon genetic potential and optimal environmental stimulants), the better one will function with these physical abilities relative to others with less genetic potential and/or optimal environmental stimulants throughout the lifespan. In other words, decline will come within the physical domain, but physical deterioration illustrates both intraindividual and interindividual change over the lifespan. The second important caveat for the physical domain (as well as psychological and social) is summarized with the adage, "use it or lose it." Maintaining physical abilities, especially after maturation, requires effort. Physical exercise is a good example. Children and adolescents, given maturational principles associated with physical growth, require little conscious effort for endurance, strength, flexibility, or balancing exercises. Adults, at all stages, do! Abilities primarily based upon learning, those in the psychological and social domains, also require mental exercise throughout the lifespan. Somewhat related to the "use it or lose it" adage, is overindulgence. Inappropriate drug use (alcohol, tobacco, prescription/ illegal drugs), poor nutrition (obesity, inadequate diet), lack of exercise (physical, psychological, social) and sustained levels of stress are the primary negative environmental determinants of unsuccessful aging. Lifestyle decisions can be life threatening ones!

Adults—young, middle aged, older—do much better than children and adolescents on tasks which load heavily on experienced, learned abilities— crystallized abilities. What do you do better now than you did as a child and adolescent? Lots of things! But, what are those abilities and, correspondingly, the factors that contribute to them? Baltes' principle of changing resource allocations over the lifespan suggests that the individual, deliberately or with little or no conscious decision making, changes allocation of resources while moving through the lifespan. We make changes in how we deal with our internal and external worlds based upon perceived strengths and weaknesses. A reasonable suggestion is that those who move through the lifespan more successfully than others are more adept at recognizing the need for making appropriate changes at appropriate times. What makes this suggestion a bit more complicating is that successful movement through the lifespan is defined, by each of us, on multiple criteria, physical, psychological, social domains and standards. We can, for example, make appropriate resource allocation changes in one domain (e.g., occupation), but not in others (e.g., physical and psychological health, family relationships, quality of life, and longevity).

The idea of changes in allocation of resources over the lifespan is based upon findings about normal aging. Perhaps not enough thought is given to one's responsibility in deciding upon those changes. While research supports Baltes' principle of changes in allocation of resources over the lifespan— maturation in the early years, stability in the middle years, and decline of many abilities (especially fluid) in the later years—the phenomenon of interindividual variability (at all stages of development) allows for differential profiles of aging–for every domain, type, and definition of aging.

Adaptive Capabilities of Selection, Optimization and Compensation

In the next chapter, dealing with intervention strategies, these adaptive capabilities will be more specifically described. Baltes and his colleagues, with the ideas of selection, optimization and compensation over the lifespan, provide both developing professionals and average citizens remarkable insight into successful aging–through all phases or stages of the lifespan. One reason for the promotion of lifespan categories of ages, phases, stages, and levels, is that people change as they move through the lifespan. We are, as we move through our lifespan, at least as much different as the same from what we were and will be. It is important to remember Baltes' ideas of *multidimensionality* and *multidirectionality* when thinking about the adaptive capabilities of selection, optimization and compensation. He has promoted a concept of a complex human being (with multiple abilities, or multi-dimensionality), traveling through a complex lifespan (with multiple factors determining abilities, or contextualisim), and selecting/optimizing/compensating, at any given point in time, among many developmental options, resulting indifferent patterns of change (multidirectionality).

Baltes (1997, p. 371), illustrated the adaptive capabilities of selection, optimization, and compensation as follows:

> . . . The essential nature of *selection* in ontogenesis follows from several arguments. One is that development always has a specific set of targets (goals) of functioning. Second, development always proceeds within the condition of a limited capacity, including constraints in time and resources. Moreover, selection is conditioned by the very fact that organisms possess behavioral dispositions (e.g., sensory modalities, motor repertoires, cognitive mechanics) that during evolution were selected from a pool of potentialities. Furthermore, . . . selection is conditioned by age-related changes in plasticity and associated losses in potential. Age-associated losses in biological potential or plasticity increase the pressure for selection . . . A specific example of selection in early life is the acquisition of language (Levelt, 1989). Although infants around the world seem to possess the same basic dispositions for the recognition and production of language, their ontogenetic development is shaped in specific (selected) directions of sound recognition and sound production by the realization (acquisition) of a particular language. Thus, the acquisition of language involves from the ontogenetic beginning selection phenomena, with

associated gains and losses in performance potential. Another concrete illustration of selection is the acquisition of cognitive stages in child development. Take Piagetian theory as an example. It has become increasingly recognized that the ontogenetic movement toward a 'final' stage of formal logical reasoning is the effect of a culture-based selection process. Another approach closely related to the notion of development, as selection is the work of Sigler (1994) who treated the ontogeny of cognitive skills and strategies in children as the outcome of variability-based selection from a larger pool of potentialities.

Optimization is the hallmark of any traditional conception of development. Development is widely considered as a movement toward increased efficacy and higher levels of functioning. My colleagues and I argue that human development, as an optimizing positive change in adaptive capacity toward a set of desirable outcomes (goals), requires in concert the application of a set of behavior-enhancing factors such as cultural knowledge, physical status, goal commitment, practice, and effort. The component elements that are relevant for the task of optimization vary by the domain and developmental status. And from an ontogenetic point of view, of course, the concept of optimization undergoes developmental changes in the components and mechanisms involved as well. Research on the development of expertise in children and adults is a good example (Ericsson & Smith, 1991).

Compensation, finally, is operative whenever a given set of means is no longer available, either because of direct losses of these means (e.g., hearing loss), because of negative transfer (e.g., incompatibility between goals), or because of new limiting constraints in time and energy (e.g., the exclusive consumptive focus on the tasks of resilience and regulation of loss). Compensation, then, has multiple origins and comes in varied forms. . . .

Compensatory behaviors or strategies, in relation to selectivity and optimization, have been of keen interest to professionals interested in research and practice during older adulthood. Recently, Dixon and Backman (1995) provided a summary of such interest, with *Compensating for Psychological Deficits and Declines: Managing Losses and Promoting Gains*. They identify the components of compensation as follows (1995, pp. 9–11):

Origins . . . compensation must have its origins in a mismatch between the skills a person possesses and the demands of the environment. Whether objective or subjective, the mismatch can be the result of an individual's deficit (or decline) vis-a-vis the relatively constant environmental demands, or the result of an increase in environmental demands that is not matched by an increase in the individual's skills. Without a mismatch—with no deficit—there is no rationale for compensation. The rationale for compensation must be to close the gap between expected level of performance and actual level of performance . . . A mismatch is necessary, but not sufficient, for compensation. Indeed, there are several qualifications or reasons that compensation might not occur for any given mismatch. These include the following situations: (a)when there is a high degree of support in the individual's environment or context and thus no need for self-initiated compensation, and (b) when the deficit is so severe that compensation is impossible to effect. (See Backman & Dixon, 1992)

Mechanisms . . . or the means through which an alleviation or attenuation of the mismatch is pursued . . . Whatever the origins of compensation, there are several mechanisms through which the actual compensatory behavior may occur. For example, an individual may: (a) increase the time or effort expended at the task or devoted to continuing to maintain the pertinent skill; (b) access a substitutable skill from the individual's present repertoire, the use of which results in a narrowing of the gap;(c) use or develop a new skill, conceding, as it were, the deficit or decline in the previously useful one; (d) modify expectations about performance, such that the gap is less troubling, thereby reducing one's criterion of success; (e) separate the personal expectation of performance from the environmental demand, such that the former resides closer to the actual level of performance or ability; and (f) select alternative tasks or goals— related or unrelated to the original skill—such that, although the original mismatch continues, it is reduced in its prominence and perhaps eventually forgotten.

Awareness . . . On the one hand compensation may be associated with awareness of a mismatch and with deliberate action intended to overcome the deficit. On the other hand, it may be associated with the absence of awareness of the mismatch, or even the compensatory behavior (e.g., compensation in some domains may be relatively automatic). Indeed, in some compensatory processes, both differences between phases in awareness and changes in awareness through time are possible. For example, it is possible that some compensatory behaviors may originate in an awareness of a mismatch, and perhaps even a desire to remediate the mismatch.

However, the actual mechanism of compensation, and indeed the fact of compensation, may not be available to, much less planfully executed by, the individual. In addition, in these or similar situations the awareness of the mismatch or compensatory mechanism may fade (or grow) with time. Compensatory behaviors, like skills, may become relatively automated and less effortful to execute (e.g., Ohlsson, 1986; Rothi & Horner, 1983). . . .

Consequences. . . . As Emerson (1900) noted (see also Baltes, 1987), for every gain in life there is a loss . . . in the big picture, the consequences of compensation are not uniformly positive: Gains in one part of a system may imply losses in another . . . In general, compensatory efforts within one domain of functioning are carried out at the expense of functioning in another area. Suppose Individual A, who is managing Skills X, Y, and Z, detects a growing disparity between expectation and performance of Skill Y. Efforts to compensate may detract from the ability to continue successful management of skills X and Z . . . The consequences of compensation may involve gains and losses in even more fundamental respects. Compensation usually results in adaptation and, where awareness is involved are certainly tends to promote success. Nevertheless, some, if not many, compensatory efforts—whether automatic or deliberate—may yield no success at all. This lack of success at closing the mismatch may, in turn, require some adaptive behavior. However, it establishes the possibility that compensatory behavior may yield, in addition to adaptation and success, no basic result, no change in the mismatch, and no demonstrable consequence. Still another consequence to compensatory behavior—and this may be the most surprising of all—is a negative or maladaptive outcome. . . .

Although the notions of selection, optimization and compensation throughout the lifespan make sense, we often find ourselves wondering why we do not follow them. In fact, we often reflect on mistakes made as related to previous options in significant life events. Hindsight can be more accurate or evaluative than foresight. We are critical of our past decisions, actions, and long-term activities, as well as being cognizant of decisions, actions, and long-term activities of others. Sometimes, our selections of goals are more dependent upon the goals of significant others, particularly in childhood and adolescence. Often, our goals after adolescence are primarily the responsibility of ourselves. Life is complex, regardless of one's stage of development. It is often very difficult to make decisions which result in long-term commitments and life histories. And, there is the matter of chance, fate, or divine intervention. Interestingly, with development from childhood and adolescence to adulthood, especially middle and late adulthood, our initiatives for selecting among alternative goals becomes more narrow or restricted. While one would think that experience enhances the world of opportunities, the reality is that for most of us, the experiences we have as we age often reflect experiencing more of the same or similar. Add to this idea that of age-related losses in the physical, psychological, and social domains, and the restriction of opportunities becomes more so. It is one thing for an older adult, or a young one for that matter, to intellectualize the ability to select among many possibilities, quite another for us to decide, much less act upon, new challenges. We always project more than we do when it comes to opportunities. We read books, listen to music, attend movies, stay at home and engage television, dream in sleep, and fantasize, often, during waking hours. Why? projection, or modeling-without-action, allows for selection of goals without personal commitment or dealing with negative consequences of our actions.

While we do try to optimize our positive adaptive capabilities, as we select among possible goals (broadly or restrictively defined), habits work against us. There are numerous reasons for why we do not optimize adaptive capabilities for desired ends. Baltes, Lindenberger, and Staudinger (1998, pp. 1056, 1057) noted that:

> . . . optimization requires a mutually enhancing coalition of factors, including health, environmental, and psychological conditions (Marsiske et al., 1995; Staudinger et al., 1995). As was true for selection, optimization can be active and passive, conscious and unconscious, internal or external. Moreover, optimization can be domain- and goal-specific as well as domain- and goal-general. The most domain-general notion of optimization is the generation of developmental reserve capacity (Baltes, 1987; Kliegl & Baltes, 1987), or plasticity of general-purpose mechanisms. . . .

At one extreme of optimization is that of the young athlete, who may optimize those physical and cognitive abilities directly related to a particular sport to the extreme of little optimization of cognitive abilities associated with education, socialization, and/or personality development. Consistent examples of this extreme form of optimization are gifted athletes who flunk out of college with poor educational/occupational achievement skills, social skills, and/or self-image. At the other extreme of optimization is the individual who has attempted competency in one or more areas, with resulting flexibility and relative proficiency in multiple areas, manipulating optimization opportunities dependent upon changing environmental or personal situations. Senator Bill Bradley is a good example of such a person. Through high school and college, Bill Bradley optimized goal-relevant means for multiple capabilities required for exceptional athletic, academic, and social achievement. During his early adult years, Bill Bradley was a professional basketball player, while in middle adulthood, Senator Bradley transitioned optimization energy for that of a successful politician.

For most of us, many opportunities arise for optimizing, within limits, personal resources directed at goals. Interestingly, we tend to optimize relatively few personal resources through the lifespan, thus reinforcing limited resources and goals at the expense of, perhaps, a more enriched life. As we hone those capabilities that assist us in seeking or maintaining some personal goals or ambitions, we are, by default, not focusing on other capabilities and/or other goals or ambitions. While it is true that as we move through our lifespan, focus on both abilities and goals change, we do get set in our ways. There are many examples for illustration, especially in adulthood and old age. In middle adulthood for example, how many times have you heard from a friend about his/her serious frustrations with occupation and/or marriage? With occupation, frustrations can be linked to a person's focus on the same optimization of skills which provided both opportunities, then limitations, in a particular area of employment. For too many years, such frustrated individuals were unable to reframe their abilities for other occupational opportunities or, perhaps, anything else. Since much of their world, particularly for males (though working females these days are included), is defined by work, frustrated workers are frustrated family and community members. Some middle adulthood faculty members in higher education, with 25 years of experience at the same university, fit this category. Many of these fine folks remain Associate Professors, not gaining Full Professor status, because they did not meet the criteria standards for promotion. Most are very bright and very frustrated. They are, in their late 50s or early 60s, locked in to their jobs. Without a record for promotion within their university, they are not viable candidates in searches at other universities. Because they have invested (optimized) much of their cognitive resources in being a faculty member, many longtime Associate Professors are unable to find employment outside of higher education. In addition, approaching older adulthood, many of these fine individuals are captives of state employee retirement systems. Their retirement income from such systems is based upon both years of service and an average of a number of highest earning years. These folks find it almost impossible to get out of the system before they retire. So, long-term Associate Professors can become very frustrated, and the frustration spills into their occupational, personal, familial, and communal lives. Since most faculty members in higher education are bright, intellectual prowess is not sufficient for optimizing occupational, personal, familial, or communal goals or opportunities.

Middle adulthood and marriage? Even though the divorce rate in America continues to rise, now over 50 percent of marriages, it is rather amazing that so many couples remain together for so long. The amazement, however, is overshadowed by the sustained frustrations of the partners and their children. As with occupational frustrations, marital frustrations illustrate unwillingness, in this case perhaps involving two adults, to focus on the human adaptiveness of sharing an adult lifespan with one another and/or children. Another idea is that human adaptability includes motivational states of frustration or competition among goals, resulting in continual emotional distress—of varying degrees and within/among individuals. With frustrated middle adulthood marital partners, one or both of the partners, though wishing for a more optimal relationship with a partner, are unwilling to seek a better relationship within or outside the marriage. The illustrations of middle adulthood frustrations associated with occupation and marriage highlight the human phenomenon of knowing one can effect change by taking advantage of opportunities and optimizing one's relative capabilities, without acting upon the opportunities or optimizing those capabilities for doing so.

These frustrations with occupation and marriage can be elevated in old age, and the examples are obvious. Some pre-retirees could not wait until retirement because they were frustrated with their work for so long. Could it be that many of the same individuals were frustrated with much of their life? (Most often, reviews of frustrated pre-retirees focus on the negative comments associated with work. But, like the chicken or egg controversy, one should wonder about how pervasive frustration is in life. Is serious personal frustration directly related to one's long-term occupation? Or, is serious personal frustration more illustrative of one who views life's glass as half-empty?) Unfortunately for some, pre-retirement frustrations are carried into retirement. These folks are unwilling to either (a) select alternative life goals or (b) commit those personal resources which optimize transference of skills from occupation to personal advancement, such as volunteerism, lifelong learning ventures, hobbies, and part-time work. Frustrated marriage partners approach old age without the significant advantage of having optimal or good mental and physical support of one's spouse. If other significant individuals, personal or social activities, and positive self-esteem are not available, frustrated marriage partners enter old age without the partner as a resource for successful aging.

Regardless of the lifespan period, we have the option of compensation when there is an erosion (loss) of previously held goal-relevant means (often linked to our own capabilities) to desired outcomes. If the desired outcome is very important, then we seek other ways to achieve the end result. Being able to see and hear reasonably well is very important. Fortunately, we have the prosthetic (compensatory) devices of glasses and hearing aids to provide some correction to failing visual and auditory abilities. Dealing with aging issues of the losses of physical strength, muscle tone, vitality, historical self-concept, and psychological adaptiveness, as well as the gains of chronic illness and personal awareness of death, is not as easy as changing prosthetic visual or auditory devices. A second age-related compensatory strategy is one of changing goals. With advancing age, we have the option of redirecting both our abilities and relative control of our worlds, to those activities that are both doable and rewarding. This option is much more plausible in older age if we, in our earlier stages of development, select and optimize multiple preventive strategies for coping with life. The examples are numerous: physical and mental exercise, good nutritional habits, caring for others, soliciting, maintaining, and enhancing personal relationships, moderation in prescription drug and alcohol use, humor, lifelong learning interests, common sense, rearranging living arrangements before age-related disabilities require it, reducing stress levels, and maintaining or enhancing a sense of self-worth.

Compensating for loss of previous levels of functioning, activities, and/or significant others occurs at all stages of the lifespan. Some people are able to compensate better than others. Within the general concept of the lifespan and the more specific one of successful aging, compensation for loss will be maximized when coping strategies are learned early in the lifespan. Further, compensation for inevitable losses (at any stage of the lifespan) will be maximized for those individuals who actively seek (select) and maintain (optimize) multiple goals. In other words, successful aging, which includes compensating for inevitable losses in physical, psychological, and social resources (and subsequent goal-directed behaviors), requires both (a) pro-action in the development and maintenance of coping abilities and (b) development of proaction as early as possible in the lifespan.

Plasticity

This principle is based on two characteristics of human life. First, at any stage of development and for all human phenotypes or characteristics, interindividual variability is found. That is, there is a range for structure, function, and behavioral performance when a human system (such as the nervous system—structure and function) or behavior (for example, verbal intelligence) is assessed. Because there is interindividual variability or differences among individuals of a particular age/period of development on any observable characteristic, the assumption is that a given individual's assessment score, relative to any other's, could be higher or lower. A more important reason for assuming plasticity is that all of us illustrate intra-individual variability. This intraindividual variability is obvious in two ways. First, regardless of what period of our life we are in, we illustrate different potentials in significant attributes within and among physical, psychological, and social dimensions. For example, each of us shows different profiles for physical aging, psychological aging, and social aging, as well as different profiles within each of these categories. Second, for every domain of aging, physical, psychological, social, there is change—permutations of the positive, negative, and stable.

The notion of plasticity, given the multiplicity of options noted above, is not new to lifespan psychology or gerontology. What is new, with the insight of Baltes and his colleagues, is that (a) plasticity (or reserve capacity) itself shows a developmental pattern, and (b) the developmental pattern is subject to intervention. Plasticity or reserve capacity, as summarized by Baltes, Lindenberger, and Staudinger (1998), is illustrated throughout the lifespan within the primary domains of aging—physical, psychological, social, historical. The assumption is that with advancing development in adulthood and genetically-programmed biological structures and systems, plasticity or reserve capacity becomes less and less. This assumption is the basis for a developmental pattern that, in adulthood, becomes negatively accelerated; i.e., the curve declines—for some abilities (fluid ones) more so than others (crystallized ones).

Interestingly, the assumption of declining plasticity during the adult years has not been integrated with another assumption; viz., during the maturational years (from birth to young adulthood), limited environmental experiences (learning) and maturing biological, psychological, and social structures, systems, and processes also limit plasticity or reserve capacity. While this assumption, like that of declining plasticity during the adult years, is based upon research, another assumption is that the younger person has more reserve capacity than his or her older counterpart. In fact, biological principles suggest that infants, children, and early adolescents have less plasticity than adults; psychological and sociological principles suggest that infants, children, adolescents, and young adults have less plasticity than older adults, including senior citizens. Thus, it is important, when dealing with plasticity or reserve capacity to focus on particular human capabilities.

The Baltes notion of differential plasticity or reserve capacity over the lifespan, illustrating a generic developmental pattern of function, is viable as a general principle for describing age-related changes in important biological, psychological and social adaptations. The cautionary note is that plasticity is both expansive and limiting at all stages of the lifespan, depending upon the status of the individual and the context he or she is in.

The second aspect of plasticity throughout the lifespan that Baltes and his colleagues have articulated is one of enhancing or limiting individual adaptability, regardless of stage of development, with self- or other-initiated intervention. Typically, intervention attempts, whether self- or other-initiated, involve actions to (a) prevent or retard age-related losses in adaptability and (b) remediate existing states of age-related losses. In the year 2000 in America, there is more widespread acceptance of long-term benefits associated with preventive intervention, regardless of area of aging. Younger citizens are more aware of such benefits, and are more willing to engage in lifestyles of moderation. The long-term benefits are noted in more successful biological and psychological aging through long-term mental and physical exercise regimens, diet, and significant other networking, to share a few. Remediation, however, remains the primary intervention for much of the losses as we age; e.g., therapies for all kinds of psychological problems, corrective surgery, drugs, and/or lifestyle changes for cardiovascular, respiratory, and nervous system problems, and prosthetic devices for visual and hearing losses.

The relevant point about plasticity and intervention within a lifespan framework is the assumption that intervention, be it preventive or remedial, is most advantageous for the individual when he or she has the most plasticity or reserve capacities associated with a particular loss and/or related gains or strengths in other capabilities. Given that the plasticity principle articulates greater reserve capacity earlier in life, a correlative assumption is that preventive intervention early on is more effective than either preventive intervention or remediation later on.

The relationship of plasticity and intervention, perhaps overstated with age-related declines in abilities, however, should include the criterion of revising priorities as we age. Conceptually, the notion of maximum gain for some loss in a goal and/or ability related to the goal earlier in the lifespan makes sense. But, what makes sense to someone (often a professional) without the loss may not make sense to the person who may experience the loss, or other priorities are more important. Cigarette smoking is an example. There is more than enough data available indicating that smoking increases the risk of life-threatening illnesses. A smoking young adult, perhaps aware of the relevant data, continues to smoke for any number of reasons; viz., addiction, habituation, self and professional diagnosis of being in excellent physical health, little, awareness of overall aging and physical deterioration, and engagement in positive lifestyle behaviors to counter negative effects of smoking. The same smoker in middle adulthood continues to have the issues of addiction and habituation. He or she no longer is in excellent physical health, and knows it; and, there is awareness of overall aging and general physical deterioration. Yet, smoking continues. Although addiction and habituation are serious contributing factors to smoking, the middle-aged adult smoker still has not prioritized the negative effects of smoking as a loss serious enough to deal with intervention strategies. The older smoker, still addicted to nicotine and habituated to the complex smoking determinants, has an additional rationale for continuing in this self-destruction; viz., the negative effects of smoking for so many years override any positive effects associated with quitting. It does make sense to intervene earlier when losses of important goals and associated abilities occur; plasticity or reserve capacity does illustrate a developmental function, with more plasticity earlier in the lifespan. Unfortunately, most of us do not take advantage of this important plasticity-intervention-lifespan notion.

Fourth Stage of the Lifespan (Old-Old Age)

A final extension of lifespan and gerontological principle notions from Baltes and his colleagues is that of stages in old age. To introduce this notion, Baltes (1997) and Baltes and Smith (1999) summarize research support of differentiating between young-old and old-old adults. Baltes refers to old-old age as the *fourth age* (80 and older) and young-old age as the *third age* (60 to 80). To continue this introduction to old-old age, recall all of the lifespan principles defined by Baltes. Although arguing for qualitatively different stages in older adulthood, Baltes also stresses such important realities as the following:

1. Multiple dimensions in understanding lifespan development (multiple physical, psychological, and sociological abilities).
2. Multiple directions, over the lifespan, in singular and multiple dimensions or abilities.
3. Variability in ability performance among individuals in any stage of development and, increased variability in performance of the individual in later stages of life.

Is there a distinct stage, albeit a conceptual one, of old-old adulthood that is based upon research findings? Baltes and Smith (1999, pp. 167–169) offer the following:

> . . . The basic architecture of the life span . . . suggests that, although more people may expect to reach the fourth stage, these added years may come with increased disability and diminished life quality. This proposition is indeed supported by Crimmins, Hayward, and Saito (1996) who suggested that the proportion of dysfunctional-inactive years of the remaining lifetime is 20% for 70-year-olds, whereas for 90-year-olds, close to 60% of their remaining years represent dysfunctional, inactive time. An opposing model, which assumes a maximum biological life span. According to Fries, the closer, on average, those individuals approximate their maximum biological life span, the more it is possible to compress morbidity into the shorter time span before death. This model, then, would suggest that the fourth stage, while existing, would be of increasing shorter duration. At present, gerontological research does not offer clear evidence on the question of the quality of functioning in advanced old age, and likely the picture is complex, with counteracting forces and processes. However, BASE (the Berlin Aging Study) because of its wide age range and broad

interdisciplinary assessment, offers a new window on the question of potential and quality of life in advanced old age.In total, 23 indicators stemming from geriatric, psychiatric, psychological, and sociological assessments were considered. When subjecting this information to a cluster analysis, groups resulted that differed in overall desirability of quality of functional status (Baltes, 1997; Mayer & Baltes,1996; Smith & Baltes, 1997). Specifically, based on cluster analysis, the 516 participants in BASE were members of four subgroups, ordered in the quality of functional status from good to very poor. (Figure 4–2)

The outcome is clear. The oldest old, perhaps because of increased closeness to death, are at a much higher risk for dysfunctionality than the younger old. Risk of membership in the less desirable clusters (labeled poor and very poor) was three times larger for the oldest old than for the young old. Relative to 90-year-olds, for instance, 70-year-olds were five times more likely to be in the functionally best group (good). The reverse was true for the very poor group. Individuals over the age of 85 had a four times greater risk of membership in this extreme group of dysfunctionality than did persons aged 70–84 years. These are dramatic age differences in risk ratios. This pattern of a major increase in risk and dysfunctionality in the fourth age is not noticeable only when physical variables are considered but also when the sole focus is on psychological measures such as intelligence, the self,

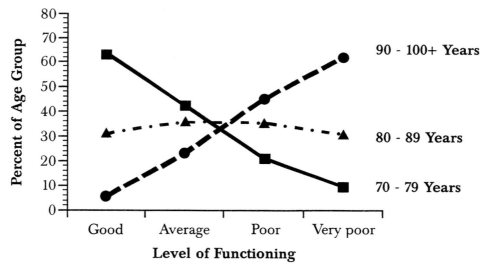

Figure 4–2. Berlin Aging Study: Distribution of research participants (by age) into four groups differing in functional status. Groups were formed by considering a total of 23 physical, mental, psychological, and social indicators (Mayer & Baltes, 1996; Smith & Baltes, 1996). Source: Baltes and Smith (1999). Reprinted with permission.

personality, and social behavior (Smith & Baltes, 1997). Psychologically speaking, advanced old age appears to be a situation of great challenge and a period characterized by chronic stress or over demand where adaptive fitness and resilience are concerned. In our view such findings suggest that advanced old age, the fourth age, represents a kind of testing-the-limits situation for resilience that is the direct consequence of the radical incompleteness of the biological-cultural architecture of the life span.

Baltes (1997, p. 377)) offered additional examples for the old-old fourth stage that stress pathological development:

> . . . The relatively pessimistic picture of advanced old age is perhaps most conspicuous when the most prevalent old-age mental illness is considered, senile dementia of the Alzheimer's type. In the Berlin Aging Study (Helmchen et al., 1996; Mayer & Baltes, 1996)—and these findings are consistent with research by others—the prevalence of all diagnoses (mild, moderate, severe) of Alzheimet's dementia increased from about 2–3% in 70-year-olds, 10–15% in 80- to 90-year-olds, to about 50% in 90-year-olds. Alzheimer's disease is the condition that older persons fear most. Its manifestation is often outside the dignity that humans aspire for themselves. Currently, there is no effective therapy available. Thus, if, as demographic analyses suggest (Manton & Vaupel, 1995; Vaupel & Jeune, 1995), the recent trend of an increase in remaining lifetime for the oldest old of the population continues, it is likely that the incidences of Alzheimer's dementia will increase as well. . . .

Again, Baltes, and others have articulated other very important aspects of aging; aspects that apply to old-old age as well. In describing and understanding human behavior at any stage we have to review the individual in his or her context. Multiple physical, psychological, and social abilities are involved. In addition, there is significant variability among these abilities for any individual; and, importantly, significant variability among individuals on any ability. Thus, the old-old or last stage of adulthood is a category of development, not necessarily illustrating normative age-graded effects for everyone at a particular chronological age or age period. We don't change qualitatively as we reach our 80th birthday. Using the young-old and old-old differentiation, some of us will exhibit characteristics of the old-old much earlier or much later than the average normative age-graded effects principle suggests. But, if we live long enough, one or more chronic illnesses will result in the deterioration of functioning characteristic of old-old age. The facts are that with more elderly living longer, more elderly will enter the fourth stage of old-old adulthood. Belsky (1999, p. 133; Table 4–1) summarized the top-ranking chronic conditions for seniors. With increasing age in later

Table 4-1
Top-Ranking Chronic Conditions for People 65 and Older*

Arthritis	48.4% of people
Hypertension	37.2
Hearing Impairment	32.0
Heart disease	29.5
Vision disease	23.0
Orthopedic impairment	17.7
Diabetes	9.9
Visual impairment	7.9

*Most of the top-ranking chronic illnesses among the elderly are not a threat to life.
Source: U.S. Bureau of the Census, 1996.

adulthood, one of two things happen with chronic conditions; viz., the conditions result in more deterioration and/or additional chronic conditions arise. In addition, the normative age-graded effects continue with advancing age. Without enhanced medical intervention, the increase in longevity (that is, more elderly in the old-old stage) provides an increase in the number of old-old adults who will illustrate increased dysfunctioning . This is a reality that needs to be addressed at communal (national, state, regional) and personal levels.

Baltes, a proponent of successful aging, offers us a warning with his formulation of the old-old stage of adulthood. As more of us move into the later phases of life, we should expect more serious disabilities. Rowe and Kahn's (1998) *Successful Aging* presents a more positive view concerning the older elderly, though their definition for this category is a chronological age of 75 or older. Their positive view stems from findings of the MacArthur foundation longitudinal study of successful aging. More of their view will be presented in Chapter 5. Rowe and Kahn's (1998, p. 15) position favors Fries' (1990) theory of compression of morbidity; viz.,

> . . . the same advances in medical technology will produce not only longer life, but also less disease and disability in old age. This optimistic theory predicts a reduction in the incidence of nonfatal disorders such as arthritis, dementia, hearing impairment, diabetes, hypertension, and the like. . . . it envisions prolonged active life and delayed disability for older people. . . .

Most likely, the position of Baltes and that of Rowe and Kahn reflect a difference in magnitude—magnitude in terms of the number of elderly negatively impacted in the age ranges of 75 or 80 and older, and the number of personal dealings with serious impairments. Even though there will be more old-old adults, and a higher percentage of them will have more chronic disabilities, the lifespan limit has not significantly changed and normal aging in older adulthood continues to be characterized by chronic illnesses and general deterioration of abilities.

Baltes, Rowe and Kahn, and other leading lifespan developmentalists and gerontologists promote successful aging. Even with the inevitabilities of chronic illness and death, proponents of successful aging provide many research findings illustrating the benefits of successful aging strategies; benefits in terms of longevity and quality of life. Advances in public health, medical technology, and responsible lifestyles certainly promote longer life and a better quality of life for those who take advantage of the interventions. Also, recall the differences among interindividual differences, intraindividual change, and interindividual differences in intraindividual change. First, regardless of age, we find differences among individuals for every ability. These differences, or variability, are most pronounced early and late in life. Second, within the individual, we find many differences among abilities. Baltes, Lindenberger and Staudinger (1998), summarizing findings from the Berlin Aging Study, propose that in old-old age, there is a dedifferentiation of abilities. In the oldest age, deterioration of biological abilities results in a compression of variability among abilities, be they biological, psychological or social. Third, as we move through the lifespan, there continue to be differences (variability) among individuals in the relationships of abilities. All three of these variability phenomena reflect both heredity and environmental determinants, with the latter determinants including individual use of advances in public health, medical technology, and responsible lifestyles.

Chapter 5

INTERVENTION STRATEGIES

INTRODUCTION

Normal or usual aging in later adulthood, as presented in the previous chapter, is characterized by gradual erosion (often starting in middle adulthood or earlier) of adaptive capabilities. More pronounced deterioration is usually found in physical abilities, especially those with rather direct links to genetic inheritance and biological integrity. Abilities which are more directly related to positive environmental impacts and learning illustrate greater stability in adulthood, with less pronounced deterioration in adulthood. This chapter presents intervention strategies for successful aging, based on the assumption of normal or usual aging patterns. Intervention strategies are useful for pathological aging conditions as well, though remedial approaches are usually attempted after the pathological condition has been diagnosed. Rowe and Kahn (1998) shared some interesting points about normal or usual aging in later adulthood:

1. Normal older adults are in a higher risk of disease than normal younger adults; normal aging individuals in both groups may not have been diagnosed with a disease, though older adults will, on average, be diagnosed before younger adults.
2. While changes in precursor disease states are normal, like ". . . modest increases in blood pressure, blood sugar, and body weight, and low bone density . . ." (p. 53), these changes increase the risk for reduced longevity and/or quality of life.
3. Normal or usual aging in later adulthood is illustrated by adults who are (a) functioning well, but (b) are at increased risk for either life-threatening disease and/or serious impairment. Many elderly are in this broad category.
4. With advancing chronological, biological, and psychological age, health problems become more evident and disabling.
5. Usual aging in later adulthood is associated with significant risks for disease and death.

6. Even with chronic illness and/or significant deterioration of biological, psychological, and social capabilities, intervention strategies can increase longevity and enhance the quality of life.

A simple fact about normal or usual aging is that we lose, to a greater or lesser degree, our adaptive capabilities, including those which retard chronic and life-ending diseases and disabilities (as well as those which promote functional adaptability). Even without significant effects of chronic diseases, we become less adaptive, compared to younger adults, as we age in later adulthood. Some individuals find it very difficult to accept this fact of life. Others accept it too easily and too quickly. Part of the aging agenda, be it normal, pathological, or successful, is dealing with the inevitability of change in one's physical, psychological, and social domains, which include the frames for personal standards of living and communal norms. These changing standards for significant adaptabilities in later adulthood should not be accepted as negative in older adulthood. Rather, understanding normal aging patterns can facilitate successful aging. Realistic acceptance of changes associated with aging—be they physical, psychological, and/or social in nature—can be as important as understanding normal profiles of later development. Realistic acceptance of changes associated with aging requires a balancing of personal awareness of physical, psychological, and social changes as well as motivation, or self-efficacy to continue one's life course with self-generated goals, and determination. As reported in most studies of successful aging, the best predictors of successive adaptations to life's certainties and uncertainties are past lifestyles.

A Context for Successful Aging and Intervention

Reviews of interventions for successful aging require a context in which the major aspects of aging are appreciated. While theories and notions of later adulthood provide such a context, for the purposes of this chapter, important age-related decline in older adulthood is highlighted, perhaps in order of priority.

1. Aging in adulthood, reflecting physical, psychological, and social dimensions *illustrates much variability* among people and within a person. These variability themes, noted once again, are important. Ageism and stereotypes of older adults do not reflect differences among individuals, much less variations within the person on important developmental variables reflecting physical, psychological, and social competencies. Thus, interventions for age-related problems, be they in the domains of physical, mental or social health, are not for all older individuals. As important, an intervention for a person in one aspect of aging should not be interpreted as sufficient for the person's overall well being.

Several common interventions illustrate this point; e.g., hearing aids for the hearing impaired and corrective lenses for those with visual disabilities. Medications for high blood pressure, diabetes, arthritis, and hormonal imbalances provide corrective interventions, as do surgical interventions for cardiovascular problems, cancer, and skeletal damage. Medication and therapy aid in all types of mental illness, from the most debilitating depressions and schizophrenia to milder forms of anxiety. Each of the above disabilities, with corresponding functional impairments, could result in more pervasive incompetence without intervention. Although there is increasing risk for one or more disabilities during the later phases of adulthood, it is important to appreciate the facts that (a) most aging adults illustrate a limited number of disabilities, and (b) these disabilities are often subject to positive intervention. It is also true that a minority of younger seniors do encounter (a) multiple chronic disabilities or (b) a severe impairment, such as Alzheimer's Disease or depression, which negatively permeate all aspects of one's life.

2. Older adults illustrate *resiliency* or *reserve capacity* albeit at lower levels than younger people. These facts—resiliency, and at a lower level—are important in: (a) understanding the phenomena of aging, (b) correcting stereotypes about older individuals, (c) promoting self-efficacy among seniors, and (d) enabling more professionals and citizens to incorporate intervention strategies for elders in need. While rather recent research has shown that older adults can benefit, to some degree, from cognitive retraining such as practice and enabling strategies, the resiliency findings indicate several other important benefits. First, loss of ability, or abilities, can be compensated for by use of other abilities. Losses in physical, psychological, and social functions are met, by most of us, regardless of age, with other means to carry on, to continue to enjoy aspects of living, and to care for others.

3. *Physical aging* in adulthood is progressive. Regardless of the aging profile—normal, pathological, or successful—all of us will, to varying degrees, illustrate progressive decline in our physical attributes. Given the phenomena of variability, our physical aging profiles will be different among individuals and, as interesting, the aging profiles for physical structures, systems, and functions within each of us will vary. The wonder of variability or differences among individuals is, however, subject to the wonders of progressive physical deterioration and, eventually, the end of life's physical journey. For most of us, the end of this physical journey is based upon progressive deterioration of one or more vital organs. Such is the nature of physical life.

Yet, physical aging, and corresponding interventions for such, include so many human attributes. At one extreme of age-related physical change should be the physical attributes of hair (any place on the body), wrinkles (any place on the body), and moderate increases in fat tissue (any place on the body). In all societies, for much of recorded history, hair loss in certain areas and gain in other areas, increased wrinkles in many body areas, and increased fat tissue are dealt with most seriously by many individuals. Cosmetic interventions for appearance changes negatively perceived by both older and younger individuals provide for multimillion dollar industries. On the one hand, the focus on youthfulness (by the individual, society, and industries) represents vulnerability of self as we age, insensitivity and naivetes of younger individuals to those older than themselves, and the wonders of commercialization in developed countries. On the other hand, such focus, particularly by older individuals, can represent resiliency in personal dealings with relatively minor age-related losses. Does it really matter, in the grand scheme of personal or societal life, if one chooses to have a face-life, tummy-tuck, or hair removal? No and yes. No in the sense of enhancing, albeit for a period of time, one's sense of self-worth. Yes in the sense of promoting surface, quick-fix changes for seniors.

The following list, summarized from Atchley (2000), Belsky (1999), and *Health and Aging in Health, United States* (1999), illustrates substantial physical changes associated with aging in adulthood. This list is not inclusive; rather, it relates to research findings for positive interventions associated with such substantive physical losses.

Primary Chronic Physical Dysfunctions for Seniors
  Arthritis (50%)
  Hypertension (38%)
  Hearing disability (32%)
  Heart Disease (30%)
  Visual Disease (23%)
  Orthopedic disability (18%)
  Diabetes (10%)
  Visual Impairment (8%)
  Chronic Sinusitis (8%)

Although the *dementias (vascular dementia and Alzheimer's Disease)* are typically listed under psychological or mental impairments, these age-related diseases are physical in nature. Dementia symptoms serious enough to impair normal competencies (with Alzheimer's Disease by far the most prevalent) are reported to occur in between four to eight percent of the elderly (Atchley, 2000). As with almost all listings of chronological-age related phenomena, the above listing confounds such important variables as gender, ethnicity, social economic status, aging within the category of seniors, and comorbidity (having more than one disability). The frequency of chronic disabilities increases with advancing age, as does the frequency of comorbidity. Arthritis and hypertension are higher in females than males, while the reverse is found for hearing impairments and heart disease. In general, disabilities are higher for the elderly from lower socioeconomic classes and minorities. Finally, there are age differences for the elderly in the relationship of progressive and catastrophic disabilities that severely limit basic activities of daily living. Progressive disabilities, often involving more than one chronic disability, are less frequently observed in the young- and middle-old, and more typical of the old-old (80 years old and above). Catastrophic disabilities leading to severe limitation in basic activities of daily living, associated with a singular catastrophic event (e.g., heart attack, stroke, hip fracture), are more typical of the young- and middle-old.

Age-related physical changes in older adulthood, other than those noted in the above list, are as important to the elderly. Sexual activity incorporates physical, psychological, and social factors. There are significant physical changes in male and female sexual systems, including hormonal, which result in significant changes in the physical aspects of sex encounters. These physical changes relate to significant psychological and social changes. For examples, Viagra[®] is a wonder drug for males dealing with penile erection, libido (sexual urges) and self-esteem problems. Older females, less frustrated by physiological changes impacting sexual desires, have the problem of finding acceptable sexual partners, as older single males prefer younger females (and, given our society, are able to find them).

Loss of sustained physical energy or endurance is another frustration of seniors. This loss comes upon us gradually, but results in serious frustration directly associated with physical aging. Most often, we accept this loss as a condition of growing older. Yet, many older adults who maintain a regiment of physical exercise are able to both maintain such exercise, albeit at lower standards of endurance, and generalize the benefits to psychological well being. A generalization concerning physical aging is that with above average resiliency or reserve capacity, the older adult is less likely to have chronic physical disabilities or more likely to compensate for them.

While there will be fluctuations in the relative frequencies of chronic conditions, gender differences, and comorbidity within the categories of the elderly (young-, middle-, and old-old), it is certain that the frequency of chronic conditions for the elderly, relative to chronic conditions of the general public, will increase significantly when the Baby Boomers become Aging Boomers. One certainty is that we will have many more aging individuals with serious physical impairments in the very near future. At least two private health industries have understood the financial impacts of physical impairments associated with aging and the dramatic increase in the elderly population; viz., pharmaceutical companies and nursing home corporations! One wonders why the medical profession, collectively or individual members, has not jumped on this yellow brick road. Unfortunately, very few medical professionals specialize in geriatric medicine, though the reasons for avoidance should be obvious; e.g., poor reimbursement from Medicare and Medicaid (along with excessive monitoring of agencies and massive paperwork) and, sadly, disinterest on the part of most practicing physicians and medical students in dealing with conditions of the elderly and the elderly themselves. A good guess is that with the increased demand (e.g., more elderly folks with chronic disabilities and more elderly with more discretionary income), seniors will find more physicians willing to provide them professional services. One hopes that with this awakening on the part of the medical community there will be a corresponding concern on its part to encourage physicians and medical students to become expert in geriatric medicine.

While the presumed professional and public awareness to health needs of the elderly will result in better health care for the elderly related to both chronic disabilities and acute problems that need not be age-related, an awareness of the most frequent disabilities of aging should stimulate greater interest in intervention approaches. As noted earlier in the text, intervention approaches or strategies can be preventative or remedial in nature. Pharmaceutical and nursing home firms deal primarily in remediation, including stabilization of existing conditions or retardation of the progression of a disability. The prevention approach, which includes recognition of normal, pathological, and successful aging, emphasizes promotion of lifestyle practices which negate the onset of chronic physical disabilities and/or retard the rate of deterioration. Both remedial and preventive intervention strategies for physical impairments will be presented, following the sections on psychological and social dysfunction associated with aging.

4. *Psychological difficulties associated with aging* range from the non-clinical, such as normal periodic bouts of depression and feelings of inadequacy, problems with perceptual-, short-, and long-term memory, speed of processing important information, reaction time, and, in general, reductions in fluid, mechanical abilities, to clinically diagnosed dysfunction. The following list of most frequent clinical dysfunction for the elderly comes from the summaries of Belsky (1999), Lemme (1999) and Hobbs and Damon (1999), **http://www.census.gov/prod/1/pop/p23-190/p,23-190 html**. An important note is that the frequencies of these clinical diseases in older age were based on community-based surveys which used specific diagnostic standards of the American Psychiatric Association's *Diagnostic and Statistical Manual of Mental Disorders*. As institutionalized adults were not included, the sample frequencies of clinical dysfunction are surely conservative. Further, most of the community-based studies were based upon self-reports. In addition to the

obvious problem of honesty in self-disclosure, the effect cohort is paramount. Older adults, relative to younger adults and adolescents, are much less likely to express, much less "officially report" emotional conditions. As the Baby Boomers become Aging Boomers, given dramatic environmental and personal changes associated with expressing emotions, the percentages of self-reported psychological difficulties, defined clinically or personally, will certainly rise. Whereas many of our more senior significant others continue to communicate little about disabilities, younger adults are much more willing to acknowledge physical, psychological, and social problems. Given my normative experiences of the 1944 cohort, I am of the opinion that acknowledgment and communication of significant disabilities, reflecting self-efficacy, are helpful for successful aging.

Primary Psychological Dysfunction for Seniors

Phobias (12%;8% for males and 14% for females), including simple, social, and agoraphobia (being afraid, extremely anxious of a wide range of situations).

Alcoholism (3%, primarily males).

Depression (1%: though 30 to 50% of nursing home residents and a minority of older adults illustrate symptoms of depression, such as loss of sexual urges, sleeping disorders, slow responsiveness, poor memory, and lack of concentration).

Suicide (less than 1%; primarily white males; 20% of American suicides committed by the 13% senior population; correlated with depression).

Drug abuse. There are no definitive epidemiological studies on drug abuse and the elderly. Three relevant issues dealing with prescription drugs are: (a) drug addiction or dependency with prescribed psychotropic medication, (b) inappropriate or irregular dosages of a medication, and (c) inappropriate combinations of medications.

These percentages of primary psychological dysfunction should not promote the assumption that older adults are better or worse off than those younger than they. Clinical psychological dysfunction is one thing; dealing with one's sense of self or psychological well-being is another. Older adults must deal with such significant psychological well-being matters as physical changes in appearance, stamina, and body system structures and processes, as well as social changes associated with retirement, financial security, loss of significant others, aging children with children, and, in general, a shrinking social context. With advancing age, successive losses in important physical, psychological and/or sociological meanings of one's life often have negative, and cumulative effects on psychological well-being. An extreme example of negativity associated with significant loss is the reality-based stories of deaths for long-married couples; viz., when a partner dies in old-old age, the remaining spouse dies in less than 18 months. Although this saga is illustrative of very old couples, the importance of the psychological domain on longevity for the remaining partner is a primary one.

The above listing focused on clinical dysfunction of the elderly. As was shared earlier in *Successful Aging: Integrating Contemporary Ideas, Research Findings, and Intervention Strategies*, there are changes in cognitive abilities over the lifespan, including changes in periods of older adulthood. These cognitive changes were presented in the framework of fluid-mechanical abilities and crystallized-pragmatic abilities. In general, with advancing age, fluid abilities more directly associated with neurological functioning, decline first and more rapidly than crystallized, learned abilities. Recall the significant work of Schaie and associates with the Seattle Longitudinal Study. Recently, Bosworth, Schaie, and Willis (1999) presented findings from a unique set of analyses of the Seattle Longitudinal Study that relates specifically to cognitive aging and mortality. The researchers were interested in assessing cognitive and social demographic risk factors associated with mortality of participants in the longitudinal study. Using data from six testing periods (1956, 1963, 1970, 1977, 1984, and 1991), cognitive and age variables were analyzed, controlling for gender and educational levels for those who died (decedents) and those who survived (survivors). The cognitive variables studied were verbal meaning, spatial orientation, inductive reasoning, number, word fluency, verbal memory, psychomotor speed, and perceptual speed. The general results of this study, summarized below, illustrate the significance of cognitive competencies, older age, and mortality:

a. Although specific differences were found for cognitive abilities and successful aging, level of cognitive functioning was found to be related to subsequent change (terminal mortality or survival). Psychomotor speed mediated or reduced the effect of level of cognitive functioning.

b. Rate of cognitive decline was a better predictor of terminal change than level of cognitive functioning preceding subsequent terminal change. Psychomotor speed, a measure of perceptual speed, was consistently related to mortality; significant decline in psychomotor speed on cognitive tasks is a primary risk factor related to subsequent mortality.

c. Younger seniors (74 years old or less) differed from older seniors with the relationship of cognitive performance and mortality. For younger seniors, the risk factors were associated with declines in fluid abilities, while for older seniors the risk factors were associated with crystallized abilities, as well as perceptual speed (fluid abilities) competence.

These findings add significantly to previous research suggesting a terminal drop hypothesis. That is, with dramatic changes in cognitive performance, the risk factor for death increases.

5. *Social issues* accompanying aging in older adulthood are related to corresponding physical and psychological age-related changes. Perhaps a more succinct message about social, physical, and psychological age-related changes is that (a) each primary contextual ingredient to the lifespan provides unique contributions and, as important, (b) there are interrelationships among them. Significant life changes in one primary dimension often impact the whole of the person-contextual association.

Primary Social Issues for Seniors

Retirement. (Although focused here on the retiree, financial, social, and psychological changes impact both spouses). Given successive generations with increased longevity and better financial status via private and public retirement accounts, post-retirement for men and women represents a significant segment of the lifespan. Retirement, for the retiree and mate, continues to be a major life-course transition. In addition to financial loss, some or much, retirement is associated with losses in long-term occupational responsibilities, relationships, and patterns of daily living. Retirement, for the retiree and partner, is associated with gains in real time, independence from work-related frustrations, and pursuits of long-standing or new interests.

Divorce (6%). An interesting fact about the married elderly is that they represent uniqueness in history (Belsky, 1999). Most elderly couples were married in the early 1920s. Unlike the current state of affairs with married adults, these couples chose to stay together, albeit for some reasons other than sexual intimacy. Given the divorce-remarriage-divorce records of Baby Boomers, one must wait a few more years for their marital success record in older adulthood!

Widowhood. (A condition of half of the senior women and 20 percent of senior men, with the numbers of widowed increasing with age). As in the past, widowhood, though traumatic for most who have lost a spouse, remains a gender equity matter. Given the number of older females, relative to older men, and sexist values, older women have a more difficult adjustment in terms of developing future partnership relationships. As with younger adults, men have more women available to choose from, often establishing significant relationships with younger women. On the other hand, older widows have more meaningful relationships with family and friends than older males.

Older Parent/Older Children Relations. Interestingly in this age of intergenerational mobility, the majority of older parents and their children are in frequent physical and emotional contact. While both generations of adults value their independence, (a) parents do intervene positively in crises of the children, and (b) one or more of the children reach out to aging parents, particularly during the latter stages of parental life. Usually, the transition of relative dominance between familial generations is gradual, including reciprocity of relative independence; older children have primary responsibilities other than associated with their parents, and older parents, while still relatively secure physically, psychologically, and socially, value continued independence. For most of us in older age, however, there comes a time when significant help is needed. Even if we are financially secure, our first line of protection is that of our loved ones. If the spouse cannot meet the challenge, then one or more adult children need to. The adult child most likely to meet the challenge, and suffer the consequences, is a daughter or step daughter.

Losing Significant Others. Perhaps the most challenging task of growing old is dealing with the death of those we care deeply about. Though losing friendships because of retirement, physical relocation, arguments, developing new interests, and social restrictions is difficult, losing a significant other due to death is traumatic. Not only is the significant other lost, but (a) fewer significant others are left and (b) such a loss heightens the sense of one's own mortality. Research findings note that as we age, our web of significant others becomes smaller, yet the smaller web includes those we hold most dear. When these significant others are lost because of death, the web not only becomes even smaller, it, and the survivors, become more fragile. Older individuals, unlike adolescents and young adults, find it more difficult to initiate new friendships. This compounds the negative effect of losing significant others in older age.

Religion and Spirituality. Perhaps reflecting a cohort effect, older adults, relative to younger adults, are more likely to participate in formal religious practices, express their religious faith in practice, and have interest in spirituality. One common sense notion of religiosity and spirituality is that these beliefs can be helpful to older adults, or one of any age, in dealing with the inevitability of one's own physical death. An obvious advantage of participation in formal religiosity is that older adults, like younger people, have the social advantages of significant others, activities, leadership roles, and assistance.

DEFINITIONS OF SUCCESSFUL AGING

Successful aging, like all things human, is in the mind of the beholder. There are many aspects to consider in understanding successful aging, in later life or any stage of the lifespan. One primary consideration is that aging, be it normal, pathological, or successful, reflects many human characteristics.

Remember the types of aging–biological, psychological, sociological, historical? We mature, stabilize, and decline in all of our abilities, and we do so within changing contexts. Another primary consideration deals with these changing contexts. Contextual change occurs within the environment (externally) and the person (internally). Societal or communal expectations related to development and aging change; our expectations, for others and ourselves, change as we move through the lifespan. So, reflections on aging are relative. A simple consideration for successful aging is that of longevity. This consideration may be most appreciated by those who are in the later years of life. The perception of one's remaining length (time) of life changes over the lifespan; it becomes much more focused and limited in later life. Given the demand in the American culture for remediation or retardation of life-threatening diseases, it is fair to suggest that increased longevity is one aspect of successful aging. It is an aspect of successful aging that is important to those who must deal with life-threatening diseases. Another consideration for successful aging is that of health quality. Many of us would categorize successful aging as a condition of reasonable physical and mental health, and unsuccessful aging as a condition of poor physical and/or mental health. This dichotomy is one of normal versus pathological aging. As noted by Rowe and Kahn (1998), the dichotomy of sickness and health is much too narrow; viz., ". . . It implies that, in the absence of some identifiable clinical disease or disability, all is well. It also implies that in the presence of disease, some kind of personal failure has occurred. . . ." (p. 38).

Life is not a combination of dichotomies. There are too many human characteristics to consider in understanding development, stability, and decline. One can show no signs of disease or disability, but deal with later life in unsatisfying ways. On the other hand, one can have multiple diseases or disabilities, and move successfully through the lifespan, including older adulthood.

Figure 5.1 is from Rowe and Kahn's (1998) *Successful Aging*. Components of successful aging, according to Rowe and Kahn, is defined by these conditions:

1. Low Risk of Disease and Disease-Related Disability
2. High Mental and Physical Function
3. Active Engagement with Life

For Rowe and Kahn, there is a hierarchy of importance for the three conditions of successful aging:

> . . . The absence of disease and disability makes it easier to maintain mental and physical function. And maintenance of mental and physical function in turn enables (but does not guarantee) active engagement with life. It is the *combination* of all three–avoid-

ance of disease and disability, maintenance of cognitive and physical function, and sustained engagement with life–that represents the concept of successful aging most fully. Furthermore, each of these components of successful aging is itself a combination of factors. Avoiding disease and disability refers not only to the absence or presence of disease itself, but also to the absence or presence of *risk factors* for disease and disability. Maintaining a high level of overall functioning requires both physical and mental abilities, which are substantially independent of each other. And, finally, they tell us what a person *can* do, but not what he or she actually *does*. Many older people, for many reasons, do much less than they are capable of doing. Successful aging goes beyond potential; it involves activity, which we have labeled "engagement with life." Active engagement with life takes many forms, but successful aging is most concerned with two–relationships with other people, and behavior that is productive. . . . (pp. 39,40)

Baltes and Baltes (1990) also suggested multiple criteria in defining successful aging. Based upon a literature review, they identified the following criteria used to define successful aging:
1. Length of life
2. Biological (physical) health
3. Mental (psychological) health
4. Cognitive efficacy (psychological health)
5. Social competence and productivity (social health)
6. Personal control (physical, psychological, and social health)
7. Life satisfaction (psychological health)

These criteria, with additional ones of financial and spiritual health, can be used to assess normal and pathological aging, as well as successful aging. The first significant point to share about multiple criteria for successful aging is that no single criterion provides a sufficient definition or assessment. A second point deals with the weight or importance of one criterion, relative to all criteria. Relatedly, the importance of criteria changes over the lifespan, including all stages of adulthood. Baltes and Baltes (1990, p. 6) noted a third point; viz., subjective or objective standards and indicators for successful aging criteria.

    . . . In psychological and social science research, there is a preponderance of the use of subjective criteria such as measures of life satisfaction, self-concept, and self-esteem and, more recently, measure of perceived or personal control. This emphasis on subjective indicators reflects the assumption that a certain paral-

lelism exists between the subjective and objective world and also
the view that, for the social scientist, reality is in part socially and
personally constructed. It also reflects the value judgement that the
perceiving self ought to be the litmus test for the quality of life. . . .
    The usefulness of subjective criteria is somewhat undermined,
in our view, by the fact that the human psyche is extraordinarily
plastic, adaptive, and able to compensate. . . . By the use of various
psychological mechanisms, humans are able to "successfully" adapt
their subjective assessments to objectively quite diverse conditions.
    It is astonishing, for instance, how little difference has been found
in life satisfaction between people who live in objectively adverse life
conditions (such as during wartime or in prisons or slums) and those
who live under normal or even superior life conditions. . . .

Baltes and Baltes identified two approaches for objective criteria of
successful aging: (a) normative definitions of ideal states and (b) adaptiveness
or plasticity of the person. Normative definitions include developmental
outcomes, including goals and objectives, for significant physical, psychological, and social domains. These normal developmental outcomes are
standards for aging, be it normal, pathological, or successful. To illustrate this
objective approach, Baltes and Baltes (1990, p. 6), dealt with personality
development and aging ". . . Erikson's theory of lifelong personality development, with generativity and wisdom as the central themes of later life, is
an example of such an approach. . . . Achieving generativity and wisdom,
then, becomes the yardstick for successful aging. . . ." Other general yardsticks for successful aging in later adulthood, based upon developmental theory, research, and/or common sense, include the following:

- Stability of physical functioning and avoidance of chronic disabilities.
- Stability of psychological well-being and avoidance of mental illness.
- Continued social networking and, with loss of significant others,
  development of new relationships.

Within each of these general yardsticks for successful aging, specific
criteria and standards can be identified. For example, with physical functioning, specific criteria include significant physical systems and functions,
such as the neurological, cardiovascular, respiratory, and muscular-skeletal.
The best advice for successful physical aging is to have a yearly physical
examination. Objective standards, for adult age groups, are based upon
updated research. The more years you have physical examinations, the more
longitudinal information medical health care providers have to assess your
present physical health relative to normative (averages categorized by age,
gender, ethnicity, social economic status, etc.) and past physical health. The

second approach for objective criteria for successful aging (Baltes & Baltes, 1990, p. 7):

> . . . Is based on the concept of *adaptivity* (or *behavioral plasticity*). This approach seems more general because it does not imply a single outcome, specific contents, or life goals. Rather, its focus is on the measurement of the efficacy of a system. Adaptivity or behavioral plasticity is a measure of potential and preparedness for dealing with a variety of demands . . . Illustrations of adaptivity in the psychological realm are the quality of one's memory and cognition and the quality of one's ability to cope with stressful events. Taken together, such measures are expected to yield indicators of the adaptive plasticity and potential of a person. . . .

Robust aging (Garfein and Hertzog, 1995) is a related concept of successful aging. Some space is given to the research of Garfein and Hertzog for several important reasons. First, the predominance of research on aging and stereotypes of the elderly focus on age-related losses (e.g., disabilities, dysfunctions, restrictions). Garfein and Hertzog concentrated on delineating positive aspects of aging. Second, most of the assessments of aging, such as clinical (physical, psychological health) indicators, basic activities of daily

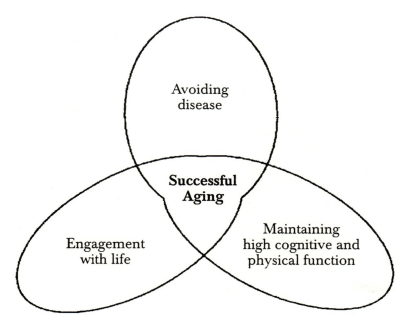

Figure 5–1. Source: Rowe & Kahn (1988). Reprinted with permission.

living (ADLS) and instrumental activities of daily living (IADLS) were developed to identify elderly with significant problems. The assessment tools used by Garfein and Hertzog focused on successful aging. Their data was a part of the University of Michigan's Survey Research Center 1986 national household survey. A number of subsample characteristics, which reduce the generalizability of findings, are worth noting; viz.:

1. Only Whites and African-Americans were included in the analysis.
2. With 1,644 respondents, more were women (59%) than men (41%).
3. Most of the respondents were either married (62%) or widowed (27%). Most of the respondents (54%) had at least a high school education.
4. Most of the respondents (75%) had a family income of less than $25,000 per year.

Respondents were categorized into the elderly age groups of young-old (60–69), middle-old (70–79) and old-old (80 and above). The following four categories of robust aging, and defining assessment examples for each, were identified:

- *Functional Status*–Questions about challenging physical functions (e.g., heavy housework) items about frequency of performing physical activities (exercise), and items dealing with functional limitations (e.g., difficulty in bathing).
- *Affective Status*–A self-report depression scale was used which included positively worded items and a range of performance allowing for positive as well as negative scores.
- *Cognitive Status*–One measure identified level of cognitive dysfunction and another measured higher level cognitive functioning.
- *Productive Involvement*–The criteria used were hours of productive involvement in compensated work, uncompensated work, and helping activities during the year.

Numerous personal variables were also included in the analyses. These included:

- *Social Contact*–Frequency of phone conversations, visits from friends, attendance at social meetings, and religious participation.
- *Health Status*–Number of chronic conditions, satisfaction with health, health rating, daily activity limited by health, number of days in bed over a three-month period, vision, and hearing.
- *Health Service*–Number of doctor visits, number of mental health visits, and number of nights in the hospital.
- *Health Behaviors*–Usual number of hours sleep in 24 hours, and frequency of reminders to stay healthy.

- *Life Events*–Number of significant life events in the past three years, and number of lifetime significant events.
- *Life Satisfaction*–Satisfaction with life.
- *Personality Indicators*–Extroversion, vulnerability, self-efficacy, neuroticism, and fatalism.

Garfein and Hertzog's findings were enlightening. With the four categories or definitions of robust aging illustrating independence from each other, the highest category of robust aging was Productive Involvement (39%), followed by Affective Status (28%), Functional Status (12%), and Cognitive Status (10%). These percentages are for the highest level of robustness. If the second highest level of robustness is added to the highest level, the percentages are as follows: Productive Involvement (80%), Affective Status (64%), Functional Status (72%), and Cognitive Status (62%)!

It is important to note that the majority of robust elders met only one of the four criteria for robustness (41%); Sixteen percent met two criterion standards, and less than five percent met three or more of the criterion standards. This finding, consistent with past research, illustrates the significance of intraindividual variability and aging. The finding also supports Baltes' (Baltes & Smith, 1999) selection-optimization-compensation model of successful aging; viz., to age successfully, one must, over the lifespan, refine goals, optimize functional capabilities, and, when necessary, compensate for losses. Since so few of the senior respondents scored in the highest rank of robustness for more than one of the four definitions of robustness, it is reasonable to suggest that (a) the four definitions of robustness are relatively independent of one another, and (b) senior aging (pathological, normal, successful) is best understood by multiple lenses, rather than a single one.

The demographic variables included in the Garfein and Hertzog analyses were important. First, chronological age was a significant factor. A linear age trend was found for the four robust aging categories; viz., young-old were more robust than middle-old, who, in turn, were more robust than old-old. With the Productive Involvement category, for example, 53 percent of the young-old scored in the highest robust rank, 29 percent of middle-old scored in this rank, and 12.5 percent of the old-old scored in this rank. Second, gender was a significant factor for the robust categories of Productive Involvement, Affective Status, and Cognitive Status. Women were more likely to illustrate high productive involvement, depressive symptoms, and functional impairment. A third significant factor was race for Functional Status and Cognitive Status; Whites were less likely to be functionally or cognitively impaired. A fourth significant factor was marital status for all four robust categories; robust elderly were more likely to be married. Educational attainment was a fifth significant factor; viz., higher educational achievement resulted in more robustness with all four categories. Family income was the sixth significant factor, with those with higher family income more likely to be classified as aging robustly on all four categories. Finally, three personal characteristics significantly differentiated robustly aging elderly from less robustly functioning respondents; viz., social contract, health and vision, and life events. The most robust elderly reported greater social contact, better health and vision, and fewer significant life events in the past three years than the less robust respondents.

Interestingly, Garfein and Hertzog found that numerous personal correlates differentiated the highest level of robustness from the second highest level. The following personal correlates or potential predictors were found for at least two of the four definitions of successful aging after controlling for age, sex, race, marital status, education, and family income:

1. Higher frequency of visits with friends–social contact.
2. Higher frequency of attending meetings–social contact.
3. Fewer chronic physical conditions–health status.
4. Higher satisfaction with physical health–health status.
5. Higher rate of physical health–health status.
6. Lower level of restricted daily activity–health status.
7. Better vision–health status.
8. Fewer significant lifetime events–life events excluding health.
9. Higher life satisfaction–psychological well-being.
10. Lower vulnerability–personality.
11. Higher self-efficacy–personality.
12. Lower neuroticism–personality.
13. Lower fatalism–personality

Garfein and Hertzog's research, reported above, used data from a cross-sectional design. Because individuals were not repeatedly tested over periods of their lifespans, causal relations among the many variables included in the study could not be determined. Nor could the confound of cohort be statistically controlled. Yet, the findings, put in the context of previous research (including studies using longitudinal and sequential designs), strongly suggest the positive nature of preventive intervention strategies for successful aging. Although the research design limitations of Garfein and Hertzog mandate caution in focusing on determining factors of demographic and personal factors associated with successful aging, the relative importance of the factors, and lifespan or timeline of the factors, the following factors must be appreciated from an preventive intervention framework:

• Chronological age, though not a causal factor of physical, psychological, and or social aging, is associated with these aging dimensions.

- For the majority of us, regardless of type of aging in older adulthood (normal, pathological, successful), our overall functional adaptiveness becomes restricted (reduced reserve capacity), resulting in optimization of our best functional abilities (including use of these abilities to compensate for losses in less functional abilities). Do we strive for a renewed sense of balance in dealing with our strengths and weaknesses?

- Women, living longer than men, use their sense of interpersonal relations to maintain productive involvement, with or without a partner.

- Race and ethnicity continue to be significant factors for development, regardless of the focus of lifespan. Relatedly, socioeconomic status (or family income) is as important in predicting successful aging. Most minorities and most folks in the lower classes age less successfully than whites in the middle and upper socioeconomic classes.

- Engagements in social activities and having friends are important for aspects of positive development, regardless of one's age.

- Health status, be it self-reported or objectively assessed, is associated with one's sense of aging–normal, pathological, or successful.

- One's assessment of significant life events, especially traumatic ones, and the number of events, relate to a person's interpretation of aging.

- Positive psychological well-being is associated with successful aging, even for individual's with serious physical disabilities.

- One's personality or overall sense of self, is established early in the lifespan and contributes significantly to personal dealings with physical, psychological, and social changes over a lifespan.

Successful aging is within the grasp of most of us, especially if we develop coping or preventive strategies early in the lifespan and maintain them. Some adaptive abilities, like personality and physical health, can have profound effects on other adaptations, such as one's assessment of significant life events (positive, negative, neutral), exercise (physical and mental), life satisfaction, friendships, and engagements in social activities.

The National Institute on Aging (1999) presents 10 tips for healthy aging (**http://www.aoa.dhhs.gov/aoa/pages/agepages/lifextsn.html**):

1. Eat a balanced diet, including five helpings of fruits and vegetables a day.
2. Exercise regularly (check with a doctor before starting an exercise program).
3. Get regular health check-ups.
4. Do not smoke (it's never too late to quit).
5. Practice safety habits at home to prevent falls and fractures. Always wear your seatbelt in a car.

6. Stay in contact with family and friends. Stay active through work, play and community.
7. Avoid overexposure to the sun and the cold.
8. If you drink, moderation is the key. When you drink, let someone else drive.
9. Keep personal and financial records in order to simplify budgeting and investing. Plan long-term housing and money needs.
10. Keep a positive attitude toward life. Do things that make you happy.

These tips reflect common sense and age-related theories/concepts, research, and interventions. Though genetic inheritance plays an important role in three types of aging–normal, pathological, successful, much more self-help involvement is required for successful aging. As will soon be reviewed, the earlier one initiates and maintains self-help intervention for successful aging, the higher the probability of increased longevity and quality of life. Part of the human condition is that most of us must learn about aging through personal experiences (our own and significant others); often, it takes many, many lessons to finally change aspects of life which erode both normal and successful aging. The most tragic examples of poor learning related to aging (from personal or other experiences) remain part of national and international histories:

- Cigarette smoking and cancers, cardiovascular diseases, and lung diseases
- Obesity (or being moderately overweight) and cardiovascular diseases, diabetes, and muscular-skeletal disabilities
- Sedentary lifestyle (lack of exercise) and being overweight
- High levels of stress and cardiovascular diseases and psychopathologies
- Alcoholism and cardiovascular diseases, liver diseases, psychopathologies, and suicide

CATEGORIES OF INTERVENTION FOR SUCCESSFUL AGING

Intervention strategies are usually identified as either remedial or preventive. Remedial intervention, as the term connotes, deals with attempts to eradicate or slow the progression of a disability. Preventive intervention is all about avoiding one or more disabilities, retarding the initiation of dysfunctions, and/or promoting positive lifestyles. While most of us can easily remember the adage of "an ounce of prevention is worth a pound of cure," too many of us are procrastinators, putting off self-help initiatives either intentionally or habitually. Given what is known about the relative strengths of remediation and prevention, in all areas associated with aging, it is rather sad that more communal and personal intervention for age-related changes are remedial rather than preventive. Sad in the fact that for many age-related disabilities, remediation is often both financially and psychologically expensive.

Many age-related declines in abilities have not been acknowledged as subject to effective preventive approaches. Starting in middle age, more hairs gray, wrinkles accumulate, and body weight distributions change. Near vision deteriorates, as does high frequency hearing. In general, fluid cognitive abilities decline, even with concentrated effort. Internal body structures, like external ones, also change in terms of both structural capacity and functioning. Retirement affects the worker and spouse, often in unanticipated ways. Significant others die.

Remedial intervention strategies, also termed *secondary prevention* and *tertiary prevention* approaches (Lemme, 1999), target age-related dysfunctions that are diagnosed before (secondary) or after (tertiary) symptoms, with the aim of retarding the progression of specific problems, rehabilitation, coping with stresses associated with the dysfunction, and/or compensating for loss by enhancing other abilities. Remedial intervention strategies are numerous and used in almost every age-related loss of abilities. In the area of physical aging, the following remediations are most common:

1. Eye glasses and cataract surgery for visual problems.
2. Hearing aids for hearing problems.
3. Exercise, canes/walkers, medication, and surgery for muscular and skeletal disabilities (e.g., arthritis, osteoporosis).
4. Medication and dietary restrictions for diabetes.
5. Medication (especially change of blood pressure medications for males) and lubricants for sexual problems with a physical cause.
6. Exercise, medication, and surgery for cardiovascular diseases.
7. Radiation, chemotherapy, and surgery for cancers.
8. Medication and structured environmental support for dementias such as Alzheimer's Disease.
9. Hospice care for the last phase of terminal illness.

Remedial strategies for psychological aging include the following:

1. Mnemonic or memory aids such as written notes, taped messages, and training in visual and associational memory skills to compensate for memory lapses.
2. Cognitive behavioral therapies (emphasizing reorganization of ma adaptive thoughts) and medication for depression, phobias, and disengagement.
3. Personal or professional help in using the cognitive pragmatic

(teamed, functioning) skills to compensate for losses in cognitive mechanical (more directly linked to genetic potential and neurological status) abilities). For example, most seniors who age successfully are able to compensate for sensory/cognitive/motor processing speed losses with enhanced attention to the most salient contextual stimuli.

4. Life-long learning activities (elder hostel, continuing education courses, Internet/mail/library access to information) for post-retirement options related to losses in work-related skills.

5. Volunteerism for psychological losses associated with the empty nest syndrome and retirement. Transferring focused attention from these losses to volunteer activities allows for the maintenance of multiple cognitive abilities associated with the serious matters of child-rearing and employment.

6. Personal or professional help in enhancing the elder's sense of self-efficacy (belief in one's ability to meet life's challenges) to deal with real and perceived losses in biological, psychological, and social abilities. To appreciate this remedial category, it is important to understand the relationship of one's sense of self-efficacy and corresponding behaviors. Those of us with low self-efficacy set lower standards of achievement than individuals with higher self-efficacy, resulting in differential effects; viz., internal and external reinforcers of behaviors tend to maintain achievement standards for both low and high self-efficacy individuals, lower the standards for those low in self-efficacy, and increase standards for high self-efficacy people.

7. Practice and training for declining cognitive abilities, especially learned, crystallized abilities less subject to deterioration based upon physical aging. For those cognitive abilities least subject to age-related declines—social and practical intelligence, verbal abilities, and wisdom—the notion of practice-makes-perfect can be translated, for the elderly, to practice makes for less loss of ability.

8. Time and focus for reflection, singularly and with significant others, to assess one's strengths and weaknesses (a) within the proximal or present personal life stage and (b) relative to projections for succeeding life stages. This remedial category is oriented more to one's reality testing for daily functioning as opposed to such psychosocial theoretical orientations stressing the psychological battles between integrity and despair. Most often, the time and focus for reflection, as a remedial approach, is initiated by significant others for the older adult with serious physical, psychological, and/or social problems.

9. Hospice care for the last phase of terminal illness.

Remedial strategies relevant for age-related social changes include the following:

1. Social Security, Medicare, Medicaid, private pensions, part-time employment for the retired elderly, as well as making do with less, to deal with financial loss. Making do with less, for many elderly, can result in poorer diets and reduced insurance coverage.
2. Volunteerism for those elderly having difficulty dealing with lost roles associated with previous employment.
3. New partners and friendships, enhanced intergenerational family contacts, and increased social activities (church, social organizations) for divorced or widowed seniors. Given the significant increases in divorce and single parent families of young and middle-aged adults, more and more seniors will be without a spouse. Establishing new friendships can compensate for loss of friends in older adulthood.
4. Dependency upon children can be less frustrating for all concerned if (a) parents in physical, psychological, and/or social need share such concerns with their offspring, and (b) children seek professional help in meeting parental needs. Area Agencies on Aging and social workers do offer remedial assistance for dependent parents and their children.
5. Community day care, assisted living facilities, and nursing homes provide much need assistance for severely dysfunctional older adults.
6. Family members, friends, church and social organizational members, and physicians are the front-line interveners for elderly abuse. Elderly abuse includes passive neglect, active neglect, verbal or emotional abuse, and physical abuse (Atchley, 2000). Elderly abuse occurs in both private households and institutional settings (out-patient health care facilities, hospitals, assisted living facilities, and nursing homes).
7. The front-line interveners for elderly abuse must also be watchful for economic exploitation of the elderly consumers. As summarized by Atchley (2000, pp. 470–471): ". . . To begin with, older people who depend on asset income are very susceptible to any 'surefire' scheme to get a higher return on their savings. Also, loneliness and isolation sometimes make older people more susceptible to deception by a friendly, outgoing person who takes an apparent interest in them. Finally, hopeless illness is more frequent among older people, and many unscrupulous people have exploited the desperation that such illness can evoke. More than 90 percent of confidence scheme victims are older people. . . ." A contemporary example of this exploitation is the dastardly schemes of some mail order magazine promoters suggesting huge financial winnings for contests. Not to be outdone, many state governments promote lotteries.

8. For many older adults, losing the right to drive is almost as dramatic as having to relocate from home to a residential facility. The spouse, child, and/or friend can reduce the sense of loss by being a willing chauffeur. Other remedial strategies include public transportation and taxis. The loss of driving privileges, especially for males, can result in increased isolation for both the one losing the privilege and spouse.

9. Especially in old-old age, accompanied by physical, psychological, and social losses, progressive isolation requires aggressive intervention, especially from family members, remaining significant others, and social network members in organizations. Two examples of aggressive intervention are Meals on Wheels and Senior Citizen Centers. Both involve community volunteers, many of whom are senior citizens.

Recently, Kaplan (2000) provided an interesting integration of preventive (primary) and remedial (secondary) strategies for successful aging with societal and personal responsibilities. He illustrates primary and secondary prevention as follows; (1) primary prevention focuses on healthy lifestyles rather than disease diagnosis and treatment, and deals with behavior, and (2) Secondary prevention usually focusing on medical diagnosis, then resulting surgery, medication, and/or lifestyle changes. Kaplan argues that primary prevention, for which no disease condition exists, may produce much greater public health benefits than historically endorsed secondary preventive strategies. The following pieces from Kaplan's (2000) argument differentiates the principle differences between the primary and secondary prevention approaches:

> . . . The secondary prevention medical model builds upon traditional linear thinking (Ackoff, 1994). If a prostate gland is too large, it must be surgically reduced. If blood pressure is too high, it must be lowered, and if a child is hyperactive, he or she must be made less active. . .
>
> An alternative view, known as the *outcomes model*, arises from a behavioral tradition. The outcomes model regards the human body as a system that cannot be divided into component parts. Although the outcomes model is similar to the traditional biomedical model, its objective is to treat the person rather than the disease. The goal of health care is to extend the duration of life or to improve the quality of life. Disease processes are of interest because pathology may either shorten life expectancy or make life less desirable. The same variables that predict disease process may also predict life expectancy or quality of life. However, in contrast to the traditional biomedical model, behaviors or biological events may affect life

expectancy independently of disease process. Further, the measures of success in the outcomes model are different than those in the traditional biomedical model. The outcomes model emphasizes quality of life and life duration instead of clinical measures of disease process. Prevention can be secondary or primary, and attention is given to efforts that produce the longest life and highest quality. Prevention can involve medical intervention, behavioral intervention, or changes in public policy. . . . (pp. 383–384)

Public and private health providers have historically concentrated on secondary prevention, using the biomedical approach. As articulated by Kaplan, the relative benefits of secondary prevention financing (public and private) to primary prevention are suspect given that little comprehensive research has been done on the effects of primary prevention. Although addressing his messages to psychologists, Kaplan's points permeate public and private health care industries:

> *Message 1. Evaluations of prevention services confuse primary and secondary programs.* Most evaluations of health care resources, using a cost/quality of remaining life years ratio, concentrate on secondary prevention health care strategies. The evaluations have resulted in poor ratios. Yet, primary preventive prevention health care strategies were not included in the evaluative research.
>
> *Message 2. Primary prevention must be recognized as distinct from health care.* While public and private health providers stress personal responsibility for primary prevention, these providers use the bulk of public and private premiums of secondary health care prevention. If preventive strategies are effective in more successful aging, then the public and private premiums should provide correspondingly appropriate reimbursement incentives.
>
> *Message 3. More resources should be devoted to primary prevention research.* Few methodological sound studies have been done for primary prevention in health care. These studies have shown that both physical and psychological factors influence types of aging profiles. More research is needed to assess *long-term* primary prevention health care strategies.
>
> *Message 4. Prevention must be recognized in public health policy.* Relative to secondary prevention, primary prevention appears to be more beneficial for public health. Public and private health policy should balance existing secondary (remedial) prevention with longer term primary prevention, lifestyle strategies.

Preventive (*primary*) intervention emphasizes lifestyle adaptations which prevent risk factors associated with physical, psychological and social aging and/or delay normative age-related aging dysfunctions. An ounce of prevention is worth a pound of cure. Our common sense alerts us, at least periodically, to the benefits of planning for the future. On the other hand, other human characteristics are those of denial and procrastination. Too many of us do not engage in plans for successful aging during our young and middle adulthood. Even in older adulthood, many of us continue less than optimal long-term lifestyles, even with the knowledge of preventive interventions for seniors. Lifestyles, habits, and addictions are difficult to change, especially those that are long-term. Why are we captives of our earlier lives?

MOTIVATION AND INTERVENTION

Heckhausen and Schulz (1993, 1995, Schulz & Heckhausen, 1996, 1999), with their ideas about *primary and secondary control* over the lifespan, offer interesting suggestions for intervention. Primary and secondary control concepts, as noted by Schulz and Heckhausen (1999, p. 139), are related to other psychological constructs, ". . . such as achievement, optimism, depression, persistence, coping, self-esteem, motivation, and personal adjustment. . . ." Personal control requires the use of abilities to deal with important environmental processes and outcomes, be they external or internal to the individual. The authors (1995) also share a complimentary tenet. Individuals find it most difficult to deal with losses related to personal control; viz., inability to perform adequately in significant life areas, erosion of abilities to perform adequately in those areas, and, correspondingly, anticipation of failure in succeeding life contexts.

Primary control refers to overt actions by the individual to make changes in the environment so as to meet needs and desires. Primary control describes ". . . behaviors aimed at generating effects in the external world . . ." "To elaborate further, primary control strategies are defined as the means by which an individual attempts to produce behavior-event contingencies. *Long-term primary control potential* refers to the capacity of the individual to produce desired outcomes on a long-term basis, typically encompassing the entire lifespan. . . ." (Schulz & Heckhausen, 1999, p. 142).

Secondary control refers to the individual's ability to manipulate one's emotions, motivations, and cognitions so as to deal with gains and losses associated with primary control; ". . . Secondary control targets the self and attempts to achieve changes directly within the individual. . . ." (Schulz & Heckhausen, 1996, p. 708). The important aspect of primary control, relative to secondary control, is that of overt actions in an environmental context. Summarizing, White (1959), Heckhausen and Schulz (1995, p. 285), noted that ". . . An underlying assumption of all control theories is the idea that humans desire to produce behavior-event contingencies and thus exert primary control over the environment. . . ." ". . . Both primary and secondary control may involve cognition and action, although primary control is almost always characterized in terms of active behavior engaging the external world, whereas secondary control is predominantly characterized in terms of cognitive processes localized within the individual. . . ."

Heckhausen and Schulz have developed a formative lifespan approach to physical, psychological, and social aging which (a) illustrates the relative importance of primary and secondary control strategies throughout the lifespan, and (b) articulates the importance of personal interventions for successful aging. One of several important contributions to the field of gerontology provided by these researchers (Schulz & Heckhausen, 1996) is clarification of what is meant by successful aging. They shared three different standards to identify individual successful aging:

1. Absolute standard. For any human attribute—physical, psychological, social, the highest level of human performance is used; i.e., the upper limit. Human longevity, registered by years since birth, is a prime example of an absolute standard with physical aging. Highest scores on standardized intelligence tests, including subtests, represent absolute standards with psychological aging. The greatest number of known intergenerational family members for a grandparent illustrates an absolute standard for social aging.

2. Interindividual relative standard. Again for any human attribute, the standard depends upon membership in one or more reference groups. The usual developmental variables of importance for relative standards are: chronological age, culture, education, ethnicity, gender, health status, and socioeconomic status.

3. Intraindividual relative standard. With the individual, rather than group, as a focus, interest in (a) relationships of multiple abilities at a given point in one's lifespan, (b) changes in singular abilities over one's lifespan, and (c) patterns of multiple abilities relationships over the lifespan. In a sense, the individual is the absolute standard for himself or herself, and the standards for multiple abilities change as one moves through the lifespan.

Schulz and Heckhausen provide another useful frame for successful aging; viz., the subjectivity of the individual. It is one thing to be assessed on absolute and relative objective, performance-based standards of physical, psychological, and social aging and another to be the assessor of one's performance, based upon self-assessment. Personal assessment focuses on one's level of satisfaction with gains and losses associated with physical, psychological, and social aging; the assessment is subjective. With the perspectives of objective and subjective assessment, it makes sense that an individual who may not meet objective standards of subjective aging in any of the dimensions of physical, psychological, and social aging can be subjectively satisfied with functioning in any or all dimensions. Actually, subjective evaluations of goal attainment are often at odds with objective assessments. When the imbalance between objective and subjective assessment becomes significant enough, a significant other may have to deal with questions of the person's physical, psychological, or social competence. The imbalance of objective and subjective assessment of significant adaptive functions most often results in the individual's reluctance to deal with intervention strategies, particularly to deal with preventive ones. Examples? In the physical domain, too many obese people, regardless of chronological age, continue to eat what they please and avoid physical exercise. Cigarette smokers continue with the physical (psychological and social) abuse. In the psychological domain, too few of us in middle and older age engage in life-long learning or memory assistance strategies. In the social domain, those of us in middle and older age tend to refrain from expanding our social network of significant others and reaching out to intergenerational family members. Preventive intervention for successful aging, in the domains of physical, psychological, and social development, requires personal commitment. Schulz and Heckhausen's (1996) ideas of developmental regulation over the lifespan, focusing on primary and secondary control, target the individual's responsibilities for successful aging.

Using Baltes' selective-optimization-compensation model, Schulz and Heckhausen (1996, 1999) offered four developmental regulation principles over the lifespan for successful aging; i.e., maximizing positive development and aging over the lifespan. These principles, summarized from their work (Schulz & Heckhausen, 1996, 1999), are as follows:

1. Competency of the individual to attempt adaptable functioning from many possibilities in a diverse array of physical, psychological, and social domains. National educational systems provide children, adolescents and adults such opportunities. Diversity in interests and competencies, an essence of the earlier periods of the lifespan, is the opposite of specialization in interests and competencies. To simplify the opposites, diversity of individual functioning is to the generalist or Renaissance Person as specialization is to the idiot savant or mercenary. The more adaptable one is in the life domains of physical, psychological, and social aging, the greater the likelihood of increased

longevity and quality of life. The more specialized one is, in a single adaptive function to the detriment of other adaptabilities, the lesser the likelihood of increased longevity and quality of life. For diversity and specialization, the normal lifespan pattern, reinforced by maturational principles and societal expectations, is for much diversity in abilities (e.g., academic learning) during childhood and adolescence and specialization in abilities (e.g., career) during adulthood.

2. Selectivity in both (a) personal physical, psychological, and social resources and (b) pursuing developmental pathways (e.g., schooling, career, interests, organizations, friends), possible because of hereditary potentials and contextual opportunities. Given the diversity of human potentials and functioning, successful development and aging requires that the individuals select and optimize some adaptabilities at the expense of others. Most of us can identify some abilities, relative to many others, which we are proud of; i.e., certain abilities for which we function best. Selectivity results in significant differences among individuals on most abilities, including the obvious ones of physical strength, physical endurance, memory skills, verbal reasoning, mathematical reasoning, and social intelligence. While we select some abilities to optimize, we must also develop competencies in many physical, psychological, and social functions. We become very adept with a few abilities (selectivity and optimization), while meeting standards of adequacy for most physical, psychological, and social functions.

3. Compensation when not meeting previous objective or personal standards of adequacy. Failure to meet previous standards of adequacy is due to the following losses:

   a. Normative developmental losses in expanding competencies; viz., failures when attempting something new. Especially during our formative years, we experience many failures in almost all physical, psychological, and social domains, while learning so much. During our formative years, these failures or losses, unless severe and pervasive, are anticipated by our elders—parents, teachers, older siblings, and more experienced significant others.

   b. Normal losses associated with aging; viz., declining functioning with previously established abilities. For example, with physical aging, physical exercises, even for the most gifted or determined athlete, are associated with lowered standards of performance. Do you have a favorite International Olympics event? If it deals with multiple sensory-motor abilities, as most do, note that those receiving medals (and participating) are most often adolescents and young adults.

c. Losses associated with non-normative, perhaps random, negative events; viz., declining functioning with major life events, such as serious illness, catastrophic accident, spouse/friend death, and financial collapse.

To be able to compensate for, and cope with, significant physical, psychological, and social losses, we are able to transfer or generalize viable abilities (including the psychological one of acceptance). Throughout our lifespan, especially during childhood, adolescence, and young adulthood, acceptance of loss, and corresponding compensatory actions, seems manageable. In older adulthood, probably because of the accumulation of so many losses, dealing with them, and physical aging phenomena, (a) compensation by acceptance is enhanced and (b) compensation via transfer of aligned abilities is eroded. An interesting idea is that acceptance of cumulative losses over the lifespan, especially losses associated with physical decline, may limit the individual's sense of competency to combat physical, psychological, and social losses with compensatory actions other than acceptance of the losses. Perhaps the concept of learned helplessness (Seligman, 1975), defined as the person's assumption of an inability to control his/her destiny, should be expanded to include the idea of compensating for losses primarily by acceptance. On the one hand, acceptance of losses can provide an individual some reduction of frustration; on the other hand, the use of the singular compensatory strategy of acceptance can severely limit one's dealings with physical, psychological, and social declines.

4. Management of trade-offs among physical, psychological, and social abilities throughout the lifespan, realizing that the resources of competence, time, and energy provided some abilities (for optimal functioning) may result in a reduction of resources for other abilities (with corresponding functional declines). Trade-offs of resources, throughout life, can be across the physical, psychological, and social domains, and within each domain. Management of trade-offs among abilities is less difficult during our early or developing years. As we mature physically and are engrossed in formal and informal learning, personal reserve capacities in physical, psychological, and social domains are, relative to middle and later adulthood, expanding or stable. During the formative years of childhood, adolescence, and young adulthood, reasonable resource trade-offs among abilities often results in a gain for the targeted ability (and corresponding function) without permanent loss for other abilities. This gain/no permanent loss phenomenon for the formative years is associated with maturation and learning. Severe or

focused targeting of select abilities in our youth, however, can result in serious erosion of functioning with non-targeted or selected abilities. Trade-off management of abilities across and within physical, psychological, and social domains during formative years is also less difficult because the socialization process includes expectation of multiple trading among abilities during childhood, adolescence, and young adulthood. In later stages of adulthood, management of trade-offs among abilities is more difficult, given (a) normal erosion of physical abilities, (b) loss of targeted abilities—"favorite" skills and functions (based upon years of selective practice and use), and (c) extremely limited reserves for other abilities which were discarded long ago in the lifespan. Older humans, like older dogs, find it difficult to learn new tricks, partly because of physical deterioration and partly because of reliance on selected abilities and functions, some of which significantly declined with loss of fluid, mechanical capabilities.

Schulz and Heckhausen (1996) provided two examples to illustrate the relationship of the four principles. The first example deals with professional athletes:

> . . . The genetic potential of such individuals is typically recognized early in life because the child exhibits extraordinary athletic performance or because one or both parents were themselves professional athletes and therefore the potential is assumed to be there. This in turn results in the allocation or resources (e.g., time, energy, and money) to the development of skills in the chosen sport. In extreme cases, the allocation of resources may be so focused on a particular activity that the development of more generalizable skills is neglected. Because professional athletics are highly competitive, the timing of training and skill acquisition must be carefully orchestrated to converge with the biological development of the individual . . . If the individual overcomes the failure experiences along the way and succeeds in making it into the professional ranks, the rewards can be great in terms of financial resources and recognition. However, athletic careers tend to be short-lived as the effects of biological declines, wear-and-tear, and injuries take their toll on the individual's ability to remain competitive. . . .
> . . . In terms of the [four] principles . . . the life course of a professional athlete is characterized by low levels of diversity in athletes' exposure to multiple performance domains and selective allocation of resources into one or few domains very early in life. It is also characterized by high levels of resilience, but of a type that

is likely to be very domain specific. We consider this a high-risk life course trajectory because (a) the probability of achieving the primary goal is low, (b) it leaves the individual with few alternative options if the primary goal is not achieved, (b) it may lead to resilience in very limited domains, and (d) it is aimed at only half of a normative life course (e.g., the first 30 to 40 years). Even if individuals reach their primary goal of becoming a professional athlete, they must still develop and implement life course plans for the post-professional period of their lives. . . . (pp. 706,707)

Their second example deals with performing artists:

> A similar analysis could be applied to the development of performing artists, such as musicians and dancers. However, there are some differences between these domains and professional sports. First, there are a variety of fallback positions available if the individual does not attain world-class levels of performance. For example, a musician who does not succeed as a soloist can join an orchestra or become a teacher. Second, the careers of performing artists tend to be longer than those of professional athletes. Thus, individuals who do achieve their primary goal can anticipate spending most of their adult lives working in their chosen domains.
>
> Professional athletes and world-class performing artists represent unique life course trajectories in that the development of the individual is focused on achieving optimal performance in a specific domain. This analysis could be extended and applied to peak performance in virtually any measurable domain. . . . (p. 707)

The examples provided by Schulz and Heckhausen illustrate the four principles regulating successful lifespan development. For example, many, if not most, individuals who strive for the status of professional athlete or performing artist are obligated to move through the educational system, often including college. Often, these gifted individuals pursue academic degree programs aligned to their professional interests. Thus, many athletes and performing artists, successful or not, are engaged in both (a) diverse educational experiences and (b) focused academic training in specific majors and minors. Unfortunately, the American culture still includes the reality of college athletes who do not graduate and, more tragic, do not illustrate adult competencies in basic academic skills. Many gifted athletes, like performing artists, never reach the professional level; yet, many of these individuals, gifted in specific domain, become coaches or mentors for younger "want-to-be's." Also, many professional athletes, like professional performing artists, transition from professional competition to coaching or mentoring. These additions to the examples of Schulz and Heckhausen (1996), however, only enhance the utility of their four principles regulating development through the lifespan.

As we leave late adolescence and early adulthood, management of trade-offs among domains deals with more selectivity and less diversity. Marriage and children typically restrict options for parents, as do careers, interests, habits (good and bad), values, and reliance on select significant others. Yet, humans are resilient, regardless of age. Many more contemporary young and middle adult females, compared to previous generations, are balancing marriage, children, and careers. Many more individuals in middle adulthood are part of the "sandwich generation," one in which adult children are responsible for both their children and parents. Unlike previous generations, working adults, male and female, can expect to change careers a number of times before retirement. This contemporary career change phenomenon and the importance of work in defining one's sense of self illustrate the importance of life-long learning with diverse abilities and objectives. Similarly, normative deterioration of physical domains during adulthood usually negatively impacts one's habits of physical exercise. As we age in adulthood, most of us interested in physical exercise concentrate on one exercise regime; viz., running, weight lifting, biking, swimming, walking, or racket sports. With physical aging and long-term singular exercise, the diversity of sports and exercises so typical of youth is lost, first to a selected type of sport or exercise, followed by reduction or cessation of physical exercise.

An interesting corollary of Schulz and Heckhausen's principles of managing trade-offs for diversity and selectivity, along with compensation for loss of abilities and performances, is the developmental aspect of managing trade-offs. From a lifespan perspective, it makes sense to meet acceptable standards with diverse abilities (and corresponding diverse functions) earlier rather than later in the one's life. Developing and maintaining multiple abilities and corresponding multiple functions, in physical, psychological, and social domains, provide the person with many options for advancing skills or compensating for lost abilities in later periods of life. While seeking diversity may well negate excellence in any one ability or function, developing and maintaining competency in many abilities and functions best prepares the individual for lifelong successes and failures—in physical, psychological, and social domains. Schulz and Heckhausen (1996) provided a developmental model for their four regulatory principles and primary and secondary control (see Figure 5–2). Primary control—personal actions manipulating the external environment for personal gain—provides the force for seeking both diversity and selectivity in abilities, functions, and objectives in the physical, psychological, and social domains. Secondary control—personal actions manipulating senses of self and cognitive processes within the individual—provides the force for dealing with failure and loss.

For Schulz and Heckhausen (1996), the lifespan model for the four regulatory principles and the controls of primary and secondary, depicts the following generalities:

> Early development is characterized by an increased ability to exert primary control over the environment. The action-outcome experiences of the child provide the basis for the development of self-competence, including generalized and exaggerated expectancies of control and perceptions of self-efficacy. Children between the ages of three and four are able to experience appropriate emotional reactions to failure . . . and therefore require compensatory mechanisms to counteract this threat to their motivational resources. During childhood and adolescence, a broad range of secondary control strategies develop, including changing aspiration levels, denial, egotistic attributions, and reinterpretation of action goals . . . Perceptions of control are highly exaggerated early in life.
> . . . Showing little correspondence to actual primary or secondary control. This delusional sense of control is adaptive in that it provides the motivation to engage the environment at a time when the organism is rapidly developing.
> Early adulthood is characterized by increasing levels of primary and secondary control as well as increased selectivity with respect to the domain specificity of control. Selectivity continues to increase throughout adulthood, whereas diversity gradually

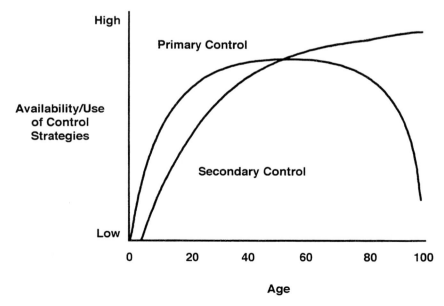

Figure 5–2. Availability and use of primary and secondary control over the life course. Source: Schulz and Heckhausen (1966). Reprinted with permission

decreases. Because of the limited capacity of the individual and external constraints, the increased selectivity at older ages has to be compensated for with decreased diversity. This trade-off between diversity and selectivity is a hallmark of development in late middle and old age.

During late middle age and old age, the strategy of choice leans more toward the elaboration and increased use of secondary control strategies . . . Increasing age-related biological and social challenges to primary control put a premium on secondary control strategies as means for maintaining the potential for primary control. As the ratio of gains to losses in primary control becomes less and less favorable, the individual increasingly resorts to secondary control processes. . . . (p. 709)

For successful aging, Schulz and Heckhausen (1996, p. 711) suggested the following three criteria:

. . . Primary and secondary controls which maximize potential and reality of longevity and physical functioning, including absence or retardation of disabilities, are first-order criteria for successful aging. . . .

Second, . . . generalized cognitive, intellectual, and social relational skills are second-order criteria of success. These abilities, along with physical or biological status, define the primary control potential of the individual and lie at the heart of our idea of successful development. Because failure and declines are inevitable features of development, it is essential that the organism has a means for dealing with failure in a way that does not jeopardize future development or undermine gains that have already been attained. Primary and secondary control strategies provide mechanisms for achieving this, and we would anticipate that individuals with higher cognitive, intellectual, and social relational skills would have higher reserves of resilience to draw upon than individuals with lesser developed abilities. . . .

Third, . . . ability or performance within a specific domain represents a third-order criterion of success. The primary control potential of a given domain depends largely on how narrow the domain is. Broad domains that are supported by generalizable skills have great primary control potential over the entire life span, whereas narrow domains that rely on abilities with little potential for transfer to other contexts have little generalized primary control potential. . . .

. . . It is possible that all three criteria or success are maximized within one individual. Such a person would demonstrate success within one or several domains; develop high levels of cognitive, intellectual, and social relational skills; maintain near-optimal levels of physical functioning; and be highly resilient to external threats throughout most of the life course. From our perspective, fulfilling the combination of these criteria represents the optimal life course. This should be contrasted with optimal functioning, which can be achieved only within a given domain within a relatively narrowly defined chronological age window and often entails trade-offs that make an optimal life course difficult to achieve.

Examples of optimal life course development might include professionals such as Supreme Court judges who develop high levels of expertise in at least one domain; generally have high levels of cognitive, intellectual, and social relational skills; and maintain their abilities well into late life. . . .

To conclude the summary of Heckhausen and Schulz intriguing lifespan model for successful aging, Schulz and Heckhausen (1996, p. 712) shared the following propositions for successful life course development:

1. Diversity provides the foundation for selectivity.
2. Selectivity is limited by sociocultural opportunity, the genetic make-up of the individual, and time. Development within a particular domain may be constrained for a given individual because of any one or a combination of these factors.
3. Diversity and selectivity have optimal life course patterns. Diversity is more important early in life, whereas selectivity becomes more important later in life.
4. Selectively focusing on a particular developmental domain has costs and benefits. Competencies within the chosen domain are enhanced, but at the cost of developing non-chosen alternatives.
5. Failure is an inherent part of the acquisition and decline of individual competencies.
6. Failure has the potential of undermining future development and therefore requires compensatory processes to ensure continued development.
7. The motivation for primary control fuels development throughout the life course.
8. The motivation for primary control regulates selection and compensation processes.
9. Primary and secondary control vary systematically over the life course and provide the mechanisms for implementing selection and compensation.
10. The successful life course is achieved when selection and compensa-

tion processes serve to maximize the primary control of the individual over the life course. . . .

The Heckhausen and Schulz motivational model for successful aging, based upon research and creative thinking, is easily adapted to the real world of the older adult. With decreasing physical abilities and related decreases in the psychological and social domains, secondary control strategies become dominant ones for most of us as we move into older adulthood. Compensation for losses, real and imagined, in older adulthood focuses more on secondary control coping, rather than on sustained personal initiatives to manipulate external contexts controlled (real or imagined) by others. The general trade-off from primary to secondary control in adulthood should not be received as negative or as another illustration of age-related decline. The trade-off from primary to secondary control in adulthood, like in earlier stages of development, is relative.

Most of us, regardless of age, rely on both motivational approaches for daily functioning. And, in middle adulthood onward, more reliance on secondary control should provide us resiliency in both senses of self (well-being) and maintenance of those primary control mechanisms—including abilities, functions, and behaviors—still within our grasp. The management of trade-offs idea provided by Heckhausen and Schulz includes the important aspect of one's ability to optimize the trade-offs in terms of longevity and quality of life. With reduced physical, psychological, and social abilities associated with normal aging, how and how much we manage trade-offs among abilities and functions in physical, psychological, and social domains significantly determines our remaining lifespan and quality of life. Management of trade-offs in older adulthood, relative to younger stages of the lifespan, is more restrictive; e.g., our aging reserve capacity or resilience in the physical, psychological, and social domains provides us less to work with, whether we draw on it or not. Whether we draw on reserve capacity or not, selection (use) among diverse abilities and optimization of functions for those abilities of competence should be a primary dilemma, if not criterion, for successful aging. Regardless of one's physical, psychological, and/or social aging status, successful age-related development requires a commitment to draw upon reserve capacity. Baltes and Baltes (1990, pp. 26, 27) articulate this requirement well:

> . . . The selection-optimization-compensation model, which in
> its constituent features is implemented at any age, gains increasing
> importance in old age because of two empirical facts specific to old
> age: (1) the primary biological feature of normal aging is increased
> vulnerability and a concomitant reduction in general adaptability

(reserve capacity) to environmental variation, and (2) the normal trajectory of psychological and biological development of aging is a continual evolution of specialized forms of adaptation, that is, individualization of life trajectories. There are two other corollaries.

First, individuals' subjective views of the self are constructed to deal with such changes, and psychological mechanisms are available to adjust to life goals and aspirations in the face of changing internal and external circumstances (secondary control). Second, the process of selective optimization and compensation, although general in its "genotypic" characteristics, is quite diverse in its "phenotypic" manifestations. Depending on individual and societal conditions, it can take many forms in content and timing.

We contend that by using strategies of selection, optimization, and compensation, individuals can contribute to their own successful aging. On the one hand, then, it is correct that the biological nature of human aging limits more and more the overall range of possibilities in old age. On the other hand, however, the adaptive task of the aging individual is to select and concentrate on those domains that are of high priority and that involve a convergence of environmental demands and individual motivations, skills, and biological capacity. . . .

A consistent message from contemporary professional researchers of lifespan development and gerontology is that successful aging, to a significant degree, resides within the individual. That is, successful aging is a responsibility of the individual. These same professionals acknowledge the importance of contextual factors in development and aging throughout the lifespan, contextual factors as diverse as societal values, federal/state/local intervention programs, access to/quality of physical, psychological, and social health providers, public transportation, network of significant others, personal/governmental finances, and availability of advancing technological products for general and specialized use. Successful aging, defined specifically by longevity and quality of life, is a product of individual and environmental determining factors.

Noting this classic developmental notion of interactionalism (e.g., heredity and environment; internal and external contributors to development), two other related ideas need to be appreciated. First, the average person does not initiate external factors for successful aging. For examples, advancements in sanitation, health-related products and practices, transportation, technologies of all sorts, and public education provide means for successful development throughout the lifespan. Access to these divergent wonders of the world is, however, another matter. And, even for those individuals with access to physical, psychological, and social advances, many do not take advantage of the opportunities. The second idea, an extension of the Baltes selection-optimization-compensation model and Heckhausen and Schulz primary/secondary motivational model, is that coping, self-help, and preventive strategies—in the physical, psychological, and social domains—developed and maintained earlier, rather than later, in the lifespan increase the opportunities for successful aging. While many older adults acknowledge limitations associated with physical aging, few recognize the pervasive effects, both positive and negative, of long-term habits, attitudes, and values (see Chapter 1; Baltes & Mayer, 1999). Positive habits, attitudes, and values, as well as physical, psychological, and social fitness, correlate positively and highly with longevity and quality of life.

Intervention for successful aging, then, is enhanced by relevant cultural advances (e.g., health care, public financing of retirement, public transportation, and technologies for living), as well as personal decisions for quality and length of life. Recall that Baltes' (1997) second principle for the architecture of human development focused on age-related increases in the need and demand for cultural interventions. His second principle was presented within the context of age-related decreases in the physical domain, which are noticeable by middle-adulthood. The more physical, psychological, and social reserves available to the aging individual, including primary and secondary control motivators, the higher the probability of successful aging.

Two recent studies provide excellent illustrations of a person's commitment to successful aging as related to cultural opportunities. The first (Seeman, Unger, McAvay, & Mendes de Leon, 1999, p. P214) is a report on self-efficacy beliefs and perceived declines in functional ability from the MacArthur longitudinal project. As reported by Seeman et al., "[l]ongitudinal data from a cohort of older men and women, aged 70–79, were used to test the hypothesis that stronger self-efficacy beliefs would protect against onset of perceived functional disabilities over a 2.5-year follow-up, independent of underlying physical ability. . . ." Self-efficacy is defined as reflecting a person's beliefs in being able to do things necessitated by contextual demands. In the Seeman et al. study, self-efficacy beliefs were measured by ". . . Beliefs relating to managing interpersonal relationships and beliefs relating to managing more instrumental daily activities. . . ." (p. 214). Nine life domains of relevance to adults were included in assessing self-efficacy beliefs. Interpersonal efficacy measures dealt with beliefs relating to abilities for managing relationships with a spouse, family members, and friends. Instrumental beliefs dealt with perceived abilities for managing transportation, living arrangements, safety, and general productivity. Physical functioning status was measured by self-reports of perceived functional disabilities related to activities of daily living. More objective, performance-based measures of physical functioning were strength, balance, and gait. The subjects of the study, assessed on criteria of physical functioning, were rated as functioning high on physical and cognitive abilities. With these high functioning older adults, lower instrumental, but not interpersonal, self-efficacy beliefs of functioning were associated with increased self-report, but not objective, declines in physical functioning abilities. A part of the Seeman et al. (p. P220) summary is of particular relevance to successful aging:

> . . . The fact that self-efficacy beliefs were found to predict reported levels of functioning (independent of measured levels of physical ability) is consistent with Bandura's argument that self-efficacy beliefs reflect individuals' beliefs in their capability to produce given levels of performance (Bandura, 1977, 1982) and that such beliefs influence the types of activity people choose to engage in, the level of effort they expend, their perseverance in the face of difficulties, and the thought patterns and emotional reactions they experience (Bandura, 1981, 1986, 1988). Specifically, individuals with weaker self-efficacy beliefs tend to curtail their range of activities, and put forth less effort, with less perseverance, in those they undertake (Bandura, 1981, 1986). One significant consequence of such a pattern of avoidance or non-perseverance is that such individuals will not have the experience of successful performance of such behavior, and this may importantly contribute to a greater likelihood of perceiving oneself as being *unable* to perform such behaviors and to self-report functional disability.
>
> The optimistic feature of a relationship between self-efficacy beliefs and reported levels of functional disability is that self-efficacy beliefs are potentially modifiable to the extent that perceptions of functional disability are not founded on literal physical incapacity, but rather reflect the effects of weak self-efficacy beliefs, there may be significant opportunities for successful interventions to increase perceptions of older adults of their ability to continue performing various activities independently. . . .

The McAuley, Katula, Mihalko, Blissmer, Duncan, Pena, & Dunn (1999) motivation study provides the second illustration of personal commitment and successful aging. This study dealt with manipulating aerobic activity and stretching/toning physical activities, over a one year period, with previously sedentary older adults (aged 60–75 years). Similar to the Seeman et al. (1999) study, the McAuley et al. (p. P283) study focused on self-efficacy beliefs, introducing their study with the following relevant literature review summaries:

> . . . It is well documented in the gerontological literature that a sense of control is important to positive physical and psychological

health (e.g., Mirowsky, 1995; Rodin, 1986; Schulz & Heckhausen, 1996).

Self-efficacy expectations (Bandura, 1986, 1997), represent a context- or domain-specific type of control and have been demonstrated to be important social cognitive influences on physical and psychological function. . . . Individuals with high self-efficacy expectations tend to approach more challenging tasks, put forth more effort, and persist longer in the face of aversive stimuli. When faced with stressful stimuli, low efficacious individuals tend to give up, attribute failure internally, and experience greater anxiety or depression (Bandura, 1986). As individuals age, performance of everyday functions becomes more challenging and requires greater effort and perseverance. Therefore, a robust sense of self-efficacy would appear to be of particular importance to older adults.

Relative to health behavior and aging, self-efficacy has been found to be predictive of adherence to exercise regimens in asymptomatic (McAuley, 1993) and clinical (Kaplan, Atkins, & Reinsch, 1984) populations, recovery from conditions associated with aging (e.g., cardiovascular disease; Carroll, 1995), and survival rates of individuals with chronic disease (Kaplan, Ries, Prewitt, & Eakin, 1994). Additionally, a weaker sense of efficacy has been implicated in slower gain speeds (Rosengren, McAuley, & Mihalko, 1998; Tinetti, Richman, & Powell, 1990), fear of failing (McAuley, Mihalko, & Rosengren, 1997), and general declines in physical and social function (Tinetti, Mendes de Leon, Doucette, & Baker, 1994).

Several studies have demonstrated that acute and long-term exposure to physical activity can have substantial effects on self-efficacy relative to physical performance measures. . . .

The McAuley et al. (1999) study dealt with the effects of two types of physical activity—light to moderate walking versus stretching and toning exercises—on self-efficacy beliefs for specific exercise and generalized physical activity. Exercise-specific self-efficacy measures dealt with perceptions of competence for increasing standards of walking exercise. Generalized physical self-efficacy measures dealt with strength, agility, and motor ability (using the Perceived Physical Ability subscale, Physical Self-Efficacy Scale; Ryckmann, Robbins, Thornton, & Cantrell, 1982). Overall, both types of exercise resulted in initial increases in self-efficacy of the participants for both specific exercise and generalized physical activity self-efficacy, followed by declines after the exercise programs were completed. The aerobic exercise program provided the most pronounced increases in self-efficacy during training and the least pronounced self-efficacy decline at follow-up (after a six-month period of no exercise). One interpretation of this study is that maintenance of self-efficacy beliefs, at least as related to physical exercise, requires ongoing participation in such exercises, particularly for those of us, like the study participants, with rather sedentary lifestyles.

INTERVENTION AND PERSONAL AWARENESS

A simple technique used by therapists is easily adapted to individual initiatives for successful aging. Marriage counselors, for example, often ask frustrated partners to list the positive and negative things about the other person and marriage. List quantity and quality which are important beginnings for marriage counseling. For the individual serious about successful aging, the adapted task is to list strengths and weakness as related to both present and expected aging. In constructing this list, I suggest you construct a matrix like the following:

	PRESENT		FUTURE	
	STRENGTHS	WEAKNESSES	STRENGTHS	WEAKNESSES
PHYSICAL				
PSYCHOLOGICAL				
SOCIAL				

If you provided lists in the matrix, the following questions may stimulate some reflection. First, for strengths and weaknesses, who did you compare yourself with—yourself (intraindividual) or others (interindividual)? Did your prioritize the lists? Which of the three domains—physical, psychological, social—is of primary concern? Of the present and future strengths and weaknesses, which ones are related to longevity and/or quality of life? Are some present strengths of such importance that you are prepared to maintain them? What are your maintenance plans? What about present weaknesses? Are they important enough for you to change behaviors for more successful aging? Are the strengths and weaknesses longstanding or of recent occurrence? Do the present strengths and weaknesses carry forward to future ones? Personal initiatives for successful aging, especially for individuals without a history of ability diversification and/or compensation strategies, are more likely to happen with serious reflections about one's life beyond day-to-day existence. The reflections need not be complex or traumatic.

For the physical domain, exercise is an important preventive or remedial strategy for successful aging. How much exercise do you do every day or week? The easiest way to move forward with exercise is to do a little bit more, every day or week, of the exercise. Another easy way to move forward with exercise and successful physical aging is to diversify your exercises, with the obvious qualifiers of consulting your physician (or good friend who knows about the exercise) and starting something new with a very conservative regimen. Another important preventive or remedial strategy is to maintain both proper diet and nutritional levels (see Rolls and Drewnowski, 1996 for specific examples of improper diet and nutritional levels). The third important preventive or remedial strategy is to deal with chronic and acute physical ailments, based upon medical evaluation, with maintenance of medication and physical rehabilitation regimes. Practitioners providing services to older adults in the physical domain are important monitors of the preventive or remedial advice provided aging clients.

For the psychological domain, the self-efficacy summaries provided earlier should prompt reflections about one's sense of confidence in dealing with everyday experiences and one's self. Self-efficacy is directly related to the concepts of life satisfaction and psychological well-being. Do you view your life as a glass half full or half empty? Are you satisfied with your life—past, present, and future? One important strategy for successful aging in the psychological domain is to follow-through with positive self-efficacy beliefs. To related aspects of this strategy are (a) follow-through with reality testing, and (b) acceptance of failure or not meeting personal standards of success. While acting upon self-efficacy beliefs often results in meeting objectives, sometimes we forget about objective standards, or the standards of significant others. The greater the imbalance of self versus objective standards, the higher the risk of unsuccessful aging.

Chapter 4 summaries of fluid and crystallized abilities should be reviewed again, in relation to preventive and remedial interventions for successful psychological aging. All of us, to varying degrees, experience deterioration of fluid (mechanical, biologically-based) cognitive abilities as middle age approaches. The deterioration of fluid abilities is enhanced through middle and late adulthood. This deterioration of fluid cognitive abilities is most frustrating in the areas of processing information and responding. Frustration is based upon limited speed of encoding/processing/ responding, and decision-making concerning relevant information and appropriate responses. Since fluid, mechanical cognitive abilities begin to decline starting in young adulthood and progressing in middle and late adulthood, one preventive strategy is to accept the reality of such deterioration. Related coping strategies include (a) compensation for important fluid abilities with other fluid and crystallized, pragmatic ones, (b) use of additional time in dealing with situations requiring engagement of fluid abilities, and (c) changes in objectives.

Driving a car, for example, remains a very significant aspect of one's sense of psychological well-being, particularly for males. With advancing age and declines of physical and fluid cognitive abilities, successful driving is based upon these abilities, but with more emphasis on learned pragmatic crystallized abilities. The older we get, the more we rely on physical prosthetics (e.g., eye glasses, corrective eye surgery) and revised driving habits; e.g., night driving is avoided, extended driving periods are reduced (to that of local driving only), and, to the point of being a dangerous driver, extremely reduced speed.

The phenomenon of elderly drivers, though illustrative of both physical and fluid cognitive decline, is probably of less concern to the older adult than his/her sense of generalized reduced competence in daily activities requiring physical and fluid cognitive functioning. Declines in abilities, exhibited in reduced functioning with daily activities, even with compensatory gains in other abilities and related functions, become, for each of us, an expanding part of our psychological domain. Successful adaptation to gradual declines in psychological abilities and functions related to daily living requires the compensatory actions of (a) acceptance of realistic loss, with corresponding changes in personal standards for successful performance, and (b) motivation to engage in other productive activities more suitable to one's psychological abilities. While most daily activities require the use of physical and social abilities for most older adults, personal engagement with daily life surely requires the two compensatory actions noted above for successful psychological aging.

For the social domain, important strategies for successful aging are directly related to one's networking of significant others, both in terms of quantity and quality. Development and maintenance of significant others networks are significant throughout the lifespan. Significant others networks include family, friends, fellow workers (present, past), formal and informal organizations, and one's spiritual realm. With advancing age in older adulthood, the quantity of significant others networking decreases; e.g., retirement, isolation and death of significant others, and self-initiated reduction in seeking out others. These factors also increase one's sense of restricting physical, psychological and social environments.

Unfortunately, public and private organizations do not deal effectively with the social and psychological withdrawal symptoms associated with retirement of employees. Some organizations do have retirement planning programs which deal with personal finances. Few provide retirees with meaningful access to the professional or social networking available during the working years. Isolation and death of significant others become more frequent with advancing physical age, resulting, in time, with losses of one's closest associates—spouse and siblings. Retirement, resulting in real loss of work-related networking, and cumulative losses of friends and family members are associated with one's loss of interest and/or action in initiating substantive relations with others not included in a shrinking network of significant others.

Relationships among family members, regardless of the physical ages of members, are very important throughout the lifespan (Belsky, 1999). Family relationships involve both support and conflict. Clarke, Preston, Raksin, and Bengtson (1999) provided an interesting summary of longitudinal survey data, focusing on intergenerational conflicts and tensions, which exemplifies social intervention and aging. With over 1,000 participants, the parents had a mean age of 62 and the adult children had a mean age of 39. The following selective summary is from Clarke et al. Participants were asked to respond to the following question; "No matter how well two people get along, there are times they disagree or get annoyed about something. In the last few years, what are some of the things on which you have differed, disagreed, or been disappointed about (even if not openly discussed) with your child (or parent)? . . ." (p. P262).

Responses were categorized by a conflict topology that allowed for parents-children comparisons. The following six conflicts or tensions identified as most prevalent are listed in Table 5–1. Parents' reported conflicts with adult children are identified in Figure 5–3.A, and adult childrens' reported conflicts with parents are identified in Figure 5–3.B. Primary parental issues with adult children were personal habits and lifestyle differences; primary adult children issues with parents were communication and interaction, personal habits and lifestyle choices, and child-rearing matters.

Table 5–1

A Typology of Conflicts and Tensions Between Older Parents and Their Adult Children

Type of Conflict	Operational Definition
Communication and Interaction Style	Conflict over the way family members engage in their relationships across generations. *Examples:* Communication styles ("He is always yelling"; "she has become quite critical") situational responses ("she jumps to conclusions"), interpersonal relationships ("mother dominates my father – I don't like that"; "the way my father treats my mother.")
Habits and Lifestyles	Conflicts over lifestyle issues: sexual activity/orientation/experiences, living arrangements, quality of life, allocation of resources and or education. *Examples:* Style of dress, hair style, types of recreation, educational occupational choices, use of alcohol or drugs, not attending to physical needs.
Child-Rearing Practices and Values	Conflict over methods or philosophy regarding parenting. *Examples:* Decisions concerning having or spacing of children, dimensions of permissiveness, control, rules/expectations, loving/unloving, forgiving/ resenting, support/involvement.
Politics, Religion, and Ideology	Disagreement about religious, moral, ethical, and political attitudes or ideas. *Examples:* Lack of religious belief or over involvement in religion, questions concerning the integrity of the United States, feelings about the involvement in Vietnam and the Gulf War, values or the lack of them as perceived by the respondent.
Work Orientation	Differences concerning priority and investment given work (or school) performance, advancement, or status. *Examples:* Child working too much or too little, degree of dedication to work.
Household Maintenance	Conflict over participation in maintenance or improvement of family living environment. *Examples:* Yardwork, housework, painting, and general maintenance.

Source: Clarke et al. (1999). Reprinted with permission.

There were generational differences: parents often listed conflicts over habits and lifestyle choices, whereas children cited communication and interaction style . . . (p. P261). . . . The data reported

... suggest three things: (1) There is considerable evidence of conflict reported by both older parents and adult children when they are allowed to vent their concerns in an open-ended survey format; (2) the issues around which conflict occurs in these aging family dyads can be typologized around six themes, with a majority of responses involving issues of interaction style and personal habits and lifestyle; and (3) there is value to a multiple-domain approach to conflict in families.

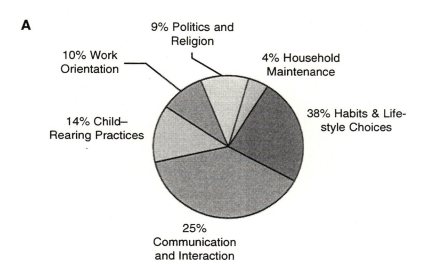

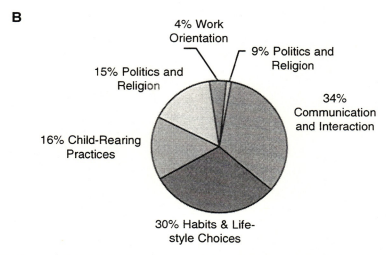

Figure 5–3. (A) Parents' reports about conflicts with their adult children. (B) Adult childrens' reports about conflicts with their aging parents. Source: Clarke et al. (1999). Reprinted with permission.

> Our data suggest that conflict in older parent-adult child rela-
> tionships may be more widespread than is commonly assumed. In
> our sample, two thirds of older parents (average age 62) and adult
> children (average age 39) reported conflict in their relationship with
> the other generation . . . (p. P268).

The Clarke, et al. (1999) study, assessing conflict with relatively young
older adults and their relatively young adult children, provides contemporary data about intergenerational differences in the social domain. With
advancing physical aging of both parents and children, with corresponding
changes in psychological and social domains, the potential for enhanced
conflicts can be identified. Aging parents will face most of the losses noted
above for the physical, psychological, and social domains. Aging adult
children, the "sandwich generation," will face similar losses, as well dealing
with aging parents and their own children moving into adulthood. Successful
aging in the social domain for the aged adult (remedial intervention), aging
adult child (preventive intervention) and grandchild (preventive intervention), should be a significant intergenerational matter, particularly as
related to the avoidance of frustrations and conflicts resulting in avoidance
behaviors among family members. For example, Belsky (1999) has
summarized research with grandparents, adult children, and grandchildren
in which trade-offs between grandparents and their adult children in dealings
with grandchildren can result in serious intergenerational conflicts. While
adult children may appreciate financial help and care for their children by
the grandparents, adult children may not appreciate child-rearing advice
given by their parents. Intergenerational family relations can be mutually
satisfying if family members respect each other and their differences.

Perhaps not so surprisingly, the physical, psychological, and social
domains interact for successful aging, particularly as related to personal
awareness and intervention. Each of us uses both personal and more
objective standards in judging the aging process and our functioning. While
personal standards may well enhance a sense of self-efficacy, more objective
standards should aid in more realistic functioning. For example, networking
with significant others (social domain) often provides more objective
standards of psychological well-being (psychological domain) and physical
fitness (physical domain) than personal standards. Similarly, being relatively
satisfied with one's life (psychological domain) correlates well with engagement with significant others (social domain) and physical health (physical
domain). Finally, good physical health (physical domain) allows for sufficient
energy reserves to engage in social networks and constructive mental health
practices, such as lifelong learning.

Chapter 6

POLICIES

INTRODUCTORY COMMENTS: IDEAS
FROM THE BERLIN AGING STUDY

To introduce policies for successful aging, the Berlin Aging Study (Baltes & Mayer, 1999) provides useful guidelines. First, Mayer et al. (1999) advocate an international perspective in attempts at understanding aging, as well as attempts at intervention. Second, these researchers offer a number of guidelines, based upon both the Berlin Aging Study and other contemporary research findings. For readers interested in updated summaries of the Berlin Aging Study, the website is recommended (**http://www.mpibberlin.mpg.de/LIP/homed.html**).

1. Resources, Reserves, and Their Limits: Positive and Negative Aspects of Old Age and Aging. Aging in adulthood is neither primarily negative nor full of disabilities and self-doubt. Most older adults are satisfied with their lives—past and present, and able to function independently. Most feel healthy, live in the present and do not fear death. Like younger persons, most older adults are independent and do not have emotional disorders. While physical health declines, the majority of older individuals are able to adapt to deterioration of physical structures and systems, as well as those abilities directly related to physical well-being. Further, older individuals, for the most part, are not socially isolated.

On the other hand, much of the positive findings of the Berlin Aging Study is based upon self-disclosure; these positive findings, at a minimum, suggest a strong psychological resiliency of older adults. Feeling, or reporting one's self as, healthy is not the same thing as being healthy. Objective findings of the Berlin Aging Study illustrated the following:

1. Inevitability of physical and mental decline.
2. Increase of chronic illnesses with age.
3. Negative consequences of physical and mental limitations on

187

active and independent living.
4. Despite reserve capacity, particularly in one's appreciation of self, limits in functional adaptability progress with age.

The differential age-related phenomena noted above strongly suggest that aging is neither (a) unidirectional nor (b) subject to singular or quick interventions. Perhaps more importantly, comparing self-reports to objective diagnoses, the resiliency of many older adults in their appreciation of self is a primary compensation in dealing with the deterioration of individual and societal support systems and functions. The important differences between self and objective analysis of functioning in older age should highlight an appreciation for those older adults who, rather than disengage, continue to engage with the compensatory use of self-efficacy—be it realistic or not. What is needed in national policy to address the dichotomy of normal decline in personal abilities, especially physical, with advancing age and relative stability of self-efficacy or psychological well-being?

2. Differential Aging Into Very Old Age. Recall the difference between interindividual and intraindividual variability. Interindividual variability reflects variability among individuals on one or more abilities; intra-individual variability deals with variability within the person over a number of abilities and over the lifespan.

When focusing on interindividual variability, researchers find that adults in their 60s and 70s are much more variable among themselves than younger adults. Young- and middle-aged elderly are also more variable as individuals when compared to younger and old-old (beyond 85 old) adults; i.e., variability among abilities within the individual. An old-old adult illustrates much less heterogeneity or variability among abilities than younger adults. This finding is more so for physical and intellectual domains, not for self-reported personality or sense of self. The present thought about this de-differentiation of abilities finding is that with old-old age comes such deterioration of the supporting neurophysiological systems and functions that most learned, crystallized abilities decline as well as fluid abilities. A simple conclusion of the de-differentiation idea is that if one is fortunate enough to live a long life, sooner or later the steady decline of physiological systems and functions will result in similar declines of abilities more directly linked to learning. With the success of medical technologies, a higher percentage of us will live significantly longer than our parents; certainly much longer than our grandparents. Yet, successes of medical technology have yet to balance the increased longevity with a similar trend in quality of life in the last phase of our lives. What is needed in national policy to address this?

3. Focusing on Very Old Age: A New Perspective? While the Berlin Aging findings strongly suggest that the young-old have good resiliency and correspondingly good accommodations to physical, psychological, and sociological changes which are age-related, the very old, those in their eighth decade of life, pose a different framework for society. As noted by Mayer et al. (1999, pp. 509, 510):

> . . . The rather isolated and specific loss of intellectual functioning observed in younger old age extends to a general decline of performance across all abilities in very old age. And, this decline appears to include those whose life courses were characterized by above-average personal and social-economic resources. This image of a qualitative change from young old to old old is particularly supported by psychiatric findings. In contrast to other mental disorders, the prevalence of dementia clearly changes in very old age. Beyond the age of 80, its prevalence increases rapidly, approaching 40% to 60% among nonagenarians and centenarians.
>
> This means that many very old persons exhibit a new quality—sometimes so much so that they are no longer recognizable as the individuals they once were. The geriatric findings on the need for care and multi-morbidity also support the view that very old age constitutes a new stage. Social conditions are also qualitatively different in very old age: Emotional loneliness increases, social participation outside the household decreases, and, foremost, institutionalization increases. On a systemic level, increasing numbers of the very old, particularly women, belong to groups whose functioning and life circumstances are associated with unsatisfactory constellations and real risks. . . .

Given the possibility of a fourth stage, in a way qualitatively different from earlier stages of adulthood, it is important to remember other significant findings about aging (including findings of the Berlin Aging Study): viz., even in advanced old age, we find variability among individuals, including the finding of much variation of abilities within a very old person. The message of Mayer et al. (1999) is that with very old age comes a compression of variabilities among individuals and within the individual. Although these variabilities continue to exist until death, in very old age, the differences among individuals, and within an individual, become more restricted.

A bit of reflection from those of us who have witnessed the final aspects of the aging process with significant others should reinforce the point of Mayer et al. For many of us in our 50s, we witness the restriction of variabilities of those of the preceding generation. The friends of our parents who are alive become more similar than different, certainly in the physical domains. Reflecting more, the similarities become more apparent in the psychological and social domains. Our parents are like their friends; showing less variability in many of adaptive capabilities. They are much less flexible, illustrate much less reserve capacity, and, in general, provide a conservation model of adaptiveness to their gradually shrinking environment. In one important sense, the very old, including the parents of some of us, are no less human than younger people. The very old are part of a family, community, and society which, for many are secondary to an individual sense of self. It is this lack of perspective sense for others, which makes for a lack of understanding and appreciation of the very old.

The lack of understanding and appreciation of the very old and the last phases of the aging process may be an adaptive function for the developing person. On the one hand, the deterioration associated with aging, particularly in the proposed fourth or last stage of life, is realistic-based upon research findings and personal experiences. On the other hand, we are insensitive to the needs of aging elders and naive about acting on personal options for our inevitable states of aging. It would seem that our developing sense of self, which is related to our engagements with external relations, has a significant lag-time. The adaptiveness of this rather unsuccessful strategy of aging is that most of us disassociate the realities of aging of others from our own aging. In the process of such disassociation between reality and the personal understanding of self, we too often disengage from meaningful relations with those who illustrate significant declines of functioning. So, what may be adaptable dissociation in younger adulthood may well limit our adaptiveness in dealing with our own physical, psychological and sociological aging later on.

4. Aging as a Systemic Phenomenon. Since aging is the result of biological, psychological, social, and life-cycle phenomena, it is worthwhile to understand the aging process and older adulthood from a multi-disciplinary rather than singular discipline perspective. The Berlin Aging Study researchers provide three examples of the usefulness of a multi-disciplinary point of view. First, the multidisciplinary approach allowed for (a) multiple disciplinary perspectives of aging assessment planning for the repeated measures of Berlin participants on many variables and (b) integration of biological, psychological, and sociological research findings. In particular, the Berlin Aging Study illustrated clustering of abilities over older age ranges, particularly young-, middle-, and old-old age, as well as for gender and other demographic variables. This multidisciplinary effort provides information beyond individual variability and/or age-related changes for a particular ability. For theory, research, and practice, a multi-disciplinary perspective provides for understanding relationships among multiple ability changes associated with age, relationships among determinants of such changes, and finally, relationships among possible interventions based upon both singular age-related disabilities (e.g., chronic illness) and functional aging (e.g., interactions, biological, psychological, and sociological forces impacting disability).

Second, the ongoing professional conferences among Berlin Aging Study researchers and practitioners, particularly geriatric physicians and psychiatrists, provided a consensus of standards for medical diagnoses and quality of medication. An interesting finding from this systemic approach to understanding the aging process was that participants were not overmedicated.

Finally, the multidisciplinary approach resulted in findings of ". . . A remarkably strong association between sensory functioning and intelligence. Although there are very many studies of intelligence in old age, this finding is new mainly because such cooperation between physicians and psychologists has been rare. . . ." (Mayer et al., 1999, p. 510).

5. Prospects For the Future. *(A) On the State of Gerontological Research.* The Berlin Aging Study included professionals in medical, behavioral, and social disciplines. Mayer et al. (1999) suggest that such a multidisciplinary research or clinical team should be expanded to include professionals with expertise in molecular genetics (with a focus on determinants of aging), as well as intervention strategies dealing with technological and behavioral remediation, loss of significant others, and transition from familial (home) residence to institutional living.

In addition to promoting a broader interdisciplinary perspective, the Berlin Aging Study researchers suggest the use of longitudinal and sequential studies to disentangle the relative effects of normal aging, cohort, and time of measurement effects. The suggestion for more sophisticated research designs is important for intervention and policy matters, as older citizens coming from earlier cohorts, are becoming more numerous, and their successive environments are changing rapidly. As noted by Mayer et al. (1999), social changes can have dramatic impacts on research findings, perhaps making some of the findings obsolete at the time of research dissemination. Rather recent advances in medical technology for detection and remediation of certain malignant, cardiovascular, and pulmonary diseases illustrate the phenomena of social, contextual changes directly impacting both longevity and quality of life. Recent advances in the understanding and promotion of positive lifestyles, as well as computer-assisted technology for skeletal, muscular, visual, and auditory prosthetic aids also illustrate the progressive impact of contextual changes on longevity and quality of life.

B. Social Policy Guidelines. A number of suggestions relating to contextual, social policies for successful aging are offered from the Berlin Aging Study.

1. Emphasis on heterogeneity, variability, or differences in the aging process among elderly groups and the individual for multiple abilities. Strengths and weaknesses among and within individuals is evident in senior citizens, as they are in younger citizens. These variability phenomena—between and within individuals, require sensibilities in the development and implementation of social policies; viz., such policies will be more effective if seniors are understood as representing varied capabilities and needs.

2. Understanding of the modifiability or reserve capacity of older individuals. The age of onset, rate, and maximum level of age-related disabilities can be changed, positively or negatively, depending upon personal and contextual intervention. Thus, much more focus—research, practice, and social policy—is needed to identify intervention strategies, with an emphasis on prevention rather than remediation of age-related disabilities.

3. Particularly for the elderly with disabling conditions, advances in home care, community day care, and institutional nursing care are needed. The disabling condition is much more likely in old-old age. Along with physical care, the elderly's sense of purpose and communal productivity needs to be addressed at personal, community, state, and national levels. Especially important in Western societies, the significance of the elderly needs to be reinterpreted to diminish the importance of economic usefulness to society. Given that there are many more elderly women than men in societies, a reeducation of human significance should promote the usefulness of the elderly without a primary criterion of economic worth.

4. Health policies should promote the relative independence of older individuals. With the promotion of positive lifestyles for long-term personal and societal gains, as well as cost-effective remedial interventions for age-related disabilities, social policies should stress the relative savings of working with seniors to deal with more successful aging. The older adult should be dealt with as an active participant in implementation of social policies that promote both longevity and quality of life.

C. The Fourth Stage. For policy purposes, the results of the Berlin Study reflect positivism for the young and middle-old, but with ". . . Very old age, the finitude and vulnerability of life and the strains and suffering associated with the approach of death become predominant. . . ." (Mayer et al., 1999, p. 513).

For those 85 years of age and above, biological impairments become paramount. The Berlin Aging Study researchers emphasize that in addition to differentiating younger and older seniors for diagnostic and prognostic sensitivities, practitioners and policymakers should recognize that a primary issue of old age is the aging of the very old. Will the prolongation of life into very old age be associated with longer periods of biological, psychological, and social dysfunction? In the last twenty years, optimistic trends for old age, based upon more successful aging, have been extended from the sixth decade to the seventh and eight decades. Can this optimistic trend continue? Perhaps, but the continuation will probably be linked to cultural interventions as much as individual physical, psychological and social health promotions. Given dramatic declines in functioning associated with very old age, the Berlin Aging Study researchers strongly promote the focused research, correlated with public awareness and policy decisions, dealing with the very old. More than a few of my students have reacted rather strongly to my categorizations of young-, middle-, and old-old adults. Their reactions are based on the a sense of inequity, that the old-old are being characterized as not only different from younger adults, but pictured in a negative frame. While old-old age is, by definitions of dysfunction, not chronological age, different from younger adulthood, the differentiation certainly does not need to imply inferiority. As with all of life, reality is in the mind of the beholder. Just because someone is different does not have to mean he or she is less of a human being than anyone else. It is important, for society and the very old, to understand and appreciate present inevitabilities associated with very old age. With understanding and appreciation of late life, constructive contextual changes for aged individuals, significant others, and society in general are possible.

PUBLIC POLICIES RELATED TO AGING

Much of the following summaries deal with public policies and aging in the United States and are from the detailed, contemporary review of Binstock (1999). Binstock has the distinction of being one of the leading professionals articulating the changes and results of aging policies. Public policies are defined as national, and target specific groupings of individuals. Binstock's historical and contemporary summaries of the changing political contexts of policies on aging are very informative. A summary of his review follows:

1. **1935–1978: The Old Age Welfare State**. Following other industrialized nations, the United States government enacted the Social Security Act in

1935. This public pension enactment, which designated age 65 for eligibility to the plan, in a real sense mandated a distinction within adulthood; viz., adults and old aged adults. The Baltimore and Ohio Railroad, as noted by Atchley (2000), started private retirement pensions in 1884. These private plans were originally provided to keep valued employees in the company, not to assist in retirement financial security. Public policies for government funded retirement pensions, from the New Deal until the late 1970s, according to Binstock (1999), promoted the concept of ageism for a heterogeneous group of adults aged 65 and older. Unlike racism and sexism, ageism is not completely prejudicial, as public policies have provided benefits to the elderly and, perhaps as important, most of us will get old. Binstock's position is that with the elderly categorized as ". . . Poor, frail, socially dependent, objects of discrimination, and above all deserving" (see Kalish, 1979) . . . ," national and State politicians . . ." implemented this compassionate construct by adopting and financing major age-categorical benefit programs, and tax and price subsidies for which eligibility is not determined by need. Through the New Deal's Social Security, the Great Society's Medicare and Older Americans Act (an omnibus social service program), special tax exemptions and credits for being aged 65 or older, and a variety of other measures enacted during President Nixon's New Federalism, the elderly were exempted from the screenings that are applied to welfare applicants to determine whether they are worthy of public help. . . ." (Binstock 1999, p. 416).

In 1979, a committee of the U.S. House of Representatives identified 134 public programs benefiting senior citizens. Binstock (1999, pp. 416, 417) characterized this relative fountain of age as follows: ". . . During the 1960s and 1970s just about every issue or problem affecting just some older persons that could be identified by advocates for the elderly became a governmental responsibility: nutritional, legal, supportive, and leisure services; housing, home repair; energy assistance; transportation; help in getting jobs; protection against being fired from jobs; public insurance for private pensions; mental health programs; a separate National Institute on Aging; and on, and on, and on. . . ." From the frame of the elderly, the good times sponsored by the federal government had a high water mark in the 1970s.

2. Late 1970s: Emergence of a Less Compassionate View of the Aged.
Most likely because of a depressed national economy, fiscal vulnerability of the Social Security system, increased federal spending (amount and relative expenditures) for aging benefits, and significant advances in the welfare of senior citizens, older adults, as an aggregate, were being dealt with as both influential and rather well off. Binstock (1999, p. 417) notes that during the last two decades, ". . . The new stereotypes, readily observed in popular culture, depicted older persons as prosperous, hedonistic, politically

powerful, and selfish. . . ." One dramatic and effective counterbalance to the acceptance of a senior citizen welfare state was the promotion (by segments of the legislature, popular press, and public policy professionals) of equity for public funding as an intergenerational issue. Specifically, opponents of increasing public support for the elderly argued for the inequity of providing more funds for the elderly from increased taxation of employers and employees, while restricting funding for others in financial need, like the unborn, infants, and children. When compared to the relative needs of those much younger than themselves, coupled with the successive public and private advantages of many elderly, the contemporary era is characterized as one of less user-friendly for senior citizens. Binstock (1999, p. 419) notes that beginning in 1983, the American Congress curtailed the progressive public support for "Social Security, Medicare, the Older American's Act, and other programs and policies reflecting the diverse economic situations of older people (Binstock, 1994). Some of these reduced benefits to comparatively wealthy older people; others targeted benefits toward relatively poor older adults. . . ."

3. Contemporary Politics and the Elderly. In 1995, balancing the federal budget became a primary issue for the Republican-dominated Congress and the Democratic President. This issue provided scrutiny of all federally funded programs, including those benefiting the elderly (Binstock, 1999). A 1995 report of the Bipartisan Commission on Entitlement and Tax Reform provided clear projections of the upcoming elderly baby boomers and negative fiscal impacts on Social Security, Medicare, and the national budget. In 1997, the Balanced Budget Act was enacted, with the design of forcing a balanced federal budget by the year 2002. The Balanced Budget Act included mandates to reduce federal spending for Medicare, a projected reduction of $115 billion in a five year period. Binstock (1999, p. 420), summarized the emergence of the political arena for elderly benefits as follows:

> . . . The matter of substantially reforming old age programs will remain on the political agenda in the years immediately ahead. The aging of the Baby Boom has major fiscal implications if Social Security, Medicare, and Medicaid policies remain largely as they are today. In fiscal year 1996, federal spending on these programs was $630 billion, amounting to 8.4% of the nation's gross domestic product (GDP). By 2030, when most of the Baby Boom will have reached old age, these three programs are projected to consume 16% of GDP, nearly twice the present proportion . . . Proposals abound for reforming these policies to reduce projected outlays, and they generate many complex issues. . . .

4. Social Security's Future. While the present status of Social Security funding is relatively financially secure, the continued focus on (a) balancing the federal budget and (b) competition among public support programs for federal dollars make for less optimistic futures–both for the elderly and those contributing taxed dollars for aging programs. For the specifics underlying the less optimistic future, Binstock's (1999) summary is recommended reading. A simple summary of his review and projections is that there are the components of TAXES, TAXES, TAXES and MORE and MORE and MORE senior citizens. He has shared the following options available to deal with the upcoming insecure financial stability of Social Security.

a. Raise the age of retirement. Since federal taxation is the primary source of funding for Social Security, raising the retirement age from age 65 would reduce costs by both (a) delaying benefits for a longer period and, correspondingly, taxing the younger elderly for a longer period. Current federal legislation mandates gradually increasing retirement age, starting in the year 2003, resting at age 67 in the year 2027. Two options available are to (a) raise the retirement age beyond 67 and/or (b) accelerate the time frame of the increases.

b. Reduce the amount of benefits. The formula used to calculate Social Security benefits could be changed to (a) reduce the weight given to averaged contributions and/or (b) remove or reduce the annual adjustment for inflation.

c. Increase taxes on Social Security benefits. Binstock (1999) provides the thresholds for present Social Security benefits taxation, noting that this taxation also reduces the after-tax income available to beneficiaries. One obvious option of taxation for beneficiaries is to make 85% of adjusted gross income taxable, regardless of income level. Another option is subject beneficiaries to the same taxation guidelines as non-Social Security citizens.

d. Increase Social Security (Social Security's Old Age and Survivors Insurance (OASI) taxes (employee and employer). First, more funds for Social Security could be obtained by increasing the percentages of taxation for employees and employers (5.35%, up to $65,400 annually presently). Second, more funds could be secured by increasing or eliminating the ceiling–from $65,400 on up).

e. Use Federal general revenues. While other countries do use general reserves as funding for social security benefits and the U.S. Government does so in support of Medicare and Medicaid, opponents of these practices argue that diluting the primary funding source for Social Security–employee and employer taxation for Social Security—would jeopardize the essential marketing tool, personal contributions for personal benefits in later life.

f. Fund reserves in the Social Security trust fund. As noted by Binstock (1999), the options summarized above will be difficult for politicians to both advocate and implement, as well as posing a significant financial burden on the elderly and younger citizens. Historically, the loans from the Social Security trust fund have been provided by the federal government to other public entitlements and programs. The revenue to repay, with interest, the Social Security bonds will be most significant and have to come from (a) raiding other federal trust funds, decreasing taxed dollars to some or all national entitlement programs, selling additional bonds, and/or increasing taxes. All of these options, from the present perspective, would result in negative responses from one or more of the many political active lobbying forces and citizens categorized by self and group-interests.

g. Privatize Social Security. Privatization of Social Security, partially or totally, has become more than a fantasy in contemporary national interests of balancing the national budget, equity of public funding, and, optimization of limited resources—national, communal, and familial. Advocates of privatization note that in addition to reducing projected taxation for Social Security benefits, privatization of funds can be limited (as opposed to total), differentiated in terms of employee and employer contributions, and/or gradually implemented (as opposed to immediate). Opponents of Social Security program privatization argue that changing the present "guaranteed" public insurance for retirement income will put senior citizens in the higher risk arena of money marketing—personal or commercial.

5. The Future of Medicare. Binstock's (1999, p. 427) summary notes that the future of Medicare is less optimistic than that of Social Security; ". . . Between 2010 and 2030 federal spending for Medicare, as a percentage of GDP, is projected to increase 73% as compared to a one-third increase in the percentage of GDP projected for OASI [Social Security's Old Age and Survivors Insurance] spending in the same period. . . ." While Social Security costs are mandated per individual, Medicare costs are presently linked to types of and amounts of health care provided to seniors. As noted by Binstock (1999), Medicare contributed to 2.4% of the GDP; the projection of Medicare's contribution to GDP in 2030 is just over 7%. This proposed dramatic increase in funding for Medicare is, once again, based upon (a) the emergence of Baby Boomers to elderly status and (b) successive extensions of longevity with succeeding cohorts.

a. Structural changes in Medicare. Binstock (1999) reports a number of policy changes for the stability of Medicare costs. The general constraint theme is to change the open-ended fee-for-health-care-service to fixed reimbursement allocations. The prototype of change is the present managed care organizations (MCO) for Medicare beneficiaries and service providers. While the MCO approach has reduced Medicare costs, it also puts MCO's at financial risk, as well as decreasing potential earnings of health care specialists, increasing private contributions from participating seniors, and enhances suspicions of poorer services for recipients. Obvious options to the MCO approach, obvious from a financial perspective (personal and public contributions), should include a degree of choice for services weighted by personal expenses for optional services. It seems that the options for the elderly with Medicare are similar to other options of younger cohorts in dealings with health insurance. MCOs provide reduced personal costs, as well as reduced service options; those who prefer more health options and service providers have to contribute more personal resources. This dilemma is far more than esoteric, as it illustrates the inequities of national health care for citizens. Those of us with enough discretionary income, and, as important, concern for personal well-being, have the option of paying more for services other than those offered by MCOs. Such is not the case for many citizens, regardless of chronological age.

b. Options to structural Medicare changes. One option is to reduce the level of reimbursements, from the Medicare program, to health care providers. Binstock (1999, p. 431)) notes that federal mandates have done so in the past: ". . . The Omnibus Budget Reconciliation Act of 1993 trimmed an estimated $55 billion in payments to hospitals, physicians, and other health care providers over the period 1994–1998 (Congressional Budget Office, 1993). BBA97 cut another $115 billion in estimated provider reimbursement from 1998 through 2002. . . ." Option two is to raise the age of Medicare eligibility to 67. This option, especially if implemented gradually, should be least objectionable to seniors, as OASI benefits are presently scheduled for eligibility, within the next 25 years, at age 67. This option would reduce the costs of Medicare by 5%; further reductions in Medicare costs using elevated age standard are possible by (a) increasing the age for benefits and/or (b) reducing the increased age criterion time frame. Option three is to increase the contributions (overall and categorical premiums) of Medicare recipients, thereby reducing federal contributions. Binstock (1999) noted that the Congressional Budget Office reviewed the impact of increasing recipient contributions from 25 to 50% by 2010. With such an increase, general revenue contributions for Medicare would be reduced by 50% annually. A very important negative for this option is that the increased premiums for the elderly would drastically reduce discretionary income. Option four is to increase taxation for the continuation of Medicare as we know it. Binstock (1999) suggests that implementation of each of the options would solve the projected public financial problems for Medicare. He also notes, however, that realistic promotion of any of the options by politicians will result in negative reactions by one or more public constituencies.

6. Long-term Care for the Functionally Disabled Elderly. Binstock (1999, p. 432), referring to a Congressional Budget Office projection with 1990 as the baseline year, summarizes the upcoming impact of the Baby Boomers and enhanced longevity for elders on long-term care costs: "... the total national costs of long-term care will almost double by 2010 and more than triple by 2030 (Congressional Budget Office, 1991). . . ." What are reasonable expectations, given this projection?

a. Personal/familial financing. Presently, personal and/or familial contributions for long-term care cost represents about a third of such costs. Most elders cannot meet long-term nursing home costs, as the costs are approaching $50,000 a year. Binstock (1999) notes research suggesting the following:
     1. Over 80 percent of long-term care outside of nursing homes for the elderly is provided by family members (most often, wife or daughter).
     2. Caregiving by family members does not decrease when professional, paid services augments caregiving.

With changing lifestyles and demographics of Baby Boomers, future elderly may find fewer familial members to provide long-term care. For example, Baby Boomers, unlike present seniors, have much higher rates of divorce, single status, and single-parent households. As noted by Binstock (1999), these changes may well result in an erosion of familial obligation in dealing with elderly parents or relatives.

b. Role of private insurance. This type of insurance is a relatively new venture for insurance companies and is, relative to (a) insurance costs for younger people and (b) senior incomes, very expensive. As with many insurance policies, there are limitations, such as how soon the benefits become available and how long the benefits are provided. Binstock (1999) notes that only five percent of older persons have private long-term care insurance, and only one percent of nursing care is covered by such insurance.

c. Role of Government. About 60 percent of long-term care costs are covered by public entitlement programs, with Medicaid contributing the majority of reimbursement. Presently, Medicaid guidelines favor nursing homes, as opposed to home or community day care.

Binstock's projection for public financing of long-term care is not optimistic:

> . . . Out-of-pocket payments for care are becoming larger and increasingly unaffordable for many. Neither the projected income and asset status of members of the Baby Boom cohort nor the dynamics of the market (at this time) indicate that these trends will abate. Broad societal trends suggest that informal, unpaid care by family members may become less feasible in the future than it is today. Only a minority of older persons may be able to afford premiums for private long-term care insurance . . . Yet, even the safety net that government programs now provide by financing long-term care for the poor is seriously threatened by contemporary federal and state budgetary politics. The political context is such that public resources for long-term care are likely to be even less available–in relation to the need for care–than they have been to date. . . . (1999, p. 436)

7. Policy Reform and the Politics of Aging. Binstock (1999) raises the important role of seniors in advocating for enhanced public funding related to the needs of the present and future elderly. He notes the assumption that with Baby Boomers becoming Aging Boomers, the political advocacy of seniors will promote enhancement of public funding to meet elderly needs, if not expectations. Unfortunately, for the elderly of the present and future, Binstock's review of related research indicates the following; viz., the elderly do not vote (or advocate) as a group, and as important, self or group (ethnicity, education, socioeconomic status, religion, political affiliation, geographic region, physical/ psychological/social age) interests of the elderly retard singular agendas.

a. Old-Age-Based Interest Groups. As noted by Binstock (1999), senior power as related to supporting elderly issues is a myth. Initiatives for public policy and funding of elderly needs were made by others with political clout; retrenchments and reforms of elderly-related policies and funding were made within the context of opposition from special interests groups for the elderly. As Binstock notes, the American Association of Retired Persons (AARP) has over 33 million members, yet this special interests group for the elderly rarely tries to promote specific positions related to national policies for the elderly. While the AARP promotes current issues and information directly related to the elderly, primarily in the health areas, it does not initiate nor promote political incentives. The headlines for the November, 1999 AARP Bulletin illustrate Binstock's summary of AARP's low political strategy:

Women on the rise? Some make it big—but others still face glass ceiling
Personal alert: Thieves want your most precious possession
Protests pay off: Controversial pensions slowed
Cozy on campus: Retirees give college towns high marks
Job outlook: Rosy; Demand for midlife workers rising
Her mission in life: Dignity after death; Activist takes aim at funeral abuses
Plight of the uninsured: Healthy aging put in jeopardy

This consumer-interest approach has been successful for AARP executives, probably because the membership of AARP is so heterogeneous. Perhaps it is wishful thinking to presume the political effectiveness of AARP. The organization—company—does assist seniors (actually, membership is open for those 50 and older) in both (a) association with the national organization and, relatedly, (b) discounts for many purchases. On the other hand, it would be good and novel for AARP to share, like the National Institute on Aging, a strategic plan directly related to the needs and desires of the elderly. Atchley (2000) suggests that AARP and other advocacy organizations for the elderly do keep the issues of seniors in the public arena. In addition to AARP, the following are advocacy organizations specifically for seniors:

National Council of Senior Citizens
American Society on Aging—professional organization
National Council on Aging—professional organization
The Gerontological Society of America—professional organization
Association for Gerontology in Higher Education—professional organization
Gray Panthers
Older Woman's League

b. Old-Age Political Collaborations for the Future. Will the Baby Boomers become Aging Boomers with common political agendas to target both national policy and funding? We'll have to wait and react. Binstock (1999), concluding his review of contemporary policy issues for the elderly, suggests a different frame of reference in projecting age-related policy and funding. Rather than a future of competition between the young and old, perhaps the competitions will be between the relatively rich and relatively poor, and/or among ethnic groups. A reasonable projection is that there will continue to be limited national funds for unlimited special interests needs and demands. Entitlement programs and funds will continue, but the relative societal and governmental embrace of special interests groups, including the elderly, will be more fluid than stable.

THE ELDERLY OF TOMORROW

In their comprehensive review of U.S. Population trends, Hobbs and Damon (1999, **http://www.census.gov/prod/1/pop/p23-190/p,23-190 html**) shared realistic facts related to the elderly of tomorrow as related to public policies. While it is human nature to focus on the present, planning for future elderly issues can result in more optimal intervention strategies. Hobbs and Damon (1999) provide us with three future elderly issues that relate directly to planning and public policies. First, The U.S. continues to be unique in the diversity of its citizens, including senior citizens. There is, and will be, diversity within the elderly. Perhaps the most appreciated diversity issues, in terms of the general population, is that there will be many more elderly and the old-old (85 years and older) will rise at the highest rate. These two facts ". . .will create compelling social, economic, and ethical choices for individuals, families, and governments. . . ." (p. 71). Yet, there is other present and future diversity matters that have not received either the professional or public policy attention of the first two noted facts. Diversity matters related to ethnicity, socioeconomic status, gender, education, and geographical/communal (metropolitan, urban, rural) histories, which can be interrelated, enhance the complexity of public and private dealings with older individuals. While the phenomenon of aging populations throughout the world should correlate with less public and private attention to the issues of youth, the same conjecture cannot be made for the diversity matters of ethnicity, socioeconomic status, gender, education, and geographical/communal histories. In fact, using contemporary U.S. Census data, public policies, and information about personal well-being of seniors, the rising economic status of some elderly is mediated by other ethnicity, socioeconomic status, gender, education, and geographical/communal histories; viz., differential elderly well-being is related to these demographic histories. Future public policies must address continuation, if not enhancement, of inequities as citizens move into older age. Questions raised by Hobbs and Damon(1999) are:

> *What are the moral and ethical limits of euthanasia and end of life treatments?*
> *Should health care be provided on an age-based rationing system?*
> *Who can judge the level of competence of a patient with respect to decision-making?*
> *Will tomorrow's generation of elderly be healthy?*
> *Will this generation be independent?*
> *Will societies provide productive and purposeful roles for them?*
> *Will more elderly be subject to extended years of disability?*
> *Will one's age of chronic disability be postponed?*

What will the chronic conditions be?
Will there be a reduction in the frequency of comorbidity?
How far will the society and individuals go in promoting positive lifestyles and
preventive intervention strategies?

The second issue raised by Hobbs and Damon is that the changing family structure requires, from both societal and personal perspectives, consideration of changing support systems for the elderly. Will support systems move towards public, as opposed to personal or familial care? The questions from Hobbs and Damon (1999) are:

What is needed to educate citizens about long-term physical and economic effects
of lifestyle in the younger years of the lifespan?
Who will care for the physically and economically dysfunctional elderly?
Will care programs and providers take into account diversity matters such as
ethnicity, culture, socioeconomic status, gender, education, and geographical/com-
munal histories?
How much personal discretionary income should the elderly be expected to
contribute to the support of themselves and others?
What are the balances for federal funding to deal with preventive versus remedial
research in categories of nonfatal chronic disabilities versus fatal chronic
conditions?

Third, the upcoming Baby-to-Aging-Boomers will bring with them to older age new dimensions, such as:

Educational attainment is much higher for the Baby Boomers; thus they will be
better educated than today's elderly.
The health of to-be-elders is generally better than their parents.
Most women who will become seniors are in the work force.
Baby Boomers are much more likely, compared to their elders, to have pension
plans which are dependent upon personal contributions.
Projections are that the age for receiving social security benefits will move upward.
Baby Boomers, unlike present seniors, are much more likely to
communicate about issues of physical, psychological, and social
health.

A recent survey conducted by AARP Roper Starch Worldwide, Inc. (**http://research.aarp.org/econ/boomer_seg_1.html**, Prisuta & Takeuchi, 1999) provided surprising information for the upcoming Aging Boomers. These boomers had major impacts on the American scene throughout their lives, starting with the infant population boom in the late 1940s to middle

1960s. Next, the boomers redefined youth culture in the 1960s and 1970s, followed by dual-income households in the 1980s and 1990s. The boomers will also redefine the retirement years of 2000–2030. The following summary is from the AARP 1999 website executive summary:

1. Overview of Study Design; Five Study Phases

a. Roper Reports data base: initial review of demographic boomers information (A Profile of the Baby Boom: Retirement, Finances, Health Information, and other Key Areas of Exploration).
b. Qualitative phase, with eight focus groups in four cities (Kansas City, Providence, Charlotte, and Phoenix).
c. Large-scale quantitative telephone survey, with a nationally representative sample of 2,001 adults aged 33–52.
d. Segmentation analysis of survey data grouped respondents based upon retirement attitudes, beliefs, and behaviors.
e. Second qualitative phase of eight post-survey focus groups in Chicago and Baltimore.

Significant findings from the quantitative survey are categorized by unique expectations for retirement, defining retirement, focusing on retirement and reflecting self-reliance, generational differences, polarization within generation, and evaluating Social Security and Medicare.

2. Unique Expectations for Retirement

a. Eighty percent plan to work part-time in retirement; 16% plan not to work at all.
b. Thirty-five percent plan to work part-time primarily because of interest and enjoyment.
c. Twenty-three percent plan to work part-time for the income.
d. Seventeen percent plan their own business; five percent plan to work full-time with a new career.
e. Twenty-one percent plan to move after retirement to a new geographic area.
f. Twenty-three percent expect financial assistance from inheritance.
g. Thirty-five percent believe they will have to downsize their lifestyle with retirement.
h. Twenty-three percent expect difficulty during retirement in financial solvency.
i. Sixteen percent believe they will have significant health problems during retirement.

3. Defining Expectations in Retirement

a. Forty-nine percent plan to do more community service and volunteerism.
b. Seventy-three percent think they will spend considerable time with hobbies or special interests.
c. Fifty-seven percent plan to live close by one or more children; 70 percent look forward to the status of grandparent.

4. Focusing on Retirement and Reflecting Self-reliance

a. Seventy-two percent have given much or some thought to their upcoming retirement years.
b. Seventy percent do not want to be dependent upon their children.
c. Sixty percent are confident in their ability to prepare for retirement.
d. Twenty percent are of the opinion that their future will take care of itself.
e. Nine percent feel retired folks should be able to depend upon family members for financial support in retirement.
f. Sixty-eight percent believe they can depend upon IRAs and 401(k)s for financial security in retirement.
g. Sixty percent plan to use investment savings for retirement income.
h. Forty-eight percent plan to rely on Social Security as a source of retirement income.
i. Sixty-six percent are satisfied with the amount of money they are investing for retirement.

5. Generational Differences

a. Eighty-four percent feel their generation needs more money than the parental generation.
b. Seventy-five percent believe they are more self-indulgent than their parents.
c. Sixty-seven percent believe they will live longer than their parents.
d. Fifty-six percent believe they will be healthier than their parents.

6. Optimism and Ambivalence

a. Sixty-nine percent are optimistic concerning the retirement years; 28 percent being very optimistic.
b. Eighty-one percent of those who have given serious thought to retirement are the most optimistic.
c. Seventy-four percent are most excited about spending time with family members during retirement and/or pursuing hobbies and interests.
d. Twenty percent view retirement as including boredom and/or isolation.

e. Financial security was the highest response to an open-ended question concerning what first comes to mind about retirement.

f. While 76 percent note the importance of saving for retirement, 47 percent find it difficult to save for the future.

g. Thirty-nine percent responded that they could not imagine themselves retired, while forty-four percent noted that they could.

h. The median age of the respondents was 42, but the typical boomer responded as feeling 35 years of age.

7. Polarization Within the Generation

a. Thirty-six percent of the most financially secure respondents (with household incomes of at least $70,000) and 18 percent of the least financially secure (with household income less than $30,000) were very optimistic about retirement.

b. Forty-nine percent of the most financially secure, versus 28 percent of those least financially secure, had given serious thought to retirement.

c. Seventy-six percent of the most financially secure, versus 47 percent of the least financially secure, are confident of the ability to prepare for retirement.

d. While 25 percent of the boomers are not financially prepared for retirement, 44 percent of those least financially secure are.

8. Evaluating Social Security and Medicare

a. Fifty-five percent of boomers have a favorable opinion of Social Security.

b. Fifty-five percent agreed with the position that since personal contributions are made to Social Security, retirement funds from it should be returned to the person.

c. Forty-eight percent count on Social Security benefits during retirement; 15 percent expect such benefits to cover most or all of retirement financial needs.

d. Thirty-six percent are confident Social Security will exist when they retire.

e. Sixty percent have a favorable view of Medicare.

f. Forty-six percent are knowledgeable about Medicare.

g. Thirty-nine percent are confident Medicare will exist when they retire.

h. While most boomers are satisfied with their current health care coverage, they are not confident about health care coverage during retirement: access to care (60% versus 25%), choosing particular doctors (55% versus 24%), and selecting specialists when needed (53% versus 21%).

The *Segmentation Analysis* of the quantitative survey data resulted in the following five boomers categories:

1. The Strugglers—nine percent of the sample.
2. The Anxious—23 percent.
3. The Enthusiasts—13 percent.
4. The Self Reliants—30 percent.
5. Today's Traditionalists—25 percent.

Characteristics of The Strugglers are as follows:

- Lowest income group (median household income $30,000 below the average boomer.
- Sixty-four percent are females.
- Money not being put aside for retirement, because of existing needs.
- Not satisfied with inability to save for retirement.
- Little or no thought given to retirement years, other than not being optimistic about their future.

The Anxious boomers are apprehensive concerning their retirement years:

- Median household income is $10,000 below the average boomer.
- Contribute some discretionary income for retirement.
- Not expecting financial security in retirement.
- Plan to continue working in retirement.
- Not optimistic concerning retirement.
- Not satisfied with savings for retirement.
- Very concerned about health coverage in retirement.

The Enthusiasts are eager to engage retirement, planning for:

- Total retirement from work, and engagements of interest.
- Satisfaction during retirement years.

The Self Reliants, having the highest income and educational levels of the boomers, are:

- Aggressively saving for future income, with some assurance that the savings will provide for financial security in retirement.
- Satisfied with their preretirement financial savings plans.
- Plan to continue working in retirement, primarily for interest or pleasure.

Today's Traditionalists feel secure about Social Security and Medicare as related to their retirement financial well-being, but also plan to continue working during retirement.

Table 6.1 summarizes comparisons among the five segmented groups with selected survey items. For each of the items, high and low percentages are noted in bold print.

Prisuta and Takeuchi (**http://research.aarp.org/econ/boomerseg3.html**, 1999), provided summary considerations and conclusions from the segmentation analysis, some of which are presently summarized.

1. The Strugglers and the Anxious boomers (32%) do not exhibit high levels of self reliance typical of the other boomer categories. The Strugglers and the Anxious are not prepared for retirement, particularly in terms of financial security. These two boomer groups, relative to the others, have the lowest levels of favorable attitudes or confidence in Social Security and Medicare programs. The two boomer categories will need secure Social Security and Medicare programs for financial assistance in retirement.

2. The Enthusiasts (13%) are very optimistic concerning their retirement years, with two-thirds noting they cannot wait until retirement. Members of this boomer category do not have serious financial or health concerns for retirement, and plan to pursue interests other than work in retirement. One concern for this boomer group is that its members may be overly optimistic, given the lengthening of retirement years and risks involved with individual retirement accounts.

3. The Self Reliants (30%), with the highest income and educational level of the boomer categories, are (a) the most serious planners and (b) saving the most for retirement. Like all boomers, the Self Reliants will have to deal with the inevitable physical deterioration associated with older age.

4. Today's Traditionalists (25%), expressing much confidence in Social Security and Medicare programs, plan to both work and rely on these supportive programs during retirement. While most of Today's Traditionalists plan to work because of interest or enjoyment, about 25 percent will be employed because of the income provided. As with the Strugglers and the Anxious, a third of Today's Traditionalists are concerned about not having enough information to help plan for retirement.

Table 6–1
Comparison of Groups Across Selected Items

	% of Total Baby Boomers	% of The Strugglers	% of The Anxious	% of The Enthusiasts	% of The Self Reliant	% Today's Traditionalists
	(N = 2001)	(N = 186)	(N = 455)	(N = 260)	(N = 592)	(N = 507)
Very / fairly optimistic about retirement years	69	42	39	93	87	77
Putting money into any of the savings vehicles asked about	90	6	100	99	100	97
Completely / somewhat satisfied with amount putting away for retirement	67	13	37	88	89	75
Expect to depend heavily during retirement on personal investments making today	64	28	57	72	83	57
Confident healthcare coverage when retired will allow to:						
See specialist when feel need to	70	48	31	87	82	91
Get care when feel need it	79	59	47	94	91	93
Visit doctor of own choosing	69	46	36	84	81	87
Plan to not work at all when retired	16	16	5	100	1	1
Plan to work mainly for interest or enjoyment sake	35	14	18	–	63	42
Can't wait to retire	42	34	32	66	44	40
Expect to have plenty of money when retired	30	9	9	49	45	28
If Social Security were not available it would have major impact on retirement	41	73	60	25	19	46
Very / somewhat confident Social Security still will be available when they retire	36	29	16	38	28	61

Table 6–1 (continued)

Very / somewhat confident Medicare still will be available when they retire	39	24	18	47	35	64
Very / somewhat favorable view of Social Security program	55	46	40	60	50	78
Very / somewhat favorable view of Medicare program	60	55	45	60	59	79
Gender						
Male	49	36	45	55	51	53
Female	51	64	55	45	49	47
Mean Age	42	42	41	42	42	42
Median Income	$51,700	$22,300	$41,100	$59,300	$69,100	$49,500
Employment Status						
Full-time	78	62	77	78	82	78
Executive / Professional	22	16	15	18	29	23
White Collar	34	23	38	41	34	31
Blue Collar	40	57	43	37	34	43
Part-Time	11	10	11	12	11	10
Not Employed	9	25	9	7	5	9
Education						
High School grad or less	41	61	50	42	24	44
Some vocational / tech training	7	14	6	6	6	10
Some college (or 2 year degree)	23	15	22	20	27	21
College graduate or more	27	8	19	29	42	22
Marital Status						
Married	68	45	65	75	77	66
Divorced	16	26	19	11	12	17
Separated	3	9	2	1	2	3
Widowed	2	4	2	3	1	3
Single / never married	11	16	11	10	8	12
Race						
White	83	80	87	84	86	78
Black / African-American	12	15	8	12	9	17
Other	4	3	4	2	3	3
Hispanic Origin	7	5	6	4	6	10

Source: Prisuta and Takeuchi.
(http:11research.aarp.orglecon/boomerseg3.html, 1999)

5. The Enthusiasts, Self Reliants, and Today's Traditionalists, relative to the Strugglers and the Anxious, are less concerned about retirement. Relatively early financial planning is one reason for optimism with the Enthusiasts and Self Reliants. Planning for work in retirement is a reason for optimism with the Self Reliants and Today's Traditionalists.

6. Given that 80 percent of the boomers expect to be employed to some degree in retirement, for multiple reasons, a portion of their retirement years will redefine retirement.

7. The boomers represent a diverse, rather than unique, segment of the population about to enter retirement. The diversity reflects chronological age, financial resources, and expectations for retirement.

Chapter 7

CONCLUSIONS AND IDEAS

S uccessful aging, given the alternatives, should be of interest to us from individual and societal perspectives. Aging in the primary domains of the physical, psychological, and social is inevitable. These aging phenomena are interpreted in the context of genetic and environmental potentials and limitations. To date, there is no fountain of youth, spiritual experience, drug, or behavioral intervention that sustains physical, psychological or social life forever. On the other hand, much has been learned about prolonging both quality and length of life. As discussed earlier, the continued findings of inter- and intraindividual variability (differences) throughout the lifespan provide the best building blocks for successful aging. And, a good portion of these variabilities is related to one's (a) environmental history and (b) personal decision-making. The first of two concluding ideas will focus on societal interventions for successful aging. The second deals with personal responsibilities and decisions.

NATIONAL INSTITUTE ON AGING: STRATEGIC PLAN–2001–2005: A BASIS FOR POLICIES IMPACTING THE ELDERLY

Richard Hodes, Director of the National Institute of Aging (**http://www.nih.gov/nia/plan/directors message.htm**) (1999), recently shared a comprehensive draft strategic plan for research dealing with elderly issues. The strategic plan represents collaborative efforts of the National Institute on Aging, National Advisory Council on Aging, and other public and private organizations. The research priorities of the strategic plan are summarized, as these priorities reflect public and private concerns related specifically to elderly issues. With such a well-articulated set of research objectives for progressive dealings with issues of the aged, one hopes that power brokers for legislative policymaking take them seriously. Like the recent *The Berlin Aging Study: Aging from 70 to 100* (1999), the proposed research objectives of the National Institute on Aging clearly articulate an interdisciplinary framework for research, education, and practice concerning significant aging issues. The following information comes from Hodes' (1999) strategic plan for the National Institute on Aging. The four primary research goals are as follows:

1. Improve health and quality of life of older people.
2. Maintain health and function.
3. Enhance older adults' societal roles and interpersonal support, reduce social isolation.
4. Understand healthy aging processes.

1. Improve Health and Quality of Life of Older People. Improving the health and quality of life of seniors on meeting the following research objectives:

1.1. Prevent or reduce age-related diseases, disorders, and disability (subgoal 1). Aging research continues to focus on conditions significantly impacting mortality and disability. Alzheimer's disease, along with cardiovascular disease, cancer, bone/muscle/joint dysfunctions, vision, hearing, and other sensory dysfunctions will be focuses on interest and funding. Specifically, research agendas will deal with the following agendas:

1.1.a. Target research dealing with the causes and risk factors, as well as enhance early detection of chronic disabilities. Targeted research is for genetic contributions to normal and abnormal aging processes and longevity. Diagnostic endeavors to focus on include noninvasive measures of monitoring biological structures and processes.

1.1.b. With the knowledge of causal and risk factors for age-related disabilities, research focusing on intervention strategies for the delay of, progression for, and severity reduction of primary disabilities. These intervention strategies are at levels of genes, cells, tissues, organs, and behavioral.

1.1.c. Improve health behaviors and medication use. Research focus will be on specifying the advantages of exercise, diet, and other healthy lifestyle behaviors for preventive and remedial intervention. Concerning medications and the elderly, research objectives include the complexities of multiple prescribed and over-the-counter medications, long-term drug usage (singular and multiple drug use), and, as important, information and communication skills for physicians in monitoring drug usage.

1.1.d. Initiate clinical studies to improve health and reduce the burden of age-related diseases. Perhaps the most important addition to federally funded research agendas is that of an objective to ensure diversity clinical elderly samples.

1.1.e. Strengthen infrastructure and resources for clinical studies. In particular, new research needs to recognize (a) the phenomena of inter- and intraindividual diversities within the elderly population, as well noted demographic variables as categories of young-, middle-, and old-old, gender, ethnicity, socioeconomic status, education, and geographical areas of living. Specific guidelines to deal with these important factors include:

Changes in the design, planning, and implementation of clinical studies.
New drug testing facilities and resources better suited to include design features for a diverse elderly population.
Enhanced collaboration with the Veterans Administration Cooperative Studies Program, as well as other federally funded units with objectives serving the elderly.
Enhanced collaboration with the National Cancer Institute for the improvement of cancer therapies with seniors.

1.1.f. The following age-related research initiatives have been identified for funding: Alzheimer's disease and other degenerative nervous system diseases; memory impairment; primary geriatric concerns of frailty (weakness and falls), delirium (acute confusional state), urinary incompetence, sleep disorders, and depression; cardiovascular disease, cancer, and diabetes; bone, muscle, and joint disorders; vision, hearing, and other sensory disabilities; prostate diseases; and infectious diseases (with corresponding immune deficiencies).

1.2. Maintain Health and Function (subgoal 2). Initiatives being pursued include the following:

1.2.a. Understand declines in disability rates for older persons. Social, educational, public health, psychological and biomedical variables that relate to length of life, disabilities, and quality of life will be researched to sustain the current trend of more successful aging. Previous research has illustrated the effectiveness of increasing educational experiences, improving on health-related behaviors, improving on the availability and effectiveness of prosthetic devices, and improving on the medical treatments of acute and chronic illnesses. Based on findings of these relationships, interventions will be researched which may enhance successful aging.

1.2.b. Improve strategies for promoting healthy behaviors, such as:
Diet
Smoking and Alcohol Abuse
Safety
Exercise

1.2.c. Evaluate hormone replacement therapy and dietary supplements. Both the remedial and safety effects of such hormonal supplements as estrogen, testosterone, human growth hormone, melatonin, and DHEA (dehyroepiandrosterone) will be researched. Additional research is being done on the relationships of such vitamins as C and E to cancers, physical aging, and cognitive abilities.

1.2.d. Improve elder interaction with the health system. Research is proposed to improve the quality of care and communication among health care providers, the elderly, and their family members, with corollary suggested improvements in self-management, satisfaction of all involved, and health results.

1.2.e. Reduce caregiver and family stress and improve individual coping with chronic disease. Proposed research focusing on the needs and patterns of caregivers should delineate strategies for better skill training and communication, physical/psychological/social support, and services.

1.3. Enhance Older Adults/Societal Roles and Interpersonal Support, and Reduce Social Isolation (subgoal 3).

Social support, social networks, and involvement in meaningful activities are related to successful aging. Specific research objectives for these areas are:

1.3.a. Identify ways for older people to retain valued roles and maintain independence. Research will focus on the special resources of the elderly, with an emphasis on prolonging lives of independence, activity, and productivity.

1.3.b. Enhance family functioning. Future research on intergenerational family support factors will include changing needs of the elderly and their primary caregivers related to patterns of work, gender, marital status, income, savings, education, and ethnicity.

1.3.c. Reduce elder neglect and abuse. With isolated findings on neglect and abuse, future research will focus on assessment tools, prevalence, and intervention related to elderly abuse of caregivers.

1.3.d. Improve health care and long-term care. Further research is needed to clarify the relevant components of health care access for the elderly. For long-term care of the elderly, which remains a family responsibility, research is planned to assess the effectiveness of caregiving interventions in the areas of caregiving skills, environmental changes, and technological aids. Special emphasis will be given to health and long-term care of elderly with dementia and their family members.

1.3.e. Improve end-of-life care. Given the paucity of research in this area, upcoming research will focus on the following end-of-life care issues: (a) transitions of care situations (home, hospital, nursing home, hospice), improved measures to assess the quality of life at its ending (patient and family members), and social and economic issues relating to end-of-life care.

1.3.f. Enable elders and families to prepare for and cope with age-associated changes in health, income, and function. Ongoing research will deal with the interrelationships of such important issues for the elderly and their significant others as patterns of work and retirement, post-retirement income sources, transfers of income among intergenerational members, and health and disability costs/reimbursement sources.

2. Understand Healthy Aging Processes.

2.1. Unlock the secrets of aging, health and longevity (subgoal 1).
Research, primarily biological, will focus on the following objectives.

2.1.a. Identify factors that pace the aging process and slow the clock. A number of ongoing research projects, including the following, will deal with basic mechanisms of normal aging and age-related diseases:

Restriction of caloric intake with animals; such restriction is associated with increased longevity and reduced rates of diseases, like cancer.

Understanding the roles of telomeres (DNA segments on the ends of chromosomes) in the regulations of aging clocks in cells.

Clarifying the role of antioxidants like vitamins C, E, and beta-carotene, as well as enzymes, in defending against oxygen radicals destroying proteins, cell membranes, and DNA.

2.1.b. Define the biologic and environmental factors that maximize cognitive, sensory, and physical functions. Specific research programs include the following:

Specifying the effects of such hormones as the growth hormone, testosterone, and estrogen in the aging process, rates of hormonal decline and the aging process, and hormonal supplements.

Clarification of the age-related decline in the immune system with age, developmental relationships of the immune system and hormones, and effectiveness of interventions such as vaccines and other preventive techniques.

Identifying the complex relationships between lifestyles, personality attributes, and physical health; research examples include eating and medication habits, anxiety and stress, and these variable relationships with hormonal changes.

Delineation of age-related declines in sensory functioning as a function of lifestyle; research examples include smoking and hearing loss and cataract risk reduction related to use of plastic lenses or hats with brims.

2.1.c. Identify genes associated with aging, longevity, age-related diseases, and behavior. New research initiatives, including intervention possibilities, include the following:

Extend studies focusing on specific genes and genetic combinations associated with longevity and changes in genetic expression.

Identification of heritabilities (ratio of genetic to environmental influences) and related developmental profiles for complex abilities defining physical functioning, cognition, well-being, and social aging.

2.1.d. Identify social, psychological, and lifestyle facts that promote health, well being, and longevity.

2.1.e. Disassociate changes of normal or usual aging from those of diseases and disorders. Interesting research examples for such disassociation include the following:

Age-related changes in memory and early symptoms of Alzheimer's Disease.
Depression and "normal" elderly complaints of aches and pains, sleep disorders, sadness, and/or lack of energy.
Comorbidity of chronic disabilities.

2.2. Maintain and enhance brain function, cognition, and other behaviors (subgoal 2). To distinguish between normal and abnormal aging, as well as maintaining cognitive functioning and retarding dysfunction, the following research objectives will be pursued.

2.2.a. Characterize changes that occur with normal brain aging with neurodegenerative disorders.

2.2.b. Characterize normal cognitive and brain function with the oldest-old (elderly 85 years old and older).

2.2.c. Understand the interaction of gene, molecular, cellular, and environmental factors for optimal cognitive function.

2.2.d. Enhance learning, attention, memory, language skills, reasoning, judgment, decision-making, and other aspects of cognition.

3. Reduce Health Disparities among Older Persons and Populations. The third of four major National Institute on Aging research goals for the next five years deals with articulating the relationships of primary demographic variables and aging.

3.1. Increase active life expectancy and improve health status for older minority individuals (subgoal 1). In the next 50 years, the proportion of ethnic minorities among the elderly will increase dramatically. Significant differences exist among elderly ethnic groups that are associated with longevity, quality of life, and onset/duration of disabilities.

3.1.a. Analyze disease prevalence and course in minority populations and sub-populations. The prevalence of such diseases as cardiovascular, hypertension, diabetes, Alzheimer's, and certain types of cancers vary significantly among ethnic groups. Differences in rates of physical disabilities are likely to be related to such demographic variables as education, socioeconomic status, geographic location, and access to proper health care. Stress-related cognitive dysfunctions are also differentially detected among elderly ethnic groups. Future research will focus on identifying determinants of these differential rates of longevity, quality of life, and onset/duration of disabilities.

3.1.b. Increase inclusion of minorities/sub-populations in research. Since minority populations have been underrepresented in clinical research, outreach efforts, such as involving religious and community organizations, will be pursued.

3.1.c. Develop preventive and interventional strategies for healthy aging appropriate for diverse populations. Barriers in culture and language will be evaluated to enhance minority population interaction with health professionals, appropriate use of medication, and self-management with chronic disabilities.

3.1.d. Improve culturally appropriate health care delivery. Research is needed to improve (a) communication among elderly minority individuals, family members, and health care providers and professionals, as well as (b) reducing health care discrepancies based upon the ethnicity of the patient.

3.1.f. Develop strategies for information dissemination. Research will focus on health-related information dissemination for diverse minority populations and correlative language, cultural, and cultural differences.

3.1.e. Improve health behaviors and health promotion strategies. Targeted research includes (a) development of culturally appropriate diagnostic and health care services, and (b) enhancement health promotion with the elderly.

3.2. Understand health differences associated with race, ethnicity, gender, environment, socioeconomic status, geography, and culture (subgoal 2).

3.2.a. Study normal aging processes in special populations. While prevalence of diseases has been recorded for various ethnic populations, little is known about normal aging patterns for these ethnic populations. Future research will deal with ethnic patterns of normal aging, as well as differentiating patterns of normal aging among these populations.

3.2.b. Determine the effects of early life factors on adult health. Research will deal with differential early life influences on longevity, quality of life, and disabilities for minority populations.

3.2.c. Develop necessary data related to health differences and causes. To assess differential aging profiles among ethnic populations, national links among ongoing research programs dealing with ethnicity and aging need to be established; viz., Population Survey, National Health Survey, Survey of Income and Program Participation, Hispanic Established Population Epidemiologic Study of the Elderly, Health and Retirement Study, and the Assets and Health Dynamics of the Oldest-Old.

3.2.d. Promote clear and functional definitions of race, culture, and ethnicity.

3.2.e. Determine the relative influences of race, ethnicity, economic status, education, and work experiences in health. Longitudinal studies are promoted to differentiate the relative weightings of such effects on normal, pathological, and successful aging.

3.3. Monitor health, economic status, and life quality of elders and inform policy (subgoal 3). Minority elders, compared to white elders, illustrate the following:

Depend significantly more on Social Security
Receive much less financial support from private pensions
Receive even less financial support from accumulated assets
Rely much more on employment in old age

3.3.a. Study over time population changes and underlying causes of health and function of elders. Since significant risk factors for chronic diseases predate symptoms by a least 10 years, continued longitudinal research will track individuals from various ethnic groups through lengthy periods of time.

3.3.b. Provide information useful for policy. The Health and Retirement Study, using a longitudinal design with representative samples of ethnic groups, is concentrating on post-retirement, economic, and family variables relating to the health of the elderly. Findings assist public planning specialists and policymakers in establishing intervention programs affecting post-retirement, including health insurance and economic well being.

3.3.c. Produce data on burdens and costs of illness, healthy life expectancy, longevity, and mortality trajectories. Future research concentrating on health need projections for all ethnic groups will have to deal with the confounding design factors of insufficient data on disease rates, differing methodologies used in studies, assumptions about direct and indirect health care costs and differences among ethnic groups in access and use of health care systems.

3.3.d. Monitor population aging and the global burden of disease. Cross-cultural comparative research with more industrialized countries will focus on noninfectious diseases such as heart disease, hypertension, diabetes and cancer.

4. Enhance Resources to Support High Quality Research. The National Institute on Aging plans to develop an infrastructure which will enhance the following goals; viz., future research, program organization and management, and dissemination of information.

4.1. Attract and train a diverse workforce for research on aging (subgoal 1).

4.2. Develop and sustain a diverse National Institute on Aging workforce and a professional environment that supports and encourages excellence (subgoal 2).

4.3. Disseminate accurate and compelling information to the public, scientific colleagues, and health care professionals (subgoal 3).

In particular, the National Institute on Aging's Office of Communication and Public Liaison will expand its communications of research findings to both professionals and the public. Health information is available on the Institute's website (**http://www.nih.gov/nia/**) and can be obtained by calling 1-800-222-2225. For contemporary information about Alzheimer's Disease, one can visit the website **http://www.alzheimers.org/adear/** or call 1-800-438-4380.

4.4. Develop and distribute research resources (subgoal 4). These resources include the following:

Centralized aging colonies of animals
Cell cultures and tissue, cell and blood banks
DNA resources for genetics
Imaging technologies for bodily explorations
Computer technologies for basic biological research
Archived data
New methodologies and improved instrumentation and computational techniques for modeling age-related changes

INTERVENTION STRATEGIES FOR THE FUTURE: SOCIETAL ISSUES

Hodes' (1999) draft strategic plan for the National Institute on Aging provides a superb, albeit ambitious, agenda for the Institute. His strategic plan is also ambitious for policymakers, as the plan articulates many of the pressing needs of present and future elderly, as well as economic implications for the diverse American society. The National Institute on Aging proposes aggressive research, dissemination, and advocacy in the primary age-related domains of physical, psychological, and social aging. How well with the 2001–2005 National Institute of Aging objectives and products fare with competing federal, State, local, and private objectives? How effective has research and policy for the elderly been? On the one hand, Social Security, Medicare, Medicaid, and private pensions have made significant contributions to a better older age for many individuals. On the other hand, many older citizens have not received much support from these contributions. Also, many older and younger citizens do not take advantage of information which clearly substantiates the positive effects of personal intervention efforts to combat normative and nonnormative losses associated with physical, psychological, and social aging.

Federal, State, and local contributions to the elderly will continue to be made in relation to other, competing, significant public agendas. This reality has been termed intergenerational equity. While the transition of Baby Boomers to Aging Boomers will provide the elderly with more voices and votes, the economic health of a society provides the base for public contributions and expenditures to any and all entitlement programs. A similar argument, including a more direct emotional relationship, can be made for intergenerational familial contributions to and from the elderly. The economic states of a society, family, and individual, certainly in this extended historical period of materialism, correlate highly with the types and amounts of assistance provided to the elderly.

Even with progressive societal and personal engagements with the elderly, there remains the important factor of self-help or responsibility. With so many governmental entitlement programs available, albeit under scrutiny by politicians dealing with so many expressed societal needs and limited resources, a serious issue is whether or not enough individuals are willing to assume personal responsibilities for changes associated with aging. The physical, psychological, and social losses are many, including reduction of physical energy and reserve capacities, diminished sensory abilities, increased chronic physical disabilities, decline of cognitive fluid abilities (especially speed of processing information), restriction of social networks and people in those networks, reduction of fiscal resources, and increased exposure to stereotypes of the elderly. As discussed in Chapter 5, personal intervention for age-related changes can be remedial or preventive. Based upon what we know about aging in adulthood, what can be the future for personal intervention strategies?

INTERVENTION STRATEGIES FOR THE FUTURE: PERSONAL ISSUES

Older adult aging in the twenty-first century, at least the foreseeable years, can be more successful than the present and past. Important age-related "improvements" of the coming years include the following:

1. The Aging Boomers will significantly increase the proportion of seniors to the general population. Relatedly, as with the general

population, the senior age categories will include much more ethnic diversity. At a minimum, the significant increase in quantity of seniors will demand that more attention—societal and personal—be given to older adults.

2. In upcoming years, more seniors will retire at earlier ages and more Aging Boomers, relative to preceding generations, expect to be partially employed during retirement.

3. Advances in technologies related to physical, psychological, and social health, for all ages, will increase longevity and quality of life. These increases, as in the past, will most likely be discriminatory; e.g., individuals with more income and education will have greater access to technological advances.

4. Educational information about better aging, from physical health to financial alternatives, will be more prevalent; access to such information will be more available.

5. Aging Boomers, based upon present lifestyles, will be more involved in preventive intervention for physical, psychological, and social retirement years.

6. With longer lives and a better quality of physical life, future seniors will have more time and energy to find new meanings of life.

Rowe and Kahn (1998, pp. 48–52), articulated the following notions relevant to personal intervention strategies for the future:

> . . . Our view of successful aging is not built on the search for immortality and the fountain of youth. George Bernard Shaw, when he was in his nineties, was asked whether he had any advice for younger people. He did. 'Do not try to live forever,' said Shaw, 'you will not succeed.' Or, as psychologist Carol Ryff put it in a thoughtful article, 'Ponce de Leon missed the point.' In short, successful aging means just what it says—aging well, which is very different from not aging at all. The three main components of successful aging—avoiding disease and disability, maintaining mental and physical functioning, and continuing engagement with life—are important throughout life, but their realization in old age differs from that at early life stages. . . .

Avoiding Disease and Disability

> . . . Minimizing the risk of disease and disability is of lifelong importance, but some of the risks change with age and, therefore, so do the means for reducing them. For example, the time required to recover from infections and injuries increases markedly with age,

as does the possibility that either can cause death. Prevention and avoidance thus become increasingly important. The incidence of specific diseases also changes with age, and the presence of certain chronic diseases becomes more likely. Hypertension and diabetes are examples. Prevention requires increasing attention, therefore, to the symptoms and test results that precede the onset of the diseases themselves. . . .

Maintaining Mental and Physical Function

. . . Gradual decreases in physical reserve and maximum performance are not only age-related; they are to some extent age-determined. Some adaptation to that fact is therefore necessary. The eager downhill skier may convert to cross-country skiing, and at an increasingly sedate pace; the enthusiastic runner may become an equally enthusiastic jogger or walker . . .

The forms of appropriate exercise change with age, as does the intensity of exercise, but the need for it and the benefits it confers continue throughout life. The maintenance of cognitive function depends in part on physical well-being. Exercise . . . Has mental as well as physical benefits. Beyond that, maintenance of cognitive ability requires the continued use of the mind, continued engagement in complex cognitive activity. We know that people who perform jobs that require little thought and allow little independent judgment tend to lose intellectual flexibility, and also reduce the intellectual content of their leisure activities . . .

The special problem for older men and women, most of who are retired from employment, is that their retirement has deprived them of a major source of social and mental stimulation. The solution, of course, is for them to discover alternative sources of that stimulation, alternative ways of using their cognitive abilities. . . .

Continuing Engagement with Life

. . . Engagement with life, as we have seen, takes two main forms: maintaining relationships with other people, and performing activities that are, in the broadest sense, productive. For much of adult life, employment provides both, although often imperfectly.

The fact of earning money is evidence of productivity, and for many people, the job gives a more direct sense of meaningful productive contribution. Employment is also, almost always, a social activity; there are co-workers, some of whom become friends. Older people, after retiring from employment, must find appropriate substitute activities and must either find ways to maintain friendships that grew out of work, or replace them. . . .

Rowe and Kahn's (1998) suggestions, based upon the MacArthur Foundation longitudinal study for successful aging, fall within the familiar domains of physical, psychological, and social aging. The suggestions also focus on the responsibilities of the individual for successful aging. Both the domains and individual responsibilities for successful aging have a contemporary history in the work of Paul Baltes (Max Planck Institute, Center for Lifespan Development) and his colleagues (see Baltes, 1997). Baltes' eight principles of development (see Chapter 2) emphasize successful development and aging.

Interventional and Functional Abilities

Personal intervention strategies for successful aging, in the physical, psychological, and social domains, was articulated by Kemp and Mitchell's (1992) intervention model focusing on a continuum of functional abilities. Their model is summarized in this section.

First, Kemp and Mitchell shared these levels of functioning:
1. Organ system.
2. Physical fitness.
3. Activities of daily living.
4. Instrumental activities of daily living.
5. Skilled performance.
6. Social roles.

Second, for each of these levels of functioning, both examples and prerequisites were identified. *Physical systems*, including organ systems, were identified in earlier sections of *Successful Aging: Integrating Contemporary Ideas, Research Findings, and Intervention Strategies*, and include the cardiovascular, metabolic, muscular, neurological, respiratory, and skeletal. Prerequisites for maintaining adequate functioning of these physical systems include proper nutrition, general physical health, and physical, psychological, and social activity. *Physical fitness* includes such functional abilities as strength, endurance or stamina, multiple sensory-motor coordination, and physical reserve capabilities. Prerequisites for maintaining adequate physical fitness include the integrity of the physical systems (and related prerequisites) and motivation.

Activities of daily living, (ADL) basic functions for independent living, include the following, listed as questions (Groningen Activity Restrictions, Quadagno, 1999, p. 279):

Can you, fully independently, dress yourself?
Can you, fully independently, get in and out of bed?
Can you, fully independently, stand up from sitting in a chair?

Can you, fully independently, wash your face and hands?
Can you, fully independently, wash and dry your whole body?
Can you, fully independently, get on and off the toilet?
Can you, fully independently, feed yourself?
Can you, fully independently, go up and down the stairs?
Can you, fully independently, walk outdoors (if necessary with a cane)?
Can you, fully independently, take care of your feet and toenails?

Prerequisites for maintaining activities of daily living include adequate integrity of physical systems and physical fitness (and related prerequisites), as well as cognitive abilities such as memory and, at times, help from others.

The following list of *Instrumental activities of daily living* (IADL) is a summary from Spirduso (1995, pp. 347–348).

Functional Health Status
> Doing heavy work (e.g., snow shoveling); no physical
> illness or condition now; not limited in activities;
> able to walk a half a mile, climb stairs, and go outside
> the home to an event.

Instrumental Role Maintenance Scale
> Frequencies of meal preparations and shopping; distance
> shopping from home; laundry regime.

PACE II: IADLs
> Using telephone; dealing with money; securing
> personal items; tidying up; preparing meals.

OARS: Instrumental ADL
> Using telephone, shopping; personal transportation;
> preparing meals; housework; taking medicine; dealing
> with finances.

Functioning for Independent Living
> Vision, hearing, and speech; mobility; control of bowels
> and bladder; unconfused behavior; identity of self;
> ability to be understood; not wandering; conventional
> behavior.

Pilot Geriatric Arthritis Project Functional Status Measure
> Mobility (e.g., driving, shopping, walking, climbing stairs,
> and transfers from bed, chair, toilet, car); personal care
> items (e.g., telephoning, writing, personal hygiene, dressing);
> work items (employment, operating appliances, housekeeping;
> home cleaning and repair; yard work); unlocking padlock;
> opening door.

PGC Instrumental Activities of Daily Living
> Using telephone; shopping; food preparation; housekeeping/

laundry; public transportation; taking medication; dealing
with finances.
Performance Activities of Daily Living (PADLs)
Personal hygiene, eating behaviors; using household
appliances; dressing; using telephone, signing name; turning
key in lock; mobility.
Physical Performance Test (PPT)
Writing a sentence; eating behaviors; dexterity; dressing;
walking; climbing a flight of stairs.

While some of these IADL measures include items from ADLs, the former
measures focus on more coordinated and/or cognitive abilities. Kempen and
Suurmeijer's (1990, p. 499) provided the following list of 18 ADL and IADL
items, prioritized from least to most difficult:
Eating/drinking
Washing hands/face
Using the toilet
Arising from chair
Getting in/out of bed
Moving inside the house
Dressing
"Light" house-cleaning activities
Washing oneself completely
Preparing dinner
Moving outdoors on flat ground
Preparing breakfast/lunch
Bed making
Up/down stairs
Care of feet/nails
Shopping
Washing/ironing clothes
"Heavy" house-cleaning activities

The above detailed summaries of ADLs and IADLs were provided
because of focused interest of older adults in maintaining independent living.
With Kemp and Mitchell's (1992) continuum of functional levels, the
prerequisites for adequate instrumental activities of daily living include those
associated with physical systems, physical fitness, and activities of daily
living, as well as social interaction with others outside network of family and
friends.

Skilled performance, the fourth level of functioning, includes competence in fluid and crystallized cognitive abilities within the context of engagement with the worlds of employment/volunteerism, and, in general, active participation and contribution in prescribed work-related activities.

Finally, positive engagement in *social roles*, requiring adequate functioning in preceding levels, deals with competence in employment or volunteer obligations, relations with significant others, and an overall sense of well-being in personal and communal contexts.

Kemp and Mitchell's (1992) continuum of functional levels provides a useful framework for personal intervention with aging. First, their continuum makes it clear that the levels, from physical system to social roles, are interdependent. This interdependency is not only sequential or unilateral in nature; i.e., more complex levels dependent upon less complex ones. The interdependency is multidirectional in that competency in more complex levels of functioning maintains or enhances competency in less complex levels. The more one engages in reasonable skilled performance and social roles, the more demands are placed upon physical, psychological, and social abilities associated with physical systems and functions, and activities related to (independent) activities for daily living.

The second use of the continuum of functional levels model for the individual, significant other and health care provider is that of monitoring the older adult's abilities, and related performances, in each of the levels. The sooner significant declines in abilities for one or more levels of functioning are noted, the likely intervention will make a positive difference. Recalling the difference between personal versus more objective standards for competency in functioning, the role of significant others and health care providers in detecting significant functional loss of an older adult should be obvious. Early detection of loss in one or more domains of functioning allows for intervention actions directed to targeted loss in abilities and compensation with other abilities and functions. For example, muscle strength loss resulting in locomotion restriction can be dealt with by an appropriate exercise regimen (remedial intervention) or restriction of physical activities (compensation).

A third derivative of Kemp and Mitchell's functional levels model, particularly for adults in their 40s–60s, is a sense of balance among the functional levels. For example, middle-aged adults are more interested in competencies associated with skilled abilities and social roles, and less interested in competencies associated with physical systems and physical fitness. Yet, it is during these middle-adult years (and earlier stages of the lifespan) that attention to physical health and fitness provides the foundation for successful aging in the physical, psychological, and social domains. The senses of balance among, and competence in, these domains throughout the lifespan are probably the most important contributors to aging–normal, pathological, and successful. These senses, to be of optimal use to the individual in aging successfully, require standards of competent functioning based upon objective information. Relatedly, one's senses–personal under-standing–of functional balance in domains and competency in functions need to be buttressed with an appreciation of differential loss (timing and level) associated with aging. We develop (prenatal, infancy, childhood, and adolescence), mature or stabilize (young adulthood) and decline (middle and older adulthood) differentially, both within and across the physical, psycho-logical, and social domains. Realizing the phenomenon of differential aging in abilities and functions in these domains impacts our senses of balance among, and competence in, them. Individuals who do not understand or accept differential aging in abilities and functions are destined for both continued frustration and unsuccessful aging. For example, short-term memory loss is a fact of normal aging in adulthood. Adults who realize and accept this loss engage in compensatory memory actions such as rehearsal, association, or storing information via written or audio notes. Adults who do not realize or accept losses in short-term memory frequently forget or confuse information requiring competent short-term memory functioning. A very good example of short-term memory loss in adulthood is remembering, even for only the time it takes to dial a phone number just heard or viewed, the phone number.

Focused Personal Interventions for Successful Aging

Baltes and Baltes (1990) shared seven general strategies or principles of successful aging which provide a foundation for personal, focused inter-vention approaches to deal effectively with adulthood. These general strategies are directly related to the research and models of Baltes and his colleagues reported in earlier chapters, and, thus, should have evoked a sense of familiarity.

The *first* general strategy advocated by Baltes and Baltes is to engage in a healthy lifestyle, so as to reduce the probability of pathological aging. While pathological aging typically deals with chronic physical disabilities, engagement in a healthy lifestyle includes attention to physical, psycho-logical, and social domains. Successful aging, for most of us, is defined as maintenance of existing functioning–in the physical, psychological, and social domains–and/or avoidance of dysfunctions in one or more of the domains. This general strategy of successful aging advocated by Baltes and Baltes, however, suggests something more; viz., active engagement with one's self and the environment to promote maintenance of existing functions and/or avoidance of significant dysfunctions.

The *second* Baltes and Baltes general strategy, based on the notion of heterogeneity in the onset, direction, and diversity of aging, is that singular interventions for successful aging, should be avoided, be they personal or societal. Because of the complexity of aging (e.g., domains of aging and functions within and among domains) and associated causes of aging (including interactions among the determinants), progressive interventions are to be associated with flexibility or reserves of the individual (and society) among the physical, psychological, and social domains. Not only is there no single cure for everybody regarding all aspects of aging, there is not a single intervention for any aspect of aging that will benefit everyone to the same degree. With multiple interventions available, individuals need to be encouraged to select interventions which will optimize successful aging in general as opposed to optimization of restricted domains or functions of successful aging. The following example is, admittedly, trite:

> *Bill is a 55-year-old male who has had a personal history of successful aging in terms of the physical, psychological, and social domains. With no history of chronic disabilities he has, in the last year, had a life-threatening illness resulting in a chronic disability and separated from long-term professional and marriage commitments. Bill is financially secure and, with medication, physically healthy.*
>
> *He is also depressed. Bill's initial approach to reestablishing a successful aging profile was to optimize physical fitness and, relatedly, physical health. After three months of such focused attention, with secondary attention given to maintaining relationships with significant others, especially male friends, Bill remained depressed. His personal focus on physical health for successful aging was positively impacting his physical fitness and little else. A friend, engaged in Bill's physical fitness regime, suggested interventions in the psychological and social domains; meaningful engagements with spouse and children, lifelong learning pursuits, marriage and personal counseling, and work-related professionalism. Over the next six months, Bill actively pursued each of these meaningful engagements—personal interventions for him. As of this writing, Bill remains physically fit and physically healthy—physical domain. He is no longer clinically depressed, given reframed and more positive relations with spouse and children—psychological domain. Bill's return to active participation in serving others with his medical expertise has revitalized his psychological and social domains for successful aging.*

The *third* general strategy offered by Baltes and Baltes for successful aging focuses on expanding the individual's reserve capacities in the physical, psychological, and social domains. While it is true that older adults find it more difficult than younger people to learn new things and maintains functioning of physical, mental, and social systems, older adults are capable of increasing personal standards for almost all capabilities. Reserve capacities and related functions can be enhanced through motivation, education, and social engagement initiatives for positive change. ". . . The greater one's reserve capacities, be they physical, mental, or social reserves, the more likely successful aging will take place. This is also true because a larger reserve capacity facilitates the search for and creation of optimizing environments. . . ." (Baltes & Baltes, 1990, p. 20).

Baltes and Baltes' *fourth* general strategy for successful aging acknowledges limitations in reserve capacities and corresponding functions. The lifespans of a species and individuals are determined by biological, including genetic, and environmental factors which contribute to development, stability, and decline of physical, psychological, and social domain systems and functions. The *fifth* general strategy for successful aging offered by Baltes and Baltes deals with individual compensatory actions based upon advances in knowledge, including technological innovations. Although compensatory actions for losses in physical, psychological, and/or social domains at any stage in the lifespan aids successful aging, compensation becomes very important when, in the later stages of adulthood, losses accumulate and gains diminish. When, for the individual and society, does the imbalance of gains and losses, favoring losses, move the primary responsibility of care from the individual to the society, and to what degree? What is the relationship between limitations in one's reserve capacities and expanding upon them? Expanding one's physical, psychological, and social reserve capacities is based upon the following factors:

1. For each person, there are objective and subjective limits for reserve structural and functional capacities. Many objective limits are based on species and individual genetic codes and contextual factors such as family, ethnicity, socioeconomic status, education, and culture. While these objective limits are significant, they do not decrease the responsibility of the individual in establishing, maintaining, and elevating subjective standards (limits). At a conceptual level, the *range of reaction* principle for individual genetic unfolding (e.g., genotypic development expressed through phenotype or observable characteristic) illustrates the significance of contextual (including personal) factors influencing reserve capacities and functions. Each of us, regardless of state or stage of life, influences our present and future—in the physical, psychological, and social domains.
2. The reserve capacities in each of the lifespan domains interact with the others. Is it too much a stretch of our imagination to appreciate the possibility that enhancing reserve capacities and/or functions in one domain (e.g., physical) may contribute to enhanced reserve capacities and functions in the other domains? Enhancing reserve capacities in

the physical domain by stopping smoking, for example, can enhance one's self-efficacy (psychological domain) and, associated with both enhancements, increase the probability of meaningful relations with the majority of peers who do not smoke (social domain). Using the psychological domain as a starting point, actively pursuing lifelong interests, even in this era of the Internet, will result in more engagements with others (social domain) and require additional physical stamina (physical domain). Pursuing the social domain as a focus of expanding reserve capacities and functions, one's expansion of meaningful intergenerational familial relations (e.g., reaching out to grandchildren) requires many cognitive operations related to assessment of family member roles and expectations, as well as financial planning (psychological domain) and the physical energy to engage the grandchildren and adult children (physical domain).

The *sixth* and *seventh* general strategies offered by Baltes and Baltes for successful aging deal with the (a) progressively negative change in the gain/loss ratio in physical, psychological, and social functioning, and (b) continuation of resilience for self associated with older adulthood. Aging in older adulthood, particularly in advanced stages of the lifespan, is characterized by progressive losses in most systems and functions. Yet, for many individuals, these losses do not significantly retard the sense of resilience or self-efficacy. Many older adults with significant physical, psychological, and/or social dysfunctions consider themselves as aging more successfully than their peers. The central issues are (a) objective versus subjective standards of competence, (b) interventions for successful aging, and (c) maintaining a positive sense of self. These issues, articulated by Baltes and Baltes, call for compensatory actions leading to changing one's standards for physical, psychological, and social competencies.

The following aspects of intervention are shared with the notion of the reader providing specific examples and related objectives for focused interventions.

1. Learn more about the normative or usual changes associated with significant aspects of physical, psychological, and social aging. Although industrialized societies provide communication avenues and access related to aging issues, many adults, particularly those over 60, do not take advantage of readily available information. Present older adults are less likely to access contemporary aging-related information because of (a) cohort-specific information-seeking habits and, relatedly (b) technological advances in communication which older adults have not learned to deal with. Traditional communication avenues for aging issues are health-care providers, area agencies on aging, senior citizen centers, media (newspaper, magazine, radio, television), public and educational libraries, and, often overlooked, knowledgeable significant others. An important key to unlocking the mysteries of normal aging is the primary control strategy of actively seeking information, which, with advancing technology, requires learning new information-seeking skills. The less this primary control strategy is used, the more we accept individual losses (in the primary domains of the physical, psychological, and social) as being both normal and acceptable. If an older adult is unwilling to learn new skills related to accessing information via technologically advanced vehicles, such as the Internet, then he or she can optimize relations with significant others (such as children and grandchildren) for assistance in gathering information.

What are the general profiles of normal physical, psychological, and social aging? Specific age-related generalizations are provided in Chapters 2 and 4. General profiles of aging, related to personal intervention strategies, are perhaps best illustrated with the model of fluid mechanical and crystallized pragmatic abilities. Although this model focuses on age-related changes in cognitive abilities (psychological domain), it is not much of a stretch of the imagination to adapt the model in differentiating among aging profiles in the physical, psychological, and social domains. Fluid mechanical abilities, compared to crystallized pragmatic ones, are more directly related to maturation, stability, and deterioration (physical domain). Crystallized pragmatic abilities, though linked to physical systems and functions, are defined primarily as subject to contextual determinants (psychological and social domains). Applying the terminology of Baltes, Staudinger, and Lindenberger (1999), the three-component model of aging–physical, psychological, and social domains–is compressed into the two-component model of lifespan cognitive development–fluid mechanical and crystallized pragmatic abilities. This compression is made for the purpose of reflecting upon personal intervention strategies for successful aging.

Normative age-related profiles of adulthood are as follows; significant decline in fluid mechanical abilities, and stability and/or moderate decline in crystallized pragmatic abilities. In older adulthood (e.g., 70s), stability and/or moderate decline in crystallized abilities give way to significant decline, albeit differentially, depending upon abilities (intraindividual differences) and the individual (interindividual differences). Yet, Baltes, Staudinger, and Lindenberg's (1999, pp. 496, 497), recent summary of research on age-related changes in fluid mechanical abilities suggests a bit more optimistic view:

> . . . Here the review focuses on cognitive intervention work
> with older adults associated with the study of psychometric intelli-

gence and related tasks that are closer to the cognitive mechanics, such as tests of fluid intelligence.

The main results can be summarized in seven points:

(a) Training gains in the practiced tests among healthy adults are substantial (e.g., they roughly correspond to the amount of average 'natural' longitudinal decline between 50 and 70 years of age);

(b) transfer however, is limited to similar tests of the same ability;

(c) gains observed as a function of self-guided practice are of similar magnitude as gains resulting from tutor-guided practice;

(d) training gains are maintained over lengthy periods of time up to several years . . . ;

(e) the factor structure of the ability space is not altered substantially through training . . . ;

(f) the amount of training gain is substantially reduced as people reach advanced old age . . . ; and

(g) in persons at risk for Alzheimer's disease or afflicted by other forms of brain pathology, learning gains are substantially reduced . . . or nonexistent . . .

At limits of functioning and in advanced old age, older adults definitely display less potential for gains from training . . . These results indicate that cognitive plasticity in the mechanics of cognition is preserved among healthy older adults and is easily activated through experiential manipulations . . . Nevertheless, the general lack of transfer of training to related abilities or to everyday functioning suggests the hypothesis that performance improvements in tests of fluid intelligence primarily reflect changes in pragmatic components of performance potential, rather than improvements in the cognitive mechanics themselves. . . .

While the Baltes, Staudinger, and Lindenberger review dealt with cognitive abilities, the inclusion of fluid and crystallized abilities make for generic conclusions for the physical, psychological and social domains of aging. Personal initiatives can make a difference in dealing positively with losses associated with older age. Such initiatives, though, are made within the context of (a) domain, (b) type and magnitude of loss, (c) availability of compensatory abilities (in one or more domains), (d) limits of compensatory actions, and (e) one' sense of competency in meeting the challenges of loss.

As suggested by the review of Baltes, Staudinger, and Lindenberger, even the physical domain (e.g., fluid mechanical abilities) is subject to personal interventions, albeit with more limited effect than personal interventions in the psychological (e.g., crystallized pragmatic abilities) and social (e.g., social convoy) domains. Personal intervention strategies, be they preventive or remedial, are directly related to lifestyle decisions and corresponding actions. Examples of positive lifestyle actions—enhanced or compensatory—in the physical domain are annual health examinations, exercise (aerobic and strength training), proper medication for acute and chronic conditions, prosthetics for ambulatory, auditory, and visual dysfunctions, moderation with diet, drug use (including alcohol), and sustained stress, and *personal attention* to physical abilities associated with daily living. For the psychological domain, intervention examples are compensation for losses in fluid abilities (e.g., cognitive processing speed) with expert crystallized abilities (e.g., social intelligence and common sense), lifelong learning interests and prerequisite learning skills), and a positive sense of self (self-efficacy). Social domain personal interventions, like physical and psychological domain ones, are based on the individual's sense of self-efficacy; i.e., the sense of competency in setting and meeting personal standards for achievement.

Examples of personal interventions for the social domain are quantity and quality of networks with significant others, both maintenance of one's existing social convoy and development of new relationships. For both the psychological and social domains, the Mental Health Association of Southeastern Pennsylvania (**http://www.mhaging.org/help/recognize.html**, 2000, p. 1) offers the following list of questions that can assist the individual and/or significant others in considering whether or not a person needs professional help:

- Have I noticed a change in my behavior?
- Do I feel more disoriented, confused, or easily agitated than usual?
- Do I feel strong and repeated concerns about death dying?
- Have I not been taking my medication for mental health problems as prescribed?
- Do I find myself arguing a lot with my family and my neighbors?
- Do I find myself in a bad mood more than usual?
- Do I avoid being with people and feel anxious when I talk with people?
- Do I feel pains and aches that don't have any medical basis?
- Have I been drinking excessive amounts of alcohol or taking drugs?
- Do I have more trouble functioning in the community than in the past?
- Do I find myself wandering around not sure of what I am doing or where I am going?
- Have I not been eating or caring for my personal hygiene?
- Am I suspicious of others including my friends and family?
- Do I find no pleasure in doing things that I used to enjoy a great deal?
- Do I feel hopeless or worthless?
- Do I feel more nervous and worried than usual without any reason?
- Do I feel that it doesn't matter if I live or die?"

Antonucci's (1985) review of personal characteristics, social support, and social behavior, illustrates the positive effects of having social skills and advantages–part of a convoy of social support. While the convoy of social support notion emphasizes a lifespan frame of reference, the four key components are readily adaptable to all phases of adulthood. Antonucci's (pp. 99–101) review of the four components are summarized as follows:

> *Properties of the Person.* These properties include age, sex, income, marital status, and other demographic characteristics, personality, and abilities. Over the life course some characteristics (e.g., gender) will be stable, and others (e.g., age) will change. The majority of these personal properties, however, will vary idiosyncratically. Some people may have stable demographic characteristics, whereas others may experience considerable variability (e.g., the individual who is middle class throughout his or lifetime *vs.* an upwardly mobile counterpart who moves from lower to middle to upper class over a lifetime). . . .
>
> *Properties of the Situation.* Situational Properties involve more objective, externally-oriented aspects of the environment. Role expectations, opportunities, demands, resources, residence, organizational membership, and life events are examples of situational characteristics. They generally include the roles one occupies throughout one's life . . . Roles generally incorporate expectations, limitations, opportunities, and requirements, each of which may be influential in activating the Support Convoy. Additionally external factors such as place of residence, organizational membership and activity, both positive and negative life experiences, and geographical location (urban vs. rural) constitute Properties of the Situation for the individual . . .
>
> *Convoy Structure.* Convoy Structure refers to network composition over the life course. Among the structural characteristics most commonly assessed are size, connectedness, stability, symmetry, complexity, and homogeneity . . . Convoy Structure refers to network structure over the life course. Thus, the ways in which these properties change over time are thought to have significant impact on the person's perception of his/her Convoy and the operation of that Convoy . . .
>
> *Convoy Functions.* Convoy Functions are the actual support given, received, or exchanged by members of the Convoy. Also of importance to the understanding of Convoy Functions is the distribution of supports given, received, and reciprocated. Although research is only now beginning to address this issue, there is reason to believe that giving support only or receiving support only has a more negative effect on an individual than does exchanging of support . . .

Convoy Adequacy. All of the components considered thus far . . . Combine to determine the Adequacy of the Convoy . . . This aspect of the model has been interpreted as a subjective component; that is, whether the focal person perceives his or her network as adequate. Thus far we have measured Convoy Adequacy in terms of the individual's perception of the Convoy. If the individual reports that the Convoy is too demanding, not understanding, becoming less important, or consisting of too few people, these are assumed to be indications of Convoy Inadequacy . . .

Outcomes. It is our assumption that the individual's sense of Convoy Adequacy is directly related to and a determinant of individual well-being . . . Examples of broad categories of Outcome variables included productive behavior, role performance, self development, health, and overall well-being. Specific Outcome measures commonly employed include health satisfaction, life satisfaction, additional domains of satisfaction, happiness, positive and negative affect. These variables are known to be important indicators of life quality. . . .

Whereas the Catell-Horn model of fluid mechanical and crystallized pragmatic abilities readily incorporates age-related changes and interventions for the physical and psychological domains, Antonucci's Social Convoy model (a modification of one by Kahn and Antonucci,1980), clearly articulates age-related changes and interventions for the social domain.

2. Reflect more on changes to be made in the future and less on changes that could have been made. How many times have you reflected upon your life and, for one or more of the primary developmental domains—physical, psychological, social, wished for the chance to change a lifestyle pattern resulting in a long-term frustrating condition? The question does not deal with any particular situation or decision. Rather, the reflective question deals with lifestyle, patterns of behavior, habits (addictions) and optimizations of abilities and functions. The reflection-without-change habit develops early in life, certainly by adolescence. While most of us, frequently, contemplate changing behaviors that resulted in ongoing frustrations, most often we continue to engage in the behaviors. Sometimes, a traumatic event will jolt us into sustained efforts to change behaviors that have provided continued erosion of a positive sense of well-being. The addictive abuses are obvious; viz., alcohol, drugs, food consumption (especially food high in fats), and a sedentary lifestyle. Other abuses to successful aging are less obvious, such as severely restricted interests, limited networks of significant others, dependency on work (including housework and child-rearing), frustrating marriage, difficulty in dealing with stress, poor sense of humor, poor lifelong learning skills, and, in general, low self-efficacy. With the frustrations identified, why do we spend so much time thinking about the past and so little thinking about the future? Successful aging, in terms of quality of life, requires dealing with present and future, not past agendas, of physical, psychological, and social functioning that please and frustrate us.

Baum and Posluszny's (1999) review of biobehavioral contributions to health and illness relate directly to personal lifestyle changes impacting longevity and quality of life. The following points are selected summaries of their review:

Diet, Obesity, and Health

What people eat and how much they weigh are inherently behavioral processes. The fact that some people are able to maintain a normal or healthy weight while others become obese is almost certainly a result of behavioral and psychological factors working in concert with genetic and metabolic characteristics.

Increasingly, one's diet and weight have been implicated in a number of health problems or adult onset diseases, and weight management and nutritional risk management programs have become a standard part of wellness or health promotion campaigns . . .

Use of vitamin supplements, increasing consumption of fruits, vegetables, fiber, and moderation of consumption of animal fat are widely believed to predispose better health. . . .

Obesity and Cardiovascular Risk: Perhaps the clearest link between diet and health or disease outcomes are for cardiovascular disease, where fat and cholesterol intake as well as salt consumption, obesity, and weight gain have been implicated as major contributors to coronary artery disease, hypertension, and stroke . . .

Diet and Cancer: The literature on the impact of diet and overall weight on the etiology and progression of cancer is more speculative and difficult to evaluate than is research on diet and heart or vascular disease. Nonetheless, research suggests that careful dietary management may help to prevent or control cancers . . .

Stress and Diet: Stress is thought to affect diet and weight at different levels. Negative mood may lead people to eat more and may result in their seeking 'comfort foods' or foods that make them feel better. Most of these foods are relatively high in fat and salt or sugar, meaning that stress may increase consumption of less healthy fatty, salty, or sweet foods . . .

Exercise: Exercise appears to be important as a means of managing weight, managing stress, and modifying the impact of stress–or other–induced disequilibrium. Regular exercise alters endocrine activity, circulatory function, muscle tone, and a number of other aspects of physical functioning. As a result, some risks for disease may be altered . . .

Exercise and Cancer: Results of several large population studies of cancer risk indicate that exercise decreases the relative risk of developing cancer . . . Sedentary activities appear to increase the risk for colon cancer . . . , And evidence suggests that breast cancer and some reproductive cancers in women are negatively correlated with exercise history, although these findings are mixed . . . Adult weight gain also appears to contribute to risk for breast cancer . . .

Stress and Exercise: Evidence of psychological benefits of exercise would suggest another layer of influence on health; in addition to fitness benefits, exercise may be related to mood and to perceived stress. Some studies support these possibilities, an many suggest that regular exercise has psychological and emotional benefits . . .

Cigarette Smoking and Tobacco Use: Tobacco use is a primary cause of premature mortality and a modifiable risk for many debilitating or fatal diseases . . . Once tobacco use is established as a habit, it is highly resistant to change. Among tobacco users, the relief from withdrawal, appetite suppression, arousal, an sensation of well being associated with tobacco make it a very desirable behavior . . . Smoking and other forms of tobacco use are major contributors to heart disease, hypertension, stroke, cancer, and several serious diseases of the lungs and airways . . . Stress is one cause of tobacco use. Smoking and tobacco use appear to reduce stress or ameliorate its aversive effects . . .

Sun Protection and Skin Cancer Prevention: Another behavior associated with serious health consequences is sun exposure. The majority of skin cancers are caused by exposure to ultraviolet (UV) radiation and sunlight. Cumulative lifetime exposure to sun is associated with basal-cell and squamous-cell cancers. More serious melanomas are more likely to be associated with intermittent but intense exposure (infrequent or periodic sunburn). . . ." (pp. 147–152).

Kamimoto, Easton, Maurice, and Macera (1999, **http://www. cdc.gov.epo/mmwr/preview/mmwrhtml/ss4808a5.htm**) reported on surveys from the Behavioral Risk Factor Surveillance System (1994–1997) and the National Health Interview Survey (1993–1995). Lifestyle products studied were:

(a) being overweight,
(b) drinking and driving,
(c) inadequate fruit and vegetable consumption,
(d) smoking, and

(e) physical inactivity.

All of these lifestyle patterns are significantly related to the leading causes of morbidity and mortality among adults aged 65 and older. Obesity is a health risk among the elderly for cardiovascular diseases, cancer, diabetes, skeletal and muscular disabilities, and reduced self-efficacy. Reduction of excess body weight for seniors reduces health risks. The findings that older men are more overweight than older women should not be surprising; the findings that most older adults are overweight should be (ranging, geographically, from 53% to 72%). Drinking and driving does decrease with older adult age, with the highest percentages of such abusive behavior being in the 55–64 age range. The obvious health risk with drinking and driving is motor vehicle-related injury. For seniors, drinking and driving increased automobile collisions threefold. With increasing age, older adults report more daily consumption of fruits and vegetables, but the highest rates of consumption, relative to a national standard, were only in the range of 30–40 percent. The 5-A-Day national program advocates daily consumption greater to or equal to five servings of fruits and vegetables. Appropriate diets of fruits and vegetables are related to reduction of cardiovascular disease and some cancers, gastrointestinal tract dysfunctions, diverticular disease, and constipation.

The prevalence of leisure time physical inactivity increases with advancing age. Physical inactivity is associated with the following unsuccessful physical aspects of aging; reduced cardiovascular health–increased morbidity and mortality; poor weight management; and musculoskeletal problems such as bone loss and osteoporosis, loss of muscle mass and strength.

Smoking decreases with advancing age in adulthood, primarily because of selective attrition–smokers, in general, die at younger ages than nonsmokers. Yet, older smokers are at greater risk than younger smokers in terms of timely morbidity and mortality. Older smokers, relative to younger ones, have smoked longer and have more smoking-related chronic diseases. Smokers, relative to nonsmokers, have higher risks for chronic disabilities such as cardiovascular and respiratory diseases and cancer. Long-term smokers relative to short-term smokers are at elevated risk for these chronic disabilities.

Kamimoto, Easton, Maurice, Huston, and Macera (1999, pp. 9,10) conclude their summary as follows:

> Prevalence of the five health risks discussed . . . are affected by aging processes, including survival bias (i.e., persons with healthier life practices outliving those with less healthy lifestyles). In this

report, the prevalence of drinking and driving, overweight, and smoking decreased with increasing age; the prevalence of fruit and vegetable consumption increased with advancing age. These trends might be associated with a combination of changes in behavior as age increases and with survival bias. However, physical inactivity increased with advancing age, and this finding most likely reflects the greater prevalence of chronic diseases and disability that are also associated with increasing age . . .

Overweight, drinking and driving, inadequate fruit and vegetable consumption, physical inactivity, and smoking are associated with the development of many diseases and injuries. Some diseases are strongly associated with a particular health risk (e.g., lung cancer's association with cigarette smoking); other disease etiologies are multifactorial, with each health risk contributing additional risk of disease occurrence (e.g., the combined effects of smoking, physical inactivity, excess bodyweight, and poor diet on cardiovascular disease). This multifactorial nature can result in confounding of one health risk by another because persons who have one health risk are more likely to have another. In addition, interventions to modify one health risk can effectively reduce another (e.g., increasing physical activity can result in loss of excess weight). . . .

Smoking (including tobacco use), obesity, drug (including alcohol) abuse, a sedentary lifestyle, and prolonged, elevated stress are five major contributors to unsuccessful, if not pathological, physical aging subject to personal primary control. The primary control can be illustrated with either preventive or remedial interventions. One's genome or genetic inheritance does set limits or ranges for phenotypic reactions; e.g., longevity and chronic diseases associated with normal aging have genetic determinants. Yet, an individual's lifestyle, reflecting daily decisions and actions, contributes significantly to genetic ranges of reactions for phenotypes. In fact, after conception, environmental determinants, including one's lifestyle, are all that is available to manipulate one's genetic contribution to physical, psychological, and social aging. In the physical and psychological domains, much is known about genetic predisposition and environmental moderating effects (see Bengtson & Schaie, 1999; Birren, 1996). Although there are few equivocal behavioral genetic findings for complex physical, psychological, and social aging, one is that most genetic ranges of reaction are subject to environmental factors; i.e., genetic influences are subject to environmental ones and vice versa.

One's lifestyle contributes significantly to onset, severity, and duration of chronic diseases associated with normal and pathological physical aging. The earlier the adoption of one the big five negative contributors to the lifespan, the greater the likelihood of nonnormal onset of chronic conditions. The more big five negative contributors adopted the greater the likelihood of multiple chronic disabilities and shortened lifespan.

Especially with long-term habits and addictions, personal interventions must include an acceptance of dependencies in the physical, psychological, and/or social domains. Each of the big five negative contributors has a physical presence in terms of biochemical and physiological functions. Each has a psychological presence in terms of one's sense of self. Since long-term habits and addictions are reinforced in a social context, smoking, obesity, drug misuse, a sedentary lifestyle, and prolonged, elevated stress have a social presence. Few individuals, even very old ones, are or were, physically, psychologically, or socially isolated from others, including significant others. As suggested by Baum and Poslyszny (1999), successful and unsuccessful personal lifestyles are reinforced by the individual and, albeit with personal interpretation and action, his/her external environment.

With the big five negative influences—smoking, obesity, drugs, sedentary lifestyle, and stress, both the individual and his/her significant others contribute to continuation of bad habits. Before adulthood, we have learned to accept those we care about (significant others). Most likely, our reluctance to intervene with unsuccessful aging lifestyles of those we care for is based upon (a) our own balance of successes and failures, (b) acceptance of significant others, with their strengths and weaknesses, and (c) fear of jeopardizing the relationship. More distal external reinforcers for unsuccessful aging, as related to the big five negative contributors, are often associated with marketing practices. Although tobacco use advertisements have become more limited, in terms of advertisement avenues, the messages still reflect youth, vitality, and pleasure. For obesity and other dietary problems, think of commercials for MacDonalds and most other fast-food companies. Drug use marketing for prescribed and over-the-counter medications, like those for cosmetics, focus on pharmaceutical wonders and/or life enhancement via product usage.

One extreme of drug marketing, that of prescribed medications based upon clinical research and development, has positive impact for successful aging. Both longevity and quality of life are significantly influenced by appropriate prescribed medications for acute and chronic physical and mental conditions. At the other extreme of drug marketing, beer commercials for example, little is shared concerning the research and development results for successful aging. While moderate use of alcohol may result in longer life, drug dependency of the older (and younger) alcohol-dependent person is reinforced by alcoholic beverage advertisements and society's acceptance of alcohol use by adults. A sedentary lifestyle for older adults has been reinforced through marketing efforts, albeit less so as the Aging Boomers approach retirement. The marketing for older adult sedentary lifestyle is much more indirect than marketing efforts noted above. Most commercial television, for example, still exemplifies youth (including young and middle adulthood). When older adults are included in programs, they are often portrayed as much more sedentary than younger persons. As damaging to dynamic aging is the relatively recent phenomenon on television. Television viewing is part of a sedentary lifestyle! Finally, prolonged, elevated stress for older (and younger) adults is also promoted by private enterprise focusing on fast-paced, extended lifestyles.

One of the most stressful marketing agendas these days is that of telephone solicitations. Relatedly, the elderly may be more vulnerable to unscrupulous or criminal scams delivered via the media, Internet, mail, or person. Perhaps the best known of current unscrupulous scams is that of the magazine sweepstakes. Atchley (2000) identified the following reasons why the elderly are vulnerable to economic exploitation:

1. Most elderly are on fixed, asset-generating income, they are susceptible to ploys suggesting a high return on investments.
2. Loneliness and isolation of many elderly make them more susceptible to someone who illustrates interest in, and caring for, them.
3. More elderly, relative to younger adults, have serious, if not hopeless, illnesses, which makes the older adult more susceptible to both pain relief and cure scams.

A fourth reason why the elderly are more susceptible to economic exploitation is that of more limited cognitive processing speed. Poor cognitive processing speed can be a distinct liability when confronted with an unscrupulous salesperson who presents deals, and seeks closure, in a rapid-fire delivery. Atchley (2000, pp. 470–473), noted that 90 percent of confidence scheme victims are senior citizens. He provided the following examples of such victimization:

> *1. The American Continental Corporation-Lincoln Savings and Loan Association Scandal* ... Lincoln Savings and Loan, a federally insured thrift institution, was owned by a holding company, American Continental Corporation. In 1987, financially troubled American Continental began an aggressive campaign of selling high-risk "junk" bonds through sales agents located in branch offices of Lincoln Savings and Loan. Lincoln employees were told to place first priority on directing depositors to the bond salespeople. Depositors assumed that since they were in a federally insured institution, what they were sold there was federally insured.

Purchasers could even have the interest from the bonds deposited directly into their Lincoln Savings passbook accounts, and the monthly statements they received showed the activity in both their Lincoln Savings accounts and the American Continental bond accounts. If asked, sales agents told bond purchasers that their investment was highly secure and federally insured and that they could redeem the bonds at any time. These statements were false. The bonds were highly speculative, they were not insured, and they could be redeemed only upon the death of the purchaser . . . This campaign was directed mainly at older clients. Indeed, 79 percent of the people who were sold these junk bonds and who subsequently lost their entire investment were age 50 or over . . . (p. 471)

2. Investment Property Scams . . . In these scams, promoters buy large tracts of cheap, often swampy, land in Florida or desert in Arizona and carve the property up into the smallest parcels allowable. Beautiful brochures and advertisements in newspapers and magazines promote the land as an investment for resale later at a profit or as a place for a retirement home. Lots are usually sold on installment contracts, and no deed is recorded until the contract is paid off. Most contracts stipulate that the property reverts to the seller if the buyer misses one or two payments, and the seller is not required to notify the buyer that he or she is delinquent. Many of these lots are sold over and over again, year after year, as buyers stop their monthly payments for any number of reasons—they die, come upon hard times, see the land and realize that their "investment" is worthless, and so on . . . (p. 472)

3. Pre-need Funeral Scams . . . People have been sold "complete burial service" for thousands of dollars, and all the survivors receive (if they are lucky) is a cheap casket. People have been sold crypts in nonexistent mausoleums and burial plots in cemeteries that exist only on paper. This type of deception thrives on the deep-seated desire of many older people to take care of burial arrangements ahead of time, to make things easier for their relatives . . . (p. 472)

4. Bank Examiner Scams . . . A person posing as a bank examiner calls on the intended victim and explains that one of the bank employees is suspected of embezzlement but that unfortunately the bank officials have been unable to catch the employee in the act. The "examiner" asks the victim to go to the bank and withdraw all of his or her savings, to thereby force the suspect in the bank to alter account books and the bank would then "have the goods" on the employee . . . (p. 472). The end of the saga leaves the victim without his or her money.

5. *House Repair Scams* . . . Home repair scams are also common. Elders are sold "driveway sealer" made of used motor oil, unneeded furnace repairs suggested by a "city inspector," carpet that disintegrates, and so on . . . (p. 472)

6. *Medical Scams* . . . Medical swindles and quackery represent a particularly vicious hazard to older people. Arthritis is a good case in point. Millions of elders suffer from arthritis. Many find themselves on mailing lists or organizations offering a wide range of useless treatments. And because they are desperate to escape the constant pain of arthritis, many elders are relieved of their money but not their suffering. . . . (p. 473)

Related alternative medical solicitations are readily available for elders (as well as the younger) with life-threatening illnesses such as cancer, diabetes, cardiovascular diseases, and lung diseases. As noted above, a primary reason why the elderly are so susceptible to the above economic exploitation is their diminished cognitive capabilities (capacity and strategy use) related to processing information within a limited period of objective and personal time.

3. Realize that successful aging requires age-related competencies and compensations in all three domains of development–physical, psychological, and social. Few, if any, individuals are able to maintain objective standards of competence in all these areas, even before later adulthood. Almost all individuals, however, are able to compensate for losses in abilities and functions in all three domains. The better one's functioning in any one of these domains, the greater the likelihood of functioning in the other domains. The less one functions in any one of the domains, the greater the likelihood of poorer functioning in the other domains. Recall Rowe and Kahn's (1998) advice, based upon the McArthur longitudinal study; viz., dysfunctional or unsuccessful aging is the result of: (a) impact of chronic disease or disability (which includes psychological dysfunctions), (b) negative lifestyle factors (such as poor diet, ineffective physical and mental exercises, bad habits, and poor socialization skills), and (c) normal biological changes of advancement through the lifespan. Since the physical, psychological, and social domains influence one another, an important task for focused intervention is that of coping with losses, in one or more domains, and compensatory gains in these domains. Fries' (1991, p. 35) concept of morbidity compression is useful in illustrating this third aspect of focused personal intervention among the three domains:

... Successful aging, viewed from a medical or public viewpoint, consists of optimizing life expectancy while at the same time minimizing physical, psychological, and social morbidity, overwhelmingly concentrated in the final years of life. Thus, the achievement of successful aging requires that the age of onset of infirmity, on average, increase more rapidly than the average life expectancy, compressing morbidity into a shorter period ...

... The basic syllogism of the compression of morbidity is that because the age of first chronic infirmity can be postponed but the life span itself is genetically fixed, the period of infirmity can be shortened. In more complete formulation, the theorem holds that (a) if morbidity may be defined as that period from the onset of the first irreversible chronic disease or aging marker until death, (b) if the date of occurrence of that marker can be postponed until later in life, and (c) if the rate of such postponement can be greater than the rate of increase in adult life expectancy, then (d) morbidity for the average person can be compressed into a shorter period of time. ... (p. 36)

One aspect of Fries' morbidity compression formulation is that focused individual intervention to precursors of chronic dysfunctions and subsequent dysfunctions, can both prolong life and enhance quality of life. That is, the earlier one deals with lifestyle conditions detrimental to successful aging, the greater the opportunities for enhancing longevity and quality of life. Another aspect of Fries' formulation is that personal attention to physical, psychological, and social aspects of aging–the sooner the better–provides opportunities for maximizing successful aging with interventions in all domains of aging. Even focused personal intervention within one domain, as noted by Kamimoto, Easton, Maurice, Husten, and Macera (1999), can have positive effects for successful aging within and among the physical, psychological, and social domains.

At the general or model level, Baltes, Staudinger, and Lindenberger (1999) articulated the lifespan model of selective optimization with compensation. Their model, related to one's projection for successful aging, is presented in Figure 7–1.

The major concepts of this model for successful aging were presented in Chapter 4. For the Antecedent Conditions and Orchestrating Processes defined in Figure 7–1, successful aging is possible within limits–limits of the individual (one's heredity and environmental encounters) and the broader context of societies. These limits, however, continue to be subject to expansion, for the person and societies. Since we live within the limited context of our existing reality, reflecting antecedent and present conditions impacting us, individual aging is our responsibility. In the later phases of the lifespan, most often defined (objectively, and by the individual), in terms of chronological age, one's plasticity (reserve capacities) is much more limited than in earlier stages of adulthood. Given that the interrelated aging domains of the physical, psychological, and social best define longevity and quality of life, the more successful (and wiser?) aging person (a) recognizes his/her relative gains/losses/plasticity in each of the domains, and (b) focuses, relatively, on the gains and reserve capacities. Such focus, as presented in Chapter 4, often results in compensatory action for some losses in one or more of the aging domains. Relativity is an important ingredient, as losses in the physical, psychological, and social domains are subject to a faster or slower rate of decline based upon both (a) continued use of diminished abilities and (b) enhanced use of optimal abilities to compensate for related diminished ones.

Orchestrating Processes include Selection, Optimization, and Compensation. Each of these components of successful aging were discussed in Chapter 4 (Baltes, Staudinger, and Lindenberger (1999, pp. 484–486) offered additional insight into these components.

Selection. "Selection involves directionality, goals, and outcomes. Strictly speaking, selection already begins in embryonic development. For instance, neurophysiological processing of information represents fundamental example of selection and selection-based specialization. . . ." Other early life fundamental examples, based upon the selective process of heredity, include the impact of recessive gene effects (e.g., blue eyes) and, much more likely,

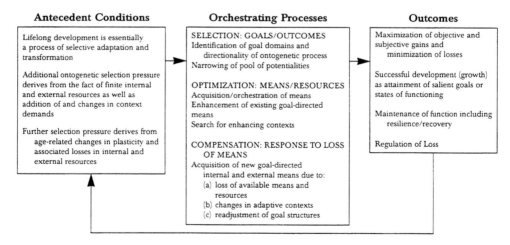

Figure 7–1. The lifespan model of selective optimization with compensation. The essentials of the model are proposed to be universal, but specific phenotypic manifestations will vary by domain, individual, sociocultural context, and theoretical perspective (adapted from P.B. Baltes 1987, 1997, P.B. Baltes and Baltes 1990, Marsiske et al. 1995). Source: Baltes, Staudinger, and Lindenberger (1999). Reprinted with permission.

multiple gene effects (sex, race, intelligence). ". . . During ontogeny, there are several additional sources for selection. First is the goal and outcome orientation of development. Individuals and societies sample from a population of possibilities or opportunities and evolve specific articulations and differentiations of goal structures. . . ."

At both the personal and communal levels, decisions are made which positively reinforce perceived gains and negatively reinforce perceived losses. ". . . A second source is limited individual capacity in terms of time and resources . . ." For every stage of development, the individual has limited abilities (based upon genetic and environmental determinants), which are expressed within (a) real time and (b) personal actions within real time. The principles of maturation and deterioration (or gains and losses) illustrate limited individual capacity. During maturation, for example, the individual is limited because of incomplete physical structures and functions, which limit optimal learning. With deterioration of physical structures and functions, starting in adulthood, optimal learning is also limited. Another example of limited capacity and time is the developmental profiles of fluid mechanical and crystallized pragmatic abilities (see Chapter 4). ". . . The third source is the incompatibility of goals and outcomes. . ." Throughout the lifespan, we make choices (selections) related to our short- and long-term goals. Often, choices and corresponding actions related to certain objectives (potential gain) result in conflict with other existing or potential objectives. For example, individual exercise regiments typically focus on singular activities, such as running, bicycling, swimming, or weight lifting. Since a particular regiment, for most individuals, is long-term, alternative exercise regiments are thought to be incompatible with one's physical fitness habit.

Since humans are creatures of habit (or reinforcement contingencies), a reasonable point is that with every habit or preferred lifestyle activity comes incompatibility with a multitude of actions. Another reasonable point is that the more ingrained the habit, the less likely other habits will be adapted. ". . . A fourth source is age-related changes in plasticity or basic potential . . ." This source of selection is similar to the deterioration or loss aspect of limited capacity and time (source two above).

> *Optimization.* ". . . The focus of optimization is on the acquisition, refinement, and maintenance of means or resources that are effective in achieving desirable outcomes and avoiding undesirable ones . . . Optimization requires a mutually enhancing coalition of factors, including health, environmental, and psychological conditions such as goal investment and goal pursuit. . . ."

Optimization may be the key of preventive intervention in Baltes' model of successful aging, as optimizing selected capabilities in the physical, psychological, and social domains requires lifestyle patterns earlier, rather than later, in the lifespan. Such optimization, as noted by Baltes, Staudinger, and Lindenberger (1999), enhances one's reserve capacity or plasticity. A caution is that optimizing a narrow band of capabilities (in one or all the developmental domains) throughout the much of the lifespan results in restricted selection of other capabilities. For older couples who have invested much of their meaning of life in a successful marriage, for example, the death of one partner often results in irreparable loss for the other. Remember the adage, "don't put all your eggs in one basket." The example does not imply that marriage partners (old or young) seek multiple intimate love relationships! Rather, for successful aging it suggests more, rather than few, personal strengths in the physical, psychological, and social domains.

> *Compensation.* "Compensation involves a functional response to the loss of an outcome-relevant means . . . There are two major functional categories of compensation. The first is to enlist new means as strategies of compensation to reach the same goal. The second compensatory strategy concerns means to change goals of development in response to loss of goal-relevant means . . . Three main causes give rise to a compensatory situation . . . A first is conditioned by the very fact of selection and optimization. Because time and effort have limits, selection of and optimization toward a given goal can imply the loss of means relevant for the pursuit of other goals. Negative transfer from the acquisition of one expert skill system to another is another possible result of selection and optimization . . . A second category of causes of compensation stems from environment-associated changes in resources. Changing from one environment to another may involve a loss in environment-based resources (means) or may make some acquire personal means dysfunctional. The third category of causes resulting in a situation of compensation are losses in means due to age-associated declines in plasticity associated with the biology of aging and the lifespan structure of opportunities that, for instance, is less developed for later life. . . ."

Compensatory actions, regardless of age, are remedial in nature, as suggested in the three categories of compensation summarized above. Issues of intrigue, related to these three compensation categories are (a) significant delay in positive lifestyle changes (i.e., compensation) to a major loss, and (b) cumulative effects of such delay with successive losses in one or more of the developmental domains.

Most often, we "live with" the erosion of capabilities associated with advancing age in adulthood until a significant capability is personally evaluated as seriously diminished. While many individuals facing this age-related phenomenon attempt, at least initially, some remediation (compensation) to combat the focused decline, few realize the cumulative effects of age-related declines in all developmental areas. Successful aging for the majority of older individuals requires compensatory actions in all three developmental domains—physical, psychological, and social.

In a number of publications, Baltes and associates (e.g.,Baltes, Staudinger, and Lindenberger, 1999), illustrate the coordination among selection, optimization, and compensation with famous concert pianist Arthur Rubinstein. When an interviewer asked Rubinstein, when he was over 80 years old, how he was able to maintain internationally recognized expertise, Rubinstein responded that he no longer played as many pieces (selection). Those he continued to play were practiced more (optimization), and he played slower musical segments prior to fast segments, making the faster segments appear faster than real. His orchestration of selection, optimization, and compensation for continued expertise with the piano is associated with the psychological domain. Given Rubinstein's professional and social significant others, one may assume that he maintained a good social convoy even in old age. But, what about his physical domain? What compensations were made in this domain to allow him to continue performing? Did those compensations relate positively and/or negatively to his psychological and social domains?

The *Outcomes* summarized in Figure 7.1 emphasize successful aging, a hallmark of the Baltes model of lifespan development. An important aspect of successful aging, suggested in Figure 7.1, is the (a) interrelationships among *antecedent conditions, orchestrating processes and outcomes,* and (b) personal responsibility for positive lifestyle changes. Personal responsibility for positive lifestyles and changes is much easier to conceptualize than practice. As noted earlier in this book, preventive strategies for successful aging are not readily adopted by those younger folks who are most vulnerable to unsuccessful aging. Later in life, remedial strategies requiring personal intervention are also not readily adopted by those most vulnerable. One primary reason for such states is the technological advances in both medical and governmental interventions. These advances have, to some degree, eroded one's sense of responsibility in initiating lifestyle changes for successful aging outcomes.

4. Accept the fact that it is never too late for focused personal intervention. While this book promotes personal preventive strategies for successful aging, remedial strategies (a) are more typical and (b) are effective. In the physical domain, a recent summary of research from the

Administration on Aging (**http://www.aoa.eldactn/fit/fact.html**, 2000) highlighting fitness facts for older adults, illustrates the fourth personal intervention suggestion.

1. The sage advice to "take it easy, you are not as young as you used to be" does not fit with contemporary research findings. Yet, many older adults follow the advice. . . . Surveys show that only 30 percent of Americans aged 45 to 64 exercise regularly, while 32 percent of adults 65 and older follow a regular plan of exercise. We now know that the human body repairs itself and performs more efficiently with proper conditioning that is achieved through a program of regular exercise and good nutrition. This is particularly true for the musculoskeletal and the cardiovascular- pulmonary system . . . With exercise, our bones . . . rebuild and repair themselves . . . Without exercise, they tend to become thin and porous—a condition known as osteoporosis. When we do not exercise, fat displaces muscle, muscles become smaller and weaker—a process known as atrophy, and we gain weight more easily because even at rest muscles burn more calories than does fat. Added weight puts added stress on our heart and lungs, and on the weight bearing joints of the knees, hips, ankles, and feet . . . When you exercise, however, you help to reduce fat tissue, while building muscle and bone. Muscle is heavier than fat but takes up half the space, so you can actually reduce your body measurements without losing weight. Strong muscles help to protect your joints and spinal column, improve your posture and balance, increase your mobility, and reduce the likelihood of falls and other accidents, and give you a younger body image. . . .

Older adults tend to also "take it easy" in the psychological and social domains, though, as with the physical domain, succeeding retirement cohorts are less likely to do so during the early phases of later adulthood. The expectations, societal and personal, are for older adults to reframe lifestyles, especially those related to employment and sustained focused expertise. For many older adults, the dilemma is one of transferring focused abilities to new objectives (gains) or accepting loses without new or refurbished agendas.

2. Contemporary research supports the sage advice, " an ounce of prevention is worth a pound of cure." Such research also promotes personal exercise routines that include the following: (a) weight training for strength and balance (e.g., weight lifting or resistance training), (b) aerobic training for strength and endurance (e.g., walking, swimming, bicycling), and (c) calisthenics for flexibility (e.g., stretching, bending, twisting). Even at advanced age, individuals are able to enhance endurance, strength, balance, and flexibility (see *Exercise: A Guide From*

the National Institute on Aging, 2000; Pratt, 1999). The following summary of general advantages of exercise for seniors comes from *Exercise: A Guide From the National Institute on Aging* (2000, p. 1):

> . . . Only about 1 in 4 older adults exercises regularly. Many older people think they are too old or too frail to exercise. . . . Researchers now know that:
>
> • Regular, active exercise such as swimming and running, raises your heart rate and may greatly reduce stiffening of the arteries. Stiff arteries are a major cause of high blood pressure, which can lead to heart disease and stroke.
> • People who are physically active are less likely to develop adult onset diabetes, or they can control it better if they do have it. Exercise increases the body's ability to control the blood glucose level.
> • Regular activity, such as walking and gardening, may lower the risk of severe intestinal bleeding in later life by almost half.
> • Strength training, like lifting weights or exercising against resistance, can make bones stronger, improve balance, and increase muscle strength and mass. This can prevent or slow bone-weakening osteoporosis, and may lower the risk of falls, which can cause hip fractures and other injuries.
> • Strength training can lessen arthritis pain. It doesn't cure arthritis, but stronger muscles may ease the strain and therefore the pain.
> • Light exercise may be good for your mental health. . . .

Preventive intervention strategies for successful aging have been advocated in *Successful Aging* for the psychological and social domains, as well as the physical domain. Much of the previous summaries of the creative work of Baltes and associates focused on preventive strategies for successful aging in the context of psychological and social aging.

3. The last piece of advice summarized by the Administration on Aging, *Elder Action: Action Ideas for Older Americans and Their Families* (**http://www.aoa.gov/aoa/eldractn/fitfact.html**) is "if you don't use it, you'll lose it." From the late 1980s onward, research has demonstrated that older adults are able to increase muscle mass and strength. Weight training in older adulthood is beneficial to successful aging, just as are aerobic, balance, and flexibility exercises. Weight training increases muscle mass, strengthens muscles, bones, ligaments, and tendons, and increases metabolism (for weight and blood sugar control). Aerobic or endurance exercises strengthen bones, muscles, ligaments, and tendons; these exercises also enhance the cardiovascular and respiratory systems

e.g., retarding both atherosclerosis (plaque buildup in veins and arteries) and arteriosclerosis (hardening of the arteries). Endurance exercises increase breathing and heart rates, metabolism, and stamina. Flexibility or stretching exercises contribute to a more limber, flexible body by stretching muscles, ligaments, and tendons, as well as moving bodily organs. Balance exercises, which are part of resistance, aerobic, and stretching exercises, stimulate both neurological and musculoskeletal systems for bodily stability and orientation.

Older adults are also able to use personal and contextual resources for enhanced psychological and social aging. Psychological well-being, a primary part of self-efficacy, has been repeatedly shown to positively impact physical, psychological, and social aging. In a recent review, Diener (2000) articulated the advantages of subjective well-being. A summary of the advantages for successful aging follow:

> . . . For millennia thinkers have pondered the question, what is the good life? They have focused on criteria such as loving others, pleasure, or self-insight as the defining characteristics of life.
>
> Another idea of what constitutes a good life, however, is that it is desirable for people themselves to think that they are living good lives. The subjective definition of quality of life is democratic in that it grants to each individual the right to decide whether his or her life is worthwhile. It is this approach to defining the good life that has come to be called "subjective well-being" (SWB) and in colloquial terms is sometimes labeled "happiness." SWB refers to people's evaluations of their lives—evaluations that are both affective and cognitive. People experience abundant SWB when they feel many pleasant and few unpleasant emotions, when they are engaged in interesting activities, when they experience many pleasures and few pains, and when they are satisfied with their lives . . .
>
> . . . People's moods and emotions reflect on-line reactions to events happening to them. Each individual also makes broader judgments about his or her life as a whole, as well as about domains such as marriage and work. Thus, there are a number of separable components of SWB: life satisfaction (global judgments of one's life), satisfaction with important domains (e.g., work satisfaction), positive affect (experiencing many pleasant emotions and moods), and low levels of negative affect (experiencing few unpleasant emotions and moods). . . . (p. 34)

Diener's review of subjective well-being research, dealing with personal (personality) and contextual (including cross-cultural) factors, concludes that a person's senses of well-being (complex in terms of physical, psychological, social domains) may be as important as environmental factors in aging—be it normal, pathological or successful.

Davis (2000) recently studied the relationships among life satisfaction, knowledge about aging, and the demographic variables of age, gender, education, living arrangement, self-reported health, financial status, ethnicity, volunteerism, and former occupation. With over 400 adult participants, Davis's age categories included the young-, middle-, and old-old adults. While linear age trends were found for both life satisfaction and knowledge about physical, psychological, and social aging, Davis found significant, positive relationships among life satisfaction (psychological well-being, self-efficacy) and participant knowledge concerning physical, psychological, and social aging. Internal motivators of life satisfaction, such as sense of general health, as well as external motivators, like education, living arrangements, financial status, and volunteerism, were significantly associated with both life satisfaction and knowledge of aging.

As noted earlier in *Successful Aging*, prevention is better than remediation when dealing with development, regardless of one's age—chronological, physical, psychological, and social. Both prevention and intervention, however, are relative in terms of (a) the interplay among the physical, psychological, and social domains, and (b) remaining lifespan. Preventive strategies for more successful aging of one's remaining life should begin earlier in the lifespan rather than later and impact physical, psychological, and social well-being. Remedial strategies for more successful aging, usually stimulated by significant loss in one of the primary lifespan domains (physical, psychological, social), can also result in longevity and enhanced quality of physical, psychological, and social life.

CONCLUDING COMMENTS

Four primary matters discussed in Chapter 7, and emphasized in *Successful Aging*, are reframed for concluding comments. These matters are:
1. Domains of Aging.
2. Types of Aging.
3. Intervention Strategies.
4. Life Review and Personal Responsibility.

1. Domains of Aging are the physical, psychological, and social. While these domains are interrelated throughout the lifespan, cases have been made to distinguish among chronological, physical, psychological, and social age and aging. As the Cattell/Horn model of fluid mechanical and crystallized pragmatic abilities illustrate, many capabilities can be differentiated in terms of primary association with physical, psychological, and/or social aging. In fact, capabilities, dependent upon genetic, maturation/deterioration, and learning contributions, show differential lifespan profiles and, correspondingly, personal gains and losses throughout the lifespan. The interrelationship of domains over the lifespan relates to Baltes' notions of multidimensionality and multidirectionality of human abilities. All of these concepts are related to the ideas of interindividual differences or variability and intraindividual change in both interindividual and intraindividual variability. People, in any stage of the lifespan, are different from one another; some differences in capabilities are more pronounced than others, and interindividual differences are more pronounced in early development and young- and middle-old age. Such differences are much less pronounced in old-old age, a result of significant deterioration of most human capabilities. Intraindividual change, summarized in the research and the model of selection, optimization, and compensation, also illustrates a normal lifespan profile of more variability in capabilities earlier in the lifespan and less later in the lifespan.

Genetic potential (genotypic range of reaction on phenotypes or observable characteristics) has been researched most in the physical domain. Both quality of life and longevity are strongly linked to genetic contributions. Simple examples of the strong genetic link to the physical domain include sex, race, height, chronic illness, and longevity, in order of genetic weightings. One's environmental context (internal and external to the individual) does make a difference in the physical domain. For example, the genetic range of reaction or lung cancer can be reduced by not smoking cigarettes. One's height and weight, directly linked to heredity, can be manipulated by contextual influences of diet/nutrition, medication, and exercise. While chronic illnesses do tend "to run in families," the environment plays a major role in time of onset and severity of chronic illnesses such as cardiovascular diseases, diabetes, and cancers.

Given contemporary research summaries and models of age-related changes in the physical, psychological, and social domains over the lifespan, several conclusions are relevant for both quality of life and longevity in the later phases of the lifespan. The *first conclusion* is that by the time most individuals become older adults genetic and environmental influences have impacted both quality of life and longevity. In terms of the rest of one's life, it is the fortunate person who has (a) inherited a genotype of integrity, (b) lived within an environment which nurtures genetic potential and individual opportunities for selection, optimization, and compensation of abilities, and (c) maximized genetic potential and environmental opportunities with decisions promoting a lifestyle for successful aging. Even the most successful agers, however, have to continue to make positive lifestyle decisions. The *second conclusion* from contemporary lifespan and gerontological research summaries is that one's past (genetic unfolding and environmental determinants) does not completely predict one's future. Lifestyle changes and/or environmental influences (e.g., medications, surgical interventions) do influence remaining quality of life and longevity. Successful agers include those adults who make decisions and lifestyle changes to combat genetic restrictions and past lifestyles. The *third conclusion* relates to the specificity and interrelationship of the physical, psychological, and social domains of lifespan development and aging. With older age comes reductions in capabilities, most noticeably early on in the physical and psychological domains. Such is the nature of biological life (impacting physical aging and psychological aging associated with fluid, mechanical abilities), as well as social life (societal mores and ageism).

2. Types of Aging. Within and across the domains of aging are types or conditions of aging, i.e., normal, pathological, and successful. As has been illustrated in earlier parts of *Successful Aging*, these conditions of aging are determined by complex interactions among genetic and environmental factors. The importance of personal responsibility as related to lifestyle was also illustrated.

The average person reflects, as suggested, average lifespan profiles in the physical, psychological, and social domains. Average aging, reflecting the majority of individuals, is not just a statistical reality. For example, insurance companies provide actuarial tables, updated annually, based upon average aging characteristics. The life (death) insurance industry focuses on chronological age in setting premium policies–the younger the individual, the lower the premium. Automobile insurance companies focus on chronological age–young and old people pay more for premiums. Health insurance companies focus on chronological age–premiums become more expensive with advancing age. And, nursing or long-term health care premiums increase, drastically, with advancing age. Why the emphasis on average age lifespan profiles for insurance companies? These companies are profit-driven, and automobile insurance companies aside, a significant amount of insurance reimbursement relates to aging-related disability/ disease/death claims. The physical aging correlate of chronological aging, then, is very important to insurance companies. Physical aging should also be important to the individual. In addition to having to pay higher premiums for those diverse insurance programs (based on normal aging profiles), each of us has to deal with ourselves and significant others. Such dealings include the domains of psychological and social aging.

Normal aging, albeit a concept based on average aging of many individuals, is real. With normal aging, some will do so faster, some slower.

Relatedly, chronic diseases contributing to death within normal aging have, on average, differential longevity impacts. Untreated high blood pressure, for example, is a chronic condition that has a long-term life-threatening effect. Untreated and treated lung and cervical cancers, on the other hand, have much more short-term life-threatening effects. Average or normal aging, then, generalizes over chronological age and individuals.

Similarly, normal aging in quality of life within the physical, psychological, and social domains reflects averages over chronological age and individuals. Unlike longevity, which is assessed objectively, quality of life also includes personal assessments. Further, quality of life within the physical, psychological, and social domain—defined objectively or subjectively—is variant, dependent upon the domain and interrelationships among domains, status of domain capabilities and functioning, and one's stage in the lifespan.

Pathological aging in older adulthood suggests atypical, negative adaptability. Pathological aging, usually illustrated in the physical domain, suggests earlier onset and rapid progression of life-threatening illnesses. Pathological aging, life normal and successful aging, is the result of the complex interaction of genes and environment. Yet, there are illustrations of rather simple determinants for pathological aging. Huchinson-Guilford and Werner syndromes are rare genetically determined conditions of premature aging (Turker, 1996, pp. 347–348).

> ... Hutchinson-Guilford syndrome represents one of the rarest and more remarkable genetic syndromes in humans . . . At birth, (Hutchinson-Guilford) patients appear normal, but by about 1 year of age severe growth retardation is seen. There is rapid loss of subcutaneous fat and hair, resulting in a prominent display of the scalp veins. Other distinctive characteristics include a high-pitched voice, bone resorption, an elevated basic metabolic rate, and a shuffling gait. Most (Hutchinson-Guilford) patients have normal to above normal intelligence. The median age of death is 12 years, with most deaths resulting from heart attacks or congestive heart failure . . .
>
> . . . Werner syndrome is an autosomal recessive disease . . . It is first manifested as a failure to undergo the usual adolescent growth spurt, although it is rarely identified at that time. By the early twenties other changes are noted, such as hair loss, graying of the hair, atrophy of the skin, and cataracts. The skin changes often lead to large ulcers later in life. Diabetes and osteoporosis are additional changes that occur during the life span of many Werner syndrome patients . . . Death usually occurs in the late forties from (cardiovascular) problems. . . .

Other conditions of pathological aging, associated with more complex genetic-environmental interactions, result in reduced longevity and quality of life. These conditions were discussed in earlier in Chapter 7; viz., obesity, drug abuse, sustained levels of high stress, lack of exercise, and poor nutrition. While a number of chronic diseases "run in families," illustrating a strong genetic influence, one's lifestyle also has a significant impact on life-threatening diseases such as cancers, cardiovascular dysfunctions, and diabetes. Genetic contributions to such chronic diseases may be balanced, to varying degrees with responsible lifestyles that include (a) avoidance of toxic substances and prolonged periods of high stress, (b) weight and nutritional control, and (c) exercise (mental and physical).

Successful aging, like normal and pathological aging, has to be appreciated within the context of the cards one is dealt, including those dealt by one's self. Heredity and environmental determinants (including one's own decisions) contribute to the individual's current state of affairs. While the motivational research presented earlier in the chapter demonstrates the positive impact of self-efficacy in older adults, successful aging requires conscious decisions about lifestyle throughout the lifespan. Preventive strategies for successful aging are more sustaining than remedial ones; the earlier in the lifespan one adopts health aging practices, the better the quality of life and longer the lifespan; and an integrated healthy lifestyle maximizes successful aging in all three lifespan domains—physical, psychological, and social.

Yet, the principles of gains and losses throughout the lifespan and cumulative effects of age-related losses are reflected even with successful aging. To maximize successful aging in older adulthood, both acceptance of, and compensation for, loss is needed. This thought is not unique to older age, as optimal development in all stages of life requires such individual actions. In older adulthood, however, the average individual is less able to engage in all aspects of the selection-optimization-compensation exercises with equality. Given deterioration of many abilities and long-term habit associated with older age, it is unreasonable to expect seniors to be as sustaining as younger adults in multiple exercises of selection, optimization, and compensation. The successful aging adult focuses on particular selections, optimizations, and compensations, with compensatory actions reflecting (a) lowered personal standards with many capabilities and (b) alternative means to maintain positive senses of self and perspectivism.

3. Intervention Strategies. With the criteria of quality of life and longevity, prevention is better than remediation for successful development and aging. Unfortunately, many individuals, living in their present lifespan context, are unwilling or unable to adopt successful aging lifestyles early in their life's journey. Further, multiple genetic and environmental factors directly associated with types of aging are not always under one's personal control in periods of the lifespan for optimal intervention. Childhood obesity is an example. While there is a genetic component for some obese children, the increase in overweight children is influenced by the fast-food industry, irresponsible parents, and the child's inability to comprehend the negative effects of obesity. Fast-food or junk food, high in fat, is part of contemporary America, as well as many industrialized societies. From a lifespan perspective, obese children often maintain their eating habits and weight condition into adolescence and adulthood. As discussed earlier in *Successful Aging*, obesity is associated with significant physical health problems throughout the lifespan. Many chronic disabilities of middle- and older-adulthood represent the cumulative effects of less than optimal lifestyles. Some of the cumulative effects are based upon singular incidents earlier in life; e.g., accidents resulting in chronic arthritic conditions. Other cumulative effects represent ongoing lifestyle decisions; e.g., poor nutrition and lack of physical exercise, with resulting chronic conditions such as arthritis, diabetes, cardiovascular disease, and depression.

While the focus on intervention strategies in *Successful Aging* is with personal responsibility and prevention, the upcoming Aging Boomers may force society to expand present entitlements for seniors. The first phase of such expansion will most likely deal with entitlements for seniors in all three domains of aging–physical, psychological, and social. The Baby-to-Aging Boomers will make for a significant percentage of Americans, and these Boomers are more influential (financially and politically) than their predecessors. Chapter 6 provided summaries of present and projected federal expenditures for existing entitlement programs for older adults. The upcoming Aging Boomers will, albeit without a single voice, expect more federal financial assistance in quality of life remedial interventions. The second phase of societal response to the Aging Boomers could include enhancement of entitlement programs promoting preventive intervention. This phase could focus on successful aging, preventive intervention, and progressive lifestyles early in the lifespan. Will the upcoming Aging Boomers be perspective enough to balance their demands for more federal entitlement remedial funding (for them) with federal entitlement preventive funding for those much younger cohorts they will never meet?

4. Life Review and Successful Aging. For all three domains of aging–physical, psychological, and social–a preventive strategy for successful aging is to review periodically strengths (gains) and weaknesses (losses) as we move through our lifespan. Baltes' (1987) notion of gains and losses throughout the lifespan fits nicely into an argument for periodic life review and successful aging. The notion is that there is no gain without loss and no loss without gain. The gain with loss aspect is most often illustrated during development in the lifespan—for the physical, psychological, and social domains. Selection and/or optimization of physical, psychological, and social abilities and resulting accomplishments retard expertise and competence with other skills. The loss with gain aspect of Baltes' notion may be illustrated with compensatory strategies to alleviate significant, often age-related, dysfunctions.

The compensatory gain in functional loss is often identified as remediation associated with capabilities specific to the dysfunction. Some cardiovascular dysfunctions, for example, are subject to surgical and drug remediation. Another gain associated with functional loss, such as loss and gain due to cardiovascular disease, is the reframing of one's priorities in life. With both more time (longevity) and quality of life, the remediated cardiovascular patient can review and act upon his/her strengths and weaknesses with a new set of life priorities in the physical, psychological, and social domains. Some folks with a new lease on life, due to remedial intervention, maintain most aspects of their lifespan lifestyle unsuccessful for aging; others opt for more positive lifestyle paths.

Summaries of research in *Successful Aging* strongly suggest a life review for successful aging which starts early, rather than late, in the lifespan. Such a developmental strategy allows for maximum preventive approaches for progressive lifestyles and, correspondingly, longer life with better quality of living. Yet, we are resilient creatures, with fluid and crystallized abilities allowing for normal, pathological, and successful adaptation throughout the lifespan. Thus, both quality and length of life, within significant limits of heredity and environmental determinants, are, throughout the lifespan, mediated by personal decisions. Few of us, especially in earlier periods of the lifespan, give enough review for lifestyle impacts on long-term quality and length of life.

APPENDICES

Appendix A

ALTERNATIVE FACTS ON AGING QUIZZES

FACTS ON AGING QUIZ, A, MULTIPLE CHOICE FORMAT

For each of the following statements, circle the letter of the best answer. If you do not know the best answer, you may put a question mark (?) to the left of the answers instead of circling a letter.

1. The portion of people over 65 who are senile (have impaired memory, disorientation, or dementia) is
   a. About 1 in 100
   b. About 1 in 10
   c. About 1 in 2
   d. The majority

2. The senses that tend to weaken in old age are
   a. Sight and hearing
   b. Taste and smell
   c. Sight, hearing, and touch
   d. All five senses

3. The majority of old couples
   a. Have little or no interest in sex
   b. Are not able to have sexual relations
   c. Continue to enjoy sexual relations
   d. Think sex is for only the young

4. Lung vital capacity in old age
   a. Tends to decline
   b. Stays the same among nonsmokers
   c. Tends to increase among healthy old people
   d. Is unrelated to age

5. Happiness among old people is
   a. Rare
   b. Less common than among younger people
   c. About as common as among younger people
   d. More common than among younger people

6. Physical strength
   a. Tends to decline with age
   b. Tends to remain the same among healthy old people
   c. Tends to increase among healthy old people
   d. Is unrelated to age

7. The percentage of people over 65 in long-stay institutions (such as nursing homes, mental hospitals, and homes for the aged) is about
   a. 5%
   b. 10%
   c. 25%
   d. 50%

8. The accident rate per driver over age 65 is
   a. Higher than for those under 65
   b. About the same as for those under 65
   c. Lower than for those under 65
   d. Unknown

9. Most workers over 65
   a. Work less effectively than younger workers
   b. Work as effectively as younger workers
   c. Work more effectively than younger workers
   d. Are preferred by most employers

10. The proportion of people over 65 who are able to do their normal activities is
    a. One tenth
    b. One quarter
    c. One half
    d. More than three fourths

11. Adaptability to change among people over 65 is
    a. Rare
    b. Present among about half
    c. Present among most
    d. More common than among younger people

12. As for old people learning new things
    a. Most are able to learn at any speed
    b. Most are able to learn, but at a slower speed
    c. Most are able to learn as fast as younger people
    d. Learning speed is unrelated to age

13. Depression is more frequent among
    a. People over 65
    b. Adults under 65
    c. Young people
    d. Children

14. Old people tend to react
    a. Slower than younger people
    b. At about the same speed as younger people
    c. Faster than young people
    d. Slower or faster than others, depending upon the type of test

15. Old people tend to be
    a. More alike than younger people
    b. As alike as younger people
    c. Less alike than younger people
    d. More alike in some respects and less alike in others

16. Most old people say
    a. They are seldom bored
    b. They are usually bored
    c. They are often bored
    d. Life is monotonous

17. The proportion of old people who are socially isolated is
    a. Almost half
    b. About half
    c. Less than a fourth
    d. Almost none

18. The accident rate among workers over 65 tends to be
    a. Higher than among younger workers
    b. About the same as among younger workers
    c. Lower than among younger workers
    d. Unknown because there are so few workers over 65

19. The proportion of the U.S. population now age 65 or over is
    a. 3%
    b. 13%
    c. 23%
    d. 33%

20. Medical practitioners tend to give older patients
    a. Lower priority than younger patients
    b. The same priority as younger patients
    c. Higher priority than younger patients
    d. Higher priority if they have Medicaid

21. The poverty rate (as defined by the federal government) among old people is
    a. Higher than among children under 18
    b. Higher than among all persons under 65
    c. About the same as among persons under 65
    d. Lower than among persons under 65

22. Most old people are
    a. Still employed
    b. Employed or would like to be employed
    c. Employed, do housework or volunteer work, or would like to do some kind
       of work
    d. Not interested in any work

23. Religiosity tends to
    a. Increase in old age
    b. Decrease in old age
    c. Be greater in the older generation than in the younger
    d. Be unrelated to age

24. Most old people say they
    a. Are seldom angry
    b. Are often angry
    c. Are often grouchy
    d. Often lose their tempers

25. The health and economic status of old people (compared with younger people)
    in the year 2010 will
    a. Be higher than now
    b. Be about the same as now
    c. Be lower than now
    d. Show no consistent trend

FACTS ON AGING QUIZ, B

Mark the statements "T" for true, "F" for false, or "?" for don't know

____ 1. A person's height tends to decline in old age.

____ 2. More older persons (65 or older) have chronic illnesses that limit their activity than do younger persons.

____ 3. Older persons have more acute (short-term) illnesses than do younger persons.

____ 4. Older persons have more injuries in the home than younger persons.

____ 5. Older workers have less absenteeism than do younger workers.

____ 6. Blacks' life expectancy at age 65 is about the same as Whites.

____ 7. Men's life expectancy at age 65 is about the same as women's.

____ 8. Medicare pays over half of the medical expenses for the aged.

____ 9. Social Security benefits automatically increase with inflation.

____ 10. Supplemental Social Security income guarantees a minimum income for needy adults.

____ 11. The aged do not get their proportionate share of the nation's income.

____ 12. The aged have higher rates of criminal victimization than younger persons.

____ 13. The aged are more fearful of crime than are younger persons.

____ 14. The aged are the most law abiding of all adult age groups.

____ 15. There are about equal numbers of widows and widowers among the aged.

____ 16. More of the aged vote than any other age group.

____ 17. There are proportionately more older persons in public office than in the total population.

____ 18. The proportion of African Americans among the aged is growing.

____ 19. Participation in voluntary organizations (churches and clubs) tends to decline even among the healthy aged.

___ 20. The majority of old people live alone.

___ 21. The aged have a lower rate of poverty than the rest of the population.

___ 22. The rate of poverty among aged African Americans is about three times as high as among aged Whites.

___ 23. Older persons who reduce their activity tend to be happier than those who do not.

___ 24. When the last child leaves home, the majority of parents have serious problems adjusting to their "empty nest."

___ 25. The proportion widowed among the aged is decreasing.

(Key: Alternating pairs of items are true or false; that is, 1 and 2 are true, 3 and 4 are false, 5 and 6 are true, and so forth, and 25 is true.)

FACTS ON AGING QUIZ, B, MULTIPLE CHOICE FORMAT

Circle the letter of the best answer. If you do not know the best answer, you may put a question mark (?) to the left of the answers instead of circling a letter.

1. In old age, a person's height
   a. Does not change
   b. Only appears to change
   c. Tends to decline
   d. Depends on how active one is

2. Compared with younger persons, more older persons (65 or over) are limited in their activity by which type of illnesses?
   a. Acute illnesses (short-term)
   b. Colds and flue
   c. Infections
   d. Chronic illnesses

3. Which type of illness do older persons have less frequently than younger persons?
   a. Chronic illness
   b. Arthritis
   c. Stroke
   d. Acute illness

4. Compared to younger persons, older persons have
   a. More injuries in the home
   b. About the same number of injuries in the home
   c. Fewer injuries in the home
   d. Twice the likelihood to be injured in the home

5. Older workers' absenteeism rates
   a. Are higher than among younger workers
   b. Cannot be trusted
   c. Are about the same as among younger workers
   d. Are lower than among younger workers

6. The life expectancy of African Americans at age 65
   a. Is higher than that of Whites
   b. Is lower than that of Whites
   c. Is about the same as that of Whites
   d. Has not been determined

7. Men's life expectancy at age 65 compared with women's
   a. Is lower
   b. Is dropping
   c. Is about the same
   d. Is higher

8. What percentage of medical expenses for the aged does Medicare pay?
   a. About 20 percent
   b. About 45 percent
   c. About 75 percent
   d. Nearly 100 percent

9. Social Security benefits
   a. Automatically increase with inflation
   b. Are not subject to change
   c. Must be adjusted by Congress
   d. Are often cut back to balance the deficit

10. Supplemental Social Security Income (SSI)
    a. Guarantees a minimum income for the needy elderly
    b. Provides extra income for all elderly
    c. Supplements the income of elderly in nursing homes
    d. Pays medical expenses for the elderly

11. As for income
    a. The majority of elderly live below the poverty level
    b. The elderly are the poorest age group in our society
    c. The elderly get their proportionate share of the nation's income
    d. The income gap between the elderly and younger people is widening

12. Compared with younger persons, rates of criminal victimization among the elderly are
    a. Higher
    b. Lower
    c. About the same
    d. Steadily increasing

13. Fear of crime among the elderly
    a. Is higher than among younger persons
    b. Is about the same as among younger persons
    c. Is lower than among younger persons
    d. Is not significant

14. The most law abiding adults are
    a. Those in their 20s
    b. Those in their 30s
    c. Those 45 to 65
    d. Those over 65

15. Comparing widows and widowers among the aged
    a. Their numbers are about equal
    b. There are about twice as many widows as widowers
    c. There are about five times as many widows as widowers
    d. There are about twice as many widowers than widows

16. Voter participation rates are usually
    a. Highest among those over 65
    b. Highest among those age 55 to 64
    c. Highest among those 40-54
    d. Highest among those 20-39

17. Being elected or appointed to public office is
    a. Rare among those over 65
    b. More frequent among those under 65
    c. More frequent among those over 65
    d. Similar in frequency among older and younger persons

18. The proportion of African Americans among the aged is
    a. Growing
    b. Declining
    c. Staying about the same
    d. Small compared with most other minority groups

19. Participation in voluntary organizations usually
    a. Does not decline among healthy older persons
    b. Declines among healthy older persons
    c. Increases among healthy older persons
    d. Is highest among healthy youth

20. The majority of old people live
    a. Alone
    b. In long-stay institutions
    c. With their spouses
    d. With their children

21. The rate of poverty among the elderly is
    a. Lower than among those under 65
    b. Higher than among those under 65
    c. The same as it is for other age groups
    d. High as a result of their fixed incomes

22. The rate of poverty among aged African Americans is
    a. Less than that of Whites
    b. About the same as that of Whites
    c. Double that of Whites
    d. Almost triple that of Whites

23. Older persons who reduce their activity tend to be
    a. Happier than those who remain active
    b. Not as happy as those who remain active
    c. About as happy as others
    d. Healthier

24. When the last child leaves home, the majority of parents
    a. Have serious problems of adjustment
    b. Have higher levels of life satisfaction
    c. Try to get their children to come back home
    d. Suffer from the "empty nest" syndrome

25. The proportion widowed among the aged
    a. Is gradually decreasing
    b. Is gradually increasing
    c. Has remained the same in this century
    d. Is unrelated to longevity

FACTS ON AGING AND MENTAL HEALTH QUIZ, MULTIPLE CHOICE

Circle the letter of the most accurate answer. If you do not know, you may put a question mark to the left of the answers instead of circling a letter.

1. Severe mental illness among persons over 65 afflicts
   a. The majority
   b. About half
   c. About 15 to 25%
   d. Very few

2. Cognitive impairment (impairment of memory disorientation, or confusion)
   a. Is an inevitable part of the aging process
   b. Increases in old age
   c. Decreases in old age
   d. Does not change with age.

3. If older mental patients make up false stories, it is best to
   a. Point out to them that they are lying
   b. Punish them for lying
   c. Reward them for their imagination
   d. Ignore or distract them

4. The prevalence of anxiety disorders and schizophrenia in old age tends to
   a. Decrease
   b. Stay about the same
   c. Increase somewhat
   d. Increase markedly

5. Suicide rates among women tend to
   a. Increase in old age
   b. Stay about the same
   c. Decrease somewhat in old age
   d. Decrease markedly

6. Suicide rates among men tend to
   a. Increase markedly
   b. Increase somewhat
   c. Stay about the same
   d. Decrease

7. When all major types of mental impairment are added together, the elderly have
   a. Higher rates than younger persons
   b. About the same rates as younger persons
   c. Lower rates than younger persons
   d. Higher rates for ages 65 to 74 than for those over 75

8. The primary mental illness of the elderly is
   a. Anxiety disorders
   b. Mood disorders
   c. Schizophrenia
   d. Cognitive impairment

9. Alzheimer's disease is
   a. The most common type of cognitive impairment
   b. An acute illness
   c. A benign memory disorder
   d. A form of affective disorder

10. Alzheimer's disease usually
    a. Can be cured with psychotherapy
    b. Can be cured with pharmacology
    c. Goes into remission among the very old
    d. Cannot be cured

11. Most patients with Alzheimer's disease
    a. Act pretty much the same way
    b. Have confusion and impaired memory
    c. Wander during the day or at night
    d. Repeat the same question or action over and over

12. Organic brain impairment
    a. Is easy to distinguish from functional mental illness
    b. Is difficult to distinguish from functional mental illness
    c. Tends to be similar to functional mental illness
    d. Can be reversed with proper therapy

13. When talking to an older mental patient, it is best
    a. To avoid looking directly at the patient
    b. To glance at the patient occasionally
    c. To ignore the patient's reactions
    d. To look directly at the patient

14. Talking with demented older patients
    a. Tends to increase their confusion
    b. Is usually pleasurable for the patient
    c. Should be confined to trivial matters
    d. Should be avoided as much as possible

15. When demented patients talk about their past, it usually
    a. Is enjoyed by the patient
    b. Depresses the patient
    c. Increases the patient's confusion
    d. Has no effect

16. The prevalence of severe cognitive impairment
    a. Is unrelated to age
    b. Decreases with age
    c. Increases with age after 45
    d. Increases with age only after 75

17. The primary causes of paranoid disorders in old age are
    a. Isolation and hearing loss
    b. Persecution and abuse
    c. Near death experiences
    d. None of the above

18. Poor nutrition may produce
    a. Depression
    b. Confusion
    c. Apathy
    d. All of the above

19. Mental illness in elders is more prevalent among
    a. The poor
    b. The rich
    c. The middle-class
    d. None of the above

20. The prevalence of mental illness among the elderly in long-term care institutions is
    a. About 10%
    b. About 25%
    c. About 50%
    d. More than 75%

21. Elders tend to have
    a. Less sleep problems
    b. More sleep problems
    c. Deeper sleep
    d. The same sleep patterns as younger persons

22. Major depression is
    a. Less prevalent among elders
    b. More prevalent among elders
    c. Unrelated to age
    d. A sign of senility

23. Widowhood is
    a. Less stressful among elders
    b. More stressful among elders
    c. Similar levels of stress at all ages
    d. Least stressful among young adults

24. Elders use mental health facilities
    a. More often than younger people
    b. Less often than younger people
    c. At about the same rate as younger people
    d. Primarily when they have no family to care for them

25. Psychotherapy with older patients is
    a. Usually ineffective
    b. Often effective
    c. Effective with Alzheimer's patients
    d. A waste of the therapist's time

LIFE SATISFACTION INDEX, B

Would you please comment freely in answer to the following questions?

1. What are the best things about being the age you are now?

2. What do you think you will be doing five years from now? How do you expect things will be different from the way they are now, in your life?

3. What is the most important thing in your life right now?

4. How happy would you say you are right now, compared with the earlier periods in your life?

5. Do you ever worry about your ability to do what people expect of you—to meet demands that people make on you?

6. If you could do anything you pleased, in what part of _____ would you most like to live?

7. How often do you find yourself feeling lonely?

8. How often do you feel there is no point in living?

9. Do you wish you could see more of your close friends than you do, or would you like more time to yourself?

10. How much unhappiness would you say you find in your life today?

11. As you get older, would you say things seem to be better or worse than you thought they would be?

12. How satisfied would you say you are with your way of life?

WOOLF AGING QUIZ (ANSWER TRUE OR FALSE)

1. _____ The majority of older adults will become senile (defective memory, disoriented, demented) during old age.

2. _____ Most older adults have no desire for sexual relations. In other words, most older adults are asexual.

3. _____ Chronological age is the most important determinant of age.

4. _____ Most older adults have difficulty adapting to change; they are set in their ways.

5. _____ Physical handicaps are the primary factors limiting the activities of older adults.

6. _____ Declines in all five senses normally occur in old age.

7. _____ Older adults are incapable of learning new information; you can't teach an old dog new tricks.

8. _____ Physical strength tends to decline in old age.

9. _____ Intelligence declines with old age.

10. _____ The majority of older adults say that they are happy most of the time.

11. _____ The vast majority of older adults will at some point end up in a nursing home.

12. _____ About 80% of older people say they are healthy enough to carry out their normal daily activities independently.

13. _____ Most older adults are rejected by their children.

14. _____ In general, most older adults tend to be pretty much alike.

15. _____ The majority of older adults say that they are lonely.

16. _____ Old age can be best characterized as a second childhood.

17. _____ Over 12% of the population of the United States is over the age of 65.

18. _____ Most older adults tend to be preoccupied with death.

19. _____ Most older adults have incomes below the poverty level.

20. _____ Older people tend to become more religious as they age; as they deal with their own mortality.

21. _____ Retirement is detrimental to an individual's health; six months ago he retired and now he's dead, retirement killed him.

22. _____ Pain is a natural part of the aging process.

23. _____ The majority of older adults say that they feel irritated or angry most of the time.

24. _____ Rarely does someone over the age of 65 produce a great work of art, science, or scholarship.

25. _____ With age comes wisdom.

LONGEVITY TEST

The basic life expectancy for males is 73 and for females, 80. If you are in your fifties or sixties, add ten points to the basic life expectancy figure. As of 2001, I am 56; thus, I add 10 points to my basic life expectancy for a score of 83.

Decide how each of the following items apply to you and add or subtract the appropriate number of years from your basic life expectancy score:

1. Family History
   −Add five years if two or more of your grandparents lived to 80 or beyond.
   −Subtract four years if any parent, grandparent, sister, or brother died of heart attack or stroke before 50.
   −Subtract two years if anyone died from these diseases before 60.
   −Subtract three years for each of diabetes, thyroid disorder, breast cancer, cancer of the digestive system, asthma, or chronic bronchitis among parents or grandparents.

2. Marital Status
   - If you are married, add four years.
   - If you are over twenty-five and not married, subtract one year for every unwedded decade.

3. Economic Status
   - Add two years if your family income is over $60,000 per year.
   - Subtract three years if you have been poor for the greater part or your life.

4. Physique
   - Subtract one year for every ten pounds you are overweight.
   - For each inch your girth measurement exceeds your chest measurement deduct two years.
   - Add three years if you are over forty and not overweight.

5. Exercise
   - Add three years if you exercise regularly and moderately (jogging three times a week).
   - Add five years if you exercise regularly and vigorously (long-distance running three times a week).
   - Subtract three years if your job is sedentary.
   - Add three years if your job is active.

6. Alcohol
   - Add two years if you are a light drinker (one to three drinks a day).
   - Subtract five to ten years if you are a heavy drinker (more than four drinks per day).
   - Subtract one year if you are a teetotaler.

7. Smoking
   - Subtract eight years if you smoke two or more packs of cigarettes per day.
   - Subtract two years if you smoke one to two packs per day.
   - Subtract two years if you smoke less than one pack.
   - Subtract two years if you regularly smoke a pipe or cigars.

8. Disposition
   - Add two years if you are a reasoned, practical person.
   - Subtract two years if you are aggressive, intense, and competitive.
   - Add one to five years if you are basically happy and content with life.
   - Subtract one to five years if you are often unhappy, worried, and often feel guilty.

9. Education
   −Subtract two years if you have less than a high school education.
   −Add one year if you attended four years of school beyond high school.
   −Add three years if you attended five or more years beyond high school.

10. Environment
   −Add four years if you have lived most of your life in a rural environment.
   −Subtract two years if you have lived most of your life in an urban environment.

11. Sleep
   −Subtract five years if you sleep more than nine hours a day.

12. Temperature
   −Add two years if your home's thermostat is set at no more than 68 degrees F.

13. Health Care
   −Add three years if you have regular medical checkups and regular dental care.
   −Subtract two years if you are frequently ill.

Total your points. Add to your basic life expectancy. If you are over fifty years of age add an additional 10 points. What is your Life Expectancy Total?

ANSWERS TO FACTS ON AGING QUIZ, A, MULTIPLE CHOICE FORMAT

1. The portion of people over 65 who are senile (have impaired memory, disorientation,
   or dementia) is
   a. About 1 in 100 +
   b. About 1 in 10 *
   c. About 1 in 2 −
   d. The majority −

2. The senses that tend to weaken in old age are
   a. Sight and hearing +
   b. Taste and smell +
   c. Sight, hearing, and touch +
   d. All five senses *

3. The majority of old couples
   a. Have little or no interest in sex −
   b. Are not able to have sexual relations −
   c. Continue to enjoy sexual relations *
   d. Think sex is for only the young −

4. Lung vital capacity in old age
   a. Tends to decline *
   b. Stays the same among nonsmokers +
   c. Tends to increase among healthy old people +
   d. Is unrelated to age +

5. Happiness among old people is
   a. Rare −
   b. Less common than among younger people −
   c. About as common as among younger people *
   d. More common than among younger people +

6. Physical strength
   a. Tends to decline with age *
   b. Tends to remain the same among healthy old people +
   c. Tends to increase among healthy old people +
   d. Is unrelated to age +

7. The percentage of people over 65 in long-stay institutions (such as nursing homes, mental hospitals, and homes for the aged) is about
   a. 5% *
   b. 10% −
   c. 25% −
   d. 50% −

8. The accident rate per driver over age 65 is
   a. Higher than for those under 65 −
   b. About the same as for those under 65 −
   c. Lower than for those under 65 *
   d. Unknown 0

9. Most workers over 65
   a. Work less effectively than younger workers −
   b. Work as effectively as younger workers *
   c. Work more effectively than younger workers +
   d. Are preferred by most employers +

10. The proportion of people over 65 who are able to do their normal activities is
    a. One tenth −
    b. One quarter −
    c. One half −
    d. More than three fourths *

11. Adaptability to change among people over 65 is
    a. Rare –
    b. Present among about half –
    c. Present among most *
    d. More common than among younger people +

12. As for old people learning new things
    a. Most are able to learn at any speed –
    b. Most are able to learn, but at a slower speed *
    c. Most are able to learn as fast as younger people +
    d. Learning speed is unrelated to age +

13. Depression is more frequent among
    a. People over 65 –
    b. Adults under 65 *
    c. Young people 0
    d. Children 0

14. Old people tend to react
    a. Slower than younger people *
    b. At about the same speed as younger people +
    c. Faster than young people +
    d. Slower or faster than others, depending upon the type of test +

15. Old people tend to be
    a. More alike than younger people –
    b. As alike as younger people 0
    c. Less alike than younger people +
    d. More alike in some respects and less alike in others *

16. Most old people say
    a. They are seldom bored *
    b. They are usually bored –
    c. They are often bored –
    d. Life is monotonous –

17. The proportion of old people who are socially isolated is
    a. Almost half –
    b. About half –
    c. Less than a fourth *
    d. Almost none +

18. The accident rate among workers over 65 tends to be
    a. Higher than among younger workers –
    b. About the same as among younger workers –
    c. Lower than among younger workers *
    d. Unknown because there are so few workers over 65 –

19. The proportion of the U.S. population now age 65 or over is
    a. 3% 0
    b. 13% *
    c. 23% 0
    d. 33% 0

20. Medical practitioners tend to give older patients
    a. Lower priority than younger patients *
    b. The same priority as younger patients +
    c. Higher priority than younger patients +
    d. Higher priority if they have Medicaid +

21. The poverty rate (as defined by the federal government) among old people is
    a. Higher than among children under 18 –
    b. Higher than among all persons under 65 –
    c. About the same as among persons under 65 –
    d. Lower than among persons under 65 *

22. Most old people are
    a. Still employed +
    b. Employed or would like to be employed +
    c. Employed, do housework or volunteer work, or would like to do some kind of work *
    d. Not interested in any work –

23. Religiosity tends to
    a. Increase in old age 0
    b. Decrease in old age 0
    c. Be greater in the older generation than in the younger *
    d. Be unrelated to age 0

24. Most old people say they
    a. Are seldom angry *
    b. Are often angry –
    c. Are often grouchy –
    d. Often lose their tempers –

25. The health and economic status of old people (compared with younger people) in the year 2010 will
    a. Be higher than now *
    b. Be about the same as now –
    c. Be lower than now –
    d. Show no consistent trend –

Key:
   * = correct answer
   + = Positive bias
   – = Negative bias
   0 = Neutral

ANSWERS TO FACTS ON AGING QUIZ, B, MULTIPLE CHOICE FORMAT

1. In old age, a person's height
   a. Does not change +
   b. Only appears to change +
   c. Tends to decline *
   d. Depends on how active one is +

2. Compared with younger persons, more older persons (65 or over) are limited in their activity by which type of illnesses?
   a. Acute illnesses (short-term) –
   b. Colds and flue –
   c. Infections –
   d. Chronic illnesses *

3. Which type of illness do older persons have less frequently than younger persons?
   a. Chronic illness +
   b. Arthritis +
   c. Stroke +
   d. Acute illness *

4. Compared to younger persons, older persons have
   a. More injuries in the home –
   b. About the same number of injuries in the home –
   c. Fewer injuries in the home *
   d. Twice the likelihood to be injured in the home –

5. Older workers' absenteeism rates
   a. Are higher than among younger workers –
   b. Cannot be trusted –
   c. Are about the same as among younger workers –
   d. Are lower than among younger workers *

6. The life expectancy of African Americans at age 65
   a. Is higher than that of Whites 0
   b. Is lower than that of Whites 0
   c. Is about the same as that of Whites *
   d. Has not been determined 0

7. Men's life expectancy at age 65 compared with women's
   a. Is lower *
   b. Is dropping 0
   c. Is about the same 0
   d. Is higher 0

8. What percentage of medical expenses for the aged does Medicare pay?
   a. About 20 percent –
   b. About 45 percent *
   c. About 75 percent +
   d. Nearly 100 percent +

9. Social Security benefits
   a. Automatically increase with inflation *
   b. Are not subject to change –
   c. Must be adjusted by Congress –
   d. Are often cut back to balance the deficit –

10. Supplemental Social Security Income (SSI)
    a. Guarantees a minimum income for the needy elderly *
    b. Provides extra income for all elderly +
    c. Supplements the income of elderly in nursing homes +
    d. Pays medical expenses for the elderly +

11. As for income
    a. The majority of elderly live below the poverty level –
    b. The elderly are the poorest age group in our society –
    c. The elderly get their proportionate share of the nation's income *
    d. The income gap between the elderly and younger people is widening. –

12. Compared with younger persons, rates of criminal victimization among the elderly are
    a. Higher –
    b. Lower*
    c. About the same –
    d. Steadily increasing –

13. Fear of crime among the elderly
    a. Is higher than among younger persons *
    b. Is about the same as among younger persons +
    c. Is lower than among younger persons +
    d. Is not significant +

14. The most law abiding adults are
    a. Those in their 20s –
    b. Those in their 30s –
    c. Those 45 to 65 –
    d. Those over 65 *

15. Comparing widows and widowers among the aged
    a. Their numbers are about equal +
    b. There are about twice as many widows as widowers +
    c. There are about five times as many widows as widowers *
    d. There are about twice as many widowers than widows +

16. Voter participation rates are usually
    a. Highest among those over 65 +
    b. Highest among those age 55 to 64 *
    c. Highest among those 40–54 –
    d. Highest among those 20–39 –

17. Being elected or appointed to public office is
    a. Rare among those over 65 –
    b. More frequent among those under 65 –
    c. More frequent among those over 65 *
    d. Similar in frequency among older and younger persons –

18. The proportion of African Americans among the aged is
    a. Growing *
    b. Declining 0
    c. Staying about the same 0
    d. Small compared with most other minority groups 0

19. Participation in voluntary organizations usually
    a. Does not decline among healthy older persons *
    b. Declines among healthy older persons –
    c. Increases among healthy older persons +
    d. Is highest among healthy youth –

20. The majority of old people live
    a. Alone –
    b. In long-stay institutions –
    c. With their spouses *
    d. With their children –

21. The rate of poverty among the elderly is
    a. Lower than among those under 65 *
    b. Higher than among those under 65 –
    c. The same as it is for other age groups –
    d. High as a result of their fixed incomes –

22. The rate of poverty among aged African Americans is
    a. Less than that of Whites 0
    b. About the same as that of Whites 0
    c. Double that of Whites 0
    d. Almost triple that of Whites *

23. Older persons who reduce their activity tend to be
    a. Happier than those who remain active –
    b. Not as happy as those who remain active *
    c. About as happy as others –
    d. Healthier –

24. When the last child leaves home, the majority of parents
    a. Have serious problems of adjustment –
    b. Have higher levels of life satisfaction *
    c. Try to get their children to come back home –
    d. Suffer from the "empty nest" syndrome –

25. The proportion widowed among the aged
    a. Is gradually decreasing *
    b. Is gradually increasing –
    c. Has remained the same in this century –
    d. Is unrelated to longevity –

Key:
  * = correct answer
  + = Positive bias
  – = Negative bias
  0 = Neutral

ANSWERS TO FACTS ON AGING AND MENTAL HEALTH QUIZ, MULTIPLE CHOICE

1. Severe mental illness among persons over 65 afflicts
   a. The majority –
   b. About half –
   c. About 15 to 25% *
   d. Very few +

2. Cognitive impairment (impairment of memory disorientation, or confusion)
   a. Is an inevitable part of the aging process –
   b. Increases in old age *
   c. Decreases in old age +
   d. Does not change with age. +

3. If older mental patients make up false stories, it is best to
   a. Point out to them that they are lying –
   b. Punish them for lying –
   c. Reward them for their imagination +
   d. Ignore or distract them *

4. The prevalence of anxiety disorders and schizophrenia in old age tends to
   a. Decrease *
   b. Stay about the same –
   c. Increase somewhat –
   d. Increase markedly –

5. Suicide rates among women tend to
   a. Increase in old age –
   b. Stay about the same *
   c. Decrease somewhat in old age +
   d. Decrease markedly +

6. Suicide rates among men tend to
   a. Increase markedly *
   b. Increase somewhat +
   c. Stay about the same +
   d. Decrease +

7. When all major types of mental impairment are added together, the elderly have
   a. Higher rates than younger persons –
   b. About the same rates as younger persons –
   c. Lower rates than younger persons *
   d. Higher rates for ages 65 to 74 than for those over 75 0

8. The primary mental illness of the elderly is
   a. Anxiety disorders +
   b. Mood disorders +
   c. Schizophrenia 0
   d. Cognitive impairment *

9. Alzheimer's disease is
   a. The most common type of cognitive impairment *
   b. An acute illness +
   c. A benign memory disorder +
   d. A form of affective disorder +

10. Alzheimer's disease usually
    a. Can be cured with psychotherapy +
    b. Can be cured with pharmacology +
    c. Goes into remission among the very old +
    d. Cannot be cured *

11. Most patients with Alzheimer's disease
    a. Act pretty much the same way –
    b. Have confusion and impaired memory *
    c. Wander during the day or at night –
    d. Repeat the same question or action over and over –

12. Organic brain impairment
    a. Is easy to distinguish from functional mental illness +
    b. Is difficult to distinguish from functional mental illness *
    c. Tends to be similar to functional mental illness +
    d. Can be reversed with proper therapy +

13. When talking to an older mental patient, it is best
    a. To avoid looking directly at the patient –
    b. To glance at the patient occasionally –
    c. To ignore the patient's reactions –
    d. To look directly at the patient *

14. Talking with demented older patients
    a. Tends to increase their confusion –
    b. Is usually pleasurable for the patient *
    c. Should be confined to trivial matters –
    d. Should be avoided as much as possible –

15. When demented patients talk about their past, it usually
    a. Is enjoyed by the patient *
    b. Depresses the patient –
    c. Increases the patient's confusion –
    d. Has no effect –

16. The prevalence of severe cognitive impairment
    a. Is unrelated to age +
    b. Decreases with age +
    c. Increases with age after 45 *
    d. Increases with age only after 75 +

17. The primary causes of paranoid disorders in old age are
    a. Isolation and hearing loss *
    b. Persecution and abuse 0
    c. Near death experiences 0
    d. None of the above 0

18. Poor nutrition may produce
    a. Depression 0
    b. Confusion 0
    c. Apathy 0
    d. All of the above *

19. Mental illness in elders is more prevalent among
    a. The poor *
    b. The rich 0
    c. The middle-class 0
    d. None of the above 0

20. The prevalence of mental illness among the elderly in long-term care institutions is
    a. About 10% +
    b. About 25% +
    c. About 50% +
    d. More than 75% *

21. Elders tend to have
    a. Less sleep problems +
    b. More sleep problems *
    c. Deeper sleep +
    d. The same sleep patterns as younger persons +

22. Major depression is
    a. Less prevalent among elders *
    b. More prevalent among elders –
    c. Unrelated to age –
    d. A sign of senility –

23. Widowhood is
    a. Less stressful among elders *
    b. More stressful among elders –
    c. Similar levels of stress at all ages –
    d. Least stressful among young adults –

24. Elders use mental health facilities
    a. More often than younger people –
    b. Less often than younger people *
    c. At about the same rate as younger people –
    d. Primarily when they have no family to care for them –

25. Psychotherapy with older patients is
    a. Usually ineffective –
    b. Often effective *
    c. Effective with Alzheimer's patients 0
    d. A waste of the therapist's time –

Key:
  * = correct answer
  + = Positive bias
  – = Negative bias
  0 = Neutral

SCORING KEY FOR LIFE SATISFACTION INDEX, B

1. What are the best things about being the age you are now?

   1 . . . . . .a positive answer
   0 . . . . . .nothing good about it

2. What do you think you will be doing five years from now? How do you expect
   things . .will be different from the way they are now, in your life?

   2 . . . . . .better, no change
   1 . . . . . .contingent B "It depends"
   0 . . . . . .worse

3. What is the most important thing in your life right now?

   2 . . . . . .anything outside of self, or pleasant interpretation of future
   1 . . . . . ."Hanging on"; keeping health, or job
   0 . . . . .getting out of present difficulty, or "nothing now," or reference to the
              past

4. How happy would you say you are right now, compared with the earlier periods in your life?

    2   . . . .this is the happiest time; all have been happy; or hard to make a choice
    1 . . . . . .some decrease in recent years
    0 . . . . . .earlier periods were better, this is a bad time

5. Do you ever worry about your ability to do what people expect of you–to meet demands that people make on you?

    2 . . . . . .no
    1 . . . . . .qualified yes or no
    0 . . . . . .yes

6. If you could do anything you pleased, in what part of _____ would you most like to live?

    2 . . . . . .present location
    0 . . . . . .any other location

7. How often do you find yourself feeling lonely?

    2 . . . . . .never; hardly ever
    1 . . . . . .sometimes
    0 . . . . . .fairly often; very often

8. How often do you feel there is no point in living?

    2 . . . . . .never; hardly ever
    1 . . . . . .sometimes
    0 . . . . . .fairly often; very often

9. Do you wish you could see more of your close friends than you do, or would you like more time to yourself?

    2 . . . . . .OK as is
    0 . . . . . .wish could see more of friends
    0 . . . . . .wish more time to self

10. How much unhappiness would you say you find in your life today?

    2 . . . . . .almost none
    1 . . . . . .some
    0 . . . . . .a great deal

11. As you get older, would you say things seem to be better or worse than you thought they would be?

    2 . . . . . .better
    1 . . . . . .about as expected
    0 . . . . . .worse

12. How satisfied would you say you are with your way of life?

    2 . . . . . .very satisfied
    1 . . . . . .fairly satisfied
    0 . . . . . .not very satisfied

WOOLF AGING QUIZ B ANSWERS

1. The majority of older adults will become senile (defective memory, disoriented, demented) during old age. **FALSE**. Dementia is not a normal part of aging and is not inevitable; in old-old age, the frequency of dementia does increase to as high as 30 percent.

2. Most older adults have no desire for sexual relations. In other words, most older adults are asexual. **FALSE**. Sexuality is not just linked to biological functioning. Sexuality, including biological and psychological functioning, continues to be an important aspect of life in older adulthood.

3. Chronological age is the most important determinant of age. **FALSE**. Chronological age is a gauge of time since birth; better estimates of aging are biological, psychological, historical, and sociological characteristics.

4. Most older adults have difficulty adapting to change; they are set in their ways. **FALSE**. Older adults are no more rigid than younger adults. Rigidity is a trait that is rather stable; an individual is more rigid (or adaptable) throughout his/her life.

5. Physical handicaps are the primary factors limiting the activities of older adults. **FALSE**. The primary handicap of senior citizens is that of age stereotyping and ageism.

6. Declines in all five senses normally occur in old age. **MOSTLY TRUE**. While there are age-related declines in the five senses, the dramatic decline in hearing is probably the result of aging and the cumulative effects of noise.

7. Older adults are incapable of learning new information; you can't teach an old dog new tricks. **FALSE**. Older adults can learn new things, albeit with more intensive training and the use of alternative learning strategies.

8. Physical strength tends to decline in old age. **TRUE**. Exercise, diet and lifestyle can retard the inevitable age-related decline in physical strength. Decline in physical strength is noticeable in middle-adulthood.

9. Intelligence declines with old age. **MOSTLY FALSE**. Older adults without physical diseases do illustrate decline in those intellectual abilities most directly linked to neurological integrity and do not illustrate intellectual decline in abilities most directly linked to past learning.

10. The majority of older adults say that they are happy most of the time. **TRUE**. the majority of seniors report high levels of life satisfaction; the more socially active, the higher the life satisfaction.

11. The vast majority of older adults will at some point end up in a nursing home. **FALSE**. About five percent of seniors live in long-term care facilities; about 25 percent of those aged 85 or older live in such facilities.

12. About 80% of older people say they are healthy enough to carry out their normal daily activities independently. **TRUE**. Except for strenuous activities, most older adults, like younger adults, are not dependent on others for normal daily activities. Since the late 1960s, volunteerism for older adults has increased from 11 to 40 percent; one out of three persons aged 75 or older are involved in volunteerism.

13. Most older adults are rejected by their children. **FALSE**. Over 70 percent of seniors have at least one child living in close proximity; over half of these seniors surveyed noted that they had visited their children within two days of the survey.

14. In general, most older adults tend to be pretty much alike. **FALSE**. Compared to younger adults, seniors are more heterogeneous or diverse as a group. Probable factors for this phenomena are (a) differential rates of biological, sociological, and historical aging, and (b) older adults, compared to younger ones, have interacted within the environment over longer periods of time, experiencing different people and life events.

15. The majority of older adults say that they are lonely. **FALSE**. Although the fear of loneliness is a myth of aging, over two-thirds of older adults report being rarely or never lonely. The fear of loneliness is often associated with loss of a spouse. Yet, widowers often remarry, and widows are more likely to expand their social relations and friendships with other widows. Older adults in small towns, relative to those in urban settings, report lower levels of loneliness.

16. Old age can be best characterized as a second childhood. **FALSE**. In one respect, aging is unidimensional; i.e., aging is a successive phenomenon. The reality of older children caring for aged parents is not equivalent to a role reversal.

17. Over 12% of the population of the United States is over the age of 65. **TRUE**. The population of seniors is steadily increasing. The fastest growing segment is the oldest old.

18. Most older adults tend to be preoccupied with death. **FALSE**. While most younger adults avoid thinking about or discussing death, older adults are less anxious about death.

19. Most older adults have incomes below the poverty level. **FALSE**. Most older adults have incomes above the poverty level; compared to seniors of past eras, the older adult of today is the wealthiest in history.

20. Older people tend to become more religious as they age; as they deal with their own mortality. **FALSE**. Level or degree of religiously remain rather stable over the lifespan.

21. Retirement is detrimental to an individual's health; six months ago he retired and now he's dead, retirement killed him. **FALSE**. For the vast majority of seniors, retirement life is positive, especially if it is planned for.

22. Pain is a natural part of the aging process. **FALSE**. Pain is a signal for injury or illness, not aging. Since there are age-related increases in frequency and duration of chronic illnesses, as well as accumulation of acute injuries, those older adults with such conditions will have to deal with pain.

23. The majority of older adults say that they feel irritated or angry most of the time. **FALSE**. Being angry or irritated, like being rigid (or adaptive), is more of a life-long trait than being associated with older adults.

24. Rarely does someone over the age of 65 produce a great work of art, science, or scholarship. **FALSE**. Although there are differences depending upon discipline, historians, botanists, inventors, philosophers, and writers tend to be more productive in older adulthood.

25. With age comes wisdom. **MOSTLY FALSE**. Wisdom is a difficult concept to define. Almost all the research on wisdom suggests that older adults are no more wise than younger adults. Older adults may have more relevant experience to make wise decisions than younger adults, but making decisions also reflects values, emotions, and intellectual abilities.

Appendix B

SEATTLE STUDY: SEQUENTIAL DESIGNS

We get our classic examples of cross-sectional and longitudinal sequential studies from Schaie (1996), a sustaining leader in both lifespan development and gerontology. As noted earlier in *Successful Aging*, Schaie is the director of the Seattle Longitudinal Study.

The cross-sequential sequence (consisting of seven independent data sets):

Aa	$(n = 500)$	Seven cohorts tested in 1956 (mean ages = 25 to 67; mean birth years = 1889 to 1931)
Bb	$(n = 997)$	Eight cohorts tested in 1963 (mean ages = 25 to 74; mean birth years = 1889 to 1938)
Cc	$(n = 705)$	Nine cohorts tested in 1970 (mean ages = 25 to 81; mean birth years = 1889 to 1945)
Dd	$(n = 609)$	Nine cohorts tested in 1977 (mean ages = 25 to 81; mean birth years = 1896 to 1953)
Ee	$(n = 629)$	Nine cohorts tested in 1984 (mean ages = 25 to 81; mean birth years = 1903 to 1959)
Ff	$(n = 693)$	Nine cohorts tested in 1991 (mean ages = 25 to 81; mean birth years = 1910 to 1966)

The *longitudinal sequences* (consisting of 15 data sets: five 7-year, four 14-year, three 21-year, two 28-year, and one 35-year follow-ups):

Seven-year longitudinal data

Ab	$(n = 303)$	Seven cohorts followed from 1956 to 1963
Bc	$(n = 420)$	Eight cohorts followed from 1963 to 1970
Cd	$(n = 340)$	Nine cohorts followed from 1970 to 1977
De	$(n = 294)$	Nine cohorts followed from 1977 to 1984
Ef	$(n = 428)$	Nine cohorts followed from 1984 to 1991

Fourteen-year longitudinal data

Ac ($n=162$)   Seven cohorts followed from 1956 to 1970
Bd ($n=337$)   Eight cohorts followed from 1963 to 1977
Ce ($n=224$)   Nine cohorts followed from 1970 to 1984
Df ($n=201$)   Nine cohorts followed from 1977 to 1991

Twenty-one-year longitudinal data

Ad ($n=130$)   Seven cohorts followed from 1956 to 1977
Be ($n=225$)   Eight cohorts followed from 1963 to 1984
Cf ($n=175$)   Nine cohorts followed from 1970 to 1991

Twenty-seven-year longitudinal data

Ae ($n=97$)   Seven cohorts followed from 1956 to 1984
Bf ($n=161$)   Eight cohorts followed from 1963 to 1991

Thirty-five-year longitudinal data

Af ($n=71$)   Seven cohorts followed from 1956 to 1991

As of the date of this publication, Schaie and his colleagues are collecting and analyzing data from the 1998 seventh wave of participants in the Seattle Longitudinal Study. According to Schaie, participants from the previous study groupings (see *cross-sequential and longitudinal sequences* listed above) will be retested, and a new cross-sectional panel will be added. Thus, another level–G, g will be added to the sequences listed above. For examples:

Gg   cohorts tested in 1998
Eg   cohorts followed from 1991 to 1998
Dg   cohorts followed from 1984 to 1998
Cg   cohorts followed from 1977 to 1998
Bg   cohorts followed from 1970 to 1998
Ag   cohorts followed from 1963 to 1998
Ah   cohorts followed from 1956 to 1998

GLOSSARY

aging. Types of aging are normal, pathological, successful, and robust. Definitions of aging are categorized as physical, psychological, and social.

> *normal aging*. Average age-related changes in physical, psychological, and social domains throughout the lifespan.
>
> *pathological aging*. Associated with chronic dysfunction, constricted longevity, and/or reduced quality of life.
>
> *successful aging*. In the physical, psychological, and/or social domains, above average longevity and quality of life.
>
> *robust aging*. An aspect of successful aging; associated with exceptional quality of life.
>
> *physical aging*. Characterized by declines in biological systems (such as cardio-vascular, muscular-skeletal, neurological, pulmonary, and reproductive) and correlated functions.
>
> *psychological aging*. Deals with age-related profiles of intellectual, personality, and motivational systems and functions, including those related to fluid mechanical and crystallized pragmatic abilities.
>
> *social aging*. Illustrated by age/stage/period-related expectations, such as schooling, marriage, employment, parenthood, and retirement.

arthritic. Adjective form of *arthritis*. Inflammation of a joint or joints resulting in pain and swelling.

asymptote. Not intersecting.

autosomal. A chromosome that is not a sex chromosome.

biochemical. The chemical composition of a particular living system.

crystallized pragmatic abilities. Associated with psychological systems and functions, these abilities, significantly determined by environmental factors, show a general profile of late decline in adulthood.

dementia. Deterioration of intellectual faculties, such as memory, concentration, and judgment, resulting from an organic disease or a disorder of the brain. It is often accompanied by emotional disturbance and personality changes.

developmental methodology. Methods and designs used by researchers which deal with ways to manipulate the three major components of age-related differences or changes chronological age, cohort, and time of measurement.

distal. Located far from a point of reference, such as an origin or a point of attachment.

domains of development and aging. Biological systems and functions reflect the physical domain; cognitive (e.g., intelligence, personality, motivation) ones reflect the psychological domain; and social interactions reflect the social domain.

empirical. Guided by practical experience and not theory.

enculturation (also *acculturation*). Process by which the culture of a particular society is instilled in a human being from infancy onward.

fluid mechanical abilities. Associated with physical systems and functions, these abilities, influenced significantly by genetic unfolding, maturation and less directly by environmental determinants, show a general profile of early decline in adulthood.

geriatrics. Theory, research, and practice focusing on the physical aspects of aging in later stages of the lifespan.

gerontology. Theory, research, and practice focusing on physical, psychological, and social aspects of aging in the later stages of the lifespan.

interindividual variability. Variability or differences among individuals and one or more variables. For example, intelligence test scores illustrate a normal distribution, with most scoring in the average range and fewer scoring in the extremes of below and above normal.

intraindividual variability. Variability or differences within a person on (a) numerous variables measured at a particular time of measurement or (b) one or more variables over time (periods of one's lifespan).

lifespan development. Theory, research, and practice emphasizing principles of development, stability, and decline throughout life, as opposed to focus on particular chronological ages/stages/periods/levels.

lifespan. Conception-to-death, womb-to-tomb; one's existing existence.

mental health. Refers to one's sense of psychological well-being, as well as clinically assessed cognitive functioning.

multifaceted. A point of view for the lifespan which articulates the importance of integrating information about many abilities and associated causes to better understand lifespan development and aging.

multidisciplinary. A theoretical, research, or practical perspective which integrates information from several disciplines of inquiry for the domains of physical, psychological, and social aging.

mutagenic. Adjective form of *mutagen* An agent, such as ultraviolet light or a radioactive element, that can induce or increase the frequency of mutation in an organism.

neurodegenerative. Relating to or marked by the degeneration of the nervous system.

neuroendocrine. Relating to, or involving the interaction between the nervous system and the hormones of the endocrine glands.

nurturance. Noun form of *nurture*. The sum of environmental influences and conditions acting on an organism.

ontogeny. Origin and development of an individual organism from embryo to adult.

pathological. Relating to or caused by disease or manifesting behavior that is habitual and compulsive.

phenotypes. Observable physical or biochemical characteristics of an organism, as determined by both genetic makeup and environmental influences.

plasticity. Capable of building tissue; formative; malleable.

proximal. Nearest; proximate.

psychotropic. Having an altering effect on perception or behavior. Used especially of a drug.

reductionary. Attempt or a tendency to explain complex phenomena or structures by relatively simple principles, as by asserting that life processes or mental acts are instances of chemical and physical laws

sandwich generation. Middle-aged working people who feel squeezed by the financial pressures of supporting their aging parents, the costs of raising and educating their children, and the need to save for their own retirement.

stereotype. Conventional, formulaic, and oversimplified conception, opinion, or image; opinion of others, based upon limited information about their category, which may or may not be true.

stochastic. Pertaining to a process involving a randomly determined sequence of observations, each of which is considered as a sample of one element from a probability distribution.

telomeres. Either end of a chromosome; a terminal chromosome.

typology. Systematic classification of types that have characteristics or traits in common.

variability. Differences among and within individuals on dependent variables or measured characteristics.

vascular. Characterized by, or containing vessels that carry or circulate fluids, such as blood, lymph, or sap through the body of an animal or a plant.

zeitgeist. Spirit of the time; the taste and outlook characteristic of a period or generation.

REFERENCES

Ackoff, R.L. (1994). Systems thinking and thinking systems. *Systems Dynamic Review, 10*, 175-188.

Albom, M. (1997). *Tuesdays with Morrie: An old man, a young man, and life's greatest lesson.* New York: Doubleday.

Antonucci, T.C. (1985). Personal characteristics, social support, and social behavior. In R.H. Binstock & E. Shanas (Eds.), *Handbook of aging and the social sciences* (2nd Ed.). (pp. 94-128). New York: Van Nostrand Reinhold.

Atchley, R.C. (2000). *Social forces and aging: An introduction to social gerontology.* Belmont, CA: Wadsworth Thompson Learning.

Backman, L., & Dixon, R.A. (1992). Psychological compensation: A theoretical framework. *Psychological Bulletin, 112*, 259-283.

Baltes, M.M., & Carstensen, L.L. (1999). Social-psychological theories and their applications to aging: From individual to collective. In V.L. Bengtson, V.L., & Schaie, K.W. (Eds.), *Handbook of theories of aging.* (pp. 209-226). New York: Springer.

Baltes, P. B. (1979). Life-span developmental psychology: Some converging observations on history and theory. In P.B. Baltes & O.G. Brim, Jr. (Eds.), *Life-span development and behavior* (Vol. 2, pp. 255-279). New York: Academic Press.

Baltes, P.B. (1968). Longitudinal and cross-sectional sequences in the study of age and generation effects. *Human Development, 11*, 145-171.

Baltes, P.B. (1987). Theoretical propositions of life-span developmental psychology: On the dynamics between growth and decline. *Developmental Psychology, 23*, 611-626.

Baltes, P.B. (1993). The aging mind: Potential and limits. *The Gerontologist, 33*, 580-594.

Baltes, P.B. (1997). On the incomplete architecture of human ontogeny: Selection, optimization, and compensation as foundation of developmental theory. *American Psychologist, 52*, 366-380.

Baltes, P.B., & Baltes, M.M. (1990). Psychological perspectives on successful aging: The model of selective optimization and compensation. In P.B. Baltes & M.M. Baltes (Eds.), *Successful aging: Perspectives from the behavioral sciences* (pp. 1-34). New York: Press Syndicate of the University of Cambridge.

Baltes, P.B., & Baltes, M.M. (1998). Savoir Vivre in old age: How to master the shifting balance between gains and losses. *National Forum, 78*, 13-18.

Baltes, P.B., Lindenberger, U., & Staudinger, U.M. (1998). Life-span theory in developmental psychology. In R.M. Lerner (Ed.), *Handbook of developmental psychology: volume 1.* Theoretical models of human development (5th ed., Editor-in-Chief: W. Damon, pp. 1029-1143). New York: Wiley.

Baltes, P.B., & Mayer, K.U. (Eds.) (1999). *The Berlin aging study: Aging from 70 to 100.* New York: Cambridge University Press.

Baltes, P.B., Staudinger, U.M., & Lindenberger, U. (1999). Lifespan psychology: Theory and application to intellectual functioning. In J.T. Spence, J.M. Darley, & D.J. Foss (Eds.), *Annual review of psychology*, Vol. 50 (pp. 471-508). Palo Alto, CA: Annual Reviews.

Baltes, P.B., Reese, H.W., & Nesselroade, J.R. (1988). *Life-span developmental psychology: An introduction to research methods.* Hillsdale, J.J: Erlbaum.

Baltes, P.B., & Smith, J. (1999). Multilevel and systemic analyses of old age: Theoretical and empirical evidence for a fourth age. In V.L. Bengtson & K.W. Schaie (Eds.), *Handbook of theories of aging* (pp. 153-173). New York: Springer.

Baltes, P.B., & Staudinger (Eds.). (1996). *Interactive minds: Life-span perspectives on the social foundation of cognition.* New York: Cambridge University Press.

Bandura, A. (1977). Self-efficacy: Toward a unifying theory of behavioral change. *Psychological Review, 84,* 191-215.

Bandura, A. (1981). Self-referent thought: A developmental analysis of self-efficacy. In J. Flavell & L. Ross (Eds.), Social cognitive development (pp. 200209). New York: Cambridge University Press, Bandura, A. (1982). Self-efficacy mechanism in human agency. *American Psychologist, 37,* 122-147.

Bandura, A. (1986). *Social foundations of though and action: A social cognitive theory.* Englewood Cliffs, NJ: Prentice-Hall.

Bandura, A. (1997). *Self-efficacy: The exercise of control.* New York: W.H. Freeman and Company.

Baum, A., & Posluszny, D.M. (1999). Health psychology: Mapping biobehavioral contributions to health and illness. In J. T. Spence, J.M. Darley, & D.J. Foss (Eds.), *Annual review of psychology,* vol. 50 (pp. 137-164). Palo Alto, CA: Annual Reviews.

Belsky, J. (1999). *The psychology of aging: Theory, research, and interventions* (3rd ed.). New York: Brooks/Cole.

Bengtson, V.L., Parrott, T.M., & Burgess, E. O. (1996). Progress and pitfalls in gerontological theorizing. *The Gerontologist, 36* (6), 768-772.

Bengtson, V.L., Rice, C.J., & Johnson, M.L. (1999). Are theories of aging important? Models and explanations in gerontology at the turn of the century. In V.L. Bengtson & K.W. Schaie (Eds.), *Handbook of theories of aging* (pp. 3-20). New York: Springer.

Bengtson, V.L., & Schaie, K.W. (1999). Dedication. In V.L. Bengtson & K.W. Schaie (Eds.), *Handbook of theories of aging* (pp. 473-480). New York: Springer.

Bengtson, V.L., & Schaie, K.W. (Eds.) (1999). *Handbook of theories of aging.* New York: Springer.

Berk, L.E. (1998). *Development through the lifespan.* Boston: Allyn & Bacon.

Bing, S. (2000). How to succeed in business: Fifteen things young people need to know about comportment. *Fortune,* May 1, 2000, 81-82.

Binstock, R.H. (1994). Changing criteria in old-age programs: The introduction of economic status and need for services. *Gerontologist, 34,* 726-730.

Binstock, R.H. (1999). Public policy issues. In J.C. Cavanaugh & S. Krauss Whitbourne (Ed.), *Gerontology: An interdisciplinary perspective* (pp. 414-448). New York: Oxford University Press.

Birren, J.E. (1959). *Handbook of aging and the individual.* Chicago: University of Chicago Press.

Birren, J.E. (1999). Theories of aging: A personal perspective. In V.L. Bengtson & K.W. Schaie (Eds.), *Handbook of theories of aging* (pp. 459-472). New York: Springer.

Birren, J.E., & Renner, V.J. Research on the psychology of aging: Principles and experimentation. (1977). In J.E. Birren & K.W. Schaie (Eds.), *Handbook of the psychology of aging* (pp. 338). New York: Van Nostrand Reinhold.

Bosworth, H.B., Schaie, K.W., & Willis, S.L. (1999). Cognitive and sociodemographic risk factors for matality in the Seattle Longitudinal Study. *Journals of Gerontology: Psychological Sciences, 54B,* P273-P282.

Brokaw, T. (1999a). *The greatest generation.* New York: Random House.

Brokaw, T. (1999b). *The greatest generation speaks.* New York: Random House.

Burnside, I.M., Ebersole, P., & Monea, H.E. (1979). *Psychological caring throughout the lifespan.* New York: McGraw-Hill.

Campbell, D.T., & Stanley, J.C. (1963). *Experimental and quasi-experimental designs for research.* Chicago: Rand McNally.

Carstensen, L.L., Isaacowitz, D.M., & Charles, S.T. (1999). Taking time seriously: A theory of socioemotional selectivity. *American Psychologist, 54,* 165-181.

Cattell, R.B. (1941). Some theoretical issues in adult intelligence testing. *Psychological Bulletin, 38,* 592.

Cattell, R.B. (1943). The measurement of adult intelligence. *Psychological Bulletin, 40,* 153-193.

Cattell, R.B. (1963). Theory of fluid and crystallized intelligence: A critical experiment. *Journal of Educational Psychology, 54,* 1-22.

Cavanaugh, J.C. (1999). Theories of aging in the biological, behavioral, and social sciences. In J.C. Cavanaugh & S.K. Whitbourne (Eds.), *Gerontology: An interdisciplinary perspective* (pp. 1-33). New York: Oxford University.

Clark, J.W. (1960). The aging dimension: A factorial analysis of individual differences with age on psychological and physiological measurements. *Journal of Gerontology, 15,* 183-187.

Clarke, E.J., Preston, M., Raskin, J., & Bengtson, V.L. (1999). Types of conflict and tensions between older parents and adult children. *The Gerontologist, 39,* 261-270.

Cohen, G. (1988). Age differences in memory for texts: Production deficiency or processing limitations? In L.L. Light & D.M. Burke (Eds.), *Language, memory, and aging* (pp. 171-190). New York: Cambridge University Press.

Cole, M. (1996). Interacting minds in a life-span perspective. A cultural/historical approach to culture and cognitive development. In P.B. Cristofalo, V.J., Tresini, M., Francis, M.K., & Volker, C. (1999). Biological theories of senesence. In V.L. Bengtson & K.W. Schaie (Eds.), *Handbook of theories of aging* (pp. 98-112). New York: Springer.

Costa, P.T., & McCrae, R.R. (1995). Longitudinal stability of adult personality. In R. Hogan, J.A. Johnson, & S.R. Briggs (Eds.), *Handbook of personality psychology.* New York: Academic Press.

Craik, F.I.M., & Jennings, J.M. (1992). Human memory. In F.I.M. Craik & T.A. Salthouse (Eds.), *The handbook of aging and cognition* (pp. 51-110). Hillsdale, NJ: Erlbaum.

Crimmins, E.M., Hayward, M.D., & Saito, Y. (1996). Differentials in active life expectancy in the older population in the United States. *Journal of Gerontology: Social Sciences, 51B,* S111-S120.

Crowdry, E.V. (1942). *Problems of aging.* Baltimore: Williams & Wilkins.

Davis, N.C. (2000). A study on aging: The relationship between life satisfaction and knowledge of aging with older adults. Unpublished master's thesis, University of West Florida, Pensacola.

Diener, E. (2000). Subjective well-being. *American Psychologist, 55,* 34-43.

Dirken, J.M. (1972). *Functional age of industrial workers.* Roningen, the Netherlands: Wolters-Noordhof.

Dixon, R.A., & Backman, I. (Eds.). (1995). *Compensating for psychological deficits and declines: Managing losses and promoting gains.* Mahwah, NJ: Erlbaum.

Durham, W.H. (1991). *Co-evolution: Genes, culture and human diversity.* Stanford, CA: Stanford University Press.

Emerson, R.W. (1900). *Compensation.* New York:Caldwell.

Ericsson, K.A., & Smith, J. (Eds.). (1991). *Towards a general theory of expertise: Prospects and limits.* New York: Cambridge University Press.

Erikson, E. (1963). *Childhood and society.* New York: Norton.

Erikson, E. (1982). *The life cycle completed.* New York: Norton.

Exercise: A guide from the National Institute on Aging. (2000). National Institute on Aging (http://weboflife.arc.nasa.gov/exerciseandaging/intro.html).

Finch, C.E., & Tanzi, R.E. (1997). Genetics of aging. *Science, 278*, 407-411.

Freud, S. (1917). *A general introduction to psychoanalysis.* New York: Washington Square Press.

Friedman, H.S., Tucker, J.S., Schwartz, J.EW., Tomlinson-Keasey, C., Martin, L.R., Wingard, D.L., & Criqui, M.H. (1995). Psychosocial and behavioral predictors of longevity: The aging and death of the "termites". *American Psychologist, 50*, 69-78.

Friedrich, D., & Van Horn, K. R. (1976). *Development methodology: A revised primer.* Minneapolis, MN: Burgess.

Fries, J.F. (1990). Medical perspectives upon successful aging. In P.B. Baltes, & M.M. Baltes (Eds.), *Successful aging: Perspectives from the behavioral sciences* (pp. 35-40). New York: Cambridge University Press.

Fry, C.L. (1999). Anthropological theories of age and aging. In V.L. Bengtson & K.W. Schaie (Eds.), *Handbook of theories of aging* (pp. 271-288). New York: Springer.

Garfein, A.J., & Herzog, R. (1995). Robust aging among the young-old, old-old, and oldest-old. *Journal of Gerontology, Social Sciences, 50B*, S77-S87.

Geary, D.C., & Lin, J. (1996). Numerical cognition: Age-related differences in the speed of executing biologically primary and biologically secondary processes. Manuscript submitted for publication.

Goodart, N.L. (1995). *The truth about living trusts.* Chicago: Dearborn Financial Publishing, Inc.

Heckhausen, J., & Schulz, R. (1993). Optimization by selection and compensation: Balancing primary and secondary control in life-span development. *International Journal of Behavioral Development, 16*, 287-303.

Heckhausen, J., & Schulz, R. (1995). A life-span theory of control. *Psychological Review, 102*, 284-304.

Hedges, L.V., & Olkin, I. (1985). *Statistical methods for meta-analysis.* Orlando, FL: Academic Press.

Helmchen, H., Baltes, M.M., Geiselmann, B., Kanowski, S., Linden, M., Reischies, F.M., Wagner, M., Wernicke, T., & Wilms, H.U. (1999). Psychiatric illnesses in old age. In P.B. Baltes & K.U. Mayer (Eds.), *The Berlin aging study: Aging from 70 to 100* (pp. 167-196). New York: Cambridge University Press.

Heron, A., & Chown, S. (1967). *Age and function.* London: Churchill.

Hertzog, C., & Dixon, R.A. (1996). Methodological issues in research on cognition and aging. In F. Blanchard-Fields, & T.M. Hess (Eds.), *Perspectives on cognitive change and aging.* (pp. 25-65). New York: McGraw-Hill.

Hillier, S., & Barrow, G.M. (1999). *Aging, the individual, and society*, 7 ed. New York: Wadsworth.

Hobbs, F.B. & Damon, B.L. (1996). 65+ in the United States. U.S. Department of Commerce. Available: http://www.census.gov/prod/1/pop/p23-190/p,23-190 html

Horn, J.L. (1970). Organization of data on lifespan development of human abilities. In L.R. Goulet & P.B. Baltes (Eds.), *Life-span developmental psychology: Research and theory* (pp. 423-466). New York: Academic Press.

Horn, J.L. (1982). The aging of human abilities. In B.B. Wolman (Ed.), *Handbook of developmental psychology* (pp. 847-870). Englewood Cliffs, NJ: Prentice-Hall.

Horn, J.L., & Cattell, R.B. (1966). Refinement and test of the theory of fluid and crystallized general intelligences. *Journal of Educational Psychology, 57*, 253-270.

Horn, J.L., & Cattell, R.B. (1967). Age differences in fluid and crystallized intelligence. *Acta Psychologica, 26*, 107-129.

Hoyer, W.J., Rybash, J.M., & Roodin, P.A. (1999). *Adult development and aging* (4th ed). New York: McGraw-Hill College.

Jung, C..G. (1933). *Modern man in search of a soul.* (W.S. Dell & C.F. Baynes, Trans.). New York: Harcourt, Brace & World.

Kahn, R.L. & Antonucci, T.C. (1980). Convoys over the life course. Attachment, roles and social support. In P. Baltes & O.G. Brim (Eds.), *Life-span development and behavior*. New York: Academic Press.

Kalish, R.A. (1979). The new ageism and the failure of models: A polemic. *Gerontologist, 19*, 398-407.

Kaplan, R.M. (2000). Two pathways to prevention. *American Psychologist, 55*, 382-396.

Kemp, B. J., & Mitchell, J.M. (1992). Functional assessment in geriatric mental health. In J.E. Birren, R.B. Sloane, & G.D. Cohen (Eds.), *Handbook of mental health and aging.* (2nd ed). New York: Van Nostrand Reinhold.

Kempen, G.I.J.M., & Suurmeijer, T.P.B.M. (1990). The development of a hierarchical polychotomous ADL-IADL scale for noninstitutionalized elders. *The Gerontologist, 30*, 497-502.

Kliegl, R., & Baltes, P.B. (1987). Theory-guided analysis of mechanisms of development and aging mechanisms through testing-the-limits and research on expertise. In C. Schooler & K.W. Schaie (Eds.), *Cognitive functioning and social structure over the life course* (pp. 95-119). Norwood, NJ: ABLEX.

Kliegl, R., Smith, J., & Baltes, P.B. (1989). Testing-the-limits and the study of age differences in cognitive plasticity of a mnemonic skill. *Developmental Psychology, 26*, 894-904.

Lemme, B.H. (1999). *Development in adulthood*, 2nd ed. Needham Heights, MA: Allyn & Bacon.

Lerner, W. (1998). *Handbook of child psychology* (Vols. 15). New York: Wiley.

Levelt, W.J.M. (1989). *Speaking: From intention to articulation.* Cambridge, MA: MIT Press.

Lindenberger, U., & Baltes, P.B. (1994). Aging and intelligence. In R.J. Sternberg (Ed.), *Encyclopedia of human intelligence* (Vol. 1, pp. 52-66). New York: Macmillan

Lindenberger, U. & Reischies, F.M. (1999). Limits and potentials of intellectual functioning in old age. In P.B. Baltes & K.U. Mayer (Eds.), *The Berlin aging study: Aging from 70 to 100* (pp. 329-359). New York: Cambridge University Press.

Magnusson, D. (Ed.). (1996). *The life-span development of individuals: Behavioural, neurobiological, and psychosocial perspectives.* Cambridge, U.K.: Cambridge University Press.

Manton, K.G., & Vaupel, J.W. (1995). Survival after the age of 80 in the United States, Sweden, France, England, and Japan. *New England Journal of Medicine, 333*, 1232-1235.

Marsiske, M., Lang, F.R., Baltes, M.M., & Baltes, P.B. (1995). Selective optimization with compensation: Life-span perspectives on successful human development. In R.A. Dixon & L. Backman (Eds.), *Compensation for psychological defects and declines: Managing losses and promoting gains* (pp. 35-79). Hillsdale, NJ: Erlbaum.

Martin, G.M., Austad, S.N., & Johnson, T.E. (1996). Genetic analysis of aging: Role of oxidative damage and environmental stresses. *Nature Genetics, 13*, 25-34.

Mayer, K.U., & Baltes, P.B. (Eds.) (1996). *Die Berliner Altersstudie* [Berlin Aging Study]. Berlin: Akademie Verlag.

Mayer, K. U., Baltes, P.B., Baltes, M.M., Borchelt, M., Delius, J., Helmchen, H., Linden, M., Smith, J., Staudinger, U.M., Steinhagen-Thiessen, E., & Wagner, M. What do we know about old age and aging? Conclusions from the Berlin aging study. (1999) In P.B. Baltes & KU. Mayer (Eds.), *The Berlin aging study: Aging from 70 to 100* (pp. 475-520). New York: Cambridge University Press.

McAuley, E., Katula, J., Mihalko, S. L., Blissmer, B., Duncan, T.E., Pena, M., & Dunn, E. (1999). Mode of physical activity and self-efficacy in older adults: A laten growth curve analysis. *Journal of Gerontology: Psychological Sciences, 54B*, P283-P292.

Mirowsky, J. (1995). Age and the sense of control. *Social Psychology Quarterly, 58*, 31-43.

Navon, D. (1984). Resources: A theoretical soup stone? *Psychological Review, 91*, 216-234.

Neugarten, B.L., Havighurst, R.J., & Tobin, S.S. (1961). The measurement of life satisfaction. *Journal of Gerontology, 16*, 134-143.

Ohlsson, K. (1986). Compensation as skill. In E. Hjelmquist & L. G. Nilsson (Eds.), *Communication and handicap: Aspects of psychological compensation and technical aids* (pp. 85-101). Amsterdam: North-Holland.

Olshansky, S.J. (1995). Introduction: New developments in mortality. *Gerontologist, 35*, 583-587.

Palmore, E.B. (1998). *The facts on aging quiz*. 2nd Ed. New York: Springer.

Park, D.C., Nisbett, R., & Hedden, T. (1999). Aging, culture, and cognition. *Journal of Gerontology: Psychological Sciences, 54B*, 75-84.

Partridge, L., & Martin, N.H. (1993). Optimality, mutation, and the evolution of aging. *Nature, 362*, 305-311.

Pipher, M. (1999). *Another country: Navigating the emotional terrain of our elders*. New York: Riverhead Books (Penguin Putnam Inc.).

Pratt, M. (1999). Benefits of lifestyle activity vs structured exercise. *The Journal, 281*, 1-4 (http://jama.ama-assn.org/issues/v281/full/jed80113.html).

Quadagno, J.S. (1999). *Aging and the life course: An introduction to social Gerontology*. New York: McGraw-Hill College.

Raven, J.C. (1960). Progressive Matrices: Revised manual. London: Lewis.

Rolls, J., & Drewnowski, A. (1996). Diet and nutrition. In J.E. Birren (Ed.), *Encyclopedia of gerontology: Age, aging, and the aged* (pp. 429-440). New York: Academic Press.

Rose, M.R. (1991). *The evolutionary biology of aging*. Oxford, U.K.: Oxford University Press.

Rothi, I., J., & Homer, J. (1983). Restitution and substitution: Two theories of recovery with application to neurobehavioral treatment. *Journal of Clinical Neuropsychology, 5*, 73-81.

Rowe, J.W., & Kahn, R.L. (1998) *Successful aging*. New York: Pantheon Books.

Ryckmann, R.M., Robbins, M.A., Thornton, B., & Cantrell, P. (1982). Development and validation of a physical self-efficacy scale. *Journal of Personality and Social Psychology, 42*, 891-900.

Salthouse, T.A. (1985). *A theory of cognitive aging*. Amsterdam: North-Holland.

Salthouse, T.A. (1988). The role of processing resources in cognitive aging. In M.L. Howe & C. J. Brainerd (Eds.), *Cognitive development in adulthood: Progress in cognitive development research* (pp. 185-239). New York: Springer-Verlag.

Salthouse, T.A. (1991). *Theoretical perspectives on cognitive aging*. Hillsdale, NJ: Erlbaum.

Salthouse, T.A. (1999). Theories of cognition. In V. L. Bengtson, & K.W. Schaie (Eds.), *Handbook of theories of aging* (pp. 196-208). New York: Springer.

Salthouse, T.A., Hancock, H.E., Meinz, E.J., & Hambrick, D.Z. (1996). Interrelations of age, visual acuity, and cognitive functioning. *Journal of Gerontology: Psychological Sciences, 51B*, P317-P334.

Salthouse, T.A., Hambrick, D.Z., & McGuthry (1998). Shared age-related influences on cognitive and noncognitive variables. *Psychology and Aging, 13*, 486-500.

Salthouse, T.A., & Mitchell, D.R.D. (1990). Effects of age and naturally occurring experience on spatial visualization performance. *Developmental Psychology, 26*, 845-854.

Santrock, J.W. (1999). *Lifespan development* (7th ed.). New York: McGraw-Hill College.

Schaie, K.W. (1965). A general model for the study of developmental problems. *Psychological Bulletin, 64*, 92-107.

Schaie, K.W. (1967). Age changes and age differences. *The Gerontologist, 7*, 128-132.

Schaie, K.W. (1972). Can the longitudinal method be applied to psychological studies of human development. In F.Z. Monks, W.W. Hartup, & J. DeWitt (Eds.), *Determinants of human behavior* (pp. 3-22). New York: Academic Press.

Schaie, K.W. (1977). Quasi-experimental research designs in the psychology of aging. In J.E. Birren, & K.W. Schaie (Eds.), *Handbook of the psychology of aging* (pp. 39-58). New York: Van Nostrand Reinhold.

Schaie, K.W. (1996). *Intellectual development in adulthood: The Seattle longitudinal study.* New York: Cambridge University Press.

Schaie, K.W. & Baltes, P.B. (1975). On sequential strategies in developmental research. *Human Development, 18*, 384-390.

Schultz, R. (1978). *The psychology of death, dying and bereavement.* Newbery Records, Inc. (Division of Random House).

Schulz, R., & Heckhausen, J. (1996). A life-span model of successful aging. *American Psychologist, 51*, 702-714.

Schulz, R., & Heckhausen, J. (1999). Aging, culture, and control: Setting a new research agenda. *Journal of Gerontology, Psychological Sciences, 54B*, P139-P145.

Seeman, T.E., Unger, J.B., MacAvay, G., & Mendes de Leon, C.F. (1999). Self-efficacy beliefs and perceived declines in functional ability: MacArthur studies of successful aging. *Journal of Gerontology: Psychological Sciences, 54B*, P214-P222.

Seligman, M.E.P. (1975). *Helplessness: On depression, development, and death.* San Francisco: W.H. Freeman.

Shipley, W.C. (1940). A self-administering scale for measuring intellectual impairment and deterioration. *Journal of Psychology, 9*, 371-377.

Shweder, R.A. (1991). *Thinking through cultures.* Cambridge, MA: Harvard University Press.

Siegler, R.S. (1994). Cognitive variability: A key to understanding cognitive development. *Current Directions in Psychological Science, 3*, 15.

Small, B.J., Dixon, R.A., Hultsch, D.F., & Hertzog, C. (1999). Longitudinal changes in quantitative and qualitative indicators of word and story recall. *Journal of Gerontology: Psychological Sciences, 54B*, 107-115.

Smith, J., & Baltes, P.B. (1996). Altern aus psychologischer Perspektive: Trends und Proile im hohen Alter [Psychological aging: Trends and profiles in very old age]. In K.U. Mayer & P.B. Baltes (Eds.), *Die Berliner Altersstudie* [The Berlin Aging Study] (pp. 221-250). Berlin: Akademie Verlag.

Smith, J., & Baltes, P.B. (1997). Profiles of psychological functioning in the old and oldest old. *Psychology of Aging, 12*, 458-472.

Smith, J., & Baltes, P.B. (1999). Trends and profiles of psychological functioning in very old age. In P.B. Baltes & K.U. Mayer (Eds.), *The Berlin aging study: Aging from 70-100* (pp. 197-226). New York: Cambridge University Press.

Spirduso, W. W. (1995). *Physical dimensions of aging.* Human Kinetics: Champaign, IL.

Staudinger, U.M., Marsiske, M., & Baltes, P.B. (1995) Resilience and reserve capacity in later adulthood: Potentials and limits of development across the life span. In D. Cicchetti & D. Cohen (Eds.), *Developmental psychopathology: Vol. 2. Risk, disorder, and adaptation* (pp. 801-847). New York: Wiley.

Steinhagen-Thiessen, E., & Borchelt, M. (1999). Morbidity, medication, and functional limitations in very old age. In P.B. Baltes & K.U. Mayer (Eds.), *The Berlin aging study: Aging from 70 to 100* (pp. 131-166). New York: Cambridge University Press.

Terman, L. (1925). *Genetic studies of genius: Vol. 1. Mental and physical traits of a thousand gifted children.* Stanford, CA: Stanford University Press.

Tetens, J.N. (1777). *Philosophische Versuche uber die menschliche Natur und ihre Entwicklung.* Leipzig: Weidmanns Erben und Reich.

Terkel, S. (1988). *The great divide: Second thoughts on the American dream.* New York: Pantheon Books.

Turker, M. (1996). Premature aging. In J.E. Birren (Ed.), *Encyclopedia of gerontology: Age, aging, and the aged*, vol. 2 (pp. 341-354). New York: Academic Press.

Vaupel, J.W., & Jeunne, B. (1995). *Exceptional longevity: From prehistory to the present.* Odense, Denmark: Odense University Press.

Verhaeghen, P., Marcoen, A., & Goosens, L. (1993). Facts and fiction about memory and aging: A quantitative integration of research findings. *Journal of Gerontology: Psychological Sciences, 48*, P157-P171.

Verhaeghen, P., & Salthouse, T.A. (1997). Meta-analyses of age-cognition relations in adulthood: Estimates of linear and nonlinear age effects and structural models. *Psychological Bulletin, 122*, 231-249.

White, R.W. (1959). Motivation reconsidered: The concept of competence. *Psychological Review, 66*, 297-333.

Willis, S.L. (1990). Contributions of cognitive training research to understanding late-life potential. In M. Perlmutter (Ed.), *Late-life potential* (pp. 25-42). Washington, D.C.: Gerontological Society of America.

Woolf, L. M. (1999) Woolf aging quiz. Available: http://www.webster.edu/~woolflm/myth.html

NAME INDEX

SUBJECT INDEX

A

AARP, 200, 201, 203, 204

activities of daily living, 144, 152, 177, 224, 225, 227

  age conditions, 48

  normal aging, 48, 119, 124, 139–141, 175, 191, 216, 218, 231, 240, 255

  pathological aging, 48, 119, 120, 140, 228, 255, 256

  robust aging, 153–155

  successful aging, 3–5, 7, 46, 49, 50, 66, 79, 109, 110, 118, 120, 125, 131, 132, 138–141, 145, 146, 149–154, 156–158, 162, 164–166, 173–178, 180–182, 186, 187, 193, 212, 214, 219, 222, 224, 228–232, 236, 237, 245, 246, 248, 249, 251–256

ageism, 39, 194, 255

age-related theories of aging, 51

aging as a systemic phenomenon, 190

aging processes, 42, 76, 77, 213, 218, 239

Aging-Hypothalamus, 53

Alcoholism, 146, 158

Alzheimer's disease, 142, 143, 159, 214, 233

Another Country: Navigating the Emotional Terrain of Our Elders, viii, xi, 39

autoimmune reaction, 54

B

Baltes' 8 principles of lifespan development, 57

  Principle 1: Lifespan Development, 57

  Principle 2: Lifespan Changes in the Dynamic between Biology and Culture, 60

  Principle 3: lifespan changes in the dynamic between biology and culture, 64

  Principle 4: development as selection (specialization) and selective

  optimization in adaptive capacity, 65

  Principle 5: development as gain/loss dynamic, 67

  Principle 6: plasticity, 67

  Principle 7: ontogenetic and historical contextualism, 68

  Principle 8: effective coordination of selection, optimization, and compensation, 70

Behavioral Risk Factor Surveillance System, 238

Berlin Aging Study, 83, 87, 89, 121, 139, 189–191, 193

Berlin Aging Quiz, 11, 13, 26, 34

big five negative contributors, 240, 241

boomers

  aging boomers, 144, 146, 201, 203, 241, 258

  anxious boomers, 207, 208–210

  baby boomers, 21, 23, 101, 144, 146, 199, 201, 203, 221

  enthusiasts, 202, 208–211

  self-reliants, 207–211

  strugglers, 207–210

  traditionalist, 207–211

C

cardiovascular risk, 237

carefulness, 113

chronic conditions, 138, 144, 234, 241, 256

chronological age, 42–44

cognitive mechanics, 118, 125, 233

cognitive pragmatics, 118

cognitive variables, 106, 107, 147

cohort effects, 74, 80, 101

compensation, 65, 66, 70, 125, 127, 128, 131, 132, 154, 166, 171, 174–176, 181, 188, 228, 230, 234, 245, 246, 248, 249, 254, 257

compression of morbidity, 138, 234, 245

314